About this book

By the year 2025 nearly 2 billion people will live in regions or countries experiencing absolute water scarcity, even allowing for high levels of irrigation efficiency. In the face of this emerging global water crisis, how should the planet's water be used and managed in the 21st century? This is the central question that this book explores.

Current international water policy sees nature competing with human uses of water. It sees the task for humanity as being how to divide the planet's water between competing uses such as food production, clean water supplies and sanitation for human communities, and protecting the environment. Dr Hunt takes issue with this perspective. She suggests that nature cannot be regarded as a residual factor in the water management equation. Nature is the source of water and only by making the conservation of nature an absolute priority will we have water in the future for human uses.

The author argues that it is essential, therefore, to manage water in different ways from those relied on in the last century. We must instead maintain the water cycle and the ecosystems that support it. This book looks at the complexity of how to do this. And it provides a wide array of ideas, information, case studies and ecological knowledge – often from remote corners of the developing world – that could provide an alternative vision for water use and management at this critical time. After discussing how the water cycle works and the inadequacies of current approaches to overcoming the growing gap between supply and demand, it examines each element of water use – irrigation for food production, water for households and sanitation, flood management, inland waterways for transport, and energy production – in order to identify the problems confronting us and the alternative approaches and policies we could pursue that would be compatible with nature. The book concludes by looking at current policy debates, the institutions needed to ensure the global preservation of the water cycle, and how to involve local people in water management decisions affecting their welfare.

This book makes for essential and compelling reading for students on courses related to water resources management and development; water managers and decision makers, and non-specialists with an interest in global water issues.

About the author

Constance Hunt is a biologist and environmentalist with considerable experience in international policy and global campaigns for water management and conservation. She is the recipient of awards from the National Research Council, US Department of Agriculture and US Army Corps of Engineers for outstanding work in the field of water resources management.

She has held a variety of posts. As Senior Adviser to the WWF's International Living Waters Campaign (1999–2001), she was responsible for basin-scale conservation for the Niger and Mekong rivers and for working with the WWF network on international water policy issues. Before this (1993–9) she was Senior Programme Officer and Director of Freshwater Ecosystem Conservation for the WWF, managing policy and field projects for sustainable river and wetland management in the US and internationally. She has also served with the World Water Council. She is currently a Senior Adviser with the United Nations Environment Programme (UNEP)'s Dams and Development Project, where she facilitates global dialogues on the recommendations of the World Commission on Dams.

She is the author/editor of two books on conservation, and of numerous articles on sustainable water resources development.

Thirsty Planet

Strategies for Sustainable Water Management

Constance Elizabeth Hunt

Zed Books
LONDON & NEW YORK

Thirsty Planet: Strategies for Sustainable Water Management
was first published in 2004 by
Zed Books Ltd, 7 Cynthia Street, London N1 9JF, UK and
Room 400, 175 Fifth Avenue, New York, NY 10010, USA.

www.zedbooks.co.uk

Cover design by Andrew Corbett
Designed and set in 10/12 pt Times
by Long House, Cumbria, UK
Printed and bound in Malta
by Gutenberg Ltd.

Distributed exclusively in the USA by Palgrave, a division of
St Martin's Press, LLC, 175 Fifth Avenue, New York, NY 10010.

A catalogue record for this book
is available from the British Library

US Cataloging-in-Publication Data
is available from the Library of Congress

ISBN   Hb 1 84277 242 2
       Pb 1 84277 243 0

Contents

List of Figures and Tables   ix
Glossary   xiii

Introduction   1

1   Riding the Water Cycle: Water Cycle Dynamics and Freshwater Ecosystems   5
    Water Cycle Mechanics   5
       Non-living Components of the Water Cycle   6
       The Living Components of the Water Cycle   13
       Completing the Cycle   23
    The Value of the Water Cycle and Freshwater Ecosystems   23
       Internal Ecosystem Dynamics   23
       Services Rendered   24
       Freshwater Ecosystem Values   29
    Conclusion   33

2   Spiralling Towards a Crisis: Water Use and Growing Shortages   37
    Water's Role in Human Civilization   37
       Water Use in Ancient Times   38
       Water Availability and Use in Modern Times   40
    A Global Water Crisis?   48
    Supply Side Solutions: Stretching the Water Cycle   51
    Conclusion   57

3   To Feed the World: Food Supply and the Water Cycle   62
    Status and Trends in Global Food Production   63
       Status of the Rate of Growth in Food Production   63
       How Much Water Will We Need for Food?   66
    Green Revolution Technologies and Their Repercussions   67

	Irrigation	68
	Artificial Fertilizers	70
	Pesticides	72
	Declines in Wild Fisheries	74
	How to Keep Food Growing and Water Flowing	79
	Sustainable Agriculture, or Agroecology	80
	Wild Fisheries	89
	Conclusion	91
4	**A Thirsty Planet: Water Supply and Sanitation in a Water-short World**	96
	Water Paucity and Plenty: The Great Divide	96
	Sources of Scarcity	97
	Inefficient Water Use	97
	Hydrological Alterations	100
	Desertification	101
	Pollutants	103
	Pathogens	107
	Improving Our Performance	108
	Water Conservation	109
	Pollution Prevention	114
	Environmental Monitoring and the Use of Bioindicators	115
	Restoring Landscape Functions	116
	Using Locally Appropriate Technologies	118
	Wastewater Recycling and Re-use	124
	Conclusion	125
5	**When It Rains, It Pours: Water Management for Flood Damage Reduction**	131
	The Nature and History of Floods	131
	Increasing Flood Hazards	135
	Increasing Vulnerability	136
	The Flood Control Concept	138
	Levees and Polders	138
	Channelization	140
	Dams	142
	Shifts Towards a Holistic Approach to Flood Management	145
	Adaptation	146
	Non-structural Flood Damage Reduction	147
	Flood Damage Reduction through Ecosystem Restoration	153
	Adaptive Management	154
	Conclusion	155

6 **Arteries of Commerce: Inland Waterways and the Water Cycle** 160

Building the Water Highways 161
   The Birth of Inland Navigation 161
   Current Status of Inland Navigation Systems 162
Effects of Inland Waterway Construction and Operation on the Water Cycle 166
   Inland Waterway Construction 166
   Inland Waterway Operation and Maintenance 174
Navigating Gently 180
   Making Better Use of Information 180
   Improving Intermodal Interfaces 181
   Improving Barge Design for Environmental Compatibility 182
   Watershed and Channel Management to Reduce Siltation 183
   Maintaining Natural Flow Regimes in Navigable Rivers 185
   Maintaining 'Environmental Windows' 186
   Making Beneficial Use of Dredged Material 187
Conclusion 187

7 **A Warmer World: The Interrelationships Between Global Warming and the Water Cycle** 192

The Nature of the Greenhouse Effect 192
Effects of Global Warming on the Water Cycle, Aquatic Ecosystems and People 196
   Climatic Changes 196
   Changes in Aquatic Ecosystems 199
   Likely Effects of Global Warming on Human Water Uses 203
Pseudo-solutions 204
   Hydropower: No Net Loss of Greenhouse Gases 205
   Nuclear Energy: No Net Gain of Environmental Protection 207
   Carbon Sequestration: Breaking Even and Paying for it 208
New Generation 212
   Increasing Energy Efficiency 212
   Investing in Renewable Resources 215
Conclusion 222

8 **When the Water Cycle Breaks Down: The Potential for Restoration** 228

Freshwater Ecosystems on the Brink 229
Protection 230
   Maintaining Ecological Processes 230
Restoration 233
   Restoring Processes 235
   Contemporary Principles of Aquatic Ecosystem Restoration 239
   Restoration of Specific Aquatic Ecosystem Types 244
   Understanding the Limits 253
Conclusion 254

9   **Avenues of Governance: Institutional Options for Protecting the Water Cycle**   258

Binding Agreements: Treaties   259

The Ramsar Convention   261

The United Nations Convention on the Law of the Non-navigational Uses of International Watercourses   268

Non-binding Agreements   271

The World Commission on Dams   271

The World Water Vision   275

Free Trade and Market Forces   281

GATT, GATS and the WTO   282

The World Bank and International Monetary Fund   284

Markets and Pricing   287

Conclusion   288

Index   293

Figures and Tables

FIGURES

1.1	The Mechanics of the Water Cycle	7
2.1	Global Population, Water Withdrawal and Consumption	41
2.2	Predicted Water Stress and Scarcity, 2050	49
3.1	Adult Returns of Wild Salmon to the Uppermost Dam on the Snake River below Hells Canyon	76
5.1	Flood Control Expenditure and Costs of Flood Damage in the US, 1935–85	137
7.1	Impacts of Climate Change on the Hydrological System	196
8.1	Trends in Global Indices of Species Population for the Forest, Freshwater and Marine Biomes, 1970–2000	231
9.1	Trends in Numbers of Ramsar-listed Sites Compared with Montreux-listed Sites	267
9.2	Suitable Projects Not Supported by the Small Grant Fund Due to Inadequate Funding	267

TABLES

1.1	Annual Water Balance of Continents and Oceans	10
2.1	Distribution of Water on Earth	42
2.2	Global Runoff and Population, by Continent, 1995	43
2.3	Global Withdrawal and Consumption of Water in Different Sectors, 1995	45
2.4	Large Dams and Storage Capacity of Large Reservoirs, by Continent	53
3.1	Annual Cereal Crop Yield Growth Rates, 1970s–1990s	64
3.2	World Production of Some Persistent Organic Pesticides	73
4.1	Daily Average Household Water Use per Person in Industrial Countries	99
4.2	World-wide Deaths from Water-related Diseases, 1998	107
4.3	Examples of Water-saving Fixtures for Households	113
4.4	Fog Water Production at Three Sites	120

5.1	Great Flood Disasters, 1950–98	134
5.2	Deaths from Major Flood Events, 1990–8	135
5.3	Percentage Failure Rate of Dam Types, 1831–1965	143
6.1	Emissions (Pounds [Kilograms]) Produced in Moving 1 Short Ton (0.91 Metric Tons) of Cargo 1,000 Miles (1,609.34 Kilometres)	165
7.1	Fluxes of Greenhouse Gases from Ecosystems	193
7.2	Greenhouse Gas Emissions from Reservoirs in Brazil and Canada Compared with Fossil Fuel Emission	205
7.3	Trends in Energy Use, by Source, 1990–7	216
9.1	Dates of Adoption of and Current Numbers of Contracting Parties to Major Environmental Treaties	265

Glossary

Adiabatic: Expansion or compression without the loss or gain of heat.

Alluvial: Made up of sand, clay and other material gradually deposited by moving water, as along a riverbed or the shore of a lake.

Aquaculture: The cultivation of aquatic plants and animals in controlled conditions for human consumption.

Aquifer: A body of rock or sediment that holds water that is abundant enough and can flow fast enough to serve as a natural underground reservoir.

Aqueduct: Used to refer both to a large pipe or conduit designed to carry water from distant locations and to the bridge-like structures built to carry water pipes or conduits across valleys or roads.

Asthenosphere: A zone within the Earth some distance below the surface which consists of weak material, subject to plastic deformation, underlying the stronger lithosphere.

Bathymetric: Information pertaining to underwater topography, collected by measuring the depth of water rather than the altitude of landforms, as in terrestrial topography.

Biogeography: The study of the geographical distribution of biological organisms.

Biomass: The total mass or amount of living organisms in a particular area or volume.

Biome A large, naturally occurring community of flora and fauna adapted to the particular conditions in which they occur.

Capillary force: The force that is the resultant of adhesion, cohesion and surface tension in liquids which are in contact with solids, as in a capillary tube. When the cohesive force is greater, the surface of the liquid tends to rise in the tube; when the adhesive force is greater, the surface tends to be depressed.

Chronic: Constantly reappearing or lasting a long time. When referring to health and environmental disturbances, the term connotes a lower-level disturbance that causes substantial damage over a long period of time, in contrast with short-term, 'acute' disturbances with greater immediate impact.

Collectors: Aquatic invertebrates that filter from transport, or gather from the sediments, fine, particulate organic matter and that depend on microbial biomass and products of microbial biomass for their nutrition.

Convective: Refers to the predominantly vertical atmospheric motions resulting in vertical transport and mixing of atmospheric properties.

Dam decommissioning: Cessation of use of a dam, often climaxing in the removal of the structure for safety or environmental reasons.

Demand-side management: Conservation of scarce resources through the control or reduction of consumer demand rather than producer supply. Strategies involving resource-efficient technologies, fee schedules that reward conservation, or rationing are examples.

Desertification: The degradation or destruction of land to desert-like conditions that can include the growth of sand dunes, deterioration of rangelands, degradation of rainfed croplands, waterlogging and salination of irrigated lands, deforestation of woody vegetation, and declining availability and/or quality of freshwater.

Diatom: Any member of the microscopic algae phylum *Chryophyta*, one-celled or in colonies, whose cell walls consist of two boxlike parts or valves and contain silica.

Dinoflagellate: Any member of the order *Dinoflagellata*, single-celled organisms, mainly marine and often with a cellulose shell. Some species are luminescent and some cause the 'red tides' that are extremely toxic to marine life.

DDT: Dichloro-diphenyl-trichloro-ethane, a powerful pesticide now banned in the United States but widely used in developing countries, largely to protect crops from insect damage and to control populations of malaria-carrying mosquitoes.

Endocrine disrupter: Any artificial substance that, when introduced into the body of an animal, interferes with the function of enzymes secreted by the endocrine system (consisting of the thyroid, adrenal and pituitary glands as well as reproductive organs that produce sexual hormones such as oestrogen, progesterone and testosterone). Often, endocrine disrupters function by mimicking the structure of natural enzymes, thus blocking enzyme receptor cells.

Eutrophication: The natural aging process of a lake or other water body with no outlet for accumulated sediments that results in the water body gradually filling in and its succession to dry land. The process is accelerated by human activities that increase loads of nutrients and silt in the water body.

Evapotranspiration: The total water loss from the Earth's surface, including that from direct evaporation and that by transpiration from the surfaces of plants.

Extirpation: The extermination of a genus, species or subspecies in part or all of its range. Complete extirpation, including the elimination of a genus, species or subspecies from artificial habitat (relocated populations or specimens in captivity) is known as extinction.

Geochemical material: Material associated with the chemistry of the Earth's crust.

Gigawatt-hour: Unit of energy equal to 1 billion watts (power unit equal to the rate of one joule, or one newton acting through a distance of one metre, per second) supplied for one hour.

Herbaceous: Plants without woody material, such as grasses and herbs, as opposed to woody shrubs and trees.

Hydrograph: A graph depicting the rise and fall of water at a specific place, such as at a cross-section of a river, over time.

Icthyologist: A biologist who studies the evolution, morphology, physiology, classification, distribution and/or life history of fishes.

Irrigation: Artificial watering of crops, generally using canals and distribution structures such as spray nozzles or perforated pipes, used to augment precipitation.

Introgression: The infiltration of genetic material from the gene pool of one species or subspecies into the gene pool of another.

Jet stream: A relatively strong wind concentrated within a narrow stream in the atmosphere.

Lithosphere: The Earth's crust; the solid, rocky part of the planet.

Macrophyte: A large plant, usually aquatic, as opposed to single-cell plants often found in planktonic or floating form in aquatic ecosystems.

Monoculture: The raising of only one crop or product without using the land for other purposes.

Morphological: Referring to the form and structure of living things.

Multilateral: Referring to an exchange or agreement that involves more than two sovereign states.

Non-structural: In the context of flood damage reduction, policy measures that contain no flood control structures, such as floodplain maps, land use regulations and flood insurance programmes.

Ombotrophic: Ecosystems that receive all of their water and nutrients from direct precipitation, having no sources of runoff or connection with groundwater.

Orographic: Referring to the physical geography of mountains.

Osmotic force: The force exerted by a solvent passing through a porous partition so as to equalize concentrations on both sides of the partition, equal to the pressure that must be applied to the solution in order to prevent passage of the solvent into it.

Photovoltaic: Referring to systems of semi-conductors that generate electricity by capturing electrons from the photons produced by solar radiation.

Physiological: Referring to the function of cells, organs, tissues and other morphological components of living things.

Polyculture: The raising of several to many crops and other products, such as livestock, poultry, or fish, in a single area of land.

Rig-vedic: Associated with the Rig-veda, the oldest and most important of the Hindu Vedas.

Shredders: Aquatic invertebrates that use particulate matter such as leaf litter with a significant dependence on associated microbial biomass.

Succession: The sequence of changes in the development of biological communities in which early-stage plants and animals create the conditions necessary to support different plants and animals in later stages. Succession is bidirectional as communities in later stages of development can be set back to earlier stages by natural or artificial disruptions such as fire, floods or hurricanes.

Supply-side management: Regulation of resource use through the control of supply to consumers. Generally involves increasing supplies of scarce resources in order to expand markets and inflate profits.

Transgenic: Refers to organisms whose genetic constitution has been altered by the (artificial) introduction of alien genes.

Water consumption: The use of water in such a way that it will only return to its source over a very long time period, or perhaps not at all. Crop irrigation provides an example, where water withdrawn from a lake or river is incorporated into the flesh of the crop and may be transported out of the drainage basin or even to another continent.

Water withdrawal: The extraction of water, some of which may return to its source, used or unused, over a relatively short time period.

Westerlies: Poleward-flowing winds over the middle latitudes of both hemispheres that travel from a predominantly westerly direction.

Introduction

The world's water experts spent much of 1999 massaging data, running models, convening consultative meetings and drafting reports in preparation for the Second World Water Forum in The Hague in March 2000. A great deal of the discussion revolved around the development of projected needs in three important water resources subsectors—water supply and sanitation, food production and nature conservation. Global and regional discussions attempted to sort out how much water would be needed in each subsector to meet growing demands by the year 2025. The people involved in formulating projections of water needs for food production relied on the use of fairly robust data sets and sophisticated models to reach their compelling conclusion. They estimated that a 17 percent increase in water consumed by irrigated agriculture would be necessary to provide for the nutritional needs of a world population likely to rise to somewhere between 7 and 11 billion by the year 2025. The chief spokesman for this subsector made an impressive presentation, replete with charts and graphs. He then turned to the nature conservation people and asked them exactly how much water the world would have to reserve 'for nature'. The nature conservation people looked rather alarmed at the philosophical gulf that yawned between the two subsectors. 'Nature is not a competitor for water,' came the response. 'Nature is the source of water.'

The thesis conveyed by these pages is simple. *Nature is the source of water; therefore our ability to support additional human lives on planet Earth depends upon the protection of nature and the continued operation of the water cycle.*

The water cycle is the combination of natural physical, chemical and biological processes that constantly recycle water, ensuring a steady supply to support life on Earth. The water cycle depends on the integrity of our planet's ecosystems in order to function. The Earth's diversity of life forms and landscapes – ranging from vast, majestic forests transpiring water into the atmosphere to tunnelling termites aiding water infiltration into the soil – make up a complex and intricate machinery. Our survival depends on this machinery to provide us with essential water.

Neglect of the integrity of the water cycle could have severe consequences for people and other living things. Most known forms of life on Earth depend on access to a water supply of adequate quality and quantity. Virtually all known forms of life that people consume as food or in commerce must have water to survive.

The aspirations of human society expand the applications of water from the simple survival and reproduction needs shared by most other forms of life to comfort, convenience, enterprise and recreation. Every newborn baby and most human struggles to achieve a higher standard of living place additional stress on the natural processes that provide our planet with water. If we take too much water, or severely damage the ecosystems that constantly renew our water supplies, the water cycle will break down. Water will become scarce or too polluted to use. According to one estimate, by the year 2025, nearly two billion people will live in regions or countries with absolute water scarcity – defined as the lack of sufficient water to maintain current per capita levels of food production and meet expanding urban demands for water even at a high level of irrigation efficiency.[1] This anticipated explosion of local and regional water shortages is collectively viewed by many in the water resources sector as an emerging 'global water crisis.'

The human ability to dodge global catastrophes is remarkable. We refrained from using biological weapons during the Second World War and nuclear weapons during the Cold War. The restraint shown in both of these cases was exemplary of the human survival instinct operating in the absence of binding agreements or functional global governance. Similar restraint in the context of water use will be needed to avoid a global water crisis. We must call upon our creativity and generosity to craft solutions that will perpetuate the water cycle. These solutions will consist of a wide array of ideas and technologies, ranging from the communications and networking potential of the Internet to the many generations of ecological knowledge passed down orally in remote corners of the developing world.

We must also recognize the complexity of the problems. The global water cycle comprises many interlocking and nested regional and local water cycles. Similarly, a global water crisis would not be truly global in nature but the combined result of ubiquitous local shortages of water. In every part of the planet, the causes of the 'water crisis' are somewhat specific. The solutions must be tailored to the causes of the problems. There is no global solution.

In the interest of the long-term sustainability of the water cycle, world leaders must commit their countries to protecting the natural ecosystems that sustain it. In many instances, this may require substantial changes to current patterns of water use. Uses that change the quantity, quality and timing of water flows to various parts of the natural ecosystem may introduce disruptions to the water cycle that eventually result in a reduction of good-quality water. The objectives that those uses have supported – including food production, flood damage reduction, provision of energy, transport of goods to markets and others – need to be met in ways that sustain the water cycle if we are to ensure an adequate future supply of water for our planet.

This argument responds sceptically to the idea that human ingenuity can overcome whatever insults we inflict upon the natural world. While we have had some limited success in turning salt water to sweet and wastewater to drinking water, the expense of these practices prohibits any reasonable hope of a panacea.

The following pages present an alternative vision for water use and management in the twenty-first century. This vision rises above the debate over whether or not to rely on controversial infrastructure such as dams to avoid a global water crisis. The intent of this work is to outline a 'third way' that will allow people to achieve a comfortable standard of living while protecting the sources of the planet's water supply for future generations.

The first chapter describes how the water cycle works and why its continued functioning relies on the presence of intact ecosystems. The second chapter discusses the nature of the 'global water crisis' in terms of water's role in human civilization, the current availability and uses of water, and the consequences of human interference in the water cycle. Chapter 2 also challenges the reader to consider the viability of broad-brush approaches to resolving the global gap between demand for and supply of water.

Chapters 3–6 present a discussion of how current approaches to water management disrupt the water cycle and what alternatives are available to achieve human objectives in a more sustainable fashion. Topics covered include food production, water supply and sanitation, flood damage reduction and navigation.

Chapter 7 addresses the issue of global warming, including its effects on aquatic ecosystems. This chapter also discusses the pros and cons of alternative energy sources in the context of water cycle maintenance.

Chapter 8 discusses the protection and restoration of aquatic ecosystems – actions that are essential to the continued operation of the water cycle.

Chapter 9 delves into current policy debates. What institutions are needed to ensure global preservation of the water cycle? How do we ensure adequate representation of and participation by local people in water management decisions that affect their welfare? Will we be able to strike a balance between global governance and decentralization or between the efficiency of markets and the protection of human rights and the environment? The implications of these policy issues for the continued function of the water cycle are examined.

Collectively, these chapters offer an analysis of how current water management practices may need to change if we are to sustain the water cycle. While some of the prescriptions may seem radical or potentially expensive, it is important to note their synergy. Larger investments in watershed management and soil and water conservation practices could improve water yield and consistency and crop production while decreasing rates of erosion and sedimentation that increase the costs of dredging. The increased use of non-hydropower, renewable energy sources – such as solar, geothermal and wind – could help address air quality and global climate change concerns, both of which affect the availability of potable water.

The author hopes that the following compilation of ideas, information and case studies will help place the international dialogue over the potential for devastating water shortages in a new light.

NOTE

1 Seckler, D., D. Molden & R. Barker, 1999. 'Water Scarcity in the Twenty-first Century.' *International Journal of Water Resources Development*, March.

1 Riding the Water Cycle
Water Cycle Dynamics
and Freshwater Ecosystems

'Four and a half billion years ago, Earth was still a molten magma ball, seething from the collision that ejected the Moon. As the planet cooled, its constituents separated like curdled milk. Within about fifty million years, the iron of which much of the Earth was comprised had sunk to the core, and the lighter elements (silicon, aluminum, calcium, magnesium, sodium, potassium, and oxygen, along with some remaining iron) formed a rocky crust at the surface – just as slag floats on top of molten iron in a smelter.

'Amongst all this rocky stuff were the volatile compounds delivered by collisions as the planet formed – hydrogen, nitrogen, hydrogen sulfide, carbon oxides and water. While the Earth was molten, these volatile compounds were dissolved in the magma, but as the molten rock cooled and solidified, the vapours were released in a process called degassing. The atmosphere that resulted from degassing was very different from today's, consisting mostly of carbon dioxide, nitrogen and water vapour....

'Those formative years were steamy times on Earth, for all the water was in the sky. And then sometime between 4.4 and 4.0 billion years ago, the temperature fell far enough for water to condense. Clouds massed in the sky, and the oceans rained down....

'Far from eradicating life, this deluge set the stage for life's entry. It turned the face of the world blue, and created a planet that exists, in atmospheric scientist James Lovelock's words, as "a strange and beautiful anomaly in our solar system".'[1]

WATER CYCLE MECHANICS

Life as we know it could not exist in the absence of freshwater. Water provides lubrication for living cells, the very building blocks of life. Water circulates through living beings, transporting materials such as nutrients to our organs, facilitating the chemical reactions that drive life's functions, and removing waste materials.

Water performs similar functions for entire ecosystems as it does for individual organisms. It circulates around the world, transporting nutrients and building materials to ecosystems, facilitating the chemical communication between ecosystems, and cleansing ecosystems so that they can maintain optimal performance.

What is more, the reliable provision of high-quality water for human uses depends on the healthy functioning of ecosystems, particularly freshwater ecosystems. Water and rock come into being and metamorphose into various forms as a function of the nihilistic physics of the Universe. The evolution of ecosystems with living components that we recognize as the biosphere buffers the raw physical processes that create and destroy matter. This sophisticated and delicate living skin on the surface of the Earth regulates the movement and quality of water in ways that perpetuate its own well-being and that of humankind.

Non-living Components of the Water Cycle

The continued supply of freshwater to the Earth's biosphere is made possible by the water cycle, that is, the natural processes by which water is purified and redistributed from up to 15 kilometres over and up to 5 kilometres under the surface of the Earth (see Figure 1.1).[2] The water cycle is driven by the constant supply to the Earth of solar energy, which evaporates water from the oceans and the land and transports it to other parts of the globe. Because more water evaporates from the oceans than falls on them as precipitation, there is a continuous transfer of freshwater from the oceans to the continents. Water is captured and temporarily detained by wetlands, ponds and lakes which eventually release it back into circulation through evaporation, seepage into groundwater systems, or discharge into rivers. On an annual basis, roughly 505,000 cubic kilometres per year evaporates from the oceans, equivalent to the top metre and a half of the sea.[3] Of this, roughly 10 percent falls as precipitation over land and the rest falls directly back into the ocean.[4] About 45,000 km³ of water per year are returned to the oceans as river runoff and groundwater flows.[5]

The hydrosphere is the interconnection between the biosphere, the atmosphere and the lithosphere that serves to integrate the planet's fluxes of water, energy and geochemical compounds. Water has a number of exceptional properties that provide it with the capacity to perform these functions. First, it has a high and universal dissolving power that is essential for distributing geochemical material and nutrients and for removing waste substances from living organisms. Second, it has a high surface tension, causing high capillary forces together with osmotic forces, which enables water and solute transport within living things. Third, a maximum density above the freezing point at 4 degrees centigrade allows freezing to proceed from the surface downward, slowing down both the heat release and the advancement of the freezing process, and thus protecting living organisms. Fourth, water has high freezing and boiling points relative to its molecular weight in comparison to similarly structured compounds such as H_2S and H_2Se. Compared to

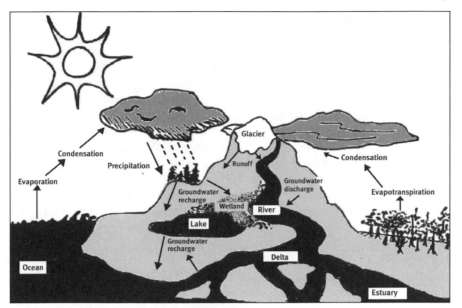

Figure 1.1 The Mechanics of the Water Cycle

these compounds, the freezing and boiling points of water would be between –50 and –100 degrees centigrade. All of these properties stem from the high cohesion and pseudo-crystalline structure of water.[6]

Origins of Water on Planet Earth

It is likely that water has been a part of our solar system since the beginning and is a product of the thermonuclear fusion process that produced the elements of the periodic table. The total amount of water present in the solar system is estimated at approximately 100,000 times the 1,350,000,000 km³ mass of water in our oceans. Water on Earth may have originated from the degassing of the planet's mantle by volcanic eruptions and surfacing lava.[7] Over time, the surface of the planet cooled and the water vapour present in the atmosphere condensed to form the oceans.

Some scientists theorize that the processes that generated the hydrological cycle continue to operate today. One commonly held belief is that degassing of the Earth's mantle by volcanic eruptions continues to contribute water to the cycle. Over the five-billion-year lifespan of the Earth, the amount of water that is 'reborn' each year is about one km³.[8] On the other hand, a small amount returns to the mantle through the plate-tectonic process. This process is driven by thermal convection currents, which move over the rigid lithosphere that forms a coherent layer over the more plastic asthenosphere. Magma moves upward into the spreading centres, or fractures, in the ocean floor, where it forms new oceanic crust and causes the lithosphere to move away from the fractures. Subduction occurs at the other end of the convection cell, where the lithosphere sinks downward. Where the old lithosphere disappears in the mantle, ocean water is dragged with the crust to depths of hundreds of kilometres and becomes involved in the re-melting of sediments into new magma.[9]

Some scientists believe that all of Earth's water may have come from comets and that the solar system continues to contribute water to the planet in the form of comets. According to this theory, comets made mostly of ice and weighing 20 to 40 tons enter the Earth's gravity field every few seconds, at a rate of thousands per day, then melt and vaporize when they near the Earth. If this rate has been constant over our planet's history, it could account for the entire volume of water here today. The comets would have delivered enough moisture to Earth to cover the entire surface of the planet with 2.5 cm of water every 20,000 years, or about six kilometres over 4.5 billion years. The Earth apparently exchanges water with the rest of the solar system as well: solar winds may be taking about four cubic metres of water out of the atmosphere each day in the form of ionized hydrogen and oxygen gases.[10]

Water in the Atmosphere

Today, a relatively tiny amount of water, roughly 15,000 km^3, is present as atmospheric water vapour at any point in time. The atmosphere recycles its entire water content 33 times each year (total precipitation divided by total atmospheric precipitable water vapour), giving water vapour a mean global residence time of about eleven days.[11] Because warm air can hold more water than cold air, the average annual vapour content decreases from 50 mm water equivalent in the equatorial regions to less than 5 mm over the polar regions.[12] This water plays a very important role in maintaining life on Earth. Water vapour constitutes two-thirds of the total amount of greenhouse gases that warm the planet by trapping heat in the atmosphere. Without these gases, the mean surface temperature of the planet would be well below freezing and liquid water would be absent from much of the planet.[13]

The molecules in liquid water are always in motion, and the warmer they are, the more they move. This movement eventually propels them into the air as vapour. Water vapour also rises from ice in a process called sublimation. As mentioned above, warm air can hold more water vapour than cold air.[14] Evaporation can only occur where a vapour pressure gradient is maintained between the evaporating surface and the overlying atmosphere. Evaporation also requires energy to convert water into vapour. While evaporation is driven by solar energy, the distribution over oceans doesn't reflect the pattern of incoming radiation because latent heat is a factor of the heat stored in the water itself and is therefore influenced by the varying temperatures of ocean currents. For example, when a cold, dry air mass passes over a warm ocean current, the high vapour pressure gradient between the warm water and dry air stimulates upward vapour transport.[15]

Water vapour condenses as it cools, whether it is forced to higher, colder altitudes by mountains or chilled by the night sky to meet us in the morning as dew. Cooling usually results from the adiabatic expansion of uplifted air caused by the decrease in atmospheric pressure with height. Heat release by condensation can subsequently provide additional energy to cause a further rise of the air mass, which can result in convective thunderstorms.[16]

'The most noteworthy characteristic of any small body of fresh water – be it a pond, a stream, an icicle, or a rain cloud – is its impermanence. Ponds evaporate, streams flow to the sea, icicles melt and dribble away, rain falls: water is forever on the move, repeatedly changing its state – liquid, ice or vapour – in the process. In a word, it is dynamic. In much the same way that every living organism has a life cycle, water has a water cycle; it circulates. Indeed all the water on earth is constantly circulating.'[17]

Water vapour condenses into droplets only when small particles, such as dust, sea salt crystals, free-floating bacteria, or smoke are present to serve as nuclei. The droplets form clouds. Within the clouds, droplets move and may bump into each other, forming larger droplets as a result. When the droplets become too heavy to remain aloft, they fall to the ground as rain, sleet, snow or hail, losing volume to evaporation as they fall.

At low latitudes the air column rises and moves towards the poles on either side of the equator. Cooling air causes the air column to descend at higher latitudes. These tendencies result in the development of convective wind cells with low pressure at the equator and high pressure in the region of 30 degrees latitude. The rotation of the Earth causes the divergent spiralling of low-pressure cells. The compensating back-flowing air produces the north-easterly and south-easterly trade winds that converge near the equator in the Inter-Tropical Convergence Zone, or ITCZ. Rising air in the equatorial convergence zone produces the high rainfall of the west-tropical rainforest areas, while the heating of the air by compression that occurs in the high-pressure belt creates the low rainfall zone of the dry, subtropical steppes and desert areas. The distance from the moist oceanic air extends these arid zones northwards into remote interiors of the northern hemisphere. Part of the warm air from the subtropical high-pressure belt moves to higher latitudes and forms the prevailing westerlies of the northern hemisphere.[18]

Cold air sinks at the poles and then spreads along an easterly course, colliding at mid-altitude with the westerlies. Where this occurs, the warm, subtropical air rides over the polar air and forms polar fronts, which are the cold front that separates the main body of colder, drier air emanating from the poles from the warmer, moister air closer to the equator. The forced uplift of moist, warm air triggers the development of anticyclonic, or low-pressure, cells. Low-pressure pulses also drive formulation of low-pressure cells in the meandering jet stream in the upper part of the westerlies. These low-pressure cells cycle inward in a convergent, spiralling movement that produces the frontal rains of mid-latitude convective cells in overheated air.[19]

Water on the Planet's Surface

Average annual rainfall on the continents (approximately 746 mm) represents a 50 percent surplus over average annual evapotranspiration (approximately 480 mm). The time during which this water runs into the ocean is extended on a seasonal basis by the detention storage of snow in the northern hemisphere. Over 60 to 70 percent of North America and Eurasia typically receives a snow cover that reaches its maximum volume in March or April, with maximum depletion at the end of summer. This lag provides the oceans with their maximum storage around October. In addition, the distribution of precipitation, evaporation and inflow from the continents produces a surplus in the Indian and Atlantic oceans and a deficit in the Pacific and Arctic oceans. As a result, there is a continuous transfer of water from the Indian and Atlantic Oceans to the Pacific and Arctic Oceans (see Table 1.1).[20]

Table 1.1 Annual Water Balance of Continents and Oceans

	Area (10^3km^2)	Precipitation		Evaporation		Discharge		Hydrosphere (discharge as % of precipitation)
		(10^3 km^3)	mm	(10^3 km^3)	mm	(10^3 km^3)	mm	
Europe	10	6.6	657	3.8	375	2.8	282	43
Asia	44.1	30.7	696	18.5	420	12.2	276	40
Africa	29.8	20.7	696	17.3	582	3.4	114	16
Australia	8.9	7.1	803	4.7	534	2.4	296	34
North America	24.1	15.6	645	9.7	403	5.9	242	38
South America	17.9	28.0	1564	16.9	946	11.1	618	40
Antarctica	14.1	2.4	170	0.4	28	2.0	142	83
All continents	148.9	111	746	71.3	480	39.7	266	36
Arctic Ocean	8.5	0.8	97	0.4	53	0.4	44	45
Atlantic Ocean	98.0	74.6	761	111.1	1133	−36.5	−372	−49
Indian Ocean	77.7	81	1043	11.5	1294	−195	−251	−24
Pacific Ocean	176.9	228.5	1292	212.6	1202	15.9	90	7
All oceans	361.1	385	1066	224.7	1176	−39.7	−110	−10

From Mook, W. G. (ed.), 2000. *United Nations Educational, Scientific and Cultural Organization/International Atomic Energy Agency Series on Environmental Isotopes in the Hydrological Cycle: Principles and Application.* Volume I. p. 14.

As soon as water falls on land, it interacts with both the biotic (living) and abiotic (non-living) components of the biosphere, making life possible as it flows back to the sea. While some of this water moves over the surface as runoff or in lakes, streams and wetlands, 35 times as much freshwater, or about 30 percent of all freshwater on Earth, is underground at any point in time.[21] This amount is equivalent to a 55-metre-thick layer spread out over the entire surface of the Earth.

The word 'groundwater' refers to water that saturates the ground, filling all available spaces. Water enters the system at a recharge point from precipitation or seepage from surface water bodies and leaves the system through evapo-transpiration (discussed in the next section) or by seeping into surface water bodies at a discharge point.

While many people picture groundwater as a network of underground streams and reservoirs, most groundwater actually occupies the pore spaces between soil particles. The ground containing the groundwater is called the saturated zone, and the water's upper surface is the water table. If the water table is not at the soil surface, as it often is in wetlands, the soil profile will have an unsaturated zone, known as the vadose zone, above the saturated zone, where available spaces contain some air as well as water.[22]

A low-permeability barrier formed by rock or thin sediments (aquitard) often defines the base of the water table. The positions of these features in the landscape relative to the position of surface water systems is a major factor determining the pattern and rate of exchange between groundwater and surface water ecosystems. Areas that freely allow movement of water into the groundwater are called recharge areas. Areas where groundwater emerges above receiving aquatic ecosystems are called springs or seeps.

The configuration of the water table changes seasonally and year to year according to groundwater recharge and discharge. Groundwater recharge, which is the accretion of water to the upper surface of the saturated zone, is related to the wide variations in the quantity, distribution and timing of precipitation.[23] The volume of groundwater and the elevation of the water table fluctuate, and because of this a stream channel can function either as a recharge area (influent or 'losing' stream) or as a discharge area (effluent or 'gaining' stream) in relation to the aquifer. The same stream channel segment can also function as a discharge area during the dry part of the year and as a recharge area during the rainy season.

The most common type of groundwater is meteoric water, which circulates as part of the water cycle. The interactions between surface and underground water are complex; any single water molecule may pass from above the ground to below it many times before it returns to the sea. Most movement is driven by hydraulic head, which is the sum of elevation and water pressure divided by the weight density of water. The greater the hydraulic head, the more quickly water will move through the saturated zone. The permeability of the substrate also influences the rate at which groundwater flows. For example, sand is more permeable than clay because the pore spaces between sand grains are larger than those between clay particles.[24] Igneous rock – the product of volcanic activity, such as basalt, is virtually impermeable. In impermeable substrates, groundwater may be contained in fractures and between layers of rock.

Groundwater moves along flow paths of varying lengths from the point of recharge to the point of discharge. In the uppermost, unconfined portion of the saturated zone, flow paths near a stream can be tens to hundreds of metres long and have travel times of days to a few years. The longest and deepest flow paths may be thousands of metres to tens of kilometres in length, with travel times ranging from decades to millennia.[25]

Groundwater moves both vertically and laterally, with flow systems of different sizes and depths frequently overlaying one another. In local flow systems, water that recharges at a water table discharges to adjacent lowland. Local flow systems are the most dynamic and shallowest, and therefore have the most interchange with surface water systems. Water in deeper flow systems has longer flow paths and longer contact times with subsurface materials; as a result, the water generally contains more dissolved chemicals. When the deep flow systems eventually discharge into surface waters, they can substantially influence the chemical characteristics of the receiving water body.[26]

For groundwater to discharge into a stream channel, the altitude of the water table in the vicinity of the stream must be higher than the altitude of the surface water in the stream. The groundwater component of stream flow is called baseflow. While baseflow is usually more consistent than flow contributed by surface runoff, it may also vary during the course of a day or over periods of weeks, months, years and decades. Groundwater inputs may also vary over the length of a stream course, with some reaches of a stream receiving water from the ground and other reaches discharging into the ground.

During a flood, the rapid rise in stream stage (level) causes water to move from the channel into the streambanks in a process known as bank storage. If the water remains between the banks and doesn't overflow onto the floodplain, most of the water stored in the bank enters the stream again within a few days or weeks. This temporary storage can reduce flood peaks and later supplement streamflows. If the rise in stream stage does cause the water to overtop the bank, widespread recharge to the water table can occur in the floodplain. When this happens, the time required for the floodwater to return to the stream channel by groundwater flow may be weeks, months or years because the lengths of the groundwater flow paths are much longer than those resulting from local bank storage.[27]

Lakes may either receive water from the ground or seep into the ground, but most lakes receive groundwater in parts of their beds and seep into the ground in other parts. The interactions between groundwater and streams and groundwater and lakes differ in several ways. First, the water levels of natural lakes do not change as rapidly as the water levels of streams, and therefore bank storage is less important. On the other hand, because the surface areas of lakes are greater than those of rivers, because there is less shading by vegetation, and because replenishment of lakes requires more time than replenishment of rivers, evaporation exerts more influence on lakes than on streams. Finally, lake sediments typically have a higher organic matter content than stream sediments. The lower permeability of organic deposits on the lakebed can affect the distribution of seepage and biogeochemical exchanges of water and solutes more in lakes than in streams.[28]

The withdrawal and consumption of water at rates that exceed natural renewal rates are unsustainable. Natural renewal rates vary substantially. Renewal rates for rivers average about 18 days.[29] In contrast, the residence time of water in deep groundwater aquifers or large glaciers may be measured in hundreds, thousands or hundreds of thousands of years.[30] Water in deep aquifers is often called 'fossil water' because once it is removed from the ground it will not be renewed over any time scale that is relevant to people. If water is removed and consumed from these components of the hydrological cycle faster than it is replenished, even accounting for the possibility that comets may contribute relatively small amounts to the water stock each year, eventually the planet will run out of water.

The Living Components of the Water Cycle

The Earth's ecosystems play a critical role in maintaining the water cycle even as they are maintained by it. If the only source of rainfall on the planet were the 10 percent of evaporation from the ocean that falls over dry land, the average precipitation across the Earth's surface would be only 25 centimetres per year – a value typical for deserts and semi-arid regions. However, two-thirds of the 70 centimetres of precipitation that falls over land each year is made available through evapotranspiration. This movement of water through the biosphere is closely coupled with the cycling of biologically important materials such as carbon and nitrogen. In the process of moving water from the soil to the atmosphere, plants combine water with carbon dioxide using solar energy to produce carbohydrates, which form the basis of nutrition for most animals. Together, precipitation from water evaporated by the ocean and that evapotranspired from vegetation account for the 110,000 km^3 of renewable freshwater available each year.[31]

Mechanical Interactions with Non-living Components

The interactions between the living and non-living components of ecosystems provide purification and regulation services that keep our water clean and moderate climatically driven droughts and floods. Freshwater ecosystems are particularly important in this regard because they form the reservoirs that make water available for use by humans, plants and animals. The value of the services generated when living and non-living components interact within freshwater ecosystems is discussed below (see 'The Value of the Water Cycle and Freshwater Ecosystems' on page 23).

The living components of a freshwater ecosystem can affect the characteristics of the water cycle. For instance, low rates of decomposition in some types of wetlands can cause basins to fill with undecomposed plant material, thus altering water conditions. Another example is that the water tables of some forested wetlands are regulated by evapotranspiration. When trees are removed from these ecosystems, standing open water and marsh vegetation can develop.

The activities of animals such as alligators, muskrats and beaver also contribute to the naturally dynamic nature of these systems. Female alligators, for example, fill in marshes by building nest mounds in which to lay their eggs. These mounds serve as nesting sites for turtles and colonization areas for plants. Trees and shrubs root on old mounds and may initiate the transformation of an open-water marsh into an upland forest.[32] Muskrats also both expand and contract aquatic ecosystems. They may consume enormous amounts of vegetation, allowing water to inundate areas that previously were fairly dry. On the other hand, they also build dens made of piles of reeds, sticks and other vegetative matter plastered with mud, which are often the first places in an aquatic ecosystem to be colonized by plants.[33] Beavers build dams and dykes, thereby storing streamflows. Beaver dams, which are often constructed in small, headwater streams, can increase surface water area, forcing water into riparian groundwater systems where it moistens the soil. Water stored in these areas can provide sources of recharge for the streams during dry periods, adding stability to flows that would otherwise fluctuate or disappear. Beaver activity may also decrease runoff during storms and lessen the damaging effects of downstream floods, without invoking the negative social and environmental effects of large dams.[34]

There are three primary processes by which ecosystems in general regulate the water cycle. These are evapotranspiration, infiltration and runoff.[35]

Evapotranspiration refers to the combined processes of evaporation and transpiration through which water that has interacted with vegetation enters the atmosphere. Because it is difficult to measure vegetative evaporation and transpiration separately, the two processes are generally considered as a package.

A portion of precipitation never reaches the ground because it is intercepted by vegetation and other natural and constructed surfaces. The amount of water intercepted in this manner is determined by the amount of interception storage available on the above-ground surfaces. This will vary depending on characteristics of the ecosystem (such as vegetation type and density). The intensity, duration and frequency of precipitation also determine the amount of water intercepted above ground. Much of this water is subject to evaporation, as is water in the vadose zone.

Transpiration is the diffusion of water vapour from plant leaves to the atmosphere. Unlike intercepted water, which originates from precipitation, transpired water originates from water taken in by the roots from the vadose zone. Vegetation transfers enormous amounts of water from the soil to the atmosphere through the process of transpiration. One Douglas fir tree, for example, can transpire 100 litres in a summer day.[36]

In the hour following a heavy rainstorm, ten tons of water vapour can evapotranspire from every hectare of an evergreen forest.[37] Evapotranspiration can dominate the water balance and can control such critical features of the water cycle as soil moisture content, groundwater recharge and streamflow.

The term **infiltration** refers to the portion of precipitation that soaks into the ground. Water that reaches the ground may be stored there for relatively long periods of time. Suctioned downward by gravity and capillary action, water infiltrates into the soil through channels formed by soil pores, as discussed above, animals ranging from bacteria and worms to rabbits and groundhogs, and root systems. Areas with natural vegetative cover and leaf litter usually have high porosity and infiltration rates. This is because these features protect the surface soil pore spaces from becoming clogged by fine soil particles created by raindrop splash.[38] They also provide habitat for worms and other burrowing organisms and provide organic matter that helps bind fine soil particles together.

Infiltration rates change throughout the duration of a storm. After a storm passes, gravity drains water out of upper soils. The water that remains in the soil maintains soil moisture, which provides terrestrial plants with water. Water that is not held in the upper reaches of the soil will continue to move downward until it reaches the groundwater table.

The term **runoff** refers to the portion of precipitation that doesn't evapotranspire or infiltrate, but instead runs overland until it empties into a surface water system, such as a stream, pond, wetland or lake. When the rate of rainfall or snowmelt exceeds infiltration capacity, excess water collects on the soil surfaces in small depressions. After these depression storage spaces are filled, excess water begins moving down-slope as overland flow, either as a shallow sheet of water or as a series of small rivulets or rills. The sheet of water increases in depth and velocity as it moves downhill. Factors that affect runoff processes include climate, geology, topography, soil characteristics and vegetation. Runoff typically occurs as overland flow, subsurface flow, and saturated overland flow. Overland flow takes place in areas with low infiltration rates, such as unvegetated slopes and paved, urban areas. Subsurface flow refers to the portion of water that runs off the landscape below the soil surface. Subsurface flow combines with groundwater flows and increases the total amount of groundwater that discharges to a stream channel during a storm. Saturated overland flow is groundwater that rises above the soil surface or the stream channel elevation and mixes with overland runoff.

Water Circulation through Freshwater Ecosystems

Water is constantly circulating on and below the surface of the land, and in the atmosphere. The constant interactions between water and the rocks and soils it encounters on its journey are major factors in the formation of landscape features (geomorphology). These features – floodplains, channels and terraces for example – provide the physical habitat for freshwater organisms.

Freshwater ecosystems are generally characterized by five broad landscapes. These are riverine landscapes, which include rivers and streams; depressional landscapes, which include lakes and ponds; and three landscape types that define wetlands: fringe, or wetlands at the margins of lakes or estuaries; slopes, or springs and seeps that emerge on hillsides; and flats, or extensive peatlands and mineral soil flats. Three general sources of water may feed these systems: precipitation, overland flow, and groundwater discharge.[39] The combination of landscape features, water source, water properties and circulation present in any aquatic ecosystem helps to determine the texture of the habitat characteristics (for instance, water depth and flow velocity). It is, therefore, a major determinant of the biological community occupying that ecosystem.

Rivers and streams, collectively referred to as lotic or running water ecosystems, are appropriately thought of as the venous system of the biosphere. The quantity and temporal distribution of stream flow, known as the hydrological regime, can be viewed as a complex, interactive function of at least three important extrinsic controls: climate, vegetative characteristics of the river basin, and physical characteristics of the basin. Climate controls the quantity and temporal distribution of precipitation and the form in which it falls, rain or snow, and thus sets an upper limit to runoff over an arbitrary time limit.[40]

Streams originate in headwater areas, usually as outlets from ponds or lakes (discussed below), or as discharge from springs, seepage areas or caves where the water table intersects the surface of the land, or as meltwater from glaciers. As the water drains away from its source, it follows the force of gravity, seeking the lowest path in the landscape subject to the malleability of the underlying substrate.

When the flow captures enough water, and thus enough energy, to create an essentially permanent channel,[41] it becomes a stream. At the top of a watershed, where the descent of a nascent stream is likely to be most steep, a stream will typically carry a scouring load of debris that continues to cut the channel until it eventually settles out in a region of lower energy.

Streams that have no tributaries are labelled first-order streams. Streams with one tributary are second-order streams, and so on from the tiniest trickle to the muscular rivers that empty into the sea. First-order streams tend to originate in steep and often mountainous landscapes; in the process of creating their channels they flow furiously in a relatively straight channel, creating sections of rapids where they meet resistance from the bedrock. At higher orders, which are lower in the landscape, the land is more level and the velocity of the river decreases substantially. The river may then create a meandering channel, eroding material from the outside of a curve (where the water must move faster to catch up with the water moving through the shorter inside of the curve), and depositing material as point bars on the more sluggish inside of the curve.

Three primary processes are involved with flowing water: erosion, sediment transport and sediment deposition. Erosion forms the beginning of most geomorphic processes. The occurrence, magnitude and distribution of erosion processes in watersheds affect the yield of sediment and associated contaminants to receiving water bodies. Soil erosion can occur gradually over a long period, or it can be cyclic or episodic, accelerating during certain seasons or during high-intensity storms. Soil conditions influence erosion rates from the land and change with changing temperature, soil moisture content, amount and growth stage of vegetation, and land use. Substrate particle size, streambed gradient, and flow rates and volumes influence erosion rates within stream channels.

Sediment transport is the movement of eroded material within the banks of a river. Sediment transport redistributes material of many different sizes and origins, including eroded material from the watershed and from the bed and banks of the channel itself. The energy that sets sediment particles in motion is derived from differences in flow velocity in different parts of the channel. The gradient of the stream, the size of sediment and bed materials, and the volume of water flowing through it at any given time largely determine the amount of sediment that a stream can transport.

Sediment deposition refers to the resettling of sediments out of the water column onto a receiving substrate. Sediments tend to drop out of suspension when the flow of water slows, as it does where a sediment-bearing stream enters a pool of quiet water such as a lake or a reservoir. Especially during floods, sediments also deposit on floodplains, where they serve as areas for plant colonization when the floodwaters recede. Sediment deposition within lakes can promote eutrophication by reducing water depth, which leads to relatively warmer water temperatures and larger zones where primary production (photosynthesis) is possible.

The patterns of sedimentation and erosion vary from stream to stream and sometimes from upper portions of one stream to another. Many first-order streams and small channels are relatively straight, and so steeply sloped that the sediment they transport along the bed (known as the bedload) includes large pieces of cobble. In higher-order streams and large river channels, a more gentle slope gives rise to patterns of channel braiding (multiple channels separated by numerous islands and sandbars in a braided pattern) and meandering (the pattern of winding back and forth across the floodplain like ribbon candy, a result of sediment erosion and deposition as described above). Changes to either the stream gradient or water volume will affect the stream's sediment transport capacity and can cause an increase in either erosion or deposition rates within the stream channel.

The processes of sediment erosion and deposition are dynamic in nature, and therefore create a constantly changing mosaic of in-stream habitat types. The physical variables within a stream and river system generate a continuous gradient of conditions, including width, depth, velocity, flow volume and temperature from the headwaters to the final river mouth. Biological communities organize themselves in response to these changes.

In the headwaters, which typically include stream orders one through three, streamside or riparian vegetation provides the bulk of food, and thus of energy. In these reaches, invertebrate communities composed of shredders and collectors dominate.[42] Most fish in headwater areas are insectivores, or animals that prey on invertebrates – primarily insects.[43] As the size of the stream increases at higher stream orders, the importance of terrestrial inputs of organic material decreases, coincidental with the enhanced significance of primary production and organic transport from upstream. Rivers of medium size rely on algae or macrophytes (vascular aquatic plants) for food and energy inputs. Scrapers, invertebrates that are adapted primarily for shearing attached algae from surfaces, dominate in these rivers.[44] Fish that eat other fish and invertebrates are the predominant vertebrates.

Large rivers receive quantities of fine-particulate organic matter from upstream processing of dead leaves and woody debris. In these reaches, depth and turbidity often limit primary production by plant photosynthesis. Here, fish that eat plankton often dominate – a situation that closely mimics the lentic (or standing-water) systems described below.

The interactions between rivers and their floodplains support both terrestrial and aquatic life. Many fish receive cues from seasonal increases in river flows to move upstream to reproduce. During a flood, fish move into ponded areas formed on the floodplain to reproduce. When the flood water recedes, the ponds are isolated from the main stem of the river, providing a nursery area where young fish can grow without facing threats from aquatic predators. In rivers with two flood seasons per year, a fall flood will reconnect the river with the floodplain, and the young fish will swim into the main stem. These ponds are also important breeding habitats for amphibians and for the insects that nourish the young fish and amphibians.

In rivers with two flood seasons, the spring flood will also dampen the floodplain soil, setting the stage for the germination and growth of moist-soil plants during the summer, after the floodwater recedes. The second flood in the fall comes just in time to create ponded areas on the floodplain where migrating waterfowl can rest on their long journey in between their summer and winter ranges. The moist-soil vegetation provides seed heads and tubers for the waterfowl to feed on while the birds remain safely in an open-water habitat, a serendipity that would not occur in the absence of floodplain dynamics.

In arid climates, floodplains are often the only areas with sufficiently moist soils to support forests. The riparian forests of the American South-west are critical to the survival of many neotropical bird species, because they provide a shaded refuge from the hot climate in the protective limbs of tall trees.

Rivers can also be categorized into reaches based on similar characteristics, such as the ratio of shallow rapids (riffles) and pools, channel width, substrate (sand, gravel, cobble or bedrock, for example) and depth. Many rivers exhibit alternation of reach type, with one type becoming more dominant between the upstream and the downstream reaches. In the headwaters, for example, bedrock and cobble-bottomed reaches may be more common, while sand and silt dominate in the lower reaches.

Lakes. In contrast to rivers and streams, lakes, which are lentic systems, cannot create their own beds; the existence of a basin must precede the birth of a lake. Lake basins form as a result of the interruption of a drainage pattern. The formation of either a basin or a barrier restricts the flow of water.[45] Movements of the Earth's crust can form lakes by creating fractures and depressions where water collects, including in the craters of extinct volcanoes. The oldest lake basins on the planet formed this way, including the great rift valleys of East Africa that formed about ten to twelve million years ago.[46]

Glaciers can create lakes by gouging holes in loose soil or soft bedrock, depositing material across streams, or leaving chunks of ice that later melt.[47] Most of the world's lakes are found in higher latitudes and are of glacial origin, including the Great Lakes of the US and the thousands of smaller lakes in the Canadian Shield.[48] Oxbow lakes form when meanders are cut off from the main channel of a river. Solution lakes form when materials such as salt, limestone and gypsum dissolve, and tend to be more saline than other lakes. Barrier lakes occur mainly behind sand or gravel bars in coastal areas and contain brackish water because of tidal flow or salt spray.[49] Lakes can be classified as seepage lakes or drainage lakes, depending on their water source. Seepage lakes generally have small watersheds and obtain their water through groundwater inflow, while tributary channels feed drainage lakes.[50]

Lake ecosystems are extremely variable, responding to changes in physical, chemical and biological conditions. Physical variability is often expressed in changes in light levels, temperatures, water currents, and sedimentation. Under natural conditions, chemical changes manifest mostly in the composition and concentration of nutrients and major ions. Biological variability includes changes in the structure, function, biomass, species composition, population and growth rates of living organisms in the lake.

Light absorption and attenuation by the water column are major factors determining water temperature and potential photosynthesis. The deeper light penetrates, the more photosynthesis can take place. The rate at which light penetration decreases with depth depends on the amount of light-absorbing dissolved substances – mostly organic carbon compounds washed into the lake – and the amount of light absorption and scattering caused by suspended materials such as soil particles from the watershed, phytoplankton (algae suspended in the water column), and detritus (dead or decaying organic material). Photosynthetic organisms include phytoplankton, periphyton (algae attached to surfaces), and macrophytes.

Temperature has a substantial effect on water density and chemistry, and therefore on the diversity and distribution of organisms in a lake. In contrast to most other compounds, water is denser as a liquid than as a solid. The maximum density of water is at four degrees centigrade; water any warmer or colder is less dense. In climates that experience two or more seasons, this quality leads to the seasonal mixing and stratification of lake waters, with important biological consequences.

During the winter in four-season, temperate climates, the temperature of the water near the bottom of a lake will typically be around four degrees centigrade, while the water at the top of the lake may be substantially cooler – approaching zero. At this point, the density difference results in the layering, or stratification, of the lake. Assuming that the surface of the lake is covered with ice, and if there is no snow cover on top of the lake to block light infiltration during the winter season, phytoplankton and some macrophytes may continue to photosynthesize. As a result a slight increase in dissolved oxygen may occur just below the ice cover. As microorganisms continue to decompose material in the lower water column and sediments, however, they may deplete any dissolved oxygen that is available to them. The ice cover would prevent the addition of oxygen from the air. If snow cover blocks light penetration below the ice, no photosynthesis will occur. Low winter oxygen conditions can cause high fish mortality, known as 'winter kill.'[51]

In the spring, increased sunlight warms the surface water and increases its density. When the temperature of the surface water equals the density of the bottom water, the lake mixes and becomes essentially homogeneous with respect to temperature and oxygen concentrations. In the summer, the surface layer will warm and become less dense than the colder bottom water, leading again to stratification. During the summer, photosynthesis in the upper layer of the water is high, leading to high concentrations of dissolved oxygen. In the bottom layers there is no source of oxygen but organisms continue to respire and decompose organic matter, depleting oxygen in the process. The decrease in surface water temperature during the fall season causes the lake to mix once more, and the cycle begins again in the winter with lake stratification.

Some lakes, particularly in warm climates, stratify only once a year during the summer. Other lakes never mix completely, with the result that organic matter accumulates in the bottom water layers and can create a permanent, anoxic, or oxygen-free, environment. Other lakes, particularly in tropical climates, may mix only once a year.

Lakes can also be classified according to their biological productivity. A eutrophic lake is highly productive. Accumulation of organic material in eutrophic lakes can lead to oxygen depletion during decomposition, and to eventual filling in of the lake. An oligotrophic lake has a relatively low rate of productivity. Populations of algae and the animals that feed on them are also relatively low. As a result, organic matter doesn't accumulate rapidly and its decomposition doesn't deplete the oxygen supply. Some species of fish require cold, well-oxygenated water.[52]

Mesotrophic lakes are intermediate between eutrophic and oligotrophic lakes. A lake can change from oligotrophic to mesotrophic to eutrophic over time, and may eventually fill in altogether. This process is known as eutrophication.

Different zones of a lake house different biological communities and these interact with and influence the physical and chemical characteristics of the lake. The near-shore zone where light penetrates to the bottom and allows macrophytes to grow is called the littoral zone. Macrophytes in this area provide a habitat for species of fish, amphibians and invertebrates that may differ substantially from deeper parts of the lake.

In eutrophic lakes, a dense cover of leaves from floating plants such as water lillies (*Nymphaeaceae* family) or pond weed (*Potamogeton* spp.) in the littoral zone may produce oxygen through photosynthesis. At the same time, however, the leaf cover prevents photosynthesis in all but a very shallow layer beneath it by blocking out the sunlight. The detritus produced by these plants may rain through the shaded water and is consumed by bacteria and other microorganisms as it sinks. These microorganisms respire in the process, consuming oxygen.

Lakes also have open water areas, known as pelagic or limnectic zones, further out from shore where light does not generally penetrate all the way to the bottom. These areas are too deep to support vascular plants, but photosynthesis by phytoplankton still occurs. Oxygen depletion may again occur in lower layers of the water column because, even though the phytoplankton are too small to block out sunlight significantly, as they die they also provide a substantial source of nutrition to microorganisms.[53]

The benthic zone occupies a lake's bottom sediments. The surface layer of the benthic zone is rich in life, primarily invertebrates that serve as an important food source for fish.[54] These invertebrates, in turn, feed largely on the microorganisms that feast on the rain of detritus from the lake's surface.

Wetland is a bit of a catch-all category that includes a very broad range of ecosystem types, generally considered to be intermediate between terrestrial ecosystems, or uplands, and open water or aquatic ecosystems.[55] According to the definition under the US Clean Water Act, wetlands are areas that are inundated or saturated by surface or groundwater at a frequency and duration sufficient to support life in saturated soil conditions. Under this definition, wetlands generally include swamps, marshes, bogs and similar areas.

The processes that create wetlands are also very diverse and dynamic. Some wetlands, such as the waterfowl-rich prairie potholes of the midwestern United States, were formed by glacial scour. Other wetlands develop at the fringe of aquatic ecosystems, including lakes, rivers and oceans, largely through soil saturation. Springs and seeps, the ecosystems that form when the water table intersects the surface of the land, are also wetlands. Peat wetlands and bogs form through the accumulation of plant material where cold water and anoxic conditions inhibit the breakdown of organic material by bacteria. Fens develop in depressions between gravel-filled hills and develop delicate and unique floristic communities dependent on the solution of minerals in water moving through the gravel fields into the depressional wetland areas.

Hydrology – the distribution and movement of water – is the driving force in all wetland ecosystems. Hydrology controls abiotic characteristics such as soil colour, soil texture and water quality, as well as biotic features such as the abundance, diversity, and productivity of plants, vertebrates, invertebrates and microbes. This control function is not unidirectional, however. The biotic component of a wetland can affect hydrology by increasing or decreasing water level or flow through such processes as interception or transpiration. Low rates of decomposition of organic material can cause basins to fill with undecomposed plant material, thus altering system hydrology.[56] The activities of animals can also change hydrological conditions, as mentioned above.

Water flows and levels in most wetlands are dynamic, fluctuating daily in coastal marshes and seasonally in almost all wetlands. Water supplies to wetlands also vary significantly from year to year. In addition, moisture gradients vary temporally as well as spatially at the margin of a wetland, with plants, animals and microoganisms responding to the gradient.

Difference in water sources can often explain temporal differences in water supply to wetlands. Overland flow, groundwater and precipitation maintain depressional wetlands. Changes in channel flow, including overbank flows carrying nutrients and organic matter, create seasonal or periodic pulses of water level in riparian wetlands. Daily tides pulse estuarine fringe wetlands. Relatively constant sources of water maintain slope wetlands, such as the seeps and springs at the groundwater/surface water interface. Precipitation alone can be sufficient to maintain peatlands.[57] The rise and fall of the tide, and resulting salinity gradients, largely determine the distribution of plant and animal species in coastal or estuarine wetlands.[58]

These landscape features and processes determine the ecological functions of wetlands, For example, wetlands that receive their water supply from precipitation typically supply water to headwater streams and to underlying aquifers by infiltration. Groundwater-dominated wetlands generally maintain higher productivity than precipitation-dominated ones because the nearly continuous flow of the former supplies nutrients and displaces sulphide and other potentially toxic compounds.

Wetlands harbour a significant amount of the planet's biological diversity, largely because the dynamic nature and resulting ecological complexity of these ecosystems create a wide range of habitats. Along the edges of rivers, for example, opportunistic species are the first to invade newly deposited sediments, but are eventually displaced by different plants and animals as the system matures. At the edges of continents, salt marsh grasses and succulents colonize new mud flats formed by alluvial outwash. These plants trap sediments and build up the topography, attracting additional plants and animals. Sphagnum moss and herbaceous plants develop a mat that eventually supports bog shrubs and bog trees. The nutrient content of the soil and the biomass of plants and animals increase over time in all of these ecosystems, as does species diversity and ecosystem complexity. This process of succession is bi-directional, as disturbances such as floods and fires can set back maturing ecosystems to earlier stages of succession.[59] The anoxic conditions in the root zones of many wetlands create conditions under which only specialized plants can survive, as does the relatively acidic nature of water in bogs.

Estuaries occur at the mouths of rivers where seawater becomes diluted by freshwater draining from the land. Estuaries are highly complex and variable ecosystems, driven by both riverine and oceanic hydrology operating on different time scales, with ocean tides cycling on a daily basis and river flow varying according to season. The degree to which estuarine ecology is driven by the contributing river or the sea also depends largely on whether the estuary mouth is open to the sea or closed by a sandbar or other obstruction. Incoming (flood) tides force seawater into estuaries, thus raising the water level. Water levels near the mouth decrease more quickly than those higher up near the outflowing (ebb) tides. The difference in water level can create strong, outflowing currents that keep the mouth open. Conversely, rivers carry sediments into estuaries, where the relatively slow, shallow water causes the sediment load to drop out of suspension. Wind and coastal currents also transport marine sediments into estuaries. When river flow is low, the river and tides may carry in more sediment than outflowing tides can remove, causing the mouth of the estuary to shallow or close.[60]

The factors that influence the chemical composition of an estuary include material brought down by the river and in on the tides, as well as the growth, death and decay of organisms living in the estuary. In addition, the salt concentration in the water increases between the river and the mouth of the estuary, and this gradient is an important factor determining the distribution of plants and animals within the ecosystem. The gradient moves, of course, in response to changes in river flow and the direction of the tide.[61] The complex interactions between these processes result in a very dynamic chemical environment to which it is difficult to adapt.

The runoff of a river into an estuary produces a distinct circulation pattern where the flow of freshwater over the top of the denser salt water causes nutrient-rich bottom water from the river to upwell to the surface. This leads to the particularly high productivity of estuaries.[62] Other factors maintaining high estuary productivity include a constant source of nutrients from rivers; a shallow basin, which increases both potential photosynthesis and sediment-trapping capacity; and thorough mixing by ocean tides.

Floristic components of estuaries range from algae and seaweed to submerged macrophytes and emergent reeds to mangrove forests. The distribution and composition of these plant communities change with shifts in salinity, nutrient content and sediment deposition that favour one set of species over another in the process of succession. Floods, flushing and scouring can reinstate earlier conditions favouring formerly successful species. These cycles occur over time periods that range from days in the case of microscopic plants and animals to many years in the case of larger plants, such as reeds and mangroves.[63]

The combination of dynamic chemical conditions and high productivity results in estuarine faunas that are generally lower in diversity but higher in abundance than adjacent freshwater or marine communities.[64] There are few truly estuarine animal species. Most animals inhabiting estuaries are principally denizens of marine or freshwater, and their distributions are also guided by changes in nutrient content and salinity. Many estuarine organisms, including prawns, crabs and some fish, have to spend some time at sea to complete their life cycles. Seasons of the year and lunar cycles often determine the timing of these movements. Estuaries are also important nursery areas for many species of marine fish.[65]

Completing the Cycle

The return of freshwater to the oceans has important consequences for global climate. Thermohaline circulation, often referred to as the Earth's conveyor belt, is driven by differences in the temperature and salinity of ocean water masses. Warm surface water currents flow from the equator towards the North Atlantic, where they cool as they exchange heat with the colder atmosphere. As the seawater cools, its density increases and it sinks to the bottom of the ocean and returns to the tropics. This system transports huge quantities of heat to high latitudes. It also produces a global-scale flux between the major ocean basins of oxygen, organic nutrients (such as nitrate, phosphate, and silicate) and various trace metals.

The quantity of water that returns to the sea, and the points at which it returns, exert significant influence on thermohaline circulation because freshwater alters the salinity and thus the density of the receiving seawater.[66] For example, if global warming were to increase the discharge of rivers into the Arctic Ocean, the density of surface waters could be significantly reduced. The loss of the density differential would effectively shut down the motor that powers the conveyor belt and tropical waters would no longer move northward in the Atlantic Ocean. Climates in New England, Nova Scotia, Newfoundland, Greenland, Iceland and much of western Europe would become dramatically colder as a result.[67]

THE VALUE OF THE WATER CYCLE AND FRESHWATER ECOSYSTEMS

Clearly, humanity's most basic biological needs, food and freshwater, depend on the continued functioning of the water cycle and freshwater ecosystems. The interactions between the water cycle and the Earth's aquatic ecosystems provide other extremely important services to human society, including temperature regulation, sanitation, transportation, energy, buffers against anthropogenic and natural disturbances, and just plain recreational fun.

Internal Ecosystem Dynamics

Although aquatic ecosystems regulate the water cycle, the life forms within these ecosystems are also extremely dependent on the complex processes that drive the cycle. The abundance, diversity and productivity of plants, vertebrates, invertebrates and microbes all depend on the distribution and movement of water. The distribution of organisms in lakes, for example, and thus the entire organization of the food chain, is determined by the depth, temperature and water quality of the lake at various times throughout the year.

Flow regimes, including floods and periods of low flows, are patterns of water movement crucial to the ecology of riverine ecosystems. For example, high flows can trigger spawning runs in migratory fish populations. Conversely, low flows in river ecosystems can provide opportunities for moist soil vegetation to grow in parts of the floodplain that are inundated under high-flow conditions. Patches of herbaceous vegetation provide food for semi-aquatic animals such as waterfowl as they migrate along river corridors. Flooding also nourishes floodplains with sediments and nutrients and provides habitat for invertebrate communities. Many birds that breed in desert ecosystems depend on the relative cool of riparian forests for reproductive success; were it not for the shade of the tree canopies next to rivers, their eggs would literally cook in the heat.[68] These forests have evolved with and are dependent on the flow regimes of their adjacent rivers.

'Alligators' jaws are covered with tiny bumps that are filled with nerves that can detect subtle movements in the water, explaining why it's so hard to sneak up on the animals....

'Daphne Soares of the University of Maryland conducted a series of experiments in which she showed that alligators could detect a single droplet of water falling into a pool in complete darkness by using the exquisitely sensitive bumps, which she dubbed dome pressure receptors (DPRs)....

"These dome pressure receptors are also evident in fossils from the Jurassic period, indicating that these semi-aquatic predators solved the problem of combining armor with tactile sensitivity may millions of years ago," she wrote.'[69]

Services Rendered

While all ecosystems interact with and influence the water cycle, freshwater ecosystems play a particularly important role in maintaining and moderating the cycle in ways that benefit people and nature. Similarly, as discussed above, the water cycle influences the structure and function of freshwater ecosystems.

The role played by freshwater ecosystems in the water cycle frequently provides services that are valued by people. These services arise from natural functions and therefore occur at no financial cost to society. However, if an ecosystem is damaged or destroyed it will not continue to function in the same manner and natural services may be lost. This is likely to have adverse impacts on the health, welfare and safety of the communities that benefited from the natural services previously provided, as well as entailing a financial cost to society. In addition, annual costs will accumulate for whatever mechanisms the communities implement to replace the services that had been provided by the natural environment.[70]

Rivers and streams provide a wide variety of benefits to human society: some relate to active use, such as the withdrawal of water for industry or instream uses for navigation or energy production; others to passive use, such as the aesthetic enjoyment of a waterfall. Many millions of people, particularly in rural areas of developing countries, rely on rivers directly for many of their needs, including food, drinking water, sanitation and transport. While people in the developed world often have alternatives to these very basic uses of rivers, they still gain many important social and economic benefits.

Public Benefits of Stream Corridor Conservation

- **Recreation:** Fishery, parks, playgrounds, urban walkways, picnic groves, bikeways, nature trails, canoeing, scenic and aesthetic amenities, wildlife habitat.

- **Water supply:** Domestic supplies, industrial supplies, groundwater recharge, irrigation and other agricultural uses.

- **Waste removal:** Disposal of treated waste effluent through assimilative capacity.

- **Other benefits:** Flood storage and retention, navigation, hydropower, historic preservation.[71]

Floodplains have also been credited with providing a wide range of benefits to people, including those listed in the box below.

Natural and Cultural Floodplain Functions

- **Natural flood and erosion control:** Reduce flood velocities; reduce flood peaks; reduce wind and wave impacts; stabilize soils.

- **Water quality maintenance:** Reduce sediment loads; filter nutrients and impurities; process organic and chemical wastes; moderate water temperature; reduce sediment loads.

- **Support flora:** Maintain high biological productivity of floodplain and wetland vegetation; maintain productivity of natural forests; maintain natural crops; maintain natural genetic diversity.

- **Provide fish and wildlife habitat:** Maintain breeding and feeding grounds; create and enhance waterfowl habitat; protect habitat for rare and endangered species.

- **Maintain harvest of natural and agricultural products:** Create and enhance agricultural lands; provide areas for cultivation of fish and shellfish; protect silvaculture; provide harvest of fur resources.

- Provide recreation opportunities: Provide areas for active and consumptive use; provide areas for passive activities; provide open space and aesthetic values.

- Provide scientific study and outdoor education area: Provide opportunities for ecological studies; provide historical and archaeological sites.[72]

Maintaining or restoring connectivity between a river channel and a natural floodplain can enhance the system's capacity to reduce flood peaks (and therefore costly damage); provide a natural water filtration function that keeps river water clean; increase floodplain fertility by allowing natural sediments to accumulate there during a flood event; and maintain habitat for fish, waterfowl and other wildlife.

'[T]he floodplains of Mali's Inner Niger Delta are a highly productive system that has supported over 550,000 Malians (including pastoralists, farmers and fishermen), domestic animals and wildlife for a thousand years. Floodplain grasses contain a relatively high protein content, making them especially good livestock fodder. Pastoral communities synchronize their livestock cycle to the annual river flood, moving their herds onto arid, rain-fed rangelands as the water recedes. The post-flood plain pastures of the delta support the highest density of herds in Africa, including cattle, sheep and goats, as well as over 170,000 hectares of rice. During drought and before rice harvests, the people depend on the natural production of wild grains in the delta. During times of flood, 80,000 fishermen depend on the fish catch, which amounts to over 61,000 tons. In addition, most of the African lakes and rivers, and a number of African wetlands support tribes whose livelihood has historically depended on fishing.'[73]

Lakes provide many of the same general benefits as rivers, including drinking water, fish, and opportunities for transportation and recreation. Large lakes can help to moderate the climate of adjacent landscapes by retaining and radiating heat in winter and creating a cooling effect in the summer. In addition, lakes can be significant sources of scientific information.

Freshwater lakes are classical examples of 'islands' of habitat – in this case, bodies of water surrounded by expanses of land. Like islands in general, the larger, older lakes tend to harbour more endemic species. In the rift valley lakes of Africa or Lake Baikal in central Asia, species diversity can be astounding. For example, each of the Great Lakes of eastern Africa contains more endemic fish species than any other lake in the world, and more species than the entire freshwater fish fauna in Europe.[74] The explosive and unique species radiation in each lake make them even more important than the Galapagos Islands off Ecuador for the study of evolutionary processes. Studying these lakes can provide humanity with important information about the evolution of behaviour, of food chains, of physiology, and of our own brains.

In addition, the fact that the rift valley lakes are some of the oldest and deepest lakes in the world make them important sources of geological information. Unlike seabed sediments, the sediments of the African Great Lakes are so laminated that they may be able to provide information about annual, if not seasonal, variations in temperature to as far back as five to ten million years ago. The lakes are also part of a global tectonic rift system, of which little is known. These lakes also provide important records of human activity over time, with some sites providing records of the earliest known human activities.[75]

The Great Lakes of the midwestern United States provided some of the first evidence for the tetragenic and bioaccumulative nature of persistent pollutants such as DDT and PCBs. The tendency of lakes to serve as sinks for whatever is deposited into them makes them extraordinary *in vivo* laboratories.

Wetlands have many beneficial functions, both for humans and nature, in terms of controlling floods, enhancing water quality and preventing erosion.

Wetland Functions

- **Groundwater recharge:** Wetland water can infiltrate down into the groundwater aquifer, usually undergoing cleansing on the way. From the aquifer, water may be drawn out for human consumption, or may flow underground until it surfaces in another ecosystem as groundwater discharge. Recharge also helps flood storage, as runoff is temporarily stored underground, rather than moving swiftly through a stream channel.

- **Groundwater discharge:** Water that was stored underground can move upward into a wetland and become surface water. Wetlands that receive most of their water in this way usually support stable biological communities because water temperatures and flow rates are relatively stable (compared to surface water, or precipitation).

- **Flood control:** When precipitation and runoff are stored in wetlands and flood flow velocity is reduced, the timing and magnitude of flood peaks is altered. This can lead to a more stable biological community downstream.

- **Water quality enhancement:** Wetlands enhance water quality by accumulating nutrients, trapping sediments, and transforming a variety of substances.

- Sediment stabilization: Wetland vegetation can reduce the energy of waves, currents, or other erosive forces, while simultaneously holding the bottom sediment in place with root systems. This can prevent, for example, shoreline erosion that could otherwise threaten human dwellings or activities and degrade water quality.

- Nutrient retention, removal and transformation: Wetlands can retain, remove or transform nutrients such as phosphorus or nitrogen. This process improves the water quality and health of biological communities, especially downstream.

- Habitat for fish: Aquatic plants and other features of wetlands can provide food, cover, or good water quality for fish that use these areas for spawning, rearing (nursery) areas, or as habitat for adults.

- Habitat for wildlife: Aquatic plants and other features of a wetland can provide food, shelter, or special habitat needs to wildlife.

- Biomass production and export: Wetlands are extremely productive ecosystems. The large amount of plant material that is produced and then decays provides nutrition to many different organisms. Some wetlands also produce food for people and livestock, fuel, and commercially valuable wood and other fibre.[76]

Watersheds, which include the Earth's entire terrestrial surface, are crucial to determining the ecological health of the aquatic ecosystems they drain into. In general, because water gravitates towards the lowest topographical position in the landscape, freshwater ecosystems accumulate materials transported from higher areas in the watershed. In many watersheds, freshwater ecosystems process dissolved and suspended materials from an area much greater than their own, which explains their disproportionately strong influence on water quality. In watersheds subject to human activity, the importance of freshwater ecosystems for maintaining water quality is emphasized by two factors: disturbances to uplands that increase erosion and augmented fertility of the landscape (largely by fertilizers for crops and livestock waste); and reduction of the area available to freshwater ecosystems by processes that include filling, dyking and draining.[77]

Watersheds also influence the timing of streamflow by regulating runoff and groundwater recharge rates. Vegetated watersheds with permeable substrates generally generate gentle stream hydrographs, characterized by higher flows in the dry seasons and lower flows during flood seasons, compared with impervious, paved surfaces, for example. In soil-covered landscapes, high organic matter content can also contribute to the landscape's ability to act as a sponge—absorbing water when it is abundant and discharging it when it is scarce.

Groundwater and caves, the subterranean ecosystems where nature stores and redistributes water, provide a number of services to society. These include water purification, biodiversity conservation (many rare and endemic life forms are found in waters underground), flow regulation, crop hydration, water temperature maintenance, and maintenance of geological structural stability. Conversely, indications of groundwater degradation or depletion include landscape desiccation and desertification, water pollution (and notably salinity intrusion into freshwater aquifers in coastal areas), species loss, and land subsidence.

Caves are unlike most other habitat types. They tend to receive all their nutrients and energy from outside sources, generally experience constant temperature and humidity, and lack light. The unique conditions found in cave habitats have led to the evolution of highly specialized organisms.

Selective pressures on cave organisms are easier to enumerate than for most habitats, and cave communities are relatively simple, frequently containing a half dozen species or less. For these and other reasons, caves and cave faunas can serve as model systems for the study of a variety of geological and biological questions, including mineralogy, adaptation, speciation, regressive evolution (for example, the disappearance of features such as skin pigments and eyes which lose their utility in a lightless environment), and species interactions.[78]

Estuaries and deltas constitute rich ecosystems where fertile silts deposit, sunshine penetrates the waters, and a reliable pattern of salt and freshwater concentrations leads to seasonal changes in habitats. This combination of fecund factors spawns a number of benefits in coastal ecosystems, including highly productive fish and shellfish habitats, buffers against typhoons, protection from land subsidence and sea level rise, and the development of coral reefs with all the recreational and scientific potential they represent.

Freshwater Ecosystem Values

The economic value of anything is a human judgement about its worth, and a statement about how much people would be willing to pay for the item. In the case of freshwater ecosystems, which remain in the public domain throughout most of the world, the assessment of economic value must be based on how much society values the existence of these ecosystems. Natural resources economists have made many attempts to quantify the financial value of these ecosystems so that they can be compared to alternative uses: the financial value of a wetland compared, for example, to the financial value of a shopping mall that might be built on the same site were the wetland to be filled in. Such attempts to quantify the value of freshwater ecosystems often shed light, but they cannot hope to illuminate a complex topic in its entirety.

Despite the fact that freshwater ecosystems in general are indispensable, since they are necessary to the continued supply of freshwater on our planet, people will continue to argue about the value of individual freshwater ecosystems compared to the opportunity costs of maintaining them in a natural state. Several approaches have been used to estimate the value of freshwater ecosystems generally, of distinct classes of freshwater ecosystems and ecosystem components, and of specific ecosystems such as South America's Pantanal or the Nile River. These estimates are often based on a general assessment of value and on replacement costs.

Valuation

The general services provided by freshwater ecosystems have been discussed above (see 'Services Rendered,' p. 24). World-wide, freshwater and wetland ecosystems are estimated to account for approximately 26 percent of the total economic value of all ecosystem services.[79] Deriving a value for freshwater ecosystems based on this estimate would require a financial estimate for the values of all the Earth's ecosystems – a formidable task likely to provide unreliable results.

To take a more manageable slice of the financial value puzzle, the world's freshwater fishery harvest provides a lower-bound estimate of the commercial value of freshwater fish. The annual harvest in 1989–91 was about 14 million tons, valued at about US$8.2 billion. This figure does not include the value of the distribution business or other components of the total fishing economy. Sport fisheries, for example, often exceed the value of commercial fisheries, sometimes by a hundredfold or more. Although the global value of fish, waterfowl and other goods extracted from freshwater systems cannot be estimated from available data, it certainly exceeds $100 billion per year and may be several times that amount.[80]

A more reliable estimate of the net financial value of the world's freshwater ecosystems would have to be based on specific goods (mussels, say) and services (storm buffering, for example) and that component's worth to the applicable population. For example, freshwater fish might be worth more to communities in the developing world who lack access to other sources of animal protein than they are to Europeans or Americans who have an astounding variety of dietary options. A composite estimate of the financial value of freshwater ecosystems would also have to be indexed proportionately to the wealth of the human populations sampled. For example, a family in Bangladesh willing to pay one dollar for the protection of their (deltaic wetland) wells against saline intrusion might be comparable to the willingness of a family in New Orleans to pay one thousand dollars for similar services.

'The definition of an ecosystem service is a matter of societal perception because it hinges on valuation. Of all the processes or functions carried on by ecosystems, only those contributing to the well-being of human society are considered services. On those rare occasions when the societal value of minimally managed functions of ecosystems is evaluated, different people reach different conclusions. The debate is even more heated when management actions to protect ecosystem services are proposed.

What scientific evidence is necessary to facilitate the societal debate on value and help establish a reasonable level of management? Does the delivery of necessary ecosystem services depend on ecosystem health? Not only is additional, well-conceived research needed to clarify these relationships, but it is also crucial to be able to communicate the results of such research and its uncertainties to the wide society that is properly involved in the debate on values.' [81]

Broadly speaking, attempts to estimate the value of freshwater ecosystems are moot and essentially a waste of good research money. Water, and therefore freshwater ecosystems, are necessary for supporting almost all of our planet's life forms. The Earth's living components produce the air we breathe and the food we eat. They are, therefore, indispensable.

The omnipresence of water has made evolution possible, and evolution has produced the planet's rich biological diversity. This diversity provides life on Earth with the possibility of adapting to evolutionary change. Water creates, destroys and rebuilds habitats for the Earth's plants, animals and other organisms. Variations in the quantity, quality, and timing of water delivered to specific ecosystems are a strong force in the evolution of life, as changes in the water regime serve as a form of natural selection, favouring one species or individual over another in the quest for survival. Similarly, communities of organisms can alter the water regimes in their habitats, making those habitats either more or less conducive to the organisms' survival. Thus, the water cycle and the process of evolution, which provides Earth with functioning ecosystems and biological diversity, are interdependent.

The role of water in supporting biological diversity is paramount. Biodiversity is the irreplaceable output of a four-billion-year-old process during which the biotic and abiotic components of the planet have interacted with each other. Existing life forms are an encapsulated history of this process and therefore constitute an entirely unique body of information. Evolution is built upon the fundamental tenet of adaptation, and the variety of life forms that exist is an indicator of the range of potential responses that life requires for meeting changes in the physical environment. Evolution therefore generally produces a system that can continue to persist under a wide range of physical conditions. The range of existing life forms developed by the evolutionary process thus constitutes a uniquely formulated insurance policy against shocks to the life system itself.[82]

'In biological diversity we are dealing with one of the ancient non-renewable resources, such as fossil fuels, rich soils and great aquifers; however, in another important respect, biological diversity is very different from these other resources. It is similar to these other non-renewables in the sense that it is a one-off endowment from nature to the earth, in that it cannot be replaced on any time scale that is relevant to humanity. However, it is distinct from these other resources because it is impossible, by definition, to substitute human innovations for this resource. That is, biological diversity is distinguishable from most other natural endowments by virtue of its naturalness.

'It is not possible to substitute human synthesized inputs, or processes, for the important characteristics of biodiversity, precisely because their importance derives from the nature of the evolutionary process that generated them – a process which occurred over four and a half billion years and generated an encapsulated history of biological activity and interaction.'[83]

Theoretical Cost and Impossibility of Replacement

Maintenance of the water cycle is perhaps the most outstanding and under-estimated service provided by freshwater ecosystems. Freshwater is not like other resources such as coal, oil, or tin for which substitutes exist. The next best alternative to the continued provision of freshwater by the natural water cycle is desalination of ocean water – an extremely energy-consumptive and expensive process.

Desalination currently accounts for less than 0.1 percent of total world water use. The cost of desalination is around US$2 to $3 per cubic metre – four to eight times more than the average cost of urban supplies, and 10 to 20 times what most farmers currently pay for water. If the world's total demand for water had to be met through desalination, water use would be substantially lower than it is today because the costs of water supply would escalate significantly. Assuming that water not consumed during use is reused and after subtracting for reservoir losses (which would be greatly reduced if water were no longer stored for long periods of time), an estimated 2,010 km^3 per year would need to be desalted. Assuming an average cost of US$1.50 per cubic metre, this volume of water would cost approximately US$3,000 billion per year – roughly 12 percent of the current gross world product.[84]

This simple cost analysis captures only a small part of the total value of the natural desalting service provided by the water cycle. If replacement cost calculations included the water evapotranspired *in situ* by the trees harvested for lumber and fuel, by the grassland used for grazing livestock, by rain-fed cropland, and by all the other vegetation that supports human activity, the cost figure would be about nine times larger. Thus, the cost estimate provided above represents a lower-bound estimate of the value of Earth's renewable water supply overall, but an upper-bound estimate of the value of freshwater systems for irrigation, industrial and municipal water supply.[85]

People cannot create freshwater in the quantities necessary to meet our combined demands. As noted above, while desalination of ocean water is technically feasible, it is not currently cost-effective for most applications. While desalination provides significant proportions of the freshwater used in several oil-rich Middle Eastern countries, such as Saudi Arabia and Kuwait, the world's desalination plants have the capacity to provide no more than two-thousandths (approximately 8 km^3 per year) of total freshwater use (approximately 3,900 km^3 per year).[86] Furthermore, while the costs of desalination are coming down as the technology improves, the cost of delivering this water to users ranges between US$1 and US$4 per cubic metre. Even the low end of this range is above the price paid by most urban consumers, and far above the price paid by farmers.[87]

A modest amount of freshwater is manufactured as a by-product of energy production in hydrogen fuel cells, such as the cells on the Apollo 11 space mission that provided astronauts with drinking water. While fuel cell technology has the potential to be one of the cleanest and least expensive forms of energy available in the coming decades, it is not likely to become a major contributor to the world's water supply in the foreseeable future. In terms of generating new water supplies, nature remains far and away our best bet.

Not only do we lack the capacity to create new supplies of freshwater, but our ability to recreate the aquatic ecosystems that keep the water cycle spinning is also extremely limited. For example, wetland ecosystems that require a specific com-bination of plant types, soil characteristics and water supply – such as vernal pools, fens and bogs – are difficult to impossible to create from scratch.[88] Even if we successfully recreate the physical structure of a wetland, we may not be able to re-establish vital functions. Denitrification, an ecological process that improves water quality, provides an example. This process requires the presence of a nitrate supply, a labile carbon source, anaerobic (oxygen-free) conditions and microbial activity. If any of these factors is absent, the denitrification function will not occur, regard-less of the appropriateness of the wetland's physical structure.[89]

CONCLUSION

This chapter has discussed how the water cycle functions to provide the planet with a continual source of high-quality freshwater. It has stressed the critical importance of ecosystems in general, and freshwater ecosystems in particular, to the continued function of the water cycle and, by extension, the continued existence of humanity. It has rejected the relevance of a global economic analysis of the value of freshwater ecosystems for two reasons. First, these ecosystems are essential in providing the food and water that we need to survive; second, they are irreplaceable.

Chapter 2 will address the 'global water crisis.' In recent years, many of the world's water experts have been sounding the alarm over the potential for competing demands for water to generate a series of devastating consequences for humankind. The debate has been framed in economic terms, and freshwater ecosystems have been defined as a sector competing for water against the food production and water supply and sanitation sectors.

Chapter 2 probes the existence and nature of the water crisis prophesied by the world's water gurus. How do we define and recognize a global water crisis? If the world indeed faces a water crisis, what forces have brought us to this point? Following the discussion of the 'global water crisis,' chapters 3–7 develop the central hypothesis of the present work: that nature is the source of, rather than a competitor for, the world's water.

Notes

1 Ball, P., 1999. *H₂O: A Biography of Water.* Weidenfeld & Nicolson, London. p. 1.

2 De Villiers, M., 2001. *Water: The Fate of our Most Precious Resource.* Mariner Books, Boston and New York. p. 34.

3 Ibid., p. 36.

4 Jackson, R.B., S.R. Carpenter, C.N. Dahm, D.M. McKnight, S.L. Postel & S.W. Runnig. *Water in a Changing World. Issues in Ecology,* No. 9, Ecological Society of America, Washington.

5 Gleick, P.H., 1993. 'An introduction to global fresh water issues'. In: Gleick, P.H. (ed.), *Water in Crisis: A Guide to the World's Freshwater Resources.* Oxford University Press, New York. p. 3.

6 Mook, W.G. (ed.), 2000. United Nations Educational, Scientific and Cultural Organization/ International Atomic Energy Agency Series on *Environmental Isotopes in the Hydrological Cycle: Principles and Application.* Volume I. p. 1.

7 Ibid., p. 2.

8 Ibid.

9 Ibid.

10 Gleick, P.H., 1998. *The World's Water: The Biennial Report on Freshwater Resources 1998–1999.* Island Press, Covelo, California. p. 195.

11 Chahine, M.T., 1999. 'The Way Forward.' In Browning, K.A. & R.J. Gurny (eds.), *Global Energy and Water Cycles.* Cambridge University Press, Cambridge. p. 284.

12 Mook, W.G. (ed.), 2000. *United Nations Educational, Scientific and Cultural Organization/ International Atomic Energy Agency Series on Environmental Isotopes in the Hydrological Cycle: Principles and Application.* Volume I. p. 7.

13 Jackson, R.B., S.R. Carpenter, C.N. Dahm, D.M. McKnight, S.L. Postel & S.W. Runnig. *Water in a Changing World.*

14 Pielou, E.C., 1998. *Fresh Water.* University of Chicago Press, Chicago. pp. 238–9.

15 Mook, W.G. (ed.), 2000. *Environmental Isotopes.* Volume I. p. 6.

16 Ibid., p. 2.

17 Pielou, E.C., 1998. *Fresh Water.* p. 1.

18 Ibid., p. 10.

19 Ibid., p. 10.

20 Ibid., p. 10.

21 Winter, T.C., J.W. Harvey, O.L. Frank & W.M. Alley, 1998. *Groundwater and Surface Water: A Single Resource.* United States Geological Survey Circular 1139. Government Printing Office, Washington. p. 4.

22 Pielou, E.C., 1998. *Fresh Water.* p. 5.

23 Winter, T.C., J.W. Harvey, O.L. Frank & W.M. Alley, 1998. *Groundwater and Surface Water.* p. 6.

24 Ibid., p. 7.

25 Ibid., p. 3.

26 Ibid., p. 7.

27 Ibid., p. 11.

28 Ibid., p. 18.

29 Population Action International, 1993. 'Sustaining Water: Population and the Future of Renewable Water Supplies.' Washington.

30 Gleick, P.H., 2000. *The World's Water 2000–2001: The Biennial Report on Freshwater Resources.* Island Press, Covelo, California. pp. 20–1.

31 Jackson, R.B., S.R. Carpenter, C.N. Dahm, D.M. McKnight, S.L. Postel & S.W. Runnig. *Water in a Changing World.*

32 Hunt, C.E., 1988. *Down by the River: The Impact of Federal Water Projects and Policies on Biological Diversity.* Island Press, Covelo, California. p. 167.

33 Ibid., p. 142.

34 Ibid., pp. 31–2.

35 Federal Interagency Stream Restoration Working Group, 1998. *Stream Corridor Restoration: Principles. Processes and Practices.* Washington. p. 2–4.

36 Pielou, E.C., 1998. *Fresh Water.* p. 69.

37 Ibid.
38 Federal Interagency Stream Restoration Working Group, 1998. *Stream Corridor Restoration.* pp. 2–8.
39 Brinson, M.M., 1993. 'A Hydrogeomorphic Classification for Wetlands.' Technical Report WRR-DE-4, US Army Engineers Waterway Experiment Station, Vicksburg, MS.
40 Poff, N.L., 1991. 'Regional Hydrologic Responses to Climate Change: An Ecological Perspective.' In Firth, P. & S.G. Fisher (eds.), *Global Climate Change and Freshwater Ecosystems.* Springer-Verlag, New York. p. 89.
41 Stream channels are not permanent, even under natural conditions. Drainage systems change continuously as a result of erosion, capture and other geological phenomena.
42 Vannote, R.L., G.W. Minshall. K.W. Cummins, J.R. Sedell & C.E. Cushing, 1980. 'The River Continuum Concept.' *Canadian Journal of Fish and Aquatic Sciences*, 37: 132.
43 Ibid., p. 133.
44 Ibid., p. 132.
45 Brown, S. (project coordinator), undated. *The Natural History of Nova Scotia V1: Topics and Habitats.* Nova Scotia Museum of Natural History. Http://museum.gov.ns.cn/mnh/nature/nhns/t8. p. 157.
46 Pielou, E.C., 1998. *Fresh Water.* p. 150.
47 Water on the Web, undated. 'Lake Ecology: A Primer on Limnology.' Http://www.nrri.umn.edu/wow/under/limnology.pdf.
48 Pielou, E.C., 1998. *Fresh Water.* p. 152.
49 Brown, S. (project coordinator), undated. *The Natural History of Nova Scotia.* p. 158.
50 Water on the Web, undated. 'Lake Ecology: A Primer on Limnology.'
51 Ibid.
52 Ibid.
53 Pielou, E.C., 1998. *Fresh Water.* pp. 178–9.
54 Water on the Web, undated. 'Lake Ecology: A Primer on Limnology.'
55 The Ramsar Convention on Wetlands of International Importance has a broader definition of wetlands. Under article 1.1, wetlands are areas of marsh, fen, peatland or water, whether natural or artificial, permanent or temporary, with water that is static or flowing, fresh, brackish or salt, including areas of marine water the depth of which at low tide does not exceed six metres. Article 2.1 provides that wetlands may incorporate riparian and coastal zones adjacent to the wetlands, and islands or bodies of marine water deeper than six metres at low tide lying within the wetlands.
56 National Research Council, 1995. *Wetlands: Characteristics and Boundaries.* Committee on Characterization of Wetlands, Water Science and Technology Board and Board on Environmental Studies and Toxicology, Commission on Geosciences, Environment and Resources. National Academy Press, Washington. pp. 22–3.
57 Ibid., pp. 24–5.
58 National Research Council, 1992. *Restoration of Aquatic Ecosystems: Science, Technology and Public Policy.* National Academy Press, Washington. p. 282.
59 Ibid., p. 264.
60 Breen, C. & M. McKenzie, 2001. *Managing Estuaries in South Africa: An Introduction Supporting the Effective Management of Estuaries.* Institute of Natural Resources, Scottsville, South Africa. Http://www.inr.unp.ac.za/emhb. p. 12.
61 Ibid., pp. 12–13.
62 Brown, S. (project coordinator), undated. *The Natural History of Nova Scotia.* p. 160.
63 Breen, C. & M. McKenzie, 2001. *Managing Estuaries in South Africa.* p. 14.
64 Ibid., p.16.
65 Ibid., p.16.
66 Oki, T., 1999. 'The Global Water Cycle.' In Browning, K.A. & R.J. Gurney (eds.), *Global Energy and Water Cycles.* Cambridge University Press, Cambridge, England. p. 24.
67 De Villiers, M., 2001. *Water: The Fate of Our Most Precious Resource.* p. 81. The relationship between the water cycle and global warming is covered in Chapter 7.
68 Ohmart, R.D., Professor of Wildlife Biology, Arizona State University, 1985. Personal communication.

69 *Washington Post*, 20 May 2002.

70 Larson, J.S., P.R. Adamus & E.J. Clairain, 1989. *A Functional Assessment of Freshwater Wetlands: A Manual and Training Outline*. The Environmental Institute, University of Massachusetts at Amherst and World Wide Fund for Nature, Publication No. 89–6. p. 7.

71 Modified from: New York State Department of Environmental Conservation, Division of Water, Bureau of Water Quality, 1986. *Stream Corridor Management: A Basic Reference Manual*. Albany, New York. 111 pp.

72 Modified from: US Water Resources Council, 1979. *A Unified National Program for Floodplain Management*. Washington.

73 Shumway, C.A., 1999. *Forgotten Waters: Freshwater and Marine Ecosystem in Africa. Strategies for Biodiversity Conservation and Sustainable Development*. Boston University, Boston. 168 pp.

74 Ibid.

75 Ibid.

76 Modified from: Larson, J.S., P.R. Adamus & E.J. Clairain, 1989. *A Functional Assessment*.

77 National Research Council, 1995. *Wetlands: Characteristics and Boundaries*. p. 38.

78 Culver, D.C., 1986. Cave Faunas. p. 429 *in* Soule, M.E. (ed.), *Conservation Biology: The Science of Scarcity and Diversity*. Sinauer Associates, Inc., Sunderland, Maryland.

79 IUCN, 2000. Vision for Water and Nature: A World Strategy for Conservation and Sustainable Management of Water Resources in the 21st Century. Gland, Switzerland. 58 pp.

80 Postel S.L. & S.R. Carpenter, 1997. 'Freshwater Ecosystem Services.' In G.C. Daily (ed.), *Nature's Services: Societal Dependence on Natural Ecosystems*. Island Press, Covelo, California. pp. 195–214.

81 Cairns, J., 1996. 'Determining the Balance Between Technological and Ecosystem Services.' In Schulze, P.C. (ed.), *Engineering with Ecological Constraints*. National Academy Press, Washington. p. 14.

82 Swanson, T., 1997. *Global Action for Biodiversity*. Earthscan Publications Ltd., London.

83 Ibid.

84 Postel & Carpenter, 1997. 'Freshwater Ecosystem Services.'

85 Ibid.

86 Gleick, P.H., 2000. *The World's Water 2000–2001*. p. 97.

87 Ibid., p. 106.

88 National Research Council, 2001. *Compensating for Wetland Losses Under the Clean Water Act*. Committee on Mitigating Wetland Losses, Board on Environmental Studies and Toxicology. National Academy Press, Washington. p. 24.

89 Ibid., p. 27.

2 Spiralling Towards a Crisis
Water Use and Growing Shortages

'The water crisis is real, but we cannot underestimate its complexity and linkages to poverty, food and environmental insecurity, and hopelessness. The problem is not just lack of water. It is also the degradation and depletion of water ecosystems – the lakes, rivers, and wetlands that are the life support systems for citizens and economies of developing countries.'[1]

Much water and a lot of fuel have been thrown upon the fiery fears about the world drying up. Reduced population growth projections, increases in water conservation in developed countries, and speculation about obtaining 'new' water from the sea, glaciers and even comets have diminished forecasts of human suffering from the inability to access water. On the other hand, global warming, corporations raiding the environment with impunity in developing countries, and increased water demand resulting from fast growth in living standards and slow growth in conservation measures spur talk of an impending world water crisis. Is such a crisis inevitable, or is it avoidable?

WATER'S ROLE IN HUMAN CIVILIZATION

Human society, though quite young compared with some of nature's other inventions, has co-evolved with the water cycle and the ecosystems that support it. Over time, we have learned how to exploit these processes and ecosystems to serve our needs and desires. When human cultures were young, we were just another life form competing for survival and our power to manipulate nature was limited. A reverence for, and fear of, nature therefore characterized our collective existence, and this attitude infused early religious beliefs and folklore.

The Koran, for example, enjoins believers to share water with anyone who needs it, because God created the world by dividing the waters of the deep from the waters of the air, thus giving life to everything. Nun, the Babylonian god, personified the idea that water was the source of all life, that the Earth came forth from water, and that water was the quickening element of all creation.[2] Chinese tradition holds that water and other elements of the Earth exist in a balance that should not be disturbed.[3] According to Rigvedic cosmology, the very possibility of life on earth is associated with the release of heavenly waters by Indra, the god of rain. Indra's enemy Vrtra, the demon of chaos, withheld and hoarded the waters and inhibited creation. When Indra defeated Vrtra, the heavenly waters rushed to Earth, and life sprang forth.[4]

As our technical capacities have facilitated our evolution into a force that can alter the Earth's climate and shift the courses of large rivers, we have begun to see nature less as a controlling force and more as a resource to be domesticated. The significance of our successes and failures in interacting with nature has grown in proportion to the scale of our endeavours.

Water Use in Ancient Times

The character of the technologies employed by modern society in water management is even more important than the size of water projects in determining their sustainability. Early civilizations employed different types of water harvesting strategies to optimize delivery of water to their crops. These systems generally were self-regulating – because they ultimately relied on annual precipitation as a source of water (in contrast to the water mining schemes of the present), they automatically maintained a balance between water abstraction for use in agriculture and recharge of the ecosystems that provided the water in the first place. Despite this apparent limitation, they were largely successful in protecting crops from both drought and flood damage over huge expanses of agricultural land, and many have outlasted modern water engineering structures.[5]

The Papago Indians, for instance, built low dykes across many acres of land to funnel runoff into a few acres for crop production. Though their technique left many miles of low walls across the desert, it allowed them to cultivate land without significantly disrupting the water cycle or the ecosystems that support it. The Nabateans, who began to farm the Negev desert about 2,000 years ago, employed a similar system. Author Fred Pearce visited one of these ancient farms one spring after six weeks with no rain and found that the soil was damp, a field of wheat was growing fast, almond trees were in leaf, and pistachio trees were budding.[6]

The relatively sustainable water-harvesting techniques of early civilizations evolved at the same time as human capacity to over-harvest, or mine, water. Early societies learned to dig wells as an update to using a communal water hole. Wells were drilled deeper as populations and water demand grew, and as tools were developed. By 3000 BC, the Egyptians had perfected core drilling in stone quarries, although the wells, which were large in diameter, lined with stone, and constructed with labour supplied by people and donkeys, were rarely deeper than 50 metres. China developed a churn drill two millennia ago, and some of the wells produced using this technology went down more than one kilometre.[7]

The Greeks and Romans were among the first to focus on the control of water as a foundation of society and to construct long-distance water supply pipelines. The ancient cities of Jericho, Ur, Memphis, Babylon, Athens, Carthage and

Alexandria relied to a great extent on artificial water supplies to provide drinking water.[8] Historians have also suggested that ownership and control of water in the arid Middle East (Egypt, Assyria, and the kingdom of Saba) formed the basis of civilizations there.

'[W]hile the technical prowess of Roman hydraulic engineers was far from unique, they did leave behind structures to inspire the Europeans of the Renaissance. Says the British geographer Denis Cosgrove: "The crumbling evidence of Roman hydro-engineering became for Renaissance observers signs of the power and the glory of Empire." The aqueducts also became a symbol of a particular attitude toward water. "The geometric precision of an aqueduct signifies the engineer's vision of water flow, a bounded channel form that has become the common conception of how even a natural river should appear." The Romans imparted from the ancient to the modern world a vision of nature tamed, remade in the image of engineering, of the land separated from the water. It was a world in which water flowing to the sea was wasted, in which marshes were for draining and floods for controlling.'[9]

As mankind's engineering prowess has expanded, the motivations behind large water projects have shifted from a pragmatic use of available resources to sustain life to be much more political.[10] Water resources development in the twenty-first century is likely to play a substantial role in directing money flows in the global marketplace, in maintaining or disrupting regional political stability, and in determining the fate of the ecosystems that support life on Earth.

'People, as we've learned clearly by now, are driven more than anything by market forces, by the desire to improve their lives with commerce, transactions, robust economies, and profits. As we have strived to fulfill these aspirations, water has been both an impediment and an opportunity. Unmanaged, it's a natural and geographical obstacle, flooding away whole communities at will, and in the process destroying carefully constructed economic systems, while making it difficult and expensive to move products and raw materials from one place to another because of its ubiquity on Earth. But water also offers a potential advantage: those who were wealthy or creative enough to control the water supplies or the irrigation channels or the barge canals – or perhaps those with the most and best weapons – produced societies with larger, healthier, better-employed, and more innovative populations, with more items to sell to more places around the world and more ways to get their products to buyers.

'To control water, thus, has long seemed to be obviously the better option; all benefits were on that side of the equations. The other course – not to build dams or otherwise restrict water's movement, and not to make water a partner in the search for profits and commerce – in other words, opting not to harness this powerful force – simply would have gone against our desire for progress and wealth.'[11]

Water Availability and Use in Modern Times

'Twentieth-century water-resources planning and development have relied on projections of future populations, per-capita water demand, agricultural production, and levels of economic productivity. Because each of these variables has always been projected to rise, water needs have also always been expected to rise. As a result, traditional water planning regularly concludes that future water demands will exceed actual water supplies. The water-management problem then becomes an exercise in coming up with ways of bridging this anticipated gap.'[12]

During the first three-quarters of the twentieth century, absolute and per capita demand for water increased throughout the world (see Figure 2.1). Freshwater withdrawals increased from an estimated 580 km^3 per year in 1900 to 3,580 km^3 per year in 1990. In the United States, water withdrawals grew from 56 km^3 per year in 1900 to more than 610 km3 per year in 1980 – a tenfold increase in water withdrawals during a period of time when the population only increased by a factor of four. Per capita water withdrawals in the US grew from less than 700 m^3 per person per year in 1900 to nearly 2,300 m^3 per person per year in the early 1980s. These trends ended in the US in the mid-1980s and early 1990s, when water use began to decrease despite continued increases in population and economic growth. At the end of the century, water withdrawals had declined by nearly ten percent from their 1980 level. By 1995, per capita water withdrawals had dropped more than 20 percent from their peak in 1980.[13]

Globally, projections of increases in demand have greatly overestimated actual increases in demand by assuming that water withdrawals would continue to increase at historical rates. Actual global water withdrawals in 1995 were estimated to be between 3,500 and 3,700 km^3, about half of what they were predicted to be 30 years earlier.[14] This gap between prediction and reality is the result of a number of trends. First, predictions of the rate of global population growth have not been matched by reality, largely as a result of the expanded availability of contraceptives and the education of women. Second, environmental and social concerns are increasingly raised by a proliferating international community of non-governmental organizations, leading to a drop-off in the number of dams built around the world.

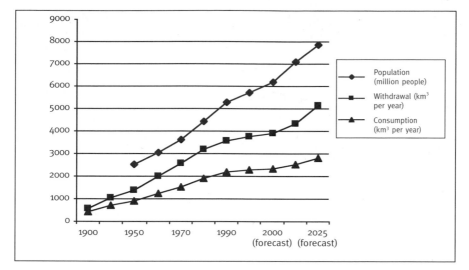

Figure 2.1 Global Population, Water Withdrawal and Consumption
From: Shiklomanov, I.A., 1998. Assessment of water resources and water availability in the world. Report for the Comprehensive Assessment of the Freshwater Resources of the World, United Nations. Data archive on CD-ROM from the State Hydrological Institute, St Petersburg.

Third, as more dams have been constructed, the marginal economic benefit of new dams, which are often planned for inferior locations, has declined, making it difficult to justify new projects.

During the final decade of the twentieth century, however, a countervailing trend began to emerge. People began to view water as a scarce resource, and eventually as an economic resource, in contrast to the past when water was thought to be an essentially sacred public good.[15] Under free-market systems, scarce goods are often allocated to the highest bidder. Projections of increased demand relative to supply therefore serve to drive up the cost of water where water is priced.

The act of redefining water as an economic good has essentially transformed water into a commodity. As the price rises, new approaches for transporting water from countries with large supplies to countries with high demands become economically feasible. As a result, water transfers are no longer limited to countries that share a drainage basin or to diversions of water from one drainage basin to another. Water is now transported globally, like any other commodity, in bottles, bags, tankers, and even glacial ice. The commodification of water creates greater pressure to expand markets by stimulating demand and expanding supplies.

How Much Water is Available?

More than 70 percent of the Earth's surface is covered with water, which is why the Earth is often called the 'blue planet.' The Earth contains a total of about 1.385 billion km³ of water; of this, approximately 35 million km³, or 2.5 percent, is freshwater. Moreover, only 12,500 km³ of this freshwater is considered to be renewable and actually available for human use. The remainder is locked up in polar ice or is available at times or in places where it cannot practicably be exploited (see Table 2.1).[16]

Table 2.1 Distribution of Water on Earth

Water location	Percentage of the total amount of water
Oceans and seas	97.5
Polar ice caps and glaciers	2.05
Deep groundwater (750–5000 metres)	0.38
Shallow groundwater (less than 750 metres)	0.30
Lakes	0.01
Soil moisture	0.005
Water in the atmosphere	0.001
Rivers	0.0001
Water in plants and animals, including people	0.00004

From: Donkers, H. 2000. 'Water Basic Facts and Figures.' Unpublished compendium of water facts prepared for the World Wide Fund for Nature.

The freshwater available to humanity is also unevenly distributed in time and space. Of the more than 40,000 km³ per year that replenishes aquifers or returns to the oceans through rivers or other runoff, about half flows unused to the sea in floods. An additional one-eighth of this potentially available water falls in areas too far from human habitation to be captured for human use.[17]

About three-quarters of the annual precipitation on our planet descends on areas that contain less than two-thirds of the world's population. For example, the Amazon Basin, a huge region with less than ten million inhabitants, receives about 20 percent of the global average runoff each year. The Congo River, with its tributaries, accounts for approximately 30 percent of the runoff in Africa, yet is home to only 10 percent of the African population.[18] On a continental basis, substantial mismatches exist between the distribution of the human population and the availability of freshwater (see Table 2.2).

The availability of water can also vary greatly from season to season and from year to year. Some river basins, such as the Ganges and Mekong, have distinct dry and wet seasons each year. Throughout much of the developing world, the freshwater supply comes in the form of seasonal rains. For example, India receives 90 percent of its rainfall during the summer monsoon season between June and September. Some developing countries can make use of no more than 20 percent of their potentially available freshwater resources because the water comes in torrents of rain and flooded rivers that are difficult to exploit.[19]

Conversely, some river basins receive very little water during the dry season. Basins with a pronounced dry season are those where less than 2 percent of the total annual runoff occurs in the four driest months of the year. Twenty-seven of

Table 2.2 Global Runoff and Population, by Continent, 1995

Region	Total annual runoff (km³)	Share of global runoff (%)	Share of global population (%)
Europe	3,240	8	13
Asia	14,550	36	60
Africa	4,320	11	13
North and Central America	6,200	15	8
South America	10,420	26	6
Australia and Oceania	1,970	5	Less than 1
Total	40,700	101[1]	Less than 101[1]

From: Postel, S., 1996. 'Dividing the Waters: Food Security, Ecosystem Health, and the New Politics of Scarcity.' Worldwatch Paper 132, September. Washington. p. 11.
[1] Does not add up to 100 because of rounding.

these basins were home to more than ten million people in 1995. They include, among others, the Balsas and Grande de Santiago basins in Mexico; the Limpopo in Southern Africa; the Hai Ho and Hong basins in China; the Chao Phrya in Southeast Asia; and the Brahmani Damodar, Godavari, Krishna, Madi, Ponnaujar, Rabamarti and Tapti in India.[20]

An average of 317,000 m³ of water per year is available for each square kilometre on Earth, roughly 7,600 m³ per person. The average amount of water per square kilometre of land varies from 134,000 m³ in Africa to 672,000 m³ in South America, and the amount per person varies from 3,930 m³ in Asia to 83,700 m³ in Oceania.[21]

Continental averages mask the extreme variability in water availability witnessed on a national or local level, however. In Europe, which averages 4,066 m³ per person per year, the water-rich Scandinavian countries skew the average annual per capita water availability. In Iceland, for instance, this figure is 624,000 m³. Water shortages are experienced in southern Europe, however, where Spain has 2,800 m³ and the average is much lower in the eastern and southern parts of the country. In South America, which receives 34,960 m³ per person per year, water draining through the extremely humid Amazon River Basin obscures national differences. Surinam, for example, has 468,000 m³ of water available to each of its citizens every year, but Peru has only 1,700 m³. In Asia, Laos has more than 55,300 m³ per person per year, while India has 2,240 m³, most of which is in the northern part of the subcontinent.[22]

Contrary to conventional beliefs, the amount of available freshwater on Earth is probably changing over time. While it is possible that icy comets and fiery volcanoes continue to contribute water to our planet, the total amount of this water is quite small compared with the amount of water that is already in circulation and the projections of increased water use by people. At the same time, human activities may actually be reducing the amount of freshwater available to the world. For example, the expansion of paved areas where water can no longer infiltrate into the soil leads to increases in runoff and reduces the amount of groundwater available to interact with surface water systems. As more freshwater discharges more rapidly into the oceans, we essentially transform freshwater into salt water.[23] In addition, a 2001 study by the Scripps Institution of Oceanography found that particles of materials such as fly ash, sulphates, nitrates, and mineral dust produced through the combustion of fossil fuels are cutting down the amount of sunlight penetrating the oceans. Reduced light penetration results in reduced evaporation from the oceans and thus to a potential decrease in the amount of freshwater on the planet.[24]

Human Uses of Water

Objectives and strategies for the management of water resources change as civilizations evolve. In pre-industrialized societies, where human demands on the resource are more limited in nature and scope, water is relatively abundant. During the industrialization phase, water is exploited more thoroughly. Often, it is the construction of infrastructure such as dams and diversion tunnels that permits socioeconomic growth in dry regions.

Over the past two centuries, the industrial and Green revolutions and the growth of cities have brought about a transformation in the distribution and use of water on an unprecedented scale. The rate of water withdrawal rose steeply at the start of the past century, and even further at mid-century. The volume of river water polluted to some degree by wastewater discharges has increased in a similar pattern.[25] Human exploitation of the world's water resources occurs at a number of interacting scales, including the individual, household, and society.

Individual human bodies are 70 percent water. An average adult normally takes in two to three litres of water per day, mostly through drinking and eating. A similar amount is released, mainly through urine, sweat and respiration. People begin to feel thirsty after a loss of only 1 percent of bodily fluids and risk death if fluid loss nears 10 percent.[26]

Household water use is determined primarily by availability and cost. There is a great deal of regional variation in water withdrawn for personal use. In Africa, these withdrawals average 17 m³ per person annually, or 47 litres per day. In Asia, 31 m³ annually per capita, or 85 litres per day, is withdrawn for personal use. In the UK, this figure is 122 m³ per year, or 334 litres per day. In the US, fully 211 m³ per person is withdrawn for personal use each year, or 578 litres per day.[27] Globally, over one billion people still lack safe domestic water supplies and 2.4 billion lack adequate sanitation.[28]

Society uses water in a range of domestic and productive endeavours. As of 1995, people were collectively withdrawing roughly 3,800 km³ of water each year for primarily economic purposes, of which 2,100 km³ were consumed (see Table 2.3 below).[29] Of course, there is regional variation in the proportion of water used for different purposes. In Africa, about 88 percent of water withdrawals are applied to agriculture. The proportions used for domestic purposes and industry are 7 and

Table 2.3 Global Withdrawal and Consumption of Water in Different Sectors, 1995

User	Amount of water used in 1995 (km³)
Agriculture	
Withdrawal	2,500
Consumption	1,750
Industry	
Withdrawal	750
Consumption	75
Municipalities	
Withdrawal	350
Consumption	50
Reservoirs (evaporation)	200
Total	
Withdrawal	3,800
Consumption	2,100
Groundwater overconsumption	200

From: Cosgrove, W.J. & F.R. Rijsberman, 2000. *World Water Vision: Making Water Everybody's Business.* Earthscan Publications Ltd., London.

5 percent, respectively. In Asia, roughly 86 percent of water withdrawn is used in agriculture, 8 percent in industry, and 6 percent for domestic consumption. In contrast, Europe applies the majority of its withdrawals – 54 percent – to industry. Agriculture and domestic uses receive 33 and 13 percent, respectively.[30]

It is also important to note that the proportion of water used in each sector changes over time. While the vast bulk of water is currently withdrawn for and consumed in agriculture, an increasing proportion of water is being sequestered for urban and industrial uses. Economic forces drive this switch. A thousand tons of water produces one ton of wheat, which has a market value of US$200. In contrast, the same amount of water used in industry yields an estimated US$14,000 of output – 70 times as much.[31] Those countries that can afford to import grain, therefore, often find that imports of 'virtual water' – the substitution of food imports for irrigated agriculture production paid for by urban and commercial growth – are an attractive alternative to continued use of water in agriculture.[32]

Agriculture consumes more water by far than any other societal use. Water is needed by plants in photosynthesis to form carbohydrates, the basic food supply of all life. The earliest forms of civilization developed in the arid lands of the Middle East, Asia and the Americas along major rivers such as the Tigris, Euphrates, Nile, Indus and Colorado, and used these rivers as a reliable source of irrigation. In the 1990s, agriculture accounted for two-thirds of the world's water use and its share of water use was expected to expand into the future.[33] Agricultural uses consume more water than any other human use, and water that is available for reuse after application in irrigation often carries concentrations of agricultural pollution that render it unfit for many applications – even for reuse in growing crops!

Industrial water use in general has more implications for water quality than quantity. In turn, the implications of industrial use for water quality depend greatly on the industry. Effluent discharges from some industries have harmful consequences for freshwater ecosystems through changes in water temperature, increases in chemical oxygen demand (the quantity of oxygen required to break down artificial chemicals), and toxic pollution.

On the other hand, industries may require water that is cleaner than can be provided by the ambient environment. In these cases, which involve 'clean' industries such as microelectronics and pharmaceuticals, the wastewater discharged into receiving waters may be higher than the ambient water quality. The resulting improvement in water quality can benefit aquatic ecosystems when it removes anthropogenic pollutants from the water.

Where water quality is naturally unsuited for human consumption, however, improvements in water quality may be harmful to native ecosystems and the species that inhabit them. Many species, including most river dolphins, have evolved in water that is very high in suspended sediment loads, for example. The low water clarity in these rivers may decrease the success rate of poachers and provide a slender margin of protection for these highly endangered mammals. Reduction of suspended sediments in these systems could improve water quality from a human perspective, while rendering the ecosystem uninhabitable for the wild species that evolved there.

Urban demands for water have been rising virtually exponentially as populations grow and people increasingly concentrate in cities, a phenomenon experienced especially in developing countries. Urban population centres have long been confronted with the inseparable challenges of providing sufficient high-quality water for human consumption and maintaining adequate sanitation facilities to protect human health and the environment. These challenges are expanding rapidly, particularly in developing countries where the current trend in urban migration far exceeds that of earlier waves of rural-to-urban migration in the developed world, and the resources needed to respond are often lacking.[34] Half of the world's population now lives in cities; by 2030, this figure is expected to reach 60 percent. The urban population in developing countries is projected to double from roughly 1.9 billion in 2001 to just under 4 billion by 2030. World-wide, about three-quarters of all current population growth is in urban areas. In most developing countries, cities are growing at about two to three times faster than the national population.[35] Although, on a global basis, urban areas use only about ten percent of total water, the demand for water in cities has been the fastest-growing component of increasing water demand over most of the planet.[36] As a result, domestic water demands increasingly compete with water use in other sectors, and the water returned from cities to receiving water bodies, which frequently are also important water sources, is often dangerously polluted.

In addition to the changes in quantity and quality of water resulting from domestic use in cities, the mere migration of water through a city in its transformation from precipitation to streamflow can significantly alter water timing, temperature, and chemistry. Stormwater flows over impervious surfaces such as roads, rooftops and parking lots. In the process, there is little potential for runoff to percolate into groundwater tables, but a great deal of potential for the water to absorb heat from paved surfaces and to entrain pollutants, such as oils and heavy metals, from contaminated surfaces. Large fluxes of polluted stormwater can also trigger releases of raw sewage into receiving water bodies in cities where a single sewer system conveys both stormwater and domestic waste. Sudden releases of polluted urban wastewater pose danger both for human health and for aquatic life.

Energy production relies heavily on water, as well. The amount of water needed to produce energy varies greatly with the type of facility and the characteristics of the fuel cycle. Fossil fuel, nuclear, and geothermal plants require enormous amounts of cooling water. Solar photovoltaic systems, wind turbines, and other renewable energy sources often require minimal amounts of water.[37] The generation of hydroelectricity generally consumes water only through evaporation from the reservoir. Regulation of rivers for electricity production can substantially alter the timing and volume of flows, with substantial implications for the physical, chemical, and biological structure of the ecosystem.

Navigation over water has provided an essential form of transportation throughout human history and is becoming even more central to trade in today's globalizing economies. While the transport of commerce on inland waterways does not directly consume water, it can trigger significant changes in hydrology, particularly in river and floodplain systems. Channelization and alteration of flow regimes are two key examples of navigation-related activities with often significant effects on other water uses. In the Mississippi River system, for example, the 'training' and channelization of the river and its delta have deprived the coast of Louisiana of sediment deposition. The loss of natural sediment deposition leaves the coastal area vulnerable to sea level rise, salinity intrusion (and resulting shifts in fish and shellfish production), and hurricane damage. The construction of the Farrakah barrage to divert dry season flows in the Ganges to the port of Calcutta has led to severe salinity intrusion in the wells of downstream Bangladesh.

Recreational uses of water have always been an important part of humankind's leisure activities. Today, recreationists are gaining economic clout over other water users in the United States because of the value of waterfront property in a very hot real estate market. Freshwater ecosystems provide a wide range of recreational opportunities, ranging from the relatively passive (such as birdwatching and photography), to the active but non-consumptive (such as white-water rafting or kayaking), to the active and consumptive (such as fishing). The effects on the resource differ according to recreational activity, but it is important to note that different recreational activities are frequently incompatible with each other. Jetskiing on reservoirs, for example, is incompatible with canoeing, kayaking, diving, birdwatching, white-water rafting, fishing, and many other sports that rely on natural aquatic habitats.

A GLOBAL WATER CRISIS?

'Global consumption of water is doubling every 20 years, more than twice the rate of population growth. According to the United Nations, more than one billion people on Earth already lack access to fresh drinking water. If current trends persist, by 2025 the demand for freshwater is expected to rise by 56 percent more than is currently available'.[38]

Despite the gap between predictions and actual water withdrawals, global water use continues to expand faster than population growth. Over the past century, world population has tripled while water withdrawals have increased more than sixfold. Since 1940, annual global water withdrawals have increased by an average of 2.5 to 3 percent per year, compared with an annual population growth of 1.5 to 2 percent. Water withdrawals in developing countries over the past decade have increased by 4 to 8 percent per year.[39]

The world's population, already at nearly six billion, is growing at a rate of approximately 80 million people per year. This number implies an increased demand for water of about 64 billion m^3 per year – an amount equal to the Rhine River's annual flow rate. The population of our planet has grown by nearly two billion people since 1970. As a result, the per capita availability of water is one-third lower than it was then.[40]

In general, based on calculations by the renowned Swedish hydrologist Malin Falkenmark, countries with 1,000 to 1,700 m^3 per person per year experience recurring problems of water scarcity. Countries with 500 to 1,000 m^3 per person per year have a chronic situation of water stress, where lack of water is slowing down economic development and may threaten public health. Countries with less than 500 m^3 per person per year are already in crisis – a situation that will become more common as the world population rises to about 8 billion in 2025.[41] While at 7,600 m^3 per person per year the global water supply on average is sufficient to avoid these unpleasant conditions, the uneven distribution of water over time and space creates water shortages in many parts of the world.

Calculations of water stress and scarcity are based on the amount of annual, available, renewable (not including fossil groundwater) freshwater per capita. Countries that have high population densities and low runoff rates will naturally be the first to fall into these categories, though wealthier countries can avoid water shortages by importing water or building desalination plants.

Currently, 31 countries – mostly in Africa and the Near East – face water stress or scarcity. Seventeen additional countries, with a combined projected population of 2.1 billion, will fall into water-short categories by virtue of population growth alone. In the Middle East, 9 out of 14 countries currently experience water scarcity

Figure 2.2 Predicted Water Stress and Scarcity, 2050
Map adapted from Samson, S. & B. Charrier, 1997. *International Freshwater Conflict: Issues and Prevention Strategies.* Green Cross International, Geneva.
Note: Small island states are not shown due to scale constraints.

and others are rapidly approaching this state.[42] By the year 2025, 48 countries with more than 2.8 billion people, roughly 33.5 percent of the global population then, will be affected by water stress or scarcity. Another nine countries, including China and Pakistan, will be approaching water stress.[43]

While these numbers look rather frightening, one needs to interpret them carefully and in the context of their implications for people and ecosystems. No region of the world is actually using 1,700 m³ annually per capita. In the US and Canada, the most prolific consumers of water in the world are using only 1,693 m³ per person per year out of a resource vastly greater than that. Oceania (the Pacific Islands, Australia, New Zealand, Fiji and Papua New Guinea) annually uses 907 m³ per person. In Europe, Asia, South America and Africa, the numbers are 726, 526, 376 and 244, respectively. When estimates of water use in rainfed agriculture are added in, however, many countries are approaching the 1,700 m³ figure.[44]

Of course, human access to water is driven by a number of social and economic factors in addition to the annual availability of water. For example, Israel has only 300 m³ per year available to its citizens, but few Israelis suffer from water shortages. On the other hand, Nigeria is rich in water, but more than half the population has no access to safe drinking water.[45] Water resources expert Peter H. Gleick has developed another measure of water need and scarcity using an estimated 'basic water requirement' (BWR). Considering only drinking water and sanitation needs for an individual suggests a BWR of 25 litres per person per day. Adding in water for bathing and cooking raises the total BWR to 50 litres per person per day. Vast regions of the world and hundreds of millions of people lack sufficient freshwater to meet these requirements. In 1990, 55 countries with an aggregate population of nearly one billion fell below this level.[46] In all industrialized countries domestic water use far exceeds the BWR, although there is wide variability in water quality. In western Europe, the recommended BWR is less than 25 percent of total domestic use. In the US and Canada, a BWR of 50 litres per person per day is less than ten percent of total current domestic use.[47]

So is the world facing a 'global water crisis'? Clearly, devastating shortages of water are becoming more common and widespread. At the same time, human use of water is becoming unsustainable as we use freshwater at rates that exceed the time required for their replenishment and increasingly tap into non-renewable sources, such as fossil groundwater.

'China, which has 22 percent of the world's population but only 7 percent of all freshwater runoff, will narrowly miss the water stress category's cutoff point of 1,700 m³ per capita in 2025. China's freshwater supplies have been estimated to be capable of sustainably supporting 650 million people – only half of the country's current population of 1.2 billion. Despite periodic flooding in the south, along the Yangtze River, China faces chronic freshwater shortages in the northern part of the country, affecting 92 million people in the Hai River Basin alone. Many of China's cities, including Beijing, face critical water shortages. The water table under Beijing has been dropping by roughly 2 metres per year, and one-third of the wells have dried up.'[48]

'In India, a country whose population hit 1 billion on August 15, the pumping of underground water is now estimated to be double the rate of aquifer recharge from rainfall. The International Water Management Institute estimates that India's grain harvest could be reduced by up to one-fourth as a result of aquifer depletion.

'The Yellow River in China first ran dry in 1972. Since 1985, it has run dry for part of each year. In 1997, it failed to reach the sea during 226 days, or roughly 7 months of the year.

'In Central Asia, the Amu Darya, one of two rivers that once fed the Aral Sea, is now drained by farmers in Turkmenistan and Uzbekistan. As the sea has shrunk to scarcely half its original size, the rising salt concentration has destroyed all fish, eliminating a rich fishery that once landed 100 million pounds of fish per year.'[49]

'Israel probably uses water more efficiently than any other country, yet its demand has exceeded the sustainable annual yield of its available sources since the mid-1970s. Israel strictly controls Palestinian use of water in the occupied 5,890 km² West Bank, from which it draws 40 percent of its groundwater and more than 25 percent of its renewable water supplies. Palestinians, noting that Jewish settlers use four times as much water on a per capita basis, charge that deep wells dug for the settlers sap the yield of their own shallower wells. Israel is projected to grow from 4.7 million people in 1990 to about 8 million in 2025.'[50]

Variations in water availability and quality in any particular time and space are natural phenomena that can be greatly intensified by human actions. The root cause of any particular water crisis experienced by people is usually an anthropogenic disruption of the water cycle. Such disruptions can occur on a variety of spatial and temporal scales, from the global (climate change, for example), to the hemispheric (atmospheric deposition of toxic pollutants), to the river basin and sub-basin (excessive withdrawals of surface and groundwater for irrigation).

Attempts to mitigate any particular water crisis must identify the relevant disruptions of the water cycle that constitute the root causes at whatever spatial and temporal scale these disruptions occur. Sustainable solutions will usually lie in restoration of the water cycle, which often requires changes in the strategies that people are using to achieve their water management objectives.

The danger in viewing the water crisis as a global problem, rather than as a series of water cycle disruptions operating at a variety of (often interacting) scales, is that such an approach leads us to search for global solutions. Attempts to simplify the search for solutions by addressing the crisis at a global scale can lead to the imposition of inappropriate technologies on cultures and ecosystems. Rather than resolving a crisis, the grafting of a globally conceived solution on a problem with complex, local causes can exacerbate the problem in the long run.

There is no denying that a freshwater crisis exists in some parts of the world and is emerging in others. It should be perceived, however, as an explosion of local and regional water management problems simultaneously in virtually all corners of the world. While global demand projections may awaken the public conscience, what matters to individual people and ecosystems is the availability of sufficient water of adequate quality to meet their legitimate needs throughout the year.

SUPPLY-SIDE SOLUTIONS: STRETCHING THE WATER CYCLE

The ever-expanding human demand for freshwater in the twentieth century led society to supply-side solutions that relied heavily on large-scale structural approaches to storing and moving freshwater.

'During the twentieth century, water-resources planning focused on making projections of variables such as future populations, per-capita water demand, agricultural production, levels of economic productivity, and so on. These projections were then used to forecast future water demands.... The next step in this traditional processes consisted of identifying projects that could be built to bridge the apparent gaps between the projected demand and the estimated available supply ....

'Even ignoring the difficulty of projecting future populations and levels of economic activities, there are many limitations to this approach. Perhaps the greatest problem is that it routinely produces scenarios with irrational conclusions, such as water demands that exceed supply, and water withdrawals unconstrained by environmental or ecological limits.'[51]

A supply-side strategy for addressing increasing water demands can make use of several technologies, depending on the setting and source of water. The strategy can divert upstream water away from its natural course, frequently in inter-basin transfers; pump aquifers, generally by sinking the deepest wells into a groundwater source to maximize control over that source; or sequestrate and store surface water for later use. (However, this last approach risks reducing the total amount of water available through evaporation losses.)

The success of these strategies lies in the adequacy of the infrastructure that is provided to support them and of the strategists that operate these structures. Common approaches to sequestering water for application to new uses and geographic areas involve dams, inter-basin transfers, and groundwater mining. All of these have consequences for ecosystems and the water cycle.

Dams come in many sizes and are used for many purposes. Increasing the water supplies available for human use has frequently involved creating huge storage structures that provide people with the capacity to regulate downstream flows. Large and small reservoirs already have an estimated combined storage of as much as 10,000 km^3 – five times the volume of all the rivers in the world.[52]

World-wide, there are more than 45,000 large dams (15 meters or more high) in over 140 countries (see Table 2.4).[53] The top five dam-building countries – China, the United States, India, Spain and Japan – account for nearly 80 percent of all large dams. China alone has built around 22,000 large dams, or close to half the world's total number.[54] In Japan only two of the 30,000 rivers are neither dammed nor modified.[55]

Individually, dams and reservoirs can exert a huge influence on the local water cycle by 'consuming' water through seepage and evaporation, changing the micro-climate around the reservoir, and altering water quality. Seismic activity triggered by dams and reservoirs can also alter surface and groundwater hydrology. At the river basin scale, dams may exert many influences that are damaging to ecology, such as altering natural flow regimes, creating barriers to migration, interfering

Table 2.4 Large Dams and Storage Capacity of Large Reservoirs, by Continent*

Continent	World-registered large dams (15 m or higher)		Number of large reservoirs (total capacity of 0.1 km³ or more)	Storage capacity of large reservoirs (km³)
	Number	**%**		
Africa	1,265	5	176	1,000
Asia	8,485	33.4	815	1,980
Oceania	685	2.7	89 (only includes Australia and New Zealand)	95 (only includes Australia and New Zealand)
Europe	6,200	24.4	576	645
North America	7,775	30.6	915	1,692
Central and South America	1,005	3.9	265	972
TOTAL	25,415	100.0	2,836	6,384

* Includes only those large dams registered with the International Commission on Large Dams (ICOLD). Data from China and the former USSR, for example, is seriously incomplete.
From: Revenga, C., J. Brunner, N. Henninger, K. Kassem & R. Payne, 2000. *Pilot Analysis of Global Ecosystems: Freshwater Systems*. World Resources Institute, Washington.

with sediment transport and deposition processes, and changing water quality. A series of dams on a river, creating a string of reservoirs head-to-tail, can effectively wipe out the ecological functions of the entire river system and replace them with an artificial ecology that is much less complex and diverse. At a global level, dams influence the water cycle by altering the distribution of water on the planet and by altering the climate through the emission of 'greenhouse gases.'[56]

While the effects of dams on ecology and the water cycle are numerous and could easily command a volume in their own right, there is one additional topic worth mentioning here: that of sediment deposition behind dams. Natural rivers carry sediments in suspension in a regular rhythm of erosion and deposition that is determined by the river's flow rate speed and volume. Much of the sediment load of a major river will be deposited in its floodplains, where it rejuvenates semi-aquatic habitats, and in its delta, where it replaces land lost to the sea.

A reservoir causes the flow rate of a natural river to slow down. As a result, much of the sediment carried by the river is deposited in the slow water behind a dam. This deposition leads to a loss of storage volume in the reservoir (as the volume allocated to water storage is gradually taken up by sediment deposition), and the correlating loss of sediment supplies to delta areas and floodplains. The World Commission on Dams estimated that some 0.5 to 1 percent of the world reservoir volume is lost from sedimentation annually.[57] This estimate is an average of a wide range of sedimentation rates, depending on the size, location and age of the reservoir and the condition of the watershed. Extreme examples of storage loss include the Cerron Grande dam in El Salvador, where sedimentation decreased the anticipated project life from 350 years to only 30 years.[58] Most of the water supply for Puerto Rico comes from reservoirs built in the early and middle twentieth century which are now losing storage volume to sedimentation. The storage capacity losses for 14 reservoirs studied by the US Geological Survey range from 12 to 81 percent, an average of 35 percent.[59]

Downstream of the dam, the lack of sediment once supplied by the river has serious economic and environmental impacts.

'The Nile transports an average of 1,100 million tons of silt each year, much of it fertile soil washed downstream from the Ethiopian highlands. For thousands of years, 90 percent of this silt reached the delta, while the remaining 10 percent was deposited on the Nile floodplain....

'[S]ince the completion of the High Dam at Aswan, and the trapping of virtually all of the silt in Lake Nasser, the delta has actually been in retreat. Borg-el-Borellos, a former delta village, is now two kilometres out to sea....

'Global warming, and the anticipated rise in sea level that higher temperatures will bring, increases the threat of inundation.... Egypt could lose up to 19 percent of its habitable land within about 60 years, displacing up to 16 percent of its population – which by then would likely total well over 1,200 million – and wiping out some 15 percent of its economic activity.'[60]

Inter-basin transfers involve moving water from one drainage basin to another, typically adjacent, basin using tunnels, canals or pipelines. The trend towards economic globalization is in part reflected in the growing number of large-scale, inter-basin transfer schemes.

The implications for the ecology of the rivers and livelihoods of the people who depend on them are tremendous, for both gainers and losers. In the gaining water body, influxes of alien water may carry with them alien species of plants and animals that can wreak havoc on native species. Increased flows can also destabilize the sediment and water balance of a receiving river, leading to channel scour and erosion. In the losing water body, decreases in water levels can cause sudden changes in the physical and chemical extent and quality of aquatic habitat, making survival difficult for life forms that have evolved in different conditions.

As the price of water increases, people are using a wider variety of methods to transfer it to distant markets. By the end of the twentieth century, tankers were already delivering water to regions willing to pay exorbitant prices for small amounts of freshwater in emergency situations. Intermittent customers included the Bahamas, Japan, Taiwan and Korea.[61]

Plans are under way in several parts of the world for steady supplies of foreign water. Turkey plans to move water from the Manavgat River to Cyprus, Malta,

'The Senqu (Orange) River originates in Lesotho, and forms the boundary between South Africa and Namibia before it enters the Atlantic Ocean. The five-dam Lesotho Highlands Water Project (LHWP) would divert about 40 percent of the water (called 'white gold' by project authorities) in the Senqu River basin to South Africa's Vaal River system in Gauteng Province. Multiple tributaries in the watershed would be dammed if all dams in the project were completed....

'The LHWP began without an environmental impact assessment for the overall project.... Since the project will divert up to 40 percent of the river's flow, the downstream effects will be substantial. Basically, the impacts include reductions in wetlands habitat, less water available downstream for people and wildlife, reductions in fisheries, and cessation of flooding. The hydrological variability of these floods is critical to many species found in ecosystems downstream of the LHWP—a variability that will cease with the damming of the waters. Floods not only bring water, but also deposit sediments. The dams will reduce the amount of nutrient-rich sediments deposited and change the timing and size of the flood, both of which could lead to a change in floodplain habitats....

'The Maloti minnow, rock catfish, and the bearded vulture are some of the known rare and endangered species that are losing habitat to the project. A threatened endemic plant, the Spiral Aloe, will be affected by the project, as will rare bird species that nest in the area.'[62]

'The Theun-Hinboun Hydropower Project, a 210 MW trans-basin river diversion project located in Bolikhamxai and Khammouane Provinces of central Laos PDR, was officially opened on April 4, 1998....[63] Below the powerhouse, tailrace channel, and re-regulating pond, the water originally in the Theun River flows into the Nam Hai, a small stream that in the past had only flowed seasonally. The water flows in the Nam Hai for several kilometers to the confluence with the Nam Hinboun. The Nam Hinboun then flows approximately 80 kilometers to its confluence with the Mekong.

'The water now flows quickly and is very muddy in the Nam Hai and in the Hinboun. It has become difficult to fish in this area and this is having an impact on the livelihoods of people living along the river. In addition, their vegetable gardens have been flooded and dry season drinking water sources inundated. Many villagers express fear of flooding during the rainy season.'[64]

Libya, Greece, Egypt and Israel using pipelines and tankers. In the summer of 2000, Israel had already begun negotiations to buy 49 billion litres of water per year from Turkey.[65] Global H_2O, a Canadian-based company, has signed a 30-year agreement with the town of Sitka, Alaska, to export 169 billion litres per year of glacier water to China. Once in China, the water is to be bottled in one of that country's 'free trade zones,' which makes extensive use of cheap labour. In order to transport the water in bulk from Sitka to markets in China and elsewhere, Global H_2O has formed a 'strategic alliance' with the Signet shipping group, a US company based in Houston, Texas, which has a fleet of supertankers. Each Signet supertanker is expected to carry over 330 million litres.[66]

Recent innovations in water bag technology could significantly lower the costs of long-distance water transfers and spur rapid growth in water markets. Because freshwater is less dense than salt water, it floats on top of seawater. Entrepreneurs have taken advantage of this principle of physics to design huge bags made of polyurethane that ships can tow across the oceans. It is possible to produce a water bag with the carrying capacity of five supertankers at about 1.25 percent of the cost.[67] The biggest economic advantage of bags over barges is that bags don't have to be unloaded immediately. They can be left behind to serve as storage vessels long after the ship that towed them to market has left on other lucrative missions.[68]

The expanded scale of water exports made possible by improved technology and increasing scarcity and price might have more widespread effects on ecosystems and the water cycle than the limited number of conventional inter-basin transfer schemes. Because transfers by tanker and water bag are limited by economics rather than by geography, it is entirely conceivable that large volumes of water could be shifted between very different ecosystems. Tapping into glaciers or icebergs, for example, would have the effect of turning semi-permanent ice reserves initially into freshwater but ultimately into salt water, potentially raising sea levels.

Moving water from water-rich ecosystems to arid ones could lead to desiccation of the moist systems and, ironically, to increased desertification in the dry systems. Reduced surface water in the lakes and rivers in humid climates can reduce groundwater recharge and soil moisture, making soils more vulnerable to compaction and ultimately less permeable. As with paving urban areas, the result could well be an increase in runoff and in the ratio of salt water to freshwater. In arid areas, the creation of a dependable water supply would remove one of the most important limiting factors on human population density and development. These trends would, in turn, place considerable additional pressure on fragile ecosystems, ultimately resulting in a decrease of vegetative cover and, again, of the soil's moisture retention capacity.[69] The end result would be a drier planet.

Groundwater mining, the withdrawal of groundwater at a rate that exceeds its replenishment, leads to the depletion of the resource. More than three-quarters of underground water is non-renewable, meaning that it has a replenishment period of centuries or more.[70] The pumping of groundwater causes the water table around the well to sink and forms a cone-shaped hollow called a cone of depression. The more water that is extracted from an aquifer, the deeper the cone of depression extends and the deeper a well must go to continue providing water. Water quality declines at deeper levels underground. At depths greater than a few hundred meters, water is likely to contain such a high concentration of minerals that it is unusable.[71]

Groundwater mining in coastal areas also leads to the depletion of available freshwater by reducing the hydraulic head that prevents the upstream movement of the saltwater 'wedge.' As a result, saltwater contamination renders part of the remaining groundwater supply useless for consumption by humans or animals and for irrigation. Because of the high salt content of seawater, a concentration of only two percent in aquifers is enough to make groundwater supplies unusable for human consumption. Saltwater intrusion can also occur in inland areas, where overexploitation of groundwater leads to the rise of highly mineralized water from deeper aquifers.[72] In Europe, saltwater intrusion is a problem particularly for Mediterranean countries such as Spain, Italy and Turkey. Inland saline intrusion has been reported in Latvia, Poland and the Republic of Moldavia.[73]

The large coastal cities of South and South-east Asia are also experiencing problems with saline intrusion into freshwater aquifers. The depression of the groundwater table because of overabstraction has caused saltwater intrusion as far inland as ten kilometres in the coastal alluvial aquifer in Madras and up to five kilometres in Manila. In Bangkok, groundwater overexploitation has caused the water levels of the underlying aquifer to drop by 60 metres, resulting in problems with saltwater intrusion and land subsidence. The land surface has fallen by as much as 60 to 80 centimetres in the centre of the city.[74] In the United States, the groundwater depletion and the resulting saline intrusion in the Miami metropolitan area is a major driver of the world's most expensive environmental restoration project.[75]

Land subsidence resulting from the removal of the water table can eliminate any hope of restoring a functioning aquifer. The extraction of water may cause an aquifer's geologic materials to compact, eliminating the pores and other spaces that could hold water. The resulting loss of water storage can be phenomenally expensive. In California's Central Valley, for example, compaction of over-drafted aquifers has resulted in a loss of nearly 25 billion m^3 of storage capacity – equal to more than 40 percent of the combined storage capacity of all of California's human-made surface reservoirs. Assuming a replacement cost of US$.24 per m^3, which is at the low end of the range of costs for new water storage options in California, the economic value of the destroyed groundwater storage capacity would amount to US$6 billion.[76]

While the consequences of groundwater mining are apparent, competition for control over the water resource can motivate this irrational behaviour. Groundwater is generally considered a public resource, but is most available to the owner of the deepest well. Groundwater is often a victim of a 'tragedy of the commons' brought about by people competing to maximize their share of a scarce resource before that resource is exhausted by their combined efforts.

CONCLUSION

In Chapter 1, I presented evidence of the importance of freshwater ecosystems in supplying the world with a continuous supply of high-quality freshwater. These ecosystems are fragile, and the water cycle is delicate. While generally quite resilient to natural disturbances such as fires, floods and cyclones, the world's water machinery can malfunction or even break down when subjected to the added stresses imposed by people. The present chapter has discussed the general nature of these added stresses in the context of the increasing water shortages around the world that many water resource experts predict will merge into a global water crisis.

Even allowing for continued growth in human populations, the world has sufficient water to provide for the basic needs of all of its citizens. That water is of uneven distribution and quality, however. In addition, while civilizations once viewed water as a public and even sacred resource, the current trend towards treating water as a commodity that can be privatized is contributing to existing inequities in water availability. As the price of water rises, technologies designed to shift water from one drainage basin to another become more profitable. In recent years, corporations have begun to invest in schemes that go far beyond the transfer of water to an adjacent drainage basin. Such techniques – including long-distance pipelines, ocean tankers, gigantic, buoyant water bags dragged behind ships and the sale of glacial ice – have all made their appearance in international markets.

The effect of piling market forces on top of the already unbalanced relationship between the location and timing of need for and availability of water is potentially harmful to the most vulnerable human communities and ecosystems. Poverty-stricken communities in water-stressed parts of the world, particularly those experiencing rapid population growth, are witnessing the erosion of their ability to access clean water. Human water stress contributes to ecosystem degradation and drought in a downward spiral (this topic is discussed in more detail in Chapter 4: see 'Desertification', p. 101). Extremely poor people are unlikely to have enough money to pay for water, or are able to do so only by forgoing shelter, food, health care or education. Meanwhile, the market increasingly decides the priority uses of water. Thus, those people, corporations and countries that have the most money can theoretically dictate whose spigots will flow, which ecosystems will survive – and which won't.

The human race is faced, essentially, with two options. One is continuing to exploit water in conventional ways, believing that future technological innovations will help us to correct any damage done to the natural machinery that provides our planet with freshwater. This option allows people to maintain and accelerate their present use of water. Under this option, we should continue the exploitation of water resources in a manner that maximizes short-term, economic profit with the assumption that increased financial wealth will help to power the advancement of water-generating technology. The second option involves realizing that human beings are a part of nature and cannot exist apart from nature. According to this perspective, humans must modify their behaviour, instead of trying to alter the natural environment, so that our use of natural resources is compatible with the processes that have created them.

The following five chapters present sequential analyses of both options organized by water use sub-sector. These sub-sectors include food production; water supply and sanitation; flood damage reduction; commercial navigation; and energy production in the context of global warming. The thesis of this set of chapters is that humanity possesses the knowledge and technologies needed to manage water to our benefit without substantially crippling the ecosystems that provide us with this precious resource. The chapters advocate such management as preferable to the conventional growth in rates of resource exploitation. After all, over the long term, nature is a safer bet than the human technological capacity that nature created.

NOTES

1 El Ashry, M.T, (Chairman, Global Environment Fund), 2001. 'The Bitter Reality of the Global Water Crisis.' Earth Times News Service, 29 November.

2 De Villiers, M., 1999. *Water Wars: Is the World's Water Running Out?* Weidenfield & Nicolson, London. pp. 50–1.

3 Barlow, M. & T. Clarke, 2002. *Blue Gold: The Fight to Stop Corporate Theft of the World's Water.* The New Press, New York. p. 4.

4 Shiva, V., 2002. *Water Wars: Privatization, Pollution, and Profit.* South End Press, Cambridge, Massachusetts. p. 131.

5 Pearce, F. 1992. T*he Dammed: Rivers, Dams, and the Coming World Water Crisis.* The Bodley Head, London. 376 pp.

6 Ibid.

7 De Villiers, M., 1999. *Water Wars.* p. 54.

8 Gleick, P.H., 1993.' An Introduction to Global Fresh Water Issues.' In Gleick, P.H. (ed.), *Water in Crisis: A Guide to the World's Freshwater Resources.* Oxford University Press, New York. pp. 3–12.

9 Pearce, F. 1992. *The Dammed.*

10 Ibid. See also McCully, P., 2001. *Silent Rivers: The Ecology and Politics of Large Dams.* Enlarged and updated edition. Zed Books Ltd., London.

11 Rothfelder, J., 2001. *Every Drop for Sale: Our Desperate Battle of Water in a World About to Run Out.* Jeremy P. Tarcher/Putnam, New York. p. 17.

12 Gleick, P.H., 1998. *The World's Water: The Biennial Report on Freshwater Resources, 1998–1999.* Island Press, Washington and Covelo, California. p. 6.

13 Ibid., p. 10.

14 Ibid., p. 12.

15 The international community first adopted the definition of water as an economic good at the International Conference on Water and the Environment in Dublin, Ireland, 1992. The topic of water as an economic good is taken up in Chapter 9.

16 Donkers, H. 2000. 'Water: Basic Facts and Figures.' Unpublished compendium of water facts prepared for the World Wide Fund for Nature.

17 Population Action International, 1993. *Sustaining Water: Population and the Future of Renewable Water Supplies.* Washington.

18 Hinrichson, D., B. Robey & V.D. Upadhyay, 1997. *Solutions for a Water-Short World.* Population Reports, Series M, No. 14. Johns Hopkins School of Public Health, Population Information Program, Baltimore.

19 Ibid.

20 Revenga, C., J. Brunner, N. Henninger, K. Kassem & R. Payne, 2000. *Pilot Analysis of Global Ecosystems: Freshwater Systems.* World Resources Institute, Washington. p. 28.

21 Donkers, H. 2000. 'Water: Basic Facts and Figures.'

22 De Villiers, M., 1999. *Water Wars.* pp. 20–3.

23 Barlow, M. & T. Clarke, 2002. *Blue Gold.* p. 11.

24 Ibid., p. 12.

25 Groombridge, B. & M. Jenkins, 1998. *Freshwater Biodiversity: A Preliminary Global Assessment.* World Conservation Monitoring Center Biodiversity Series No. 8. World Conservation Press,

Cambridge. pp. 30–1.
26 Hinrichson, D., B. Robey & V.D. Upadhyay, 1997. *Solutions for a Water-Short World.*
27 Ibid.
28 Meinzen-Dick, R.S. & M.W. Rosegrant (eds.), 2001. *Overcoming Water Scarcity and Quality Constraints.* 2020 Focus, No. 9. International Food Policy Research Institute, Washington.
29 Cosgrove, W.J. & F.R. Rijsberman, 2000. *World Water Vision: Making Water Everybody's Business.* Earthscan Publications Ltd., London.
30 Hinrichson, D., B. Robey & V.D. Upadhyay, 1997. *Solutions for a Water-Short World.*
31 Brown, L.R. & B. Halwell, 1998. 'China's Water Shortage Could Shake World Food Security.' *Worldwatch,* July/August. p. 13.
32 Rosegrant, M.W. & X. Cai, 2001. 'Water for Food Production.' In Meinzen-Dick & Rosegrant (eds.), *Overcoming Water Scarcity.*
33 Gleick, P.H., 1993. 'An Introduction to Global Fresh Water Issues.'
34 Falkenmark, M. & G. Lindh, 1993. 'Water and Economic Development.' In P.H. Gleick (ed.), *Water in Crisis: A Guide to the World's Freshwater Resources.* Oxford University Press, New York.
35 Richards, A., 2001. 'Coping with Water Scarcity: The Governance Challenge.' CGIRS Working Papers Series No. 01–4. Center for Global International and Regional Studies, University of California, Santa Cruz. p. 21.
36 Ibid., p. 22.
37 Gleick, P.H., 1993. 'An Introduction to Global Fresh Water Issues.'
38 Barlow, M., 1999. *Blue Gold.*
39 Hinrichson, D., B. Robey & V.D. Upadhyay, 1997. *Solutions for a Water-Short World.*
40 Ibid.
41 Donkers, H., 2000. 'Water: Basic Facts and Figures.'
42 Samson, S. & B. Charrier, 1997. *International Freshwater Conflict: Issues and Prevention Strategies.* Green Cross International, Geneva.
43 Hinrichson, D., B. Robey & V.D. Upadhyay, 1997. *Solutions for a Water-Short World.*
44 De Villiers, M., 1999. *Water Wars.* pp. 16–19.
45 Ibid., p. 18.
46 Gleick, P.H., 1998. *The World's Water: The Biennial Report on Freshwater Resources, 1998–1999.* p. 44.
47 Ibid., p. 46.
48 Hinrichson, D., B. Robey & V.D. Upadhyay, 1997. *Solutions for a Water-Short World.*
49 Brown, L.R. & B. Halweil, 1999. 'Populations Outrunning Water Supply as World Hits 6 Billion.' Worldwatch News Release, 23 September. Washington.
50 Population Action International, 1993. 'Sustaining Water.'
51 Gleick, P.H., A. Singh & H. Shi, 2001. *Threats to the World's Freshwater Resources.* Pacific Institute for Studies on Development, Environment and Security, Oakland, California. p. 7.
52 McAllister, D.E., A.L. Hamilton, & B. Harvey, 1997. 'Global Freshwater Biodiversity – Striving for Integrity of Freshwater Ecosystems.' *Sea Wind* 11(3). Bulletin of Ocean Voice International.
53 World Commission on Dams, 2000. *Dams and Development: A New Framework for Decision-Making. The Report of the World Commission on Dams.* Earthscan Publications, Ltd, London and Sterling, Virginia. p. 8.
54 Ibid., p. 9.
55 Suzuki, D. *et al.,* 1996. *The Japan We Never Knew.* Stoddart Publishing Co., Toronto.
56 Chapter 7 provides more detail about dams and climate change.
57 World Commission on Dams, 2000. *Dams and Development: A New Framework for Decision-Making.* p. 65.
58 McCully, P. 1996. *Silenced Rivers.* p. 111.
59 Soler-Lopez, L.R., 2001. 'Sedimentation Survey Results of the Principal Water-Supply Reservoirs of Puerto Rico.' In Sylva, W.F., (ed.), *Proceedings of the Sixth Caribbean Islands Water Resources Congress, Mayaquez, Puerto Rico, February 22 & 23.* Unpaginated CD.
60 Postel, S. 1996. *Dividing the Waters: Food Security, Ecosystem Health, and the New Politics of Scarcity.* Worldwatch Paper 132, September. Washington. p. 11, pp. 31–2.
61 Gleick, P.H., 1998. *The World's Water, 1998–1999.* p. 200.

62 International Rivers Network, http://irn.org/programs/lesotho/background.html
63 International Rivers Network, 1999. *Power Struggle: The Impacts of Hydro-development in Laos.* International Rivers Network, Berkeley. p. 14.
64 Ibid., p. 18.
65 Barlow, M. & T. Clarke, 2002. *Blue Gold.* p. 132.
66 Ibid., p. 135.
67 Ibid., p. 139.
68 Rothfelder, J., 2001. *Every Drop for Sale.* p. 124.
69 The process of desertification is covered in more detail in Chapter 4.
70 Jackson, R.B., S.R. Carpenter, C.N. Dahm, D.M. McKnight, S.L. Postel & S.W. Runnig. *Water in a Changing World. Issues in Ecology.* Ecological Society of America, Washington.
71 Pielou, E.C., 1998. *Fresh Water.* University of Chicago Press, Chicago. p. 47.
72 Revenga, C., J. Brunner, N. Henninger, K. Kassem & R. Payne, 2000. *Pilot Analysis.* p. 19.
73 Ibid., p. 19.
74 Ibid.
75 Based on the author's experience. Reference is to the restoration of the South Florida/Everglades ecosystems, which is estimated to cost at least US$7 billion.
76 Postel, S. 1996. *Dividing the Waters.* p. 19.

3 To Feed the World
Food Supply and the Water Cycle

'Great progress in feeding the earth's burgeoning population has been made in the past several decades. Between 1970 and 2000, the number of people on earth has grown by 2.3 billion, and average food production and distribution have more than kept pace....

'Yet while enough food is produced today to meet the needs of all of the world's 6 billion people, that food is not evenly distributed or consumed....

'As distressing as this picture is, even more distressing trends are surfacing. The rapid growth in food production evident over the past several decades has begun to slow. Cereal production grew at a rate of 2.6 percent per year between 1967 and 1982. In the late 1980s and early 1990s, this rate dropped to around 1.3 percent per year. Per capita grain production is now actually decreasing, as population outstrips growth in grain production.... The rate of land degradation in some regions is accelerating. And competition for limited water supplies is growing, with more water moving from the agriculture sector to cities.'[1]

Disruptions of the Earth's water cycle are both a major cause and a result of the slowdown in increased farmland productivity. Water scarcity is becoming a primary cause of slowdowns in projected irrigated cereal yield growth in developing countries. To stave off hunger in the coming decades, food production approaches that are compatible with the continued functioning of the water cycle are needed. In the following pages, we examine the causes for these disruptions, as well as potential antidotes.

STATUS AND TRENDS IN GLOBAL FOOD PRODUCTION

As discussed in the previous chapter, agriculture consumes more water by far than any other human use. Modern times have seen leaps in the productive capacity of farmland with the advancement of chemicals and machines, but several disturbing trends are feeding a sense of insecurity about society's ability to adequately feed future generations. Urban lands are expanding and gobbling up productive farmland. Tired farmland, suffering from soil erosion and compaction, is further reducing the world's agricultural capacity. Technologies such as irrigation that once boosted productivity are now forcing farmers to take waterlogged and saline land out of production. The world's human population is rapidly increasing, and rising standards of living are fuelling an increasing demand for meat, which requires substantially more water to produce than plant crops.

Status of the Rate of Growth in Food Production

During the last half of the twentieth century, a package of advances in agricultural technology known as the 'Green Revolution' made significant dents in the prevalence of hunger in the world. By the early 1990s, developing countries as a whole produced between three and four times as much food as they did in 1950.[2] Less than a decade later, the number of malnourished people around the world had been reduced by 160 million from the 1990 levels.[3]

The Green Revolution has not stopped hunger from plaguing the planet, however. Food production has failed to keep pace with population growth in two-thirds of developing countries, including more than 80 percent of African countries.[4] In 1997, 790 million people in developing countries were classified as food-insecure, 60 percent of whom live in South Asia and sub-Saharan Africa. In sub-Saharan Africa, the number of food-insecure people actually increased from 125 million people in 1997 to 186 million in 2000.[5] At the end of the last century, an estimated 840 million people, a number that exceeds the combined populations of Europe, the US and Japan, did not have enough to eat.[6]

In many parts of the world, growth in the rate of food production is slowing substantially or farm productivity is actually decreasing due to water shortages, desertification, increased soil salinity and other related factors. The per capita global production of cereal grains peaked in 1984 and has declined since, while in Africa such declines began in 1967, exacerbating a growing malnutrition problem.[7] Even as the population expands, the rate at which modern agricultural methods can increase global food production is declining (see Table 3.1). The number of hungry people can be expected to grow substantially in the coming years as populations boom, particularly in developing countries. The task of feeding the human population in the twenty-first century is a daunting challenge.

The reduction in the rate of increase in global food production has been unevenly distributed. In tropical regions, for example, harvests have lagged behind population growth. One of the reasons is that modern agricultural technology spawned by the Green Revolution (discussed in more detail below) was developed primarily for use in temperate climates and is generally ill-suited to tropical areas.

Table 3.1 Annual Cereal Crop Yield Growth Rates, 1970s–1990s

Crop	Region	1970s (%)	1980s (%)	1990s (%)
Wheat	Asia	4.33	3.71	0.72
	Latin America	0.60	3.40	2.36
	Sub-Saharan Africa	3.54	0.92	-0.81
	World	2.10	2.78	0.42
Rice	Asia	1.61	2.42	1.55
	Latin America	0.70	2.97	3.71
	Sub-Saharan Africa	0.02	2.51	-0.56
	World	1.49	2.37	1.54
Maize	Asia	3.43	2.75	1.55
	Latin America	1.49	0.61	3.82
	Sub-Saharan Africa	2.26	1.72	2.09
	World	3.19	0.60	1.76
Cereals	Asia	2.90	2.79	1.46
	Latin America	1.69	1.28	3.12
	Sub-Saharan Africa	1.90	0.56	0.66
	World	2.18	1.79	1.12

From: Gruhn, P., F. Goletti & M. Yudelman, 2000. 'Integrated Nutrient Management, Soil Fertility, and Sustainable Agriculture: Current Issues and Future Challenges.' Food, Agriculture, and the Environment Discussion Paper 32, September. Food Policy Research Institute, Washington. p. 7.

Favourable growing conditions exist in the tropics year-round, intensifying pest and crop disease problems. In addition, many tropical regions also have fragile soils, which when cleared for crops are subject to erosion, leaching and compaction. Cleared tropical forests, for example, typically produce crops for only a few years until the soil is exhausted; its utility for grazing is only somewhat less short-lived.[8]

It is estimated that the relative crop yields for cereals in irrigated areas in developing countries will continue to decline, from 0.86 in 1995 to 0.74 in 2025. 'Relative crop yield' is the ratio of the projected crop yield to the maximum economically attainable yields at specified crop and input prices under conditions of zero water stress. This drop represents an annual cereal production loss of 139 million metric tons, which is higher than China's total rice production in 1995.[9]

In the twenty-first century, new strategies will be needed to keep the world fed as the rate of population growth exceeds increases in farmland productivity. Every year the global population climbs by an estimated 90 million people. This means that the farmers of the world will have to increase food production by more than 50 percent to feed some 2 billion more people by 2020.[10] Many scientists are convinced that the Green Revolution can gain a second wind from the expanded use of transgenic, or genetically modified, organisms. Two types of transgenic crops have so far been created: those resistant to insecticides and herbicides and those designed to produce an insect-killing toxin.[11] By the end of the twentieth century, more than 60 different crops had been engineered and the global area planted in transgenic crops jumped from 2 million hectares in 1996 to nearly 28 million in 1998 – a nearly fifteen-fold increase in just two years.[12]

Supporters of transgenic crops argue that their products will enhance modern agriculture's environmental compatibility while boosting food production. Theoretically the herbicide-resistant varieties will allow farmers to reduce or abandon ploughing – a practice designed to reduce weeds that is responsible for a great deal of soil erosion. The insecticide-producing crops are intended to reduce the need for pesticide applications.

Opponents of transgenic crops counter both these arguments. First, they contend that the herbicide-resistant crops will increase farm reliance on herbicides, which are toxic to many soil organisms and can pollute groundwater. As herbicide use grows, weeds will develop resistance to the herbicides and eventually outpace the productivity gains made by genetically modified organisms (GMOs).[13] Second, they contend that insects will develop resistance to the toxin produced by insecticide-producing plants within three to five years of introduction, rendering the crops ineffective.[14]

Even more frightening, from the perspective of the Earth's biodiversity, is the propensity of synthetic genetic material to invade wild plant populations. Such events can increase the relative survival rates of weeds compared to domesticated crops and decimate the wild crop prototypes that are essential to the continuing vigour of domestic crop varieties. In 1997, just one year after the first commercial GMOs were planted in Canada, a farmer reported cross-pollination with a related weed species growing on the margins of the field, producing a herbicide-tolerant descendant. DNA[15] testing confirmed this report.[16]

The contamination of the wild stock of maize varieties in the remote Sierra Norte de Oaxaco Mountains in Southern Mexico by transgenic DNA indicates the potential for GMOs to decimate natural genetic lines. This contamination indicates that there is a high level of gene flow from industrially produced maize towards populations of progenitor races, and that more accessible regions are exposed to higher rates of introgression than these remote plant populations. The scientists who analysed this discovery concluded that transgenic characteristics are maintained from one generation to the next.[17]

'The addition of biotechnology-based approaches in pest management is merely a new tool to be used as input substitutions to address the problems (e.g. pest resistance, pollution, soil degradation) caused by previous agrochemical technologies. Transgenic crops developed for pest control closely follow the paradigm of using a single control mechanism (a pesticide) that, as a strategy, has been shown to fail repeatedly over time against pest insects, pathogens and weeds. Transgenic crops are likely to increase the use of pesticides and to accelerate the evolution of 'super weeds' and resistant insect pests.'[18]

How Much Water Will We Need for Food?

The production of one metric ton (1,000 kg) of grain requires roughly 1,000 m³ of water, given regional variances for climate and type of grain and allowing for evapotranspiration from the crop but not for inefficiencies in irrigation systems. In 1995, annual global grain consumption averaged around 300 kg per capita including the consumption of livestock products. If we assume that global grain consumption will remain at this level, simply meeting the grain requirement of the estimated global population in 2025, 2.6 billion above the population in 1995, will require an additional 780 billion m³ of water. The non-grain (fruit and vegetable) portion of the diet may require only one third as much water to produce as the grain, because it is largely made of water. If so, the minimum additional amount of water required to meet the food requirements of the 2.6 billion people expected to be added to the global population between 1995 and 2025 would be 1,040 billion m³. This quantity is equal to more than twelve times the flow of the Nile River and 56 times the flow of the Colorado.[19]

This figure neglects the common assumption that per capita demand for meat products will grow proportionately with the economies of developing countries. Roughly 70 m³ of water is required to produce a single kilogram of grain-fed beef and 4 m³ to produce a kilogram of pork. About 40 percent of the world's grain production already went to feed livestock at the turn of the century.[20] The typical American diet, with its high share of animal products, requires twice as much water to produce as the nutritious, but less meat-intensive, diets common in some Asian and European nations. The same volume of water that now feeds one American could instead feed two if more US consumers moved down the food chain.[21]

Increases in grain consumption in China alone could trigger widespread shortages of food and water in the coming decades. China's population is projected to grow from 1.2 billion in 1998 to 1.5 billion by 2030 – an increase that exceeds the entire population of the United States. The increase in population alone would boost demand for water by one-fourth over 1998 levels without any growth in per capita water consumption. Per capita water consumption is already growing, however. Between 1990 and 1997, for example, China's pork consumption climbed by 9 percent per year. Consumption of both beef and poultry, starting from a much smaller base, grew by 20 percent per year. The brewing of beer, which is also made from grain, was growing at about 7 percent per year. Demand for irrigation water in China's agriculture sector is projected to grow from 400 m³ per year in 1998 to 665 m³ by 2030.[22]

As mentioned in Chapter 2, increasingly agricultural water consumption will have to compete with more lucrative applications of water for urban and industrial uses. This means that those countries and regions that can afford to import food will have the flexibility to use their water for other purposes. The potential therefore exists for huge imbalances between population and food supply as places such as the US, the European Union and China import more food from developing countries whose people cannot afford to buy it.

Clearly, we will need to economize our water uses and ensure that the planet's water cycle is fully functional, working day and night to renew our supplies of precious freshwater, if the food and other water-related requirements of the human race and biosphere are to be met in coming decades.

GREEN REVOLUTION TECHNOLOGIES AND THEIR REPERCUSSIONS

Many of the current Green Revolution technologies involved in food production impede the operation of the water cycle and reduce the overall availability of good-quality freshwater to the planet. The optimal functioning of the water cycle will therefore require changes in food production practices. Before exploring options for more water-compatible food production processes, we will examine the aspects of Green Revolution technologies that damage aquatic ecosystems and the water cycle, reducing the availability of both food and water to the Earth's inhabitants.

In many parts of the world, growth in the rate of food production is slowing substantially or farm productivity is actually decreasing due to water shortages, desertification, increased soil salinity and other related factors. The decline in farmland productivity is closely tied to interventions in the water cycle and ecological disruptions caused by Green Revolution technology.

The term 'Green Revolution' was coined in 1968 by the late William S. Gaud, then Director of the US Agency for International Development, to describe the breakthrough in food production triggered by the development and rapid dissemination of new semi-dwarf rice and wheat varieties in Asia.[23] Since the late 1960s the spread of Green Revolution technologies throughout the world has been credited with the central role in staving off Malthusian predictions of widespread famine.

This 'revolution' actually began in the late 1950s in Mexico with unheralded jumps in wheat production. During the 1960s and 1970s, food production expanded markedly in India, Pakistan and the Philippines. In the 1980s, grain production in China saw remarkable growth. Increases in yield accounted for nearly 80 percent of increased output between 1959 and 1980.[24] If the global cereal yields of 1959 had continued to prevail in 1999, nearly 1.8 billion hectares of additional land of the same quality would have been needed to equal the global harvest at the end of the century instead of the 600 million that was used.[25]

Modern varieties of grain, including transgenic varieties, can only achieve markedly higher yields over traditional varieties if systematic changes in crop management are made, however. These include the application of fertilizers, water

'The technological package of the Green Revolution was hailed at one time as a "miracle" and was introduced into all regions of the Third World without regard for their basic characteristics. Since that time, it has usurped traditional technologies, displaced genetic variety, promoted excessive use of chemicals, depleted soil nutrients, caused problems with water supply and irrigation, induced pest immunity, and generally provoked ecological and cultural degradation.'[26]

management, and the control of weeds and pests. The combined effect of adding nutrients to boost soil fertility and greater moisture availability as a result of irrigation is to improve the farm environment for weeds, pests and diseases. As a result, pest control becomes essential to realizing maximum yields.[27]

Irrigation

Agricultural irrigation withdraws and consumes a large quantity of freshwater. Irrigation systems also change the chemical quality of available water and the timing of its presence in natural ecosystems. As a result, irrigation has a number of substantial effects on the water cycle. In the early 1990s, people removed approximately 2,700 km^3 – about 5 times the annual flow of the Mississippi River – from the earth's freshwater ecosystems every year for use in irrigation.[28] As of 1995, water consumed in irrigation (either not returned to its original source or returned in such a degraded condition that it is no longer usable) was 1,430 km^3 world-wide and expected to grow to 1,485 km^3 by the year 2025.[29]

Although only 17 percent of the world's cropland is irrigated, these lands produce a full one-third of the world's total food supply. Carried out correctly, and with adequate drainage, irrigation can provide farmers with the control of water applications necessary to grow modern, high-yielding crop varieties and increase the number of annual harvests from one to two or three. However, because of badly planned and poorly built irrigation systems, the yields on half of all irrigated land – amounting to around 120 million hectares – have been falling in recent years.[30] Irrigation, if carried out incorrectly, can cause waterlogged and salted farmland, declining and contaminated aquifers, shrinking lakes and inland seas, and the destruction of aquatic ecosystems.[31]

Poor water management is the root cause of soil waterlogging and salinization. Without adequate drainage, seepage from unlined canals and over-watering of fields cause the groundwater table to rise. The root zone eventually becomes waterlogged, starving plants of oxygen and inhibiting their growth. Evaporation of water near the soil surface during dry periods leaves behind a layer of salt that reduces crop yields and can eventually kill the crops.[32]

The irrigation water itself also adds salt to the soil. Even the best supplies have salt concentrations of 200–500 parts per million (ppm). For comparison, water with salt concentrations of less than 1,000 ppm are considered fresh. The application of 10,000 m^3 of water per hectare per year (a fairly typical irrigation rate) therefore adds between 2 and 5 tons of salt to the soil annually. Without adequate flushing, the salt can build up within a couple of decades to levels that leave the land essentially useless.[33]

'Farmers are currently experiencing an abundance of salt in their fields.... The Rasi Salai dam and its reservoir [in Thailand], along with the irrigation area, are all located directly on top of a large salt dome, and the problem of salinization is directly related to the construction of the project.'[34]

Significant degradation of existing irrigated cropland has occurred over the past decade. Estimates of annual global losses of agricultural land due to waterlogging and salinization range from 160,000 to 1.5 million hectares. Most of this loss has occurred in irrigated cropland with high production potential.[35]

The modern irrigation systems meant to replace the traditional lifestyles of dryland people often underestimate the complexity of the landscape and climate of the environment into which they are transplanted.[36] Very basic elements of hydrology, such as the relationship between precipitation, vegetative cover on the watershed, soil condition and stream flow, are not well understood in many arid climates. As a result, modern irrigation systems are not always compatible with the landscapes into which they are introduced and many fail as a result.

'The River Senegal rises in the Fouta Djallon and flows northward through increasingly arid land; when it finally turns west towards the ocean, it borders on desert. In these areas of low rainfall, the river's annual flood is necessary to life. Towards the end of the rainy season, it overflows its banks and floods the broad alluvial plain of the middle valley, where crops are grown in the dry season after the waters have receded. The valley's agricultural production systems traditionally followed the seasonal rhythm of the river: rainfed cropping and pasturing on the *jeeri* uplands, followed by flood-recession farming and grazing on the *waalo* lowlands. Over the period 1946–1971, it is estimated that on average 312,000 hectares were flooded on both banks of the river and 108,000 hectares cultivated....'[37]

'The total area covered by irrigation schemes on the left bank in 1995 was 71,751 hectares; and the area actually cultivated, both seasons included, was 29,792 hectares....'[38]

'Senegal River development schemes have not brought about development.... Instead of development, there has been destruction. By sweeping aside production systems which offered a degree of food security, Senegal River development schemes have made life even more precarious than before for many inhabitants of the Valley. Those who are excluded from irrigated farming because of the high costs involved cannot now fall back on the *waalo*, because since the dams were built, the annual floods can no longer be relied on to provide crops and grazing and replenish fish stocks. All the future seems to hold for them is emigration to the volatile outer fringes of Dakar's urban sprawl.'[39]

The redistribution of water from natural floodplains to irrigation reservoirs for the purpose of expanding commercial agriculture can lead to substantial reductions in the productivity of natural ecosystems and the elimination of traditional farming methods.

Artificial Fertilizers

'Paradoxically, one reason for Bangladesh's cloudy food future may be the side effects of the Green Revolution itself. The switch to intensive agriculture prompted many Bangladeshis to plant three rice crops per year instead of two, forcing them to rely on chemical fertilizers rather than the natural annual inundations of the flood season to replenish the soil. Dikes erected to channel floodwaters to the sea have diverted rich nutrients, leaving the country hostage to the higher import bills and long-term environmental consequences that stem from dependence on manmade fertilizers.'[40]

Nutrient augmentation can significantly increase crop yields if properly managed. Fertilizers such as phosphorus and nitrogen, however, pose considerable threats to the health of people and ecosystems when they are released in large amounts to the aquatic environment. Ingestion of nitrates, such as through drinking water, can also be toxic to humans and animals when it is transformed within the body into nitrites, which affects the oxygen-carrying capacity of red blood cells. Nitrites and the carcinogenic compounds they can create may also spur goitre, birth defects, heart disease, and cancer of the stomach, liver and oesophagus.[41]

Fertilizer use in the developed world, where relatively low prices lead to over-application, generally has contributed to more environmental and human health problems than use in the developing world. In the United Kingdom, for example, around 1.6 million people receive water with nitrate levels that exceed guidelines. Nearly two-thirds of the pollution in US rivers, and close to 60 percent of the pollution in US lakes, is attributed to excessive nutrient applications.[42]

While cropland per person shrank by 40 percent between 1950 and the mid-1980s world-wide, fertilizer use per person multiplied nearly five times – rising from 5.5 to 26 kilograms.[43] Part of this trend may relate to the ironic decrease in soil fertility over time as fertilizer use continues. When fertilizers are added to a crop, a plant absorbs not only the extra nitrogen, phosphorus and potassium from the fertilizer, but also proportionately increased levels of micronutrients (nutrients needed in very small amounts) from the soil, including zinc, iron and copper. Over time, the soil becomes deficient in these micronutrients, inhibiting the plant's capacity to absorb the nutrients provided by the fertilizer.[44]

Excess nutrients can also trigger a wide range of ecological disturbances when released into the aquatic environment. These include algae blooms, oxygen depletion, eutrophication, changes in the composition and structure of the food

'Agronomists and other agricultural scientists have for generations been taught the 'law of the minimum' as a central dogma. According to this dogma, at any given moment there is a single factor limiting yield increases, and that factor can be overcome with an appropriate external input. Once one limiting factor has been surpassed – for example, nitrogen deficiency, with urea as the correct input – the yields may rise until another factor, pests for example, becomes the new limiting factor due to increased levels of free nitrogen in the foliage that attracts and supports the herbivore populations. That factor then requires another input – a pesticide in this case – and so on, perpetuating a process of treating symptoms rather than dealing with the real causes that evoked the ecological imbalance.'[45]

chain, and biological activation of toxic metals present in the substrate. While these disturbances can trigger a short-term boost in overall biomass production in the aquatic environment, over the long term they are more likely to significantly reduce the ecosystem's productivity.

Oxygen-depleted waters in the coastal ocean are found world-wide, and the incidence and extent of such areas in coastal waters is apparently increasing due to accelerated eutrophication. The largest, most severe, and most persistent zone of oxygen-depleted, or hypoxic, water is found in the northern Gulf of Mexico on the continental shelf of Louisiana. The area of impact and duration of hypoxia on the Louisiana shelf is of considerable concern since Louisiana fisheries landings are 28 percent of the US total. Fish, shrimp, and benthic (bottom-dwelling) animal densities are severely depressed in these hypoxic zones. In addition, hypoxic water masses are present on the shelf during critical periods of the life history of several commercially important species.[46]

The scientists and government agencies responsible for addressing this problem believe that the most important reason for this persistent lack of oxygen in the Gulf hypoxic zone is the use of massive quantities of nitrogen fertilizer in the Mississippi River Basin. The Mississippi Basin, which is America's breadbasket and accounts for nearly a third of the US's continental land mass, drains to the Gulf of Mexico in Louisiana. The mean annual concentration of nitrate in the lower Mississippi River remained approximately the same in the first half of the twentieth century, but has doubled since then. Nitrogen and phosphorus fertilizer use in the United States began in the mid-1930s and climbed to a dramatic peak around 1980. The increase in nitrogen concentrations in the Gulf of Mexico is highly correlated with increasing use of nitrogen fertilizers in the Mississippi River Basin.[47]

Other zones of severe oxygen depletion related to nutrient loading include the Adriatic and Black seas, which receive high concentrations of nutrients in run off from the Po and Danube rivers, respectively. In the Adriatic Sea, the most severe eutrophic conditions are restricted to semi-enclosed bays and to the areas within the estuarine plume of the Po, which dominates freshwater inputs. The Adriatic Sea also receives inputs of nutrients from point source discharges. In response to the increased nutrient load, particularly in the summer, primary productivity increases with a maximum in the Emilia–Romagna area. During summer, this area has suffered from persistent heavy algae blooms, the eventual decomposition of which causes anoxic conditions and mass kills of fish and benthic fauna. In 1990, the accumulation of gelatinous material produced by extensive blooms of dino-flagellates and diatoms on the beaches of Benicasim in Spain had an adverse effect on the tourist trade.[48]

The Black Sea is naturally anoxic as a result of inadequate mixing of top and bottom layers of water to oxygenate the lower reaches of the water column. Over the years, organic matter has been sinking and decomposing in the deep waters of the Black Sea. This natural oxygen depletion is exacerbated by pollution. The largest share of nitrogen loading, an estimated 31 percent of the total, comes from agriculture. The resulting eutrophication in the Black Sea contributes to gradual shallowing of the zone of light penetration, widespread reductions in concentrations of dissolved oxygen, and the occasional formation of anoxic benthic layers of hydrogen sulphide distinct from the permanent anoxic layer in the main basin. These physical and chemical changes lead to the following changes in the Black Sea's biological communities: increased algal blooms, a massive loss of shallow water plants, changes in the food chain, and severe reductions in fish stocks.[49]

Eutrophication has caused changes in the base of the food chain, resulting in an increase in the development of single-species blooms of plankton. Higher levels within the food chain have subsequently changed as well, leading to massive quantities of jellyfish (*Aurelia aurita*) and a predatory comb jelly (*Mnemiopsis leidyi*). The decomposition of two prolific species has resulted in widespread hypoxia and has caused a dramatic reduction in the number of large, benthic marine species which are an important source of food for fish. These changes to the marine ecosystem of the Black Sea have contributed to the demise of the fisheries and reduced its tourism potential.[50]

Pesticides

Pesticides are poisons by design, and therefore can exert acute or chronic toxic effects on unintended victims. Insecticides are by far the most toxic category of pesticides, but fungicides and herbicides can also exert disastrous effects on freshwater and other ecosystems.

Since 1945, global production of pesticides has increased an estimated 26-fold, from 0.1 to 2.7 million tons.[51] As of 1998, the pesticide market was worth around US$30 billion per year.[52] Since the middle of the twentieth century, a vast quantity of extremely toxic and long-lived pesticides has been introduced into the global environment (see Table 3.2). In industrialized countries, the growth in pesticide use decreased in the last 15 years of the twentieth century as health and environmental concerns inspired an increasing number of bans. Eight of the twelve chemicals targeted for elimination under the global treaty on Persistent Organic Pollutants (POPs) are pesticides used in agriculture, disease control and structural pest management. Banned in most industrialized countries and many developing countries, these pesticides remain in use in many regions, legally and illegally.[53]

Table 3.2 World Production of Some Persistent Organic Pesticides

Material	Date of introduction	Cumulative world production (tons)
Aldrin (insecticide)	1949	240,000
Chlordane (insecticide)	1945	70,000
DDT (insecticide)	1942	2.8 to 3 million
Endrin (insecticide and rodenticide)	1951	(3,119 tons in 1977)
Hexochlorbenzene (fungicide and byproduct of pesticide production)	1945	1 to 2 million
Oxaphene (insecticide)	1948	1.33 million

From: McGinn, A.P., 2000. 'Phasing out Persistant Organic Pollutants.' In L.R. Brown et al., State of the World 2000. W.W. Norton & Company, New York. p. 223, note 13.

Industrialized countries still lead the world in pesticide use by a large margin; they accounted for 80 percent of pesticides in use in the late 1990s.[54] The restrictions on production and use of certain, last-generation pesticides have reduced the total quantity of pesticides used in industrialized countries, but the toxicity of newer pesticides has continued to increase. Some current pesticide formulations are 10 to 100 times as toxic as were the pesticides used in 1975.[55] Many of these compounds degrade rapidly in the environment and are less toxic to non-target organisms than their persistent predecessors.[56]

Older-generation pesticides continue to degrade human health and the environment in the industrialized countries that have banned them, however. They are considered persistent compounds because they remain intact for many years, or break down into equally noxious by-products, and continue to circulate in the ecosystem and seep into the food chain. Farmers who have few options for safe disposal of these pesticides may also continue to store them on-farm, use them up, or dispose of them illegally. During a 1992 state-run safe disposal operation for pesticides, for example, one Wisconsin farmer brought in a ton of DDT that he had been storing in his barn for nearly two decades.[57]

Many of the pesticides that have been banned in industrialized countries are still used extensively in the developing world because they are the cheapest to produce.[58] These substances continue to find their way into the environment, including food and water supplies, essentially saturating the world through dispersion or importation of food products. Pesticides that have been banned in industrialized countries – DDT and toxaphene, for example – are consistently found in remote areas such as the high Arctic, where conventional agriculture is not even practised, providing evidence that global circulation transports chemicals applied in temperate, tropical and subtropical countries over long distances.[59]

Because they are so highly toxic, pesticides often affect organisms that are not their intended targets, including people. The acute, or immediate, effects of human exposure to pesticides are well documented and range from obvious poisoning through skin and lung to more vague 'flu-like' symptoms and death. Chronic health problems associated with pesticide exposure include cancer, birth defects, and nervous-system damage.

Pesticides also poison wildlife and degrade entire ecosystems. Rain and snowmelt wash these substances, along with fertilizers, off agricultural lands and into surface waters. Environmental effects of pesticides at the ecosystem level can include the removal of habitats and food sources for a wide range of non-target plant and animal species and even extirpation of beneficial wildlife species. Pesticides can actually help non-beneficial species by triggering the evolution of immunity to pesticides in target species and creating niches for new pests.

Many agricultural chemicals, particularly pesticides, act as endocrine disrupters by mimicking the action of hormones. These substances often accumulate in freshwater ecosystems. Most endocrine disrupters attach to sediments, or to fat molecules, when ingested by fish or invertebrates. Because these chemicals do not dissolve in water, the bodies of animals tend to retain them for long periods of time. Thus, animals that live in aquatic ecosystems that are contaminated with these chemicals are at risk of accumulating hazardous amounts over their lifetimes.

Endocrine-disrupting chemicals also tend to accumulate up the food chain. For example, plankton will accumulate small amounts, and the small fish and invertebrates that feed on plankton will accumulate larger loads simply because of the quantity they ingest. Larger fish that eat the small fish will accumulate more, and so on up the food chain to the highest predator – be it a bald eagle or a human being.[60]

In very minute amounts, endocrine disrupters alter a whole spectrum of morphological, physiological, reproductive and life history traits. Tumours, deformities, reproductive abnormalities and reduced survivorship have been widely documented in fish, birds and mammals exposed to these chemicals. Scientists attribute a 50 percent decline in human sperm counts world-wide since 1940, when widespread use of these chemicals began, to the ability of many of these compounds to act like oestrogen within the body. Endocrine disrupters taken in by one generation can produce changes in the next.[61]

Pesticides, especially persistent organic (carbon-ring-based) compounds, do not directly alter the water cycle so much as they ride on it as they circulate throughout the Earth's biosphere. A molecule of DDT or its primary breakdown product, DDE, can easily attach itself to a soil particle and become washed with runoff into an aquatic ecosystem. There, it may be consumed by a microorganism and start to work its way up the food chain, or volatilize from the water surface and be transported thousands of kilometres away to do its damage elsewhere.

Declines in Wild Fisheries

In 1993, food fish accounted for 16 percent of animal protein consumed worldwide. In some Asian countries, fish accounted for between 30 and 50 percent of

'The loss of yields due to pests in many crops, despite the substantial increase in the use of pesticides, is a symptom of the environmental crises affecting agriculture. It is well known that cultivated plants grown in genetically homogeneous monocultures do not possess the necessary ecological defence mechanisms to tolerate pest populations that experience outbreaks. Modern agriculturalists have selected crops for high yields and high palatability, making them more susceptible to pests by sacrificing natural resistance for productivity. On the other hand, modern agricultural practices negatively affect pests' natural enemies, which in turn do not find the necessary environmental resources and opportunities in monocultures to effectively suppress pests. As long as the structure of monoculture is maintained as the structural base of agricultural systems, pest problems will continue to persist.'[62]

animal protein consumed. By 1996, fish production in developing countries was not far behind the total production of four main animal commodities – beef and veal, sheep, pigs and poultry. Of the total fish consumed, marine captures accounted for 72 percent, inland captures for 6 percent, coastal aquaculture for 9 percent and inland aquaculture for 13 percent.[63] In 1997, the catch from wild inland fisheries totalled 7.7 million metric tons, or nearly twelve percent of all fish directly consumed by humans from inland and marine capture fisheries.[64] Most of the inland catch is consumed locally or marketed domestically and it often contributes to the subsistence and livelihood of poor people.[65]

Globally, inland fisheries' landings increased at 2 percent per year from 1984 to 1997, with a much higher rate of increase in Asia – 7 percent per year. More discouraging trends are masked by this data, however. While on a global basis the inland fish catch has increased recently, some industrialized regions – including the US, Europe and the former Soviet Union – have reported decreases in catches.[66] The Food and Agriculture Organization of the United Nations (FAO) estimates that actual inland capture is greater than the amounts reported by a factor of two, and, in some instances, three.[67] FAO has also stated that food fisheries on wild inland stocks (those that rely on natural reproduction and fertility) are generally at or exceed the limits of sustainable yield and that corresponding shifts in fish community structure are occurring with risks of diminished production and damaged stocks.[68] In addition, the productivity of existing fisheries is often propped up by artificial enhancements, such as stocking of hatchery-reared fish or introduction of non-native species.

As discussed above, a substantial and increasing amount of water consumed for agricultural irrigation is used to produce grain for livestock feed needed to accommodate both the surging global population and its increased hunger for meat products. It is therefore somewhat ironic that the structures and water diversions that support irrigated agriculture are considered to be major factors contributing to the declines of the world's wild fish resources – a key source of food for the poor.[69]

The World Commission on Dams found that the most significant ecosystem impact associated with dams was the blocking of passageways of migratory fish

'Almost all inland waters are heavily fished for food, recreation and for commercial gain. It has been recognized that inland waters throughout the world have long suffered degradation in the quality and quantity of water and of the aquatic and associated terrestrial environments. Construction of dams and weirs, diversion for irrigation and other purposes, river channelization, encroachment by agriculture, industries and housing estates into the margins of lakes, and some other human impacts have led to major modifications of inland water habitats with repercussions on fish stocks. Many inland water bodies have also been overfished. The combination of factors has usually led to a decline in fish, both in quantity and quality, with the lower-valued fish surviving best in the stressed environments.'[70]

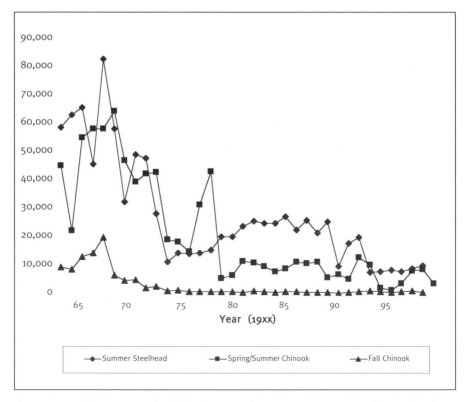

Figure 3.1. Adult Returns of Wild Salmon to the Uppermost Dam on the Snake River below Hells Canyon (Ice Harbor Dam 1964–8; Lower Monumental Dam 1969; Little Goose Dam 1970–4; Lower Granite Dam 1975–99)

Source: Peter F. Hassemer, Senior Fishery Research Biologist, Iowa Department of Fish and Game.

species.[71] Dams also block the migration of other aquatic organisms that are critical to maintaining aquatic ecosystems and food chains, such as mussel larvae and aquatic insects. Scientists believe that dams are largely responsible for the virtual elimination of lucrative runs of salmon and steelhead trout from the Pacific North-west of the United States. In recent years, quite a controversy has arisen concerning the value of a fishery worth one billion dollars per year relative to the value of the region's multi-purpose dams, which were built and are operated with considerable federal subsidies. The affected fish are anadromous, maturing in the ocean but returning to inland river systems to spawn. Dams create life-threatening barriers both to upstream spawning runs and to the downstream migration of young fish.

When Lewis and Clark explored the Snake River close to two centuries ago, an estimated two million fish returned to their spawning grounds each year. By 1975, 13 dams had been built on the mainstem of the Snake River, a major tributary of the Columbia River. Another 14 dams stretched across the Columbia itself. Indi-vidual salmon runs had declined to the tens of thousands and were to decline to the hundreds, tens, and single units by the end of the century. Some stocks have apparently been wiped out completely. While many factors contributed to the decline of these wild fish stocks, including overfishing at sea and watershed deforestation, close correlations exist between the construction of the dams and the diminishing returns of the fish (see Figure 3.1).

'Of the various human-caused changes in the Columbia River Basin, perhaps none has had greater impact than dams. The potential for dams to affect salmon runs was recognized early in the Pacific North-west's development. The constitution of the Oregon Territory, drafted in 1848, prohibited dams on any river or stream in which salmon were found, unless the dam were constructed to allow salmon to pass freely upstream and downstream...'[72]

'Hundreds of dams have been built on rivers of the Pacific North-west. They range from small irrigation dams ... to the massive dams ... on the Columbia and Snake rivers that are several hundred feet high and completely block upstream and downstream passage of anadromous fish. Dams on various rivers – some of them impassable – have greatly reduced wild runs. Even smaller dams (e.g., those associated with many hatchery operations and irrigation diversion dams) can block salmon runs. In addition to their effects on migration, large storage dams affect the quantity and timing of water flow in the river as well as flow velocities, water chemistry, and water temperatures.'[73]

Other factors responsible for the decline of wild fisheries and related to modern agricultural methods include pollution (excessive discharges of nutrients from fertilizers, releases of pathogenic microbes from livestock facilities, and pesticide contamination) and aquaculture, or fish farming.

As the demand for inland fish continues to grow and environmental degradation continues to accelerate, only two ways remain to maintain inland fisheries production: through the restoration of rivers and aquatic habitats, or through the enhancement of fisheries. Habitat restoration requires substantial financing and public support and is therefore currently limited in its geographical scope. Fisheries enhancement, on the other hand, is practised in almost every country with inland fisheries resources. These enhancements include introduction of new species, artificial stocking and other measures – many of which threaten the natural ecosystem through loss of species and genetic diversity and changes in species assemblages.[74]

Marine fisheries and fish species that need different habitats during different times in their lives (including anadromous fish, as well as diadromous fish, such as eels, which breed in saltwater and mature in freshwater) are also suffering from the impacts of modern agriculture. These include the loss of brackish and delta ecosystems as upstream dams trap sediment and incur saltwater intrusion upstream, the blocking of migration routes, changes in estuarine salinity, and eutrophication of coastal waters. The sturgeon population of the Caspian Sea, treasured for caviar production, now relies on stocking from hatcheries because dams built by the former Soviet Union halted natural spawning migrations.[75]

Aquaculture, the artificial breeding of captive fish and shellfish, provides a large and growing proportion of global fish production, but it may not be sustainable over the long term. Furthermore, if human society increasingly relies on aquaculture to produce animal protein, we may risk sacrificing natural, self-sustaining fisheries in the process.

'The combination of commercial over-fishing and channeling fisheries' output into exports means that fish are becoming less available and less affordable for those that need them most. In Bangladesh, for example, per capita supplies have fallen off by nearly one-third in the past 20 years. Despite this drop, its export-oriented fish culture has expanded rapidly. Bangladesh is currently the eleventh-largest aquaculture producer in the world. Fish, often considered the food of the poor, are floating further from their grasp.'[76]

When poorly designed and managed, aquaculture systems can significantly degrade the aquatic ecosystems that support them. As vast areas of natural ecosystems are converted to aquaculture facilities, important ecosystem services are often lost. The natural ecosystems are left unfit to serve as nurseries and feeding grounds for native aquatic species. In many cases, the aquaculture operations are abandoned after a short time as the environment deteriorates and they become unprofitable.[77]

Aquaculture production generally relies on feed made of fishmeal. This can result in an inefficient use of the total fisheries resource as it can take up to four kilograms of fishmeal to produce one kilogram of aquaculture-reared fish and shellfish.[78] Shrimp farms can also be large-scale consumers of freshwater. Raising one kilogram of shrimps requires 50 to 60 thousand kilograms (equal to 50 to 60 m³) of water.[79]

Aquaculture systems may also rely on wild-caught fry and juvenile fish, though this practice largely pre-dates the development of artificial spawning techniques. Many Asiatic rivers sustained massive abstractions of young fish annually for many years. Even levels of abstraction of young fish amounting to 74 percent of the total instantaneous reduction rate of a fish population (which also includes losses through emigration, fishing, and natural mortality) can be sustained in some fisheries, such as carp populations in the Padma River. Despite the apparent resilience of fish stocks to the removal of large numbers of young, there are several records of declines in the numbers of fish exported in recent years, particularly in China where 18 billion fry of major carp species were removed every year before 1965. Numbers had dropped to seven billion after 1965. In the Pearl River, only three to four billion were removed yearly for fish seed in the 1980s as compared to 14 billion per year in the 1960s. In all these systems, however, contemporaneous environmental degradation makes it impossible to assign blame for the declines to overfishing of the young-of-the-year alone.[80]

Artificial fisheries almost always involve the accidental (or intentional) release of cultured fish into wild fish habitats. The mingling of captive-bred fish with wild populations spreads diseases, lessens the number of native fish through increased competition, and may weaken the genetic base of wild fish through interbreeding. Aquaculture systems can also be significant sources of pollutants to natural aquatic ecosystems. Fish ponds need frequent water exchanges to remain healthy. Pond effluents often contain high concentrations of nutrients, pesticides, antibiotics and other wastes which managers flush out into surrounding waters.[81]

When implemented in a way that supports rather than destroys native ecosystems, aquaculture can be an important source of food and trade. Small-scale aquaculture systems, particularly when integrated into polycultural farming systems, can provide a sustainable source of protein, unlike many large-scale aquaculture systems that are net consumers of fish protein. Increased nutrient recycling through the use of by-products and wastes from plant and animal production processes in integrated agriculture/aquaculture systems is possible, but not yet common even in Asia. Significant scope exists for enhancing fish production by promoting these systems among small scale farmers. Other options include utilization of wastewater, fish production in small-scale irrigation schemes, and combined rice-and-fish farming (also being promoted for controlling insect pests without artificial chemicals).[82]

HOW TO KEEP FOOD GROWING AND WATER FLOWING

Most recent projections from academics and international agencies concerned with world agriculture conclude that increased irrigation development costs and growing competition for water from cities and industries mean that future increases in crop production will have to come from rainfed farming, small-scale irrigation, improved infrastructure and management of existing large systems.[83] One further implication of these predictions is that it is unlikely that large increases in the production of livestock and poultry raised on feed from large-scale irrigation operations will be adequate to satisfy demands for animal protein for people in the developing world. Thus, it is even more important that the world restore and maintain wild fisheries.

Sustainable Agriculture, or Agroecology

The next revolution in food production may very well start with a new, ecological perspective on agricultural systems. Sustainable agriculture systems deliberately integrate, and take advantage of, naturally occurring beneficial interactions. They emphasize management over technology, and biological relationships and natural processes over chemically intensive production methods. The objective of these systems is to enhance and manage complexity, rather than reduce and simplify the biophysical interactions on which agricultural production depends. This can be done by minimizing dependency on external inputs, such as fertilizers and pesticides, and by regenerating internal resources. This type of approach increases the likelihood that improvements will persist, as dependencies on external systems are kept to a reasonable minimum.[84]

In addition, since it is poor people in developing countries who are most affected by food shortages, it is appropriate to increase the use of agriculture systems that maintain and rely on the available natural resource base in those countries. This strategy is likely to provide more long-term food security than increasing reliance on external sources of chemicals and machinery. Evidence from around the world is growing to support the view that adopting sustainable agriculture can bring substantial yield improvements to farmers, especially in ecologically diverse and fragile areas. These farmers, many of whom lack access to the capital necessary to purchase external inputs, must often rely on internal resources such as rainfall, biologically fixed nitrogen, nutrients from lower soil strata and biological pest control based on natural predator/prey relationships.[85]

'There are many cases of food deficit areas such as parts of Ethiopia, Kenya, Uganda, and Burkina Faso becoming food surplus areas following the adoption of sustainable agricultural practices. As yields increase, farmers feel secure enough to diversify into new crops. In Honduras, for example, farmers who used to grow maize exclusively now cultivate upwards of 25 crops per farm. In Gujarat, India, farmers have moved away from sorghum/millet based systems to grow many types of vegetables. In Taita-Taveta, Kenya, a local non-governmental organization reintroduced traditional staples of sweet potato, arrowroot, sugar cane and bananas, and fruit trees. The result was a reduction in food insecurity and an improvement in the nutritional status of the local population.'[86]

Sustainable agriculture systems, because they require an intimate understanding of local agroecology, will differ substantially from one location to the next. A vast amount of knowledge is required to make such systems work. Fortunately, there exists an immense body of experience and understanding among many cultures in the developing world. This knowledge base is often the best starting point for the expansion of food production systems. Traditional agricultural practices can benefit from the introduction of modern technology, such as Geographic Information Systems and satellite photography, in improving yields while reducing risks.

'Many modern farming systems are net energy consumers. The factory production of eggs, poultry, hogs, milk, and cattle requires extensive feeding of grain. Vegetables and fruits are also very energy-intensive food products – particularly when they are grown under irrigation. Between 1952–1972 the total energy inputs into agriculture in the industrialized capitalist states increased by around 70 percent, but food production increased only 30 percent. The new technology brought higher yields, but a marked decline in energy efficiency. Between 1945–1970, corn yields in the United States had risen by 138 percent, but energy inputs increased three-fold. When beef production was transformed from rangeland grazing to feedlot operations, energy efficiency ratios declined to between 0.2 and 0.4.

In contrast, many traditional agricultural practices are net energy producers:
- Slash-and-burn agriculture in tropical areas has provided a return in the range of 16 kilocalorie (kcal) for every 1 kcal expended;
- Maize produced by traditional farmers in the Yucatan area of Mexico produced between 13 and 29 kcal for every 1 kcal used; and
- Chinese wet-rice farmers produced an average of 50 kcal of energy for every 1 kcal used in production.'[87]

Adopting sustainable agriculture does not necessarily mean a return to some form of primitive farming system. Its blend of innovations may originate with scientists, with farmers, or both. A key emphasis is placed on participation by farmers and rural people in all problem-solving processes to ensure equitable access to productive resources. Better use of local knowledge, practices and resources brings greater self-reliance among farmers and rural organizations.[88]

'Over twenty years of research by land grant universities and other scientific institutions [in the United States] demonstrates repeatedly that sustainable farming is, on average, more profitable than conventional agriculture. Through a combination of factors that include lower costs, higher yields and, in some cases, price premiums, farmers who use one or more sustainable practices (as defined by the National Academy of Sciences) make a larger profit in the market-place than do growers who rely solely on conventional practices.'[89]

Rain-Fed Agriculture

An increased reliance on rain-fed agriculture can strengthen the ability of developing countries to produce their own food while minimizing dependence on expensive inputs. Increased use of rain-fed agriculture relative to irrigated agriculture also has two significant benefits for nature and the water cycle. First, a relative reduction in water abstracted for irrigation means a relative increase in water available for other uses, including ecosystem maintenance. Second, to the extent that rain-fed agriculture must rely on ecological relationships rather than on external inputs of water, fertilizers and pesticides, a return to rain-fed agriculture can help restore and maintain the hydrological and chemical integrity of freshwater ecosystems. When sustainable agriculture practices are employed, rain-fed systems can reduce the proportion of the landscape that is barren and subject to erosion after harvest and increase the water retention capacity of soils. Together, these tendencies result in improved quantity, quality and predictability of water flows.

Farmers can increase the productivity of rain-fed agriculture through the use of diversified cropping patterns. Increased diversity in agricultural systems can provide a range of benefits over monocultures including enhanced nutrition, income generation, production stability, minimization of risk, reduced insect and disease incidence, efficient use of labour, and maximization of returns under low levels of technology. In addition, total yields per hectare are often higher than sole-crop yields.[90] Mixed-crop systems can take many forms and may be characterized by the degree to which they mimic natural ecosystems. Examples of some approaches to agriculture that can increase productivity per unit of land and calorie of energy expended are outlined below, and include crop rotation and intercropping, mixed plant/animal systems, agroforestry, and non-timber forest products.

Crop rotation, cover crops, and intercropping all entail farming systems designed to maximize the fertility of the land without the addition of artificial fertilizers. Crop rotation is the practice of alternating the crops grown on a particular piece of land to maximize the sustainable productivity of the land. Crop rotation can reduce disease, insect pests, and the prevalence of particular weed species. Rotation can also boost soil fertility, since different rooting structures extract nutrients at various depths. When legumes are integrated into the rotation, or used as a cover crop, nitrogen is added to the soil.[91]

Cover crops are living groundcovers grown between periods of regular crop production. They offer a number of benefits to the soil, including the reduction of soil erosion, the addition of organic matter, improvements in soil conditioning, and improved water use efficiency. Legume cover crops also provide a source of nitrogen.[92]

Intercropping is the practice of simultaneously producing more than one crop on a piece of land. This may involve planting a tall crop like maize in a field to be harvested first, with a few shade-tolerant crops such as beans, rice, squash or sweet potato that can be harvested a month or so later. The corn stalks can provide support for vines of beans or peas, which in turn contribute nitrogen to the soil. The benefits of crop rotation and intercropping can include decreased soil erosion, soil enrichment, and reduced pest problems with limited or no use of chemicals.[93]

An example of intercropping is 'alley cropping' as practised in Africa, Haiti, and elsewhere. In this low-cost and labour-intensive system, food crops are grown in wide rows that alternate with hedgerows of nutrient-producing trees and shrubs. The hedgerows are pruned periodically, and the nitrogen-rich material is returned to the soil as mulch, which inhibits weed growth and retains soil moisture. The hedges are usually planted along the contours of sloping land in order to act like terraces by decreasing water runoff velocity and subsequent soil erosion.[94]

Mixed plant/animal systems include farming strategies that mimic natural ecosystems. In nature, the survival of plant and animal species is interdependent. Associations of plants and animals evolve together and include plants synthesizing organic substances (producers), animals that feed on these plants (consumers), carnivores and parasites that feed on the consumers, and organisms capable of mineralizing organic substances that create conditions favourable for plants. Evolution has produced regulatory mechanisms that maintain the population sizes of these organisms in the appropriate proportions so that the productivity of the entire system is optimized.[95]

Mixed plant/animal agriculture systems seek to mimic the ecology of natural ecosystems. These systems achieve a synthesis: farming, tree growing and animal husbandry that do not merely complement each other but become an integrated whole. Animals feed on the biomass produced by the plants and fertilize the plant communities with their manure. People reap the benefits of foods and other resources produced by the plants and animals.[96]

'Although the damage done by modern farming to soil, water, fish and other animals has been documented all over the world, the warnings go for the most part unheeded. Just south of Vientiane (Laos), roughly 20 kilometres from the Mekong, Southchay and Bang Hathasinh have a farm in the village Khamsawaat. They did heed the warning they received.

'"We bought the first piece of land six years ago with the savings of both our families," says Soughchay. "We started out by growing rice and vegetables. We sold vegetables in Vientiene, borrowed money, and bought more land and buffaloes. After two years, large debts had built up and I became very ill. The doctor told me to stop working with chemicals. You see, the head of our district has been promoting chemical fertilizer and pesticides by selling them very cheaply. I used a lot, never carefully, putting it on the land with my bare hands. The chemicals crept inside me and I was ill for a long time.

'"My grandfather had taught me about herbal medicines; they helped me to recover. Afterwards we decided to do things differently. First, no more debts. Second, we used no more chemicals. We developed a different way of farming. We dug ditches around the rice fields and put fish in them. In the dry season, they are fed with whatever is available on the farm; cassava, vegetables, rice husks. In the rainy season, when the fields are under water and the ditches and pond overflow, the fish swim into the fields and find food there. In turn they fertilize the soil with their droppings and protect the rice by eating insects and weeds. At first we had to buy fingerlings, but now we breed the fish in our own ponds. We make a good profit on them."

'Southchay and Bang now own 8 hectares of land and have 24 buffaloes that they rent out to other farmers. They employ two or three people to help when the rice seedlings are ready for transplanting. "Everything on this farm is linked to each other. We grow many different crops, we raise many kinds of animals. Wastes from one thing can be used for another."'[97]

'Examples of the environmental consequences of dramatic technological changes abound in less-developed countries. One example is the substitution of tractor for buffalo power in Sri Lanka. At first sight this substitution seemed to involve a simple trade-off between more timely planting and labour savings on one hand and the provision of milk and manure on the other. But buffaloes create buffalo wallows, and these in turn provide a surprising number of benefits. In the dry season they are a refuge for fish, which then move back to the rice fields in the rainy season. Some fish are caught and eaten by the farmers and by the landless, providing valuable protein; other fish eat the larvae of mosquitoes that carry malaria. The thickets surrounding the wallows harbour snakes that eat rats that eat rice, and lizards that eat the crabs that make destructive holes in the ricebuds. The wallows are also used by the villagers to prepare coconut fronds for thatching. If the wallows go, so do these benefits.'[98]

Agroforestry is the combined cultivation of tree species and agricultural crops, an old system of production that is common and evolving throughout the world. Cultivating a mixture of tree and non-tree crops can increase the productivity of an agricultural system by replicating the processes that characterize a natural system. Agroforestry and similar systems can be designed to meet the needs of communities, or to produce marketable surpluses of timber and non-timber products.

In agroforestry systems, woody and herbaceous perennials are grown on land that may also support agricultural crops, and often animals. The spatial arrangement and temporal sequence of these components enhance ecological stability and the sustainability of production. This integration also allows the components of the system to complement one another in their use of resources, and in the timing of that use. Under ideal conditions, deep-rooted perennials can recycle nutrients from the subsoil to the surface, and make them available to other plants. The difference in root depth and in height between types of plants minimizes competition for water and light. Agroforestry systems can maintain soil organic matter and other important soil characteristics at more favourable levels than can monoculture farming systems. This is because agroforestry systems reduce losses of soil and water to erosion and runoff, cycle nutrients efficiently, naturally augment the nitrogen content of the soil, and create favorable soil temperatures and structures.[99]

Many forest management specialists advocate the establishment of agroforestry systems, particularly as a substitute for swidden (slash-and-burn) agriculture, because they require low capital investments, provide a great deal of employment, and are likely to be environmentally benign.[100]

The non-timber forest products industry makes use of resources available in the natural ecosystem, usually without any cultivation or artificial manipulation. A wide range of products can be harvested sustainably from forests, including pharmaceutical products, food, rattan, bamboo, spices, oils, ornamental plants, animal products, chemical components and fibres.

'The trade in non-timber forest products has provided South-east Asian forest-dwelling people with an important source of income and goods for nearly two thousand years. Evidence of the export of forest products from the western Indonesian islands to China dates from the beginning of the fifth century. Middle Eastern trade contact with the Malay Peninsula was initiated some time around 850 AD, and the European market began importing the riches of the Spice Islands in the fifteenth century.'[101]

'The case of Thailand, a country that has lost most of its original forests, is perhaps illustrative of trends that may soon be experienced in other South-east Asian nations still relatively rich in forest resources. The two most outstanding general trends are the increase in imports of formerly exported non-timber forest products, and the increasing percentage of total forest revenue provided by non-timber forest products.'[102]

Soil and Water Conservation Practices

Regardless of the composition of output, most agricultural systems benefit from the application of soil and water conservation practices. These are designed to prevent or decrease rates of soil erosion and increase the soil moisture retention capacity of the landscape. Soil and water conservation practices can also increase the fertility of the soil, primarily by supplementing the soil's organic matter content. Particularly when practised on a large scale throughout a river basin, soil and water conservation practices can improve water quality, reduce flood peaks, and increase river low flows during the dry season.

Practices vary widely based on landscape type, intensity of use, and products generated. They can include changes in basic methods (such as 'no-till' farming and contour ploughing), small-scale engineering (such as check dams and terraces), or simply placing a deteriorating piece of land out of production and allowing it to recover naturally.

'No technique yet devised by mankind has been anywhere near as effective at halting soil erosion and making food production truly sustainable as no-tillage. The long-term gains from widespread conversion to no-tillage could be greater than from any other innovation in third world agricultural production.

'Over 45.5 million hectares of land is under no-tillage world-wide. Approximately 52 percent of this land is in the USA and Canada, 44 percent in Latin America, 2 percent in Australia, and 2 percent in the rest of the world. There is a very big potential to bring this soil conserving technology to these parts of the world, although limiting climatic and socio-economic factors have to be taken into account. The East European countries seem to have the biggest potential for a fast growth of this technology.'[103]

Micro- and Small-scale Irrigation

The use of water-efficient technologies in the cultivation of fruits, vegetables, and orchard crops, known as 'micro-irrigation,' has been rapidly expanding in recent years. The most common method is drip, or trickle, irrigation, in which a network of porous or perforated piping, installed on, or below, the soil surface, delivers water directly to the root zone. Water losses from evaporation and seepage are extremely low in these systems. Drip systems may apply 20 to 25 percent less water to the field than conventional sprinklers, and 40 to 60 percent less than simple gravity systems, to sufficiently water the same crop. Drip irrigation has an additional advantage in arid areas because it is often better suited for irrigating with brackish water than other types of irrigation systems. The fairly constant level of moisture maintained in the root zone helps to prevent salt concentrations from rising to yield-reducing levels.[104]

The expansion of drip irrigation was accelerated by the availability of inexpensive plastics in the second half of the twentieth century. By the mid-1970s, six countries (Australia, Israel, Mexico, New Zealand, South Africa, and the United States) were irrigating substantial areas by drip irrigation and globally over 56,600 hectares were under this method. By the 1990s, the use of drip irrigation had increased more than 28-fold, with nearly 1.6 million hectares watered by drip and micro-sprinklers in 1991. While this represented only 0.7 percent of the world's irrigated areas, some countries rapidly adopted micro-irrigation. Israel, for example, was watering over 100,000 hectares, nearly half of its irrigated area, using micro-irrigation.[105]

While drip irrigation systems remain too expensive for most poor farmers and for use on low-value row crops, innovations are making the technology cheaper and more accessible. For example, one system rotates a single drip line between ten rows of crops rather than allocating an individual drip line to each and costs just 10 to 20 percent of the cost of traditional drip systems. In field trials in a hilly area of Nepal, the system doubled the amount of land that could be irrigated with the same amount of water.[106]

Small-scale irrigation systems used by gardeners to grow crops for their families or for local markets are often also referred to as 'micro-irrigation.' These systems have tremendous potential for increasing food security in poor areas, as demonstrated by the gardens planted in the small valleys in Zimbabwe known as *dambos*. These gardens are usually irrigated with water drawn from nearby wells in buckets. The individual gardens usually occupy less than a half-hectare each, but collectively cover around 20,000 hectares, nearly 10 percent of the 'official' irrigated area in Zimbabwe. During the 1986–7 drought, *dambos* were the only lands in some areas that yielded any corn, the area's staple grain. *Dambos* also produce a wide variety of foods. One survey of a single, large *dambo* found 23 different crops and 26 tree species, as well as bees, fish, reeds and fodder.[107]

There is considerable evidence that farmer-controlled, small-scale irrigation has a better record of performance than government-controlled large- or small-scale systems. These farmer-owned and -managed systems can also fail sometimes, but the failed systems do not continue to operate regardless. Moreover, the substantial small-scale sector that exists, generally without significant government support, indicates that these systems are economically viable.[108]

A review of successful, small-scale irrigation systems identified the following common characteristics. First, the technology is simple and low-cost. It usually consists of small pumps drawing water from shallow aquifers of rivers and streams. Second, the institutional arrangements for operating the system are private and individual. Third, supporting infrastructure is adequate to permit access to inputs and to markets for the sale of surplus production. Fourth, the systems generate high and timely cash returns to farmers. Finally, the farmer is an active and committed participant in project design and implementation.

It is not so much the size of the irrigation system that determines its success, but a host of institutional, physical, and technical factors.[109] For example, an assessment of returns to irrigation in the Philippines concluded that, while average returns to small-scale irrigation were slightly higher than those to medium- and large-scale irrigation, the difference was insignificant because the variation in performance of the systems within each type was so large.[110]

Ecologically Based Pest Management

Another application of the ecological relationships between plants and animals to sustainable agriculture is in the control of harmful pests, generally using predator–prey relationships. In order to be sustainable, such practices must be implemented in concert with an ecological strategy designed to maintain system stability and resilience.

The use of natural enemies to reduce the impacts of pests has a long history. The ancient Chinese, observing that ants were effective predators of many citrus pests, augmented ant populations by taking their nests from surrounding habitats and placing them in their orchards. The insectaries and airfreight delivery of natural enemies across oceans are modern adaptations to this approach, made necessary by the global distribution of common crop varieties far from the ecosystems where their ancestors evolved.[111] Ecological pest management in the twenty-first century goes beyond the previous focus on insects to include weeds and pathogens.[112]

The emerging global interest in integrated pest management is largely the result of modern society's increased understanding of the role that disturbance plays in structuring ecological communities. While the most disturbed terrestrial ecosystems may have one major disturbance event, such as a fire, every several years, many agricultural ecosystems experience multiple events per growing season – including ploughing, planting, fertilizer and pesticide applications, cultivation and harvest. Highly disturbed systems generally exhibit reduced species diversity and shortened food chains, resulting in the few well-adapted species (that is, pests) having few natural enemies to suppress their populations. As a result, people often increase the number of disturbance events, such as increasing pesticide applications, which, while controlling the initial negative symptom, may catalyse its reoccurrence.[113]

The three general approaches to biological control are importation, augmentation and conservation of natural enemies of the target pest.

Importation is used when a pest of exotic origin is the target. Some of the many organisms that are introduced into non-native ecosystems become pests, owing to a lack of natural enemies to suppress their populations. Once the origin of the pest is known and promising natural enemies are identified, a thorough evaluation of the likely environmental impacts of importation of the enemies must be conducted before taking the decision on whether or not to establish an introduction programme.

Augmentation is the direct manipulation of natural enemies to increase their effectiveness. This approach is used when the populations of the natural enemy are not present or cannot respond quickly enough to the growth of the pest population. Augmentation can be accomplished either through the mass production and periodic colonization of natural enemies or by their genetic enhancement, or both.

Conservation of natural enemies involves identifying the factors that might limit the effectiveness of a natural enemy and modifying them to increase the effectiveness of the beneficial species. In general, conservation of natural enemies involves either reducing factors that limit their populations or enhancing their access to resources that they need to grow and thrive.[114]

The following examples demonstrate the range of techniques that have been used throughout the world to combat pests successfully without the use of pesticides:

- Cotton farmers in Peru's Canete Valley combat pesticide-resistant insects by reintroducing native beneficial insects and by using a short-season crop variety that matures before the late-season arrival of pests.

- Farmers in Bangladesh, involved in the NOPEST project, eliminated pesticide use and achieved an eleven percent increase in rice production by diversifying crop production and varieties and restoring the balance between pests and natural predators.

- Farmers in western Kenya increased food production and enhanced soil fertility by using natural repellents made from a native shrub to combat termites.

- Physical barriers and repellent plants such as lemon grass have helped tropical farmers in Honduras and Nicaragua protect trees and plant nurseries from leaf-cutter ants.

- By adopting ecological pest management methods and cutting pesticide applications, Peruvian potato farmers have reduced Andean potato weevil infestations, generating an estimated benefit of US$162 per hectare.

- Rice farmers in Thailand work with the Food and Agriculture Organization to effectively control field rats with a coordinated, community-based programme of mechanical control methods such as filling and flooding burrows.[115]

Wild Fisheries

Over one billion people, mainly in developing countries, rely on freshwater fish as their principal source of animal protein. International statistics do not reflect the full importance of wild-caught fisheries because many of the fish are consumed by fisher families or traded locally, never entering the formal economy.

'Statistical data on the fish production in the Lower Mekong Basin are weak. Recent estimates indicate a total production from capture fisheries [of] not less than one million tonnes, and an additional contribution from aquaculture of some 200,000 tonnes. The value of the freshwater capture fishery production is estimated at US$700–800 million at the retail market. Fish constitute the major part of the animal protein intake for the approximately 60 million inhabitants of the Lower Mekong Basin, who are depending on this resource for nutrition, income and employment. Approximately 85 percent are rural dwellers. The average per capita income in the area ranges from US$186–400, but considerable difference between the urban and the rural populations may disguise an even lower average per capita income in rural areas.'[116]

At the same time that the world's subsistence fisheries are increasing in value, the international trade in fish is expanding rapidly. Fish are an increasingly valuable export product, particularly for developing countries, far surpassing other major commodities such as coffee and rice.[117] Some of the opportunities for increasing inland fisheries production include interdisciplinary and participatory decision making, sustainable fishery management, and ecosystem restoration.

Interdisciplinary and Participatory Decision Making

Many management practices can contribute to increased fish production. These include consulting fishery experts in water and related land resources management decisions; combining efforts with environmental and fishery agencies to prevent and reverse environmental degradation and to rehabilitate aquatic habitats and increase fish yields; and the extensive organization of community-based management of common property resources.[118]

The first of these points is especially important when considering development options for water resources at a river-basin scale. In contemporary water resources planning processes, the involvement of fisheries experts and other environmental professionals generally begins after many of the fundamental decisions have been made. Fish biologists are rarely included in the selection of the preferred plan of action from among the alternatives considered. Thus, the role of environmental professionals has been to evaluate the likely environmental impacts of the preferred alternative and design proposals for mitigation of these impacts.

If the world's wild fisheries are to thrive, fisheries managers and biologists, along with representatives of other water sectors and the affected community, must play an active role in all phases of the water resources planning process. The participation of these key stakeholders in articulating a water management strategy may result in the inclusion among its objectives of restoring/maintaining wild fisheries. In addition, including fishery experts in the selection and evaluation of alternatives for meeting the objectives of the strategy increases the likelihood that the alternatives evaluated, and the alternative eventually selected for implementation, will include strategies compatible with the long-term productivity of the fishery.

Sustainable Fishery Management

Ensuring high productivity of wild fisheries requires a rich information base that is accessible to all fishery managers. Important information includes the patterns of movement of various fish stocks throughout the year, the habitat needs of various aquatic organisms (fish as well as their invertebrate prey base, for example), and the interactions between various components of the aquatic ecosystem (predator/prey relationships, competition, symbiosis, etc.). This information may be gleaned from a variety of sources, including anecdotes and historic accounts from people who have been fishing from the river or lake in question for many years; as well as from field research involving fish tagging, radio-telemetry, invertebrate sampling, and habitat surveys.

It is the responsibility of fisheries professionals to share this information with other water resources managers in a manner that influences the overall use of freshwater ecosystems. It is also necessary to continually monitor fish populations and regulate the catch. This tracking and regulation must be accomplished within a context of learning to understand the aquatic ecosystem that supports the fishery, including habitat needs, migratory routes, food sources, inter-specific relationships, and external influences.

Ecosystem Restoration

Where the degradation of aquatic habitat has resulted in a decline of wild fisheries, it may prove economically efficient to restore the habitat. Habitat restoration to support wild fish production can range from re-establishing a natural flow regime (by changing the operations of existing water control structures), to physically reconnecting components of the ecosystem by breaching dykes or removing dams. Habitat restoration can provide a wide range of benefits in addition to increased fishery production, thus boosting its economic appeal.

In order to ensure that our descendants inherit thriving fisheries, it is extremely important that efforts to boost global fish production favour the restoration of wild-caught fisheries over the construction of aquaculture systems, and that investments are made in the latter to ensure the conservation of the former. It is equally important to avoid the introduction of exotic species of fish to natural freshwater ecosystems. While the exotics may temporarily increase production, the long-term interactions between the introduced species and the rest of the ecosystem are unpredictable and could contribute to the eventual degradation of the ecosystem to the detriment of the fishery.[119]

CONCLUSION

It is nature's way to balance trends in one direction with tendencies towards different directions in maintaining the resilience of life on Earth. Over the past half-century or more, global trends in food production have become increasingly artificial, with intensifying reliance on man-made inputs. This trend has certainly increased food production, but has also destabilized ecosystems and the water cycle. The compensating trend is quite likely to be one that increases food production in regions where hunger is rampant while simultaneously protecting the processes that produce food in the first place. Society's ability to feed the world's poorest regions will need to rely on the use of native, staple crops rather than on alien cash crops, which put food on the table only if the market price remains high enough to produce a profit. The economic viability of farmers in the developing world will also depend on lowered costs of inputs such as fertilizers, pesticides, machine parts and fuel. Thus, rather than further homogenization of global agriculture, feeding tomorrow's children will require a return to native products and ecology, and indigenous and, in some cases, ancient techniques updated with modern information and agro-ecological understanding. Similar strategies will apply in other sectors of water use, as we will see in chapters 4–6.

Notes

1 Gleick, P.H., 2000. *The World's Water 2000–2001: The Biennial Report on Freshwater Resources.* Island Press, Washington. pp. 65–6.
2 Moffett, G.D., 1994. *Critical Masses: The Global Population Challenge.* Viking-Penguin, New York.
3 Rijsberman, F. & D. Molden, 2001. 'Balancing Water Uses: Water for Food and Water for Nature.' Thematic background paper prepared for the International Conference on Freshwater, Bonn. p. 2.
4 Moffett, G.D., 1994. *Critical Masses.*
5 Rijsberman, F. & D. Molden, 2001. 'Balancing Water Uses.' pp. 2–3.
6 Shah, M. & M. Strong, 1999. *Food in the 21st Century: from Science to Sustainable Agriculture.* World Bank, Washington. p. 9.
7 Moffett, G.D., 1994. *Critical Masses.*
8 Ehrlich, P.R. and A.H. Ehrlich, 1991. *Healing the Planet: Strategies for Resolving the*

Environmental Crisis. Addison-Wesley Publishing Company, Inc., Reading, MA. 365 pp.

9 Rosegrant, M.W. & X. Cai, 2001. 'Water for Food Production.' In Meinzen-Dick, R.S. & M.W. Rosegrant. *Overcoming Water Scarcity and Quality Constraints. 2020 Focus No. 9.* International Food Policy Research Institute, Washington.

10 Shah, M. & M. Strong, 1999. *Food in the 21st Century.* p. 9.

11 Halwell, B. 1999. 'The Emperor's New Crops.' *Worldwatch*, July/August. p. 22.

12 Ibid., p. 22.

13 Ibid., p. 24.

14 Ibid., p. 23.

15 DNA is deoxyribonucleic acid, spiralling chains of molecules that comprise the genetic codes of all living things on Earth.

16 Halwell, B. 1999. 'The Emperor's New Crops.' p. 23.

17 Quist, D. & I.H. Chapela, 2001. 'Transgenic DNA introgressed into traditional maize landraces in Oaxaca, Mexico.' *Nature 2001*, 414: 541–3.

18 Altieri, M. & C.I. Nicholls, 2000. 'Applying Agroecological Concepts to Development of Ecologically Based Pest Management Strategies.' In National Research Council, Board on Agriculture and Natural Resources, *Professional Societies and Ecologically Based Pest Management. Proceedings of a Workshop.* National Academy Press, Washington. p. 15.

19 Postel, S. 1996. *Dividing the Waters: Food Security, Ecosystem Health, and the New Politics of Scarcity.* Worldwatch Paper 132, September. Washington. pp. 14–15.

20 Gleick, P.H. 2000. *The World's Water 2000–2001.* p. 68.

21 Postel, S. 1999. 'When the World's Wells Run Dry.' *Worldwatch*, September/October. p. 35.

22 Brown, L.R. & B. Halwell, 1998. 'China's Water Shortages Could Shake World Food Security.' *Worldwatch*, July/August. p. 11.

23 Borlaug, N.E. & C. Dowswell, 2001. 'The Unfinished Green Revolution – The Future Role of Science and Technology in Feeding the World.' Paper at Seeds of Opportunity Conference, School of Oriental and African Studies, 31 May– 1 June. London. p. 2.

24 Postel, S., 1996. *Dividing the Waters*: p. 15.

25 Borlaug, N.E., 2000. 'The Green Revolution Revisited and the Road Ahead.' Special 30th Anniversary Lecture, the Norwegian Nobel Institute, 8 September.

26 International Development Research Centre, 1992. *For Earth's Sake: A Report from the Commission on Developing Countries and Global Change.* International Development Research Centre, Ottawa, Ontario, Canada. 145 pp.

27 Borlaug, N.E. & C. Dowswell, 2001. 'The Unfinished Green Revolution.' pp. 3–4.

28 Postel, S., 1993. 'Water and Agriculture.' In P.H. Gleick (ed.), *Water in Crisis: A Guide to the World's Freshwater Resources.* Oxford University Press, New York. pp. 56–66.

29 Rosegrant, M.W. & X. Cai, 2001. 'Water for Food Production.'

30 Hinrichsen, D., 1998. 'Feeding a Future World.' *People and the Planet*, 7 (1): 6–9.

31 Postel, S., 1993. 'Water and Agriculture.'

32 Ibid.

33 Ibid.

34 Sretthachau, C., K. Nungern & A. Olsson, 2000. 'Social Impacts of the Rasi Salai Dam, Thailand: Loss of Livelihood Security and Social Conflict.' Paper submitted by the South-east Asia Rivers Network to the World Commission on Dams Regional Consultation on 'Large Dams and their Alternatives in East and South East Asia: Experiences and Lessons Learned.' Hanoi. 14 pp.

35 Rosegrant, M.W., 1997. 'Water Resources in the Twenty-first Century: Challenges and Implications for Action.' Food, Agriculture and the Environment Discussion Paper 20. International Food Policy Research Institute, Washington, DC. 27 pp.

36 Pearce, F., 1992. *The Dammed: Rivers, Dams, and the Coming World Water Crisis.* The Bodley Head, London. 376 pp.

37 Adams, A., 2000.' The Senegal River: Flood Management and the Future of the Valley.' Drylands Issue Paper IP93, International Institute for Environment and Development, London. p. 1.

38 Ibid., p. 11.

39 Ibid., p. 24.

40 Moffett, G.D., 1994. *Critical Masses: The Global Population Challenge.* Viking-Penguin, New

York.

41 Gruhn, P., F. Golettie & M. Yudelman, 2000. 'Integrated Nutrient Management, Soil Fertility, and Sustainable Agriculture: Current Issues and Future Challenges.' International Food Policy Research Institute Discussion Paper 32. Washington. pp. 7–8.

42 Ibid., p. 8.

43 Brown, K.R., C. Flavin & S. Postel, 1991. *Saving the Planet: How to Shape an Environmentally Sustainable Global Economy*. W.W. Norton & Co., New York. 224 pp.

44 Lutz, K., 2000. 'Green Revolution Turns Sour.' *New Scientist*, 8 July.

45 Altieri, M. & C.I. Nicholls, 2000. 'Applying Agroecological Concepts.' p. 15.

46 Rabalais, N.N., R.E. Turner, W.J. Wiseman & D.F. Boesch, 1991. 'A Brief Summary of Hypoxia on the Northern Gulf of Mexico Continental Shelf: 1985–1988.' In: Tyson, R.V. & T.H. Person (eds.), *Modern and Ancient Continental Shelf Anoxia*. Geological Society Special Publication No. 58. pp. 35–47

47 Turner, R. E. & N.N. Rabalais, 1991. 'Changes in Mississippi River Water Quality this Century: Implications for Coastal Food Webs.' *Biosicence*, 41 (3): 140–7.

48 Stanners, D. & P. Bourdeau (eds.), 1995. *Europe's Environment: The Dobris Assessment*. European Environmental Agency, Copenhagen.

49 Ibid.

50 Ibid.

51 McGinn, A.P., 2000. 'POPs Culture.' *Worldwatch*, March/April. p. 33.

52 Yudelman, M., A. Ratta & D. Nygaard, 1998. 'Pest Management and Food Production: Looking to the Future.' 2020 Brief 52. International Food Policy Research Institute, Washington.

53 WWF Global Toxic Chemicals Initiative, 2000. UNEP Global POPs Treaty – INC4/Bonn: Implementing Integrated Pest Management (IPM). Washington.

54 Yudelman, M., A. Ratta & D. Nygaard, 1998. 'Pest Management and Food Production.'

55 McGinn, A.P., 2000. 'POPs Culture.' p. 33.

56 Ongley, E.D., 1996. 'Control of Water Pollution from Agriculture.' Food and Agriculture Organization of the United Nations, FAO Irrigation and Drainage Paper 55. Rome.

57 Author's personal experience as manager of clean-up programmes for the Great Lakes with the US Environmental Protection Agency.

58 Yudelman, M., A. Ratta & D. Nygaard, 1998. 'Pest Management and Food Production.' Ongley, E.D., 1996. 'Control of Water Pollution from Agriculture.'

59 Ongley, E.D., 1996. 'Control of Water Pollution from Agriculture.'

60 Colburn, T.E., A. Davidson, S.N. Green, R.A. Hodge, C.I. Jackson & R. Liroff, 1990. *Great Lakes: Great Legacy?* The Conservation Foundation, Washington, and the Institute for Research on Public Policy, Ottawa, Ontario. 301 pp.

61 Abramovitz, J.N., 1996. *Imperilled Waters, Impoverished Future: The Decline of Freshwater Ecosystems.* Worldwatch Paper 128. Worldwatch Institute, Washington. 80 pp.

62 Altieri, M. & C.I. Nicholls, 2000. 'Applying Agroecological Concepts.' pp. 14–19.

63 Matthews, M. & A. Hamond, 1999. *Critical Consumption Trends and Implications: Degrading Earth's Ecosystems.* World Resources Institute, Washington. p. 5.

64 Revenga, C., J. Brunner, N. Henninger, K. Kassem & R. Paye, 2000. *Pilot Analysis of Global Ecosystems: Freshwater Ecosystems.* World Resources Institute, Washington. p. 41.

65 Food and Agriculture Organization of the United Nations, 1999. 'Inland Fisheries Are under Increasing Threat from Environmental Degradation.' Press Release 99/16. 24 March. Rome.

66 Inland Water Resources and Aquaculture Service, Fishery Resources Division, Fisheries Department, 1999. *Review of the State of World Fishery Resources: Inland Fisheries*. FAO Fisheries Circular No. 942. FIRI/C942. Food and Agriculture Organization of the United Nations, Rome. p. 43.

67 Ibid.

68 Ibid., p. 2.

69 Ibid., p. 34.

70 Of course, the degradation of fish habitat is linked to uses of water other than for agriculture, including hydroelectricity production, navigation, and industrial and domestic water supply.

71 World Commission on Dams, 2000. *Dams and Development: A New Framework for Decision-*

Making. The Report of the World Commission on Dams. Earthscan Publications Ltd, London and Sterling, Virginia. p. 82.

72 National Research Council, 1996. *Upstream: Salmon and Society in the Pacific Northwest.* National Academy Press, Washington. p. 60.

73 Ibid., p. 9.

74 Revenga, C., J. Brunner, N. Henninger, K. Kassem & R. Paye, 2000. *Pilot Analysis.* pp. 43–4.

75 World Commission on Dams, 2000. *Dams and Development.* p. 82.

76 Abramovitz, J.N., 1996. *Imperilled Waters.* p. 41.

77 Ibid., p. 44.

78 Van Hofwegen, P. & M. Svendsen, 2000. *Final: A Vision of Water for Food and Rural Development.* World Water Council, Marseilles. 79 pp.

79 Matthews, M. & A. Hamond, 1999. *Critical Consumption Trends.* p. 60.

80 Welcomme, R.L., 1995. 'Relationships between Fisheries and the Integrity of River Systems.' *Regulated Rivers Research & Management,* 11 (1): 132.

81 Matthews, M. & A. Hamond, 1999. *Critical Consumption Trends.* p. 60.

82 Food and Agriculture Organization of the United Nations, 1999. *Integrated Resource Management for Sustainable Inland Fish Production.* Committee on Fisheries, COFI/99/2. Rome. 7 pp.

83 McCulley, P., 1996. *Silenced Rivers: The Ecology and Politics of Large Dams.* Zed Books Ltd, London and New Jersey. p. 205.

84 Thompson, J. & F. Hinchcliffe, 1998. 'Sustaining the Harvest.' *People and the Planet,* 7 (1): 10–11.

85 Ibid.

86 Ibid.

87 Warnock, J.W., 1987. *The Politics of Hunger.* Methuen Publications, Agincourt, Ontario. 334 pp.

88 Thompson, J. & F. Hinchcliffe, 1998. 'Sustaining the Harvest.'

89 Corselius, K., S. Wisniewski & M. Ritchie, 2001. 'Sustainable Agriculture: Making Money, Making Sense. Twenty Years of Research and Results. Literature Review.' In The Institute for Agriculture and Trade Policy, *Fires of Hope: Food for a Sustainable Future.* Washington. p. 3.

90 Altieri, M.A., 1987. *Agroecology: The Scientific Basis of Alternative Agriculture.* Westview Press, Boulder, CO. 227 pp.

91 Corselius, K., S. Wisniewski & M. Ritchie, 2001. 'Sustainable Agriculture.' p. 11.

92 Ibid., p. 17.

93 Ehrlich, P.R. & A.H. Ehrlich, 1991. *Healing the Planet.* p. 208.

94 Lalonde, A. 'African Indigenous Knowledge and its Relevance to Sustainable Development.' In Inglis, J.T. (ed.), *Traditional Ecologic Knowledge: Concepts and Cases.* International Program on Traditional Ecologic Knowledge and International Development Research Center, Ottawa, Canada. pp. 55–61.

95 Douglas, J.S. & R. de J Hart, 1984. *Forest Farming.* Intermediate Technology Publications, London. 207 pp.

96 Ibid.

97 Sluiter, L., 1992, *The Mekong Currency.* Project for Ecological Recovery/TERRA, Bangkok. p. 39.

98 Altieri, M.A., 1987. *Agroecology.*

99 National Research Council 1993. *Sustainable Agriculture and the Environment in the Humid Tropics.* National Academy Press, Washington. 702 pp.

100 Offenberger, M. (ed.), 1990. *Keepers of the Forest: Land Management Alternatives in Southeast Asia.* Kumarian Press, West Hartford, Conn. 289 pp.

101 DeBeer, J.H. & M.J. McDermott, 1996. *The Economic Value of Non-timber Forest Products in Southeast Asia.* The Netherlands Committee for IUCN, Amsterdam. p. 23.

102 Ibid., p. 77.

103 Derpsch, R. 2001. 'Frontiers in Conservation Tillage and Advances in Conservation Practice.' In D.E. Scott, R.H. Mohtar and G.C. Steinhardt (eds), *Sustaining the Global Farm.* Selected Papers from the 10th International Soil Conservation Organisation meeting held 24–29 May 1999 at Purdue University and the USDA-ARS National Soil Erosion Research Laboratory.

104 Postel, S., 1993. 'Water and Agriculture.' p. 61.

105 Ibid.

106 Postel, S., 1996. *Dividing the Waters.* p. 56.

107 McCulley, P., 1996. *Silenced Rivers.* pp. 207–8.

108 Rosegrant, M.W., 1997. 'Water Resources.'

109 Rosegrant, M.W. & Claudia Ringer, 1998. 'Impact on Food Security and Rural Development of Transferring Water out of Agriculture.' *Water Policy*, 1 (6): 573.

110 Rosegrant, M.W., 1997. 'Water Resources.'

111 Landis, D.A. & D.B. Orr, 2000. 'Biological Control: Approaches and Applications.' University of Minnesota National IPM Network, http://ipmworld.umn.edu/chpaters/landis.htm.

111 National Research Council, Committee on Pest and Pathogen Control through Management of Biological Control Agents and Enhanced Cycles and Natural Processes, Board on Agriculture. *Ecologically Based Pest Management: New Solutions for a New Century.* National Academy Press, Washington. p. 3.

113 Landis, D.A. & D.B. Orr, 2000. 'Biological Control: Approaches and Applications.'

114 Ibid.

115 WWF Global Toxic Chemicals Initiative, 2000. UNEP Global POPs Treaty.

116 Mekong River Commission Secretariat, 1999. *MRC Programme for Fisheries Management and Development Cooperation (2000–2004).* MKG/R.95063, Rev. 4. Phnom Penh. p. i.

117 Abramovitz, J.N., 1996. *Imperilled Waters*, p. 40.

118 Food and Agriculture Organization of the United Nations, 1999. *Integrated Resource Management.*

119 Wilcove, D., M. Brown, & P.C. Lee, 1992. 'Fisheries Management and Biological Diversity: Problems and Opportunities.' In McCabe, R.G. (ed.), *Transactions, 57th North American Wildlife & Natural Resources Conference*, 27 March–1 April 1992, Charlotte, North Carolina, pp. 373–83.

4 A Thirsty Planet
Water Supply and Sanitation in a Water-short World

'Ecosystem conservation is vital for meeting the basic needs of people. Properly functioning, well-maintained freshwater ecosystems are the basis of secure systems for water supply and sanitation.'[1]

WATER PAUCITY AND PLENTY: THE GREAT DIVIDE

The gap between where the world is and where it might be with regard to the extent and distribution of sustainable water supply and sanitation services is simply staggering. Communities complain about the lack of funds to repair antiquated, leaking infrastructure, while national governments proceed with costly and economically irrational dam construction projects. People in the industrialized world use highly treated drinking water to flush their toilets, wash their cars and water their lawns and golf courses while women in Africa walk many kilometres each day carrying water urns on their backs to provide a minimal supply of freshwater for their families. If a global water crisis is to be avoided, these conditions must change.

Fortunately, humanity has already developed the technology needed to reduce the waste of water in our domestic affairs and to increase services to the poor. Part of the solution rests in the recognition that the technological solutions applied in the wealthy Western countries are largely unnecessary overkill and that we can reduce the waste of water, the energy consumed in our water supply and sanitation systems, and the pollution of our water supplies. Another part of the solution is the recognition that these wasteful approaches need not be repeated in the developing world. But the most important part of the solution is the application of alternative, sustainable technologies in communities around the globe.

The world made great strides towards the end of the twentieth century in providing water and sanitation services to a growing population. The percentage of people served with some form of improved water supply rose from 79 (4.1 billion people) in 1990 to 82 (4.9 billion) in 2000. Over the same period, the percentage of the world's population with access to excreta disposal facilities increased from 55 (2.9 billion people) to 60 (3.6 billion).[2]

Much remains to be done, however. At the turn of the century, one billion people still lacked safe drinking water and almost three billion – half the world's population – lacked adequate sanitation. More than two million children were dying every year from water-related diseases.[3] These problems are unevenly distributed. Only three-fifths of Africans have access to safe and reliable water supplies,[4] while in North America and Europe 90 percent of the population have access to safe drinking water.[5] Less than half of all Asians have access to improved sanitation. Sanitation coverage in rural areas is less than half that in urban settings.

One of the fundamental and often overlooked causes of water supply shortages is a short-circuiting of the water cycle. Environmental degradation frequently reduces the capacity of the water cycle to provide adequate quantities of good-quality water to support expanding human populations. Poor land-use practices, direct pollutant discharges, and atmospheric deposition of pollutants contaminate surface and groundwater. Poor land-use management practices can also lead to desertification, which is often accompanied by a reduction in available freshwater. Water shortages are exacerbated by the lack of sanitation facilities, which frequently leads to the spread of water-borne disease. Direct discharges of human waste into aquatic ecosystems also severely disrupt the chemical balance of these ecosystems and can render them lifeless for long periods of time.

In some cases, however, the cures are nearly as damaging as the disease. Modern water supply systems, which involve industrial-scale treatment and distribution systems, are energy-intensive and often inefficient. Modern sewage treatment systems waste both nutrients and water, and also use excessive amounts of energy. Between two and three percent of the world's energy consumption is used to pump and treat wastewater. In the developing world, the cost of energy to supply water may easily consume half of a municipality's budget.[6] The repercussions of excessive energy consumption on the planet's water cycle are discussed in Chapter 7.

SOURCES OF SCARCITY

Some of the most widespread causes of potable water supply shortages include inefficient water use, hydrological alterations, desertification, pollutants, and pathogens.

Inefficient Water Use

Water supply systems often perform badly, resulting in wasted water and unreliable delivery. Poor management and inadequate cost recovery are often reflected in a lack of infrastructure maintenance, patterns of water delivery that are not in synch with patterns of demand, wasteful application processes, pollution of the human water supply and of aquatic ecosystems, and water losses through seepage, leaks and evaporation. These problems can have severe negative repercussions for human health and the environment.

'Unaccounted-for water' is water that is presumed lost from a distribution system. Causes of such losses can be either physical, such as seepage and leaks, or administrative. Physical losses combined with intermittent water supply can lead to the contamination of drinking water as substantial changes in pressure in water distribution pipes permit polluted water to infiltrate the pipelines.[7] Administrative losses stem from ineffective management of water supply systems and include illegal connections, faulty or broken meters, and meter readers who are poorly trained, incompetent or corrupt.[8]

At the turn of the century, mean unaccounted-for water was estimated at 15 percent in North America, 39 percent in Africa and 42 percent in Asia and Latin America and the Caribbean.[9] In the cities of North Africa and the Middle East, up to 52 percent of bulk water supplied is unaccounted for.[10] In the Guateng Province of South Africa, which includes more than 20 percent of the country's population, including the metropolitan areas of Pretoria and Johannesburg, 52 percent of water supplied to the urban sector is wasted through inefficiency. These losses amount to 1.5 million m^3 per day, which is more than enough to meet the total, combined water needs of two neighbouring countries, Botswana and Lesotho.[11] In India, over 40 percent of the total municipal water supply is lost in the distribution system before it reaches consumers. In Malta, one of the world's most water-stressed countries, 30 percent of the water is lost before it reaches consumers. In Mexico City, an estimated 40 percent of water was lost through leaky pipes built at the beginning of the twentieth century.[12]

'Mexico City's water situation adds directly to its economic problems. Residents pay only 20 percent of the actual costs of being provided with water. This subsidy may effectively prevent the more efficient use of water for other purposes. The difficulty of supporting the city results in part from its geography. In 1982, Mexico City had to pump water from a distance of 100 km and from 1,000 m below the city. By the 1990s, rapid population growth required the city to withdraw additional water from 200 km away and 2,000 m lower. The costs of satisfying this increasing water demand are enormous – equal to roughly half of Mexico's annual interest payments on its external debt. And unfortunately, to some extent the many leaks and breaks in the water system defeat the enormous effort expended. The amount of water lost corresponds to the gross needs of Rome.'[13]

'Intermittent supply is common in many cities in [the Middle East and North Africa]. Especially during the summer, the intervals between 'turns' of piped water supply increases significantly. During the summer in Algiers, for example, water is provided to customers every other day, in Jordan twice a week, and in the city of Taiz in Yemen only once a month.... [H]ousehold members, particularly women, sometimes have to do without water for days and adjust household chores such as bathing children and washing clothes or dishes accordingly. Alternatively, they can purchase expensive water from vendors, which the poor cannot afford.'[14]

'A recent comprehensive review of [World] Bank experience in water and sanitation projects compellingly shows that supply costs in developing countries are much higher than they should be, largely because of low efficiency of water supply agencies. For example, in Singapore, 'unaccounted for water' (water lost between the distribution point and the users) is 8 percent of total water produced, but in Manila the share is 58 percent and in most Latin American cities it is about 40 percent. For Latin America as a whole such water losses cost up to $1.5 billion in forgone revenue every year.'[15]

Inefficient water supply systems have implications for the environment, as well. As long as populations are growing, standards of living are improving, and incentives are lacking for water conservation and demand management, most communities will seek to expand their supplies of water. The increase in water supplies to people can affect freshwater ecosystems through infrastructure construction and increases in water withdrawal. Inadequate or poorly maintained water supply and sanitation systems can also become conduits for pollutants to enter aquatic ecosystems and community water supplies. An increase in water supply almost inevitably leads to an increase in wastewater discharges as well, and without adequate sanitation services these discharges can significantly alter aquatic ecosystems and the water cycle through pollution and changes in flow patterns.

Inefficiencies are often coupled with gross inequities. While many households pay for water below the cost of delivery, many urban dwellers who lack connections to a public water supply, typically poorer families in slums and squatter communities, must spend substantial portions of their income to purchase water from vendors. For example, studies in Nigeria, Bombay and Haiti have indicated that poor households can spend between one-fifth and one-third of their income on water.[16]

Table 4.1 Daily Average Household Water Use per Person in Industrial Countries

Toilet	30 gallons (113.55 litres)	42 %
Bath	20 gallons (75.70 litres)	32 %
Kitchen	10 gallons (37.85 litres)	12 %
Laundry	15 gallons (56.76 litres)	14 %
Total	75 gallons (283.86 litres)	100 %

From: Van der Ryn, S. 1995. *The Toilet Papers: Recycling Waste and Conserving Water.* Ecological Design Press, Sausalito, California.

Gross inefficiencies also exist in the area of water quality improvement and maintenance. In the industrialized world, per capita water use has been increasing, with many countries reaching consumption levels in excess of 200 litres per person per day. Although only a small fraction of this water is used in households for drinking and cooking, generally all water is treated to stringent drinking water standards.[17] In fact, flush toilets have been shown to account for around 40 percent of the residential water use in industrial countries (see Table 4.1).[18] Thus, while people in industrialized countries are using highly purified water to flush toilets, wash cars and water lawns, many people in developing countries are withdrawing their drinking water from the same rivers into which they discharge their sewage.

Hydrological Alterations

Most natural landscapes function rather like a sponge: they absorb water when it is present in excess and release it when it is not. When the spongy characteristics of the landscape are altered, both the water absorption and release functions are diminished. The landscape can capture less rainfall than before, so more water runs off the land and less is conducted through the soil into groundwater aquifers. As a result, extremely low flows and water shortages, as well as extremely high flows that cannot be efficiently captured, become more common in the drainage basin.

'On an average, water discharged from the village springs [in the Danda and Chandrabhaga watersheds in India's Garwhal region] ... is much more than the desired level.... Despite this, the per capita annual availability of fresh water in these two regions ... is much less than the national average.... Forest degradation and soil erosion are among the main reasons why this region cannot store water. Although there are more than 60 days of rainfall each year, there is no water in the summer months. This results in many hardships, especially for women who have to travel long distances in search of water.'[19]

Changes in the characteristics of the drainage basin of a river or lake can lead to temporary or long-term water shortages, just as they can lead to floods. Removing vegetation from a land area, or paving it, decreases water infiltration, with the result that precipitation runs off rapidly into receiving surface waters. This leaves little water to be stored in the landscape. Landscape drainage by ditches and canals, generally intended to convert wet soils to dry soils for agriculture or development, also reduces the landscape's ability to retain water.

Water supply shortages sometimes motivate the construction of dams, which leads to severe alterations of hydrological patterns and can exacerbate the shortages. The storage of water behind a dam often reduces water availability to communities downstream. Elimination of seasonal flood pulses, and the decreased inundation of downstream floodplains, can reduce the amount of aquifer recharge and, ultimately, groundwater availability.

Evaporation from reservoir surfaces can substantially reduce downstream water availability. As shown in Table 2.3 (p. 45), global evaporation from reservoirs amounts to nearly ten percent of total human water consumption. The amount of evaporation relative to river flows depends on the reservoir's surface-area-to-volume ratio and the climate of the region in which the dam is built. Cumulative quantities of evaporative losses from the Glen Canyon Dam on the Colorado River in Arizona are estimated at nearly three billion m³, a difference of almost 2.5 billion m³ from the evaporation that would have occurred from the river under natural, undammed, conditions. Total losses from evaporation and seepage are about 6.3 percent of the river's average annual flow.[20] The evaporation rate from Lake Nasser, the reservoir impounded by Egypt's Aswan High Dam, is estimated to be about 10,000,000,000 m³ per year, or ten percent of net storage volume.[21] Average annual evaporative water loss from the five reservoirs that supply domestic water to the city of Bulawayo, Zimbabwe, are 5,589,000,000 m³, or about 15 percent of total designed full supply capacity.

Hydrological alterations of the landscape, combined with dam construction, contribute to high sedimentation rates in reservoirs, which can decrease the storage available behind the dam for water supply and other purposes, as described in Chapter 2. Alterations of the natural hydrology of the landscape can also lead to water quality degradation, which renders freshwater unusable for drinking and other purposes.

'The increasing salinity of Australia's catchments and inland waters is one of the most significant threats to the health of aquatic ecosystems, and irrigation and drinking water supplies. Dryland salinity will be the major contributor to salinization of the landscape of the next 100 years, with irrigation-induced salinity only having a localized effect. The major cause of dryland salinity is the clearing of deep-rooted perennial vegetation and its replacement with shallow-rooted annual crops. In areas that are cleared, water (e.g. rainfall) can leak into the saline groundwater table, raising its level until it reaches the surface. As well as causing soil salinization, raised saline groundwater tables discharge saline water directly into rivers, streams, wetlands and lakes, and can degrade riparian habitat.'[22]

In addition to the inevitable loss of water and water storage capacity from reservoirs, these systems are generally inappropriate in the context of providing water to rural communities. The two main reasons that the systems are ill suited for rural communities are the high capital costs and water losses associated with piped distribution systems to rural areas.[23]

Desertification

A step more extreme than hydrological alteration, desertification implies a long-term alteration of the entire climate, including the hydrology, in a specific location. Desertification has been defined as the degradation or destruction of land to desert-like conditions that can include the growth of sand dunes, deterioration of range-lands, degradation of rainfed croplands, waterlogging and salinization of irrigated lands, deforestation of woody vegetation, and declining availability and/or quality of freshwater.[24]

More than 20 percent of the world's susceptible drylands are affected by human-induced soil degradation.[25] Six million hectares of productive land have been lost to land degradation every year since 1990.[26] In the early 1980s, severe desertification involving production losses of up to 50 percent affected more than 135 million people world-wide.[27] By the end of the twentieth century, desertification was placing the livelihoods of more than 1 billion people who directly depend on the land at risk.[28] Twelve million people die each year because of inadequate supplies of drinking water as a result of land degradation and desertification.[29]

Desertification is a significant threat to the arid, semi-arid and dry sub-humid areas of the globe – the 'susceptible' drylands that cover more than 40 percent (over six billion hectares) of the planet's surface and provide the habitat and resources of roughly one-fifth of the world's population.[30] Susceptible areas include the savannas of Africa, the steppes of south-east Europe and Asia, the Great Plains and the Pampas of the Americas, the outback of Australia, and the margins of the Mediterranean.[31] Desertification is also a problem over vast portions of the Indian subcontinent.[32]

Regardless of when the rainy season occurs, rainfall in these regions is limited (between less than 100 mm per year and 300 mm per year) and extremely irregular, especially from one year to another. The irregularity of rainfall means that watercourses in arid and semi-arid regions are dry most of the time, but subject to floods, which are often sudden and short, during the rainy season. Some watercourses gradually seep into their lower reaches as a result of infiltration in the proximity of desert areas, while others flow into internal depressions where their water evaporates completely, often leaving large quantities of salt on the soil surface.[33]

Groundwater is most likely to be found, and to serve as the principal source of water, in arid and semi-arid regions. Some aquifers lie fairly close to the surface and can be tapped by surface wells, while others lie in geological strata as much as 1,000 to 2,000 metres below the surface. In arid and semi-arid areas, both these types of aquifers are replenished mainly from large rivers with a substantial low flow and from smaller rivers during the rainy season. Some aquifers are no more than the groundwater underflow of a river within its bed. These regions also contain large sedimentary basins consisting of layers of permeable rock from a few hundred metres to one or two thousand metres thick which are saturated with freshwater from periods in the distant past. These fossil aquifers allow only very limited replenishment.[34]

The biophysical mechanism driving desertification is still under debate. Some scientists believe that soil surfaces almost denuded of vegetation by human activity have a higher albedo (the ratio of reflected light to the total amount of light falling on a surface) than surfaces with a natural vegetation cover. The albedo increase results in less short-wave energy stability and reduced convective rainfall. Other scientists believe that reduced evapotranspiration from plants leads directly to a decrease in rainfall.[35] In any case, the reduction of vegetation through deforestation, agricultural conversion or overgrazing results in the removal of root systems that hold soil in place and of leaf cover that shades and cools the soil.

Indicators of desertification include the decrease of effective soil depth by erosion. The loss of topsoil reduces the amount of soil organic matter and, as a result, the amount of water available to plants and microorganisms. Soil crusts – hard-packed soil surfaces caused by extreme erosion – indicate that the deterioration of soil structure has proceeded to the extent that the surface is sealed. As a result, water penetration of the soil decreases, as does the amount of water available to plants. Decreases in water penetration reduce the rate of aquifer recharge. As desertification progresses and aridity increases, increasing evaporation (relative to precipitation) together with the destruction of plant cover contribute to the desiccation of the soil and a considerable decrease in the soil's capacity to retain water. This results in a substantial increase in runoff, which triggers more violent and destructive floods.[36]

Dryland soils are particularly vulnerable because they recover very slowly from disturbances. Soil forms slowly in areas with limited water supplies. Salts tend to remain once accumulated on the soil surface. Soils that are dry, poorly held together and sparsely covered by vegetation are particularly susceptible to erosion. Infrequent rains are extremely erosive, especially where vegetation cover is sparse.[37] Heavy rainfall and a sudden rise in water levels, particularly in rivers with a sedimentary soil type and sparse vegetation, as in desertified areas, always results in rivers transporting enormous amounts of sediment. The sediment reduces the infiltration rates within the rivers, thus reducing the rate of river water seepage into aquifers. Sediment also drastically reduces the water yields of natural lakes whose drainage basins are entirely within arid or semi-arid zones. Increasing amounts of water are lost from these lakes through evaporation and evapotranspiration as the desertification process progresses. Water quality also deteriorates as salt from evaporated water accumulates, resulting in water that is unfit for human consumption and sometimes even unusable for agriculture.[38]

Desertification is usually the result of unsustainable land use and over-population. While the causes of desertification are often associated with food production, the impacts extend to all facets of life for which water is required, including drinking water supplies.

'Like so many other Yatenga [Burkina Faso] villages, Kalsaka has lost half of its cropland to desertification.... Water, too, is growing scarcer. It's not just the decline in rainfall. The crusting of soil and the death of vegetation has had an even greater effect. Rain no longer soaks in, but rushes off down gullies and streams. The water table has dropped. Wells have to be continually deepened, and dry up each year.'[39]

Pollutants

Water pollutants, including pathogens, further limit the amount of freshwater that is available for human consumption and other uses.[40] In Austria, for example, agricultural activities have led to excessive concentrations of nitrates and pesticides, affecting 73 percent of the country's groundwater areas. As a consequence,

49 percent of the population is affected by the reduced water availability for human consumption. The 1999 cyanide spill into the Danube River in Romania contaminated the drinking water supply for thousands of people.[41]

The pollutant-caused impairment of water sources has followed a U-shaped curve in most industrialized countries. Freshwater quality reached an all-time low around the 1950s and has been recovering ever since. Controls have been introduced on domestic and industrial effluents, and are continually being tightened. At the same time, farm chemicals are now subject to similar controls.

In most developing countries, however, water quality has been deteriorating rapidly. Out of 60 developing countries that were industrializing in 1992, for example, only ten had effective laws, regulations and enforcement procedures to cope with growing pollutant-related problems.[42] In developing countries, improving the quality of water is an important element in strategies to reduce poverty. The poor often must use polluted water, suffering debilitating diseases as a consequence, while many industries gain access to municipally treated water and then return the untreated effluent to waterways. Moreover, a new generation of toxic industrial pollutants, finding their way into the food chain, can cause serious health problems to humans who eat contaminated fish and shellfish. Sewage and industrial waste pollute rivers on every continent.[43]

For purposes of remedying water quality problems, pollutant sources are generally broken down into point and non-point (diffuse) sources. Point-source discharges are effluents that are discharged from one specific and identifiable place (a sewage or industrial outfall, for example). In the 1970s, the conventional approach to reducing point-source pollutant discharges in industrialized countries was to set technology-based treatment standards that specified the treatment levels required before an effluent could legally be discharged into a waterway, as well as the best technology available to meet those standards. Newer standards in the industrialized world are designed for the protection of specific water bodies and must take into account the cumulative effect of multiple pollution sources, the sensitivity of local aquatic species, and regional hydrological conditions. Effluent limitations and treatment technologies are then specified to ensure that the ambient water quality standards are not transgressed.[44] While these approaches to controlling point-source discharges have performed well in the industrialized world, they are extremely expensive to implement compared with steps that can be taken earlier in most effluent-producing processes to prevent the generation of pollutants in the first place (see section on pollution prevention, below).

Non-point-source pollutants are substances that enter a waterway in a diffuse manner. Non-point sources include runoff from agricultural operations and other land uses, as well as atmospheric deposition to water surfaces and seepage of contaminants into surface water bodies from contaminated groundwater sources. The lack of an identifiable discharge point and the cumulative nature of the environmental impacts render pollutants from non-point sources much more difficult to control than those emitted from point sources. The primary methods that have been developed to reduce pollutant discharges from land-based sources include land-use practices designed to minimize the amount of polluted runoff that leaves a particular site. Examples of non-point-source control practices include the use of silt fences in urban construction projects, the planting of filter strips next to streams in agricultural areas, and the construction of artificial wetlands to cleanse storm water runoff from roads and parking lots in urban settings.

Sources and types of water pollution differ according to location and land use. In general, pollutants are delivered to aquatic ecosystems by industrial discharges, sewage, runoff, percolation or seepage into aquifers or water pipelines, and deposition on, or precipitation into, water bodies from the atmosphere. Most anthropogenic pollutants emanate from municipal, industrial or agricultural sources.

Municipal wastewater is composed primarily of water and human excreta, but often contains trace amounts of other contaminants.[45] In countries with modern sewage treatment systems, wastewater discharges from households are frequently contaminated with other substances – ranging from detergents to pesticides and caustic plumbing agents – which families dump into their sinks and toilets. Municipal wastewater also carries numerous pathogenic microorganisms. As this wastewater travels through sewers to sewage treatment plants, it may also receive discharges from industrial facilities that have contracted with municipalities to treat their wastewater. Many cities combine stormwater conduits with their wastewater sewer systems, adding additional pollutants such as oil and heavy metals to the toxic brew. During heavy precipitation events, combined systems sometimes overflow, resulting in discharges of untreated wastewater directly into rivers and lakes.

Much of the world's municipal wastewater is discharged untreated into rivers, lakes and estuaries. The median percentage of wastewater treated effectively before being discharged into waterways ranges greatly throughout the world, from just 14 percent in Latin America and the Caribbean to 90 percent in North America. In Europe, a median of 66 percent of wastewater is treated effectively; in Asia, the median is 35 percent.[46]

Even where municipal wastewater is effectively treated, many municipal sewage treatment plants also receive discharges from industries and stormwater

'Since Thomas Crapper invented the water closet, many sanitation experts have come to view it as one of the stupidest technologies of all time: In an effort to make them 'invisible' it mixes pathogen-bearing faeces with industrial toxins in the sewer system, thus turning "an excellent fertilizer and soil conditioner" into a serious, far-reaching and dispersed disposal problem. Supplying the clean water, treating the sewage, and providing all the delivery and collection in between requires systems whose cost strains the resources even of wealthy countries, let alone the 2 billion people who lack basic sanitation. The World Health Organization has stated that water-borne sanitation cannot meet any of its declared objectives – equity, disease prevention and sustainability – and suggests that only with more modern (waterless) technologies can the world's cities be affordably provided with clean water for drinking, cooking and washing. Meanwhile, a new village-affordable, solar-powered water purifier can stop the tragedy of water-borne disease.'[47]

runoff that contain additional pollutants which the plants cannot effectively remove or neutralize before discharging the treated water back into nature.

Industrial waste varies tremendously depending on the type of industry or processing activity, and may contain a wide variety of both organic and inorganic chemicals. The quantity of industrial effluents discharged into freshwater ecosystems is increasing rapidly around the world. In the mid-1980s, around 237 billion tons of industrial wastewater was discharged. This figure was expected to double by the year 2000 to 468 billion tons.[48]

Agricultural effluents primarily contain excess nutrients (such as the phosphorus and nitrogen present in fertilizers and manure) and pesticides. Suspended sediments resulting from soil erosion on agricultural land can also pollute water bodies. Irrigated and non-irrigated land, rangeland, animal feedlots, and other sources can generate polluted runoff. Particularly in industrialized countries such as the United States, where sewage and industrial discharges are generally treated, agricultural runoff can constitute the major source of water pollution. The trend towards agricultural domination of pollution loads to aquatic ecosystems in the US is increasing, as large-scale factory farms with thousands of head of livestock concentrate their waste in sewage lagoons, which are prone to rupture and spill over into local rivers and streams.

While the types and sources of pollutants discussed above are the most ubiquitous, smaller sources discharging highly concentrated loads of pollutants into drainage basins or water bodies can cause severe, ephemeral or chronic, problems locally. These sources include leakage from hazardous waste sites, accidental discharges, or warfare in the form of intentional environmental destruction.

'The Yenisey River in Russia has been contaminated by three decades of discharges of radioactive particles from a state-run factory making bomb-grade plutonium. The contamination is hidden in the sands of the riverbed, on the islands and in the floodplains. Radionuclides, the product of nuclear fission, including plutonium-239, cesium-137 and strontium-90, have been found hundreds of miles downstream, apparently carried by the river's powerful floods, and have been detected in the food chain.

'In downstream villages, experts have found a disturbing statistical pattern of illnesses: an increase in children with leukaemia, breast cancer among women, genetic aberrations, and a higher death rate. All are possible effects from radiation exposure.'[49]

Communities with polluted surface water often turn to groundwater as a fallback. Unfortunately, many groundwater aquifers are also becoming polluted. As the ground absorbs the precipitation that falls on the surface of the land, it also absorbs pollutants that are deposited on the soil surface. Groundwater can leach naturally occurring elements, such as arsenic, out of subsurface deposits, making them available to people through water consumption. In addition, as mentioned above, other water sources such as leaking sewer lines or highly contaminated rivers that recharge aquifers can pollute groundwater.

Nitrate is one of the pollutants most commonly found in groundwater. Nitrate levels above 10 mg/litre can cause infant methemoglobinemia, or 'blue baby syndrome.' About 3,000 cases of methemoglobinemia have been reported world-wide, nearly half of them in Hungary, where private wells have particularly high nitrate concentrations.[50] Many wells in the Yucatan peninsula of Mexico have nitrate concentrations above 45 mg/litre. More than one-third of the wells in Romania and Moldavia have nitrate concentrations of more than 50 mg/litre.[51] In the northern Chinese counties of Beijing, Tianjin, Hebei and Shandong, the concentration of nitrate in groundwater frequently exceed 50 mg/litre and is as high as 300 mg/litre in some locations.[52]

Because they do not break down readily, organic pesticides can remain in groundwater reservoirs long after their use has ceased. After a half century of spraying in the eastern Indian states of West Bengal and Bihar, for example, DDT was found in groundwater at levels as high as 4,500 micrograms per litre – several thousand times higher than what is considered a safe dose.[53]

Pathogens

Pathogens include any microorganism or virus that can cause disease. Many pathogens – including those that cause malaria, encephalitis, hepatitis, cholera, dysentery, schistosomiasis and other diseases – are associated with contaminated water or water-dependent vectors such as mosquitoes or snails. While water-related diseases have been virtually eliminated in most industrialized countries, they constitute the most pressing water quality issue in much of the rest of the world. In 1998, water-related diseases caused an estimated 3.4 million deaths (see Table 4.2).

Water-based diseases are transmitted by means other than ingestion by hosts that live in water for all, or a portion, of their life cycles. The principal pathway for the transmission of water-borne diseases is through the contamination of drinking water supplies with pathogen-carrying animal or human excreta, and the subsequent ingestion of pathogens by uninfected people (faecal–oral transmission).

Water-related diseases borne by vectors are not generally a symptom of con-taminated water, but may result from large-scale development of water resources for urban and agricultural uses that create favourable conditions for the vectors.[54]

Table 4.2 World-wide Deaths from Water-related Diseases, 1998

Diarroeal diseases	2,219,000
Malaria	1,110,000
Trypanosomiasis	40,000
Intestinal worm infections	17,000
Dengue fever	15,000
Schistosomiasis	7,000

From: Water Supply and Sanitation Collaborative Council, 2000. *Vision 21: A Shared Vision for Hygiene, Sanitation & Water Supply and a Framework for Action*, Geneva. p. 6.

'The Manantali and Diama dams were built with the ambition of generating electricity, increasing the area of pump-scheme irrigation in Mauritania and Senegal, and providing landlocked Mali with direct access to the sea. This would be accomplished by maintaining a minimum constant flow of 200 m³ per second in the main river channel, deepening the river, and constructing a port and boat lock. Yet, to date, no power has been produced at Manantali, irrigation has been costly and far below levels anticipated, and not a single vessel has passed through the Diama boat lock since it was completed in 1986.

'Like similar structures on other tropical rivers that terminate or substantially reduce the natural annual flood, conventional management of the Manantali and Diama dams degrades the habitat and renders the traditional production systems unsustainable. This increases the dependency of the local populations on wage-labor migration, further burdening those – mainly women, children and the elderly – who remain in the valley. The Diama dam, by blocking the upstream migration of saline waters for expansion of irrigation in the lower basin and delta, has contributed to an explosion of water-borne parasitic diseases, including schistosomiasis, malaria, and Rift Valley Fever. Because of this, and the adverse nutritional impacts of the reduction in traditional food-production activities, the overall health of the riparian populations has seriously deteriorated.

'Hydrological research proved that the Manantali reservoir contains enough water to simultaneously produce electricity at profitable levels and to allow for a controlled release towards the end of the rainy season. This controlled release, when added to the undammed flows from the river's other principal tributaries, would replicate a natural flood. In principle, this could support flood-recession farming, fishing and herding on more than 100,000 hectares of floodplain in Mauritania and Senegal. Epidemiologists believe that periodically manipulating reservoir levels and allowing saline flows upstream from Diama would markedly reduce the insect and snail vectors that host disease pathogens.'[55]

IMPROVING OUR PERFORMANCE

Global society has access to an array of technologies, ranging from ancient to experimental, that can help us to manage water supply and sanitation more effectively. We can, for example, conserve resources by increasing efficiency. We can reduce the energy invested in water supply and sanitation in the industrialized world substantially by switching to simpler technologies. We can effectively expand usable water supplies by reducing and preventing pollution. We can also 'close the loop' on certain natural resources by recycling human waste and wastewater. This approach will help to maintain the water cycle by returning agricultural nutrients to the land rather than discharging them into our freshwater sources and keep freshwater in circulation rather than discharging it immediately after first use into sewers, streams and, ultimately, the ocean.

Water Conservation

The search for sustainable water management necessarily involves striving for improvements in the efficiency of resource use. Sustainable water supply systems are environmentally efficient, in the sense that water use rates do not exceed rates of replenishment. Environmental efficiency thus requires that where water supply infrastructure is newly provided, it is accompanied by sanitation services that reduce the net loss of usable freshwater by preventing contamination of the supply.

In the United States, water-use efficiency has been improving since about 1980, during a period of economic and population growth. The amount of freshwater withdrawn per American fell by 21 percent during the years 1980–95, and water withdrawn as dollars of real GDP fell by a startling 38 percent – over twice as fast as energy efficiency improved.[56] Similar improvements have been gauged in other countries.

Major gains in the efficiency of water use in the twenty-first century will generally consist of improvements in the technology and management of water supply systems, the removal of incentives to waste water, and the reform of public institutions that govern water use at all levels. The increasing prevalence of private financing of water supply systems around the world means that the public institutions must become more active in influencing and regulating private investment in water supply systems to avoid unfair pricing schemes that favour the rich at the expense of the poor. To ensure sustainable water supplies, public institutions must also be willing to ensure the health of the ecosystems that support the water cycle – a public trust responsibility which most private corporations still treat as an externality.

'[T]he Sydney Water Corporation in Australia (a state-owned corporation wholly owned by the people of New South Wales) ... operates under a five year licence granted by the Government. The renewal of the licence is dependent upon key performance indicators for water quality, water pressure, sewage surcharges and customer services. Under this agreement, Sydney Water is committed to reducing demands for fresh water by 45 percent between 1990–1 and 2010–11 and has identified a programme of water efficiency (water audits, retro-fitting, information, coupons for water-saving devices), leakage control (system pressure reduction, pipe replacement, and actively searching for and repairing leaks) and water recycling activities to reduce demand. Failure to comply can lead to the licence being revoked. Such pressures encourage the water utilities to concentrate upon options for improving supply of existing resources.'[57]

Water conservation consists of any beneficial reduction in water losses, waste, or use. In the context of drinking water supply, it may be viewed as an alternative set of technologies for meeting safe drinking water needs. Increasingly, water conservation is helping to meet the environmental goals of many communities, in addition to lowering costs and improving the reliability of water and wastewater systems.

Objectives of Water Conservation Programmes

One of the chief purposes of conservation is to avoid, postpone or reduce capital costs associated with new water supply facilities. In connection with infrastructure funding, the value of conservation is appropriately assessed in terms of supply, treatment, and distribution costs that can be avoided because of planned reductions in water demand or in the rate of increase in demand. Water conservation programmes can have notable effects on the size and timing of certain investments in urban water and wastewater treatment. Several categories of investment are sensitive to changes in average flows or peak volumes, and can therefore be influenced by water conservation programmes. These include wastewater treatment facilities, storage facilities (tanks and reservoirs), source water facilities (dams, impoundments, intakes, and wells), and transmission facilities (pipes). Conservation becomes more valuable over time because future water supplies and the facilities needed to deliver them are expected to cost more, even when adjusting for inflation. Thus, permanent conservation savings that are realized today will have increasing value into the future.[58]

'In an attempt to reduce per capita water consumption, Mexico City replaced about 350,000 toilets with smaller and more efficient models, saving enough water to meet the needs of 250,000 inhabitants.'[59]

Water conservation programmes can lead to increased supplies and/or lower prices of water available to poor communities. In Nairobi, for example, low-income families are likely to be a major target group for the sale of the huge quantities of water that the private operator will obtain from the reduction of water losses.[60]

'The first three years of the Greater Hermanus (South Africa) Water Conservation Programme, which includes a 12-point plan, have shown considerable improvement in water demand management results, including [a 32 percent reduction in per capita peak demand for water, a 20 percent increase in revenue from water sales, South Africa's most socially just tariffs and a 96 percent support level from residents]. A principal driving force is the notion of social justice.... Furthermore, the programme creates jobs, helps in promoting the payment of services, and improves quality of life and social harmony. It is such returns on investment that garnered the exceptional support from the people of Hermanus. The Hermanus model is becoming the standard model for urban water management in South Africa.

'The 12-Point Plan of the Greater Hermanus Water Conservation Programme

1 An assurance of supply tariff. Ensuring that those visiting only in peak periods pay for the ability to obtain sufficient water.

2 **An 11-point escalating block-rate tariff.** The more water you use, the more you pay per unit. Basic water is far more affordable.

3 **Information billing.** Monthly assessments to show water users how much they have used over the past 13 months.

4 **Intensive communication.** Newsletters, newspaper articles, ratepayer meetings, water conservation tips, hotline for leaks.

5 **Schools resource audits.** Pupils examine their use of water at school and at home, and find ways to reduce these levels.

6 **The Hermanus Working for Water Project.** Labour-intensive clearing of water-consumptive invading plants.

7 **Retrofitting project.** Installing water-saving devices (e.g., dual-flush toilets) into all dwellings and fixing leaks.

8 **Water-wise gardening.** Demonstration gardens, promoting water-wise gardening in nurseries, pertinent information.

9 **Water-wise food production.** Promoting sustainable food gardens by the poor and helping to ensure their access to this resource.

10 **National water by-laws.** Regulations designed to reduce water wastage (e.g., banning automatic-flushing urinals).

11 **Water loss management.** Reduction of unaccounted-for water (e.g. fixing leaks, detecting unpaid use of water).

12 **Security meter project.** On-line pre-payment meter giving users control (e.g., information, security, e-mail).'[61]

Other Benefits of Water Conservation Programmes

Water conservation programmes can also be structured to benefit the water cycle and the freshwater ecosystems that support it by providing any of the following benefits. Conservation programmes can help maintain the health of aquatic ecosystems by postponing or eliminating the need for new dams and diversions, thereby protecting the habitat value of streams that would otherwise be lost. These programmes can also assist in restoring the natural values and functions of wetlands and estuaries: by reducing our need to withdraw and redistribute water from natural systems, water conservation can reduce negative impacts on both the source and the receiving ecosystems.[62]

Conservation programmes can help to protect groundwater supplies from excessive depletion and contamination. By reducing the amount of water withdrawn from aquifers, they can avoid the negative effects of over-withdrawal, including saline intrusion into groundwater and land subsidence.

Conservation programmes can also increase the quality of runoff and waste-water discharges. In rural areas they can reduce the total amount of polluted agricultural runoff that enters freshwater ecosystems. Programmes directed at indoor water use can significantly reduce the amount of flows discharged into receiving ecosystems and water treatment plants. Reductions in quantities of wastewater received by ecosystems and sewage treatment plants increase the capacity of both to remove water pollutants.

Basic Process for Developing Water Conservation Programmes

The process of developing a water conservation plan for an urban area might involve the following steps.

Specifying conservation planning goals: As water conservation programmes can be conceptualized from a number of different perspectives, it is important to involve all relevant parties in the selection of goals.

Developing a water system profile: An inventory of existing resources and conditions helps systems to assess their present circumstances and to design strategies to meet emerging needs.

Preparing a demand forecast: Forecasts can be based on simple projections of population expansion, or complex models of water use.

Identifying and evaluating conservation measures: Wide selections of specific conservation measures exist, including both supply-side and demand-side management techniques. They range from simple education tools to advanced water-efficient technologies.

Designing an implementation strategy: Managers should make note of any specific factors or contingencies that might affect or prevent the implementation of selected measures. A plan for monitoring and evaluation should address data collection, modelling and other issues that will be important in tracking the effects of water conservation on demand over time.[63]

Water conservation practices for urban areas include a wide range of tools applied at several scales and targeted at a variety of audiences: auditing and incentive programmes for residential areas and individual homes; regulatory and retrofitting programmes for commercial, industrial and institutional users; and information and education programmes for a variety of water users.[64]

Examples of water conservation practices for urban areas include universal metering, water accounting and loss control and pricing. Water supply administrators can also employ water-use audits; provide retrofit kits (for instance, low-flow showerheads and toilet blocks); make use of pressure management; promote landscape water-use efficiency; and introduce water-use standards and regulations for times of drought or other water-supply emergencies.[65] An expanding catalogue of technologies is available to cut water use in households (see Table 4.3).

Table 4.3 Examples of Water-saving Fixtures for Households

Country	Technology	How introduced	Impacts on consumption
US (California)	Ultra Low-Flow Toilets (ULFT)	1980 and 1992 State Plumbing Codes mandating efficiency standards for new toilets. Some water supply agencies offer rebates on bills to users who install ULFT.	Conventional 21 litres per flush. 1980 code toilets 13 litres per flush. 1992 code toilets 6 litres per flush. Savings of about 20,000 litres per household per year.
	Low-flow showers	1980 State Plumbing Codes mandating efficiency standards for new showers	Pre-code flow rates 17 litres per minute. Post-code flow rates 10 litres per minute. Savings of about 20,000 litres per household per year.
UK	Hand basin spray taps	Commercial product	Standard tap 8 litres per minute. Spray tap 2 litres per minute.
India	Two-pit pour flush toilet	Community-based organizations	Conventional toilet 10 litres per flush. Two-pit pour toilet 2 litres per flush. 10 million people in India now use these.
World-wide	Waterless urinal	Commercial product. Main markets so far in the Philippines and the UK	Normal urinal 8 litres per flush. Waterless urinal 0 litres per flush.

From: Sutherland, D.C. & C.R. Fenn, 2000. *Assessment of Water Supply Options. World Commission on Dams Thematic Review Options Assessment IV.3.* World Commission on Dams, Cape Town, South Africa. p. 27.

Pollution Prevention

'Ecological systems are our best models of sustainable systems. There is no pollution in mature ecosystems because all wastes and by-products are either recycled and used somewhere in the system, or are fully dissipated. Pollution is defined as material or energy that is a by-product of the activity of one part of a system that has an unintentional impact on another part of the same system.

'This implies that a characteristic of sustainable economic systems should be a similar "closing the cycle" by finding productive uses for, and recycling, currently discarded pollution. This is as opposed to simply storing it, diluting it, or changing its state and allowing it to disrupt other existing ecosystems and economic systems that cannot effectively use it. Those things that have no possible productive uses should not be produced at all.'[66]

Pollution prevention programmes focus on preventing, or reducing, the generation and release of pollutants at the source. Pollution prevention strategies often take a 'life-cycle' approach, examining every step in the production process for opportunities to increase efficiency and reduce waste and environmental impact. In an ideal world, prevention would replace treatment or mere disposal as the dominant practice for addressing water and other pollution problems. Waste streams that cannot be reduced or eliminated through prevention alone can be recycled, treated or disposed of.[67]

Preventing the production of pollutants is potentially the most effective method for reducing risks to human health and the environment from exposure to pollutants for several reasons. It is the surest way, for example, to avoid the inadvertent transfer of pollutants across media that may occur with end-of-pipe control approaches. Prevention strategies also eliminate the risks that are inherent in any release of pollutants into the environment and protect natural resources for future generations by avoiding excessive levels of wastes and residues and by minimizing the depletion of resources.

Pollution prevention is also potentially the most cost-effective method of environmental protection because it reduces raw material and energy losses, the need for end-of-the-pipe treatment and disposal technologies, and the long-term potential liabilities associated with releases into the environment.[68] This is particularly true if prevention is compared with 'end-of-pipe,' or treatment approaches.[69]

Pollution prevention strategies aimed at reducing the effects of pollution in freshwater environments are generally more information-intensive than end-of-pipe approaches. The former must be based on a holistic analysis of the entire life cycle of the factory, farm, municipal plant or household where the strategy will be implemented. This means not only analysing production processes for individual outputs, but also examining the interactions of these processes with each other and with the external environment. The design of a pollution prevention strategy is based on an investigation of production and waste streams associated with the operation of the facility. This investigation should identify opportunities to reduce the use of waste-producing inputs by either reducing the total quantity of the input used in the process or by substituting an alternative to that particular input that produces less waste.

'The petroleum-based solvents used to clean ink from press components in the lithographic printing process generally consist of 100 percent volatile organic compounds (VOCs), which are then released into the waste stream. Deluxe Corporation of St Paul, Minnesota, invented a new ink that is based on vegetable oil. It matches, or exceeds, conventional inks in press and printing performance. Most importantly though, the ink includes a solubility conversion mechanism that enables it to be cleaned with a simple, VOC-free water solution.'[70]

Environmental Monitoring and the Use of Bioindicators

The processes of identifying the toxic effects of artificial substances and isolating these effects from the effects of other factors in a laboratory are often long and arduous. Historically pollution control programmes in the US have been based on the measured increase in the incidence of a specific endpoint or ailment, cancer for example, in animals exposed to a pollutant compared to an unexposed, control population. This *in vitro* approach to developing pollution standards avoids most environmental factors that could lead to false-positive results and is therefore indispensable in identifying causes of ecosystem impairment. On its own, however, it misses a wide range of interactions between chemicals and components of the environment into which they are released.[71]

For example, chemicals can have cumulative and synergistic effects on biological systems. A series of different chemicals can interact in ways that are not predictable based on laboratory studies of each individual chemical. In addition, the 'endpoints' that represent significant results in the laboratory (cancer rates, mortality, reproduction success, etcetera) may not be the 'endpoints' that are evident in the natural environment (teratogenic effects such as deformities in offspring, for example). Finally, the timing of exposure is more important in terms of biological impact than is the quantity of contaminant to which the organism or ecosystem is exposed. Animals exposed to very minute quantities of endocrine-disrupting chemicals during very sensitive portions of their life histories – in the womb, in puberty or in pregnancy, for example – can suffer the effects of these contaminants or pass them on to their offspring. On the other hand, individuals exposed to relatively large quantities of these substances during less sensitive parts of their lives may never experience any measurable result.

The Great Lakes of the midwestern United States provided a turning point in the history of pollution control by focusing attention on pollutant effects within the environment rather than through the lens of a microscope. Discoveries of birth deformities and reproductive impairments in top predators (such as bald eagles and herring gulls) led to the discovery that hydrophobic chemicals were concentrating up the food chain and triggering teratogenic effects.

Information gathered from the environment makes a good supplement to laboratory work in assessing the health of freshwater ecosystems and in identifying problems. According to the US Environmental Protection Agency, surveys of living aquatic communities (biosurveys) provide the following advantages. First, biological communities reflect overall ecological integrity, including physical and biological integrity. Second, biological communities integrate the effects of different pollutants and thus provide a holistic measure of their aggregate impact. Biological communities also integrate stresses over time and provide an ecological measure of fluctuating environmental conditions. Assessing the integrated response of biological communities to highly variable pollutant inputs offers a particularly useful approach for monitoring non-point-source pollution impacts and the effectiveness of prescribed solutions. Third, routine monitoring of biological communities can be relatively inexpensive, particularly when compared to the cost of assessing toxic pollutants, either chemically or with toxicity tests. Fourth, the status of biological communities is of direct interest to the public as a measure of a pollution-free environment, while reductions in chemical pollutant loadings are not as readily understood or appreciated by the public as positive environmental results. Fifth, where water quality standards do not exist, biological communities may provide the only practical means of evaluation.[72]

Above all, incorporating biological assessments can broaden the focus, and thus the effectiveness, of a water quality programme. Routine monitoring of sources and ambient water quality for compliance purposes is important, but what matters in the long run is whether the overall quality of the aquatic environment is adequate to sustain human uses and ecosystem functions. This topic is covered in more detail in Chapter 8.

Restoring Landscape Functions

Throughout the world, there is a growing recognition of the importance of landscape restoration in preventing further depletion of water supplies, increasing the sustainability of water withdrawals, and providing a potential surplus to serve the needs of increasing human populations. Communities may approach the restoration of hydrological functions in a variety of ways, depending on the root cause of the water cycle disruption.

For example, the problem may start high up in the watershed where the removal of vegetation and subsequent soil erosion have decreased the ability of the landscape to absorb water, leading to increased surface runoff and flooding during rainstorms and drought during the dry season. In such instances, the cultivation of perennial vegetation cover on the uplands may be the appropriate solution to the water supply problem.

River channelization may disrupt the interaction between a river channel and adjacent aquifers by lowering the bed of the river so that it no longer replenishes the aquifer but the aquifer instead drains into the channelized river, thus reducing the water storage capacity of the system.[73] When channelization is the root cause of water supply shortages, the most practical solution is often the restoration of the natural contours of the river.

'The pre-drainage wetlands of southern Florida covered an area estimated at approximately 3.6 million hectares. This region was a complex system of hydrologically interrelated landscapes, including expansive areas of sawgrass sloughs, wet prairies, cypress swamps, mangrove swamps, and coastal lagoons and bays.

'As a result of land use and water management practices during the past 100 years in the Everglades region of southern Florida, the defining characteristics of the regional wetlands, and thus the hydrology of the entire system, have been severely altered. The federal and state governments constructed an extensive system of drainage channels primarily to create arable land. Rather than storing wet-weather flows in the extensive wetland system, the drained system dumped excess water to the estuaries. The lack of water storage availability in the peninsula caused lower dry-season flows and a reduction in hydraulic head for the groundwater supply in South-east Florida (the Miami metropolitan area), which both reduces water availability and permits saltwater intrusion into the aquifer.'[74]

Meanwhile, the demand for urban water in South-east Florida is expected to double by 2050 as the region's population continues to increase.

'In order to restore the hydrology and ecology of the region and protect the water supply, the federal and state governments have embarked on a restoration programme that is projected to cost US$7 billion. The restoration project will expand the region's storage capacity by 1.7 billion gallons (6.4 billion litres) per day, 20 percent of which will be used to enhance urban and agricultural supplies and reduce shortages. The increased storage will improve recharge to the Biscayne Aquifer, the region's primary source of drinking water.'[75]

Groundwater overabstraction may also be the root cause of a water supply shortage, either because the water table drops below a level that is practically accessible or because the reduction of hydraulic pressure, or 'head,' allows saltwater to intrude and contaminate freshwater supplies. In such instances, the most practical solution is often artificial recharge of the aquifer. Artificial recharge can be accomplished either through direct surface recharge, which typically uses infiltration basins to increase the natural rate of percolation of water into the aquifer, or through direct subsurface recharge, which uses recharge or injection wells to access deeper aquifers. The former method is less expensive but more land intensive than the latter. Direct surface recharge has the potential advantage of creating additional environmental benefits, such as increasing wildlife habitat and vegetative water purification services within the infiltration basins. The process of filtering water through the surface soil strata can also remove pollutants from the source water.

The countries that have applied groundwater recharge technologies on the largest scale are the Netherlands, the US, Germany, Israel, China and India.[76]

Using Locally Appropriate Technologies

'Put yourself in the position of a future archaeologist sifting through the material remains of our culture some hundreds of years from now. What will he make of the curiously shaped ceramic bowl in each house, hooked up through miles of pipe to a central factory of tanks, stirrers, cookers and ponds, emptying into a river, lake or ocean?

'"By early in the twentieth century urban earthlings had devised a highly ingenious food production system whereby algae were cultivated in large centralized farms and piped directly into a food receptacle in each home."'[77]

Options are abundant for providing water supply and sanitation services to the world's communities without investing in expensive and environmentally damaging infrastructure. Many households receive improved services without being connected to a multiple-user system at all. Supply solutions such as public standpipes, boreholes, protected dug wells, protected springs and rainwater collection technologies, and disposal methods such as septic systems, pour-flush latrines, simple pit latrines, and improved, ventilated latrines are often less expensive than system connections and more readily available to rural populations.[78] A few examples of promising technologies are presented below, but the list is by no means exhaustive.

Alternative Water Supply Systems
Even if governments change their policies to provide incentives for the conservation and efficient management of water, population growth will continue to place growing pressure on existing domestic water supplies. Expanding supplies in ways that protect the water cycle requires site-specific solutions that are affordable to construct, operate and maintain, and that allow natural ecosystems to continue to function.

Small-scale water harvesting systems, which sequester water from rain, fog, dew and snow, can provide a reliable source of water to individual communities. Rain can be collected from a number of surfaces such as rooftops, parking lots and roads that would otherwise prevent infiltration of water into aquifers and increase quantities of unusable runoff. The water thus sequestered is stored in cisterns or other containers until it is needed.

Rainwater harvesting systems exist in virtually all corners of the globe. People living on small islands in the Caribbean, for example, have relied on rooftop catchments and cistern storage systems for more than three centuries. More than half a million people in the Caribbean islands are still partially dependent on such supplies.[79] In fact, small-island developing states throughout the world, including the Maldives, Micronesia and the Marshall Islands, employ rainwater harvesting techniques.[80] Large areas of some countries in Central and South America, including Honduras, Brazil and Paraguay, use rainwater harvesting as an important source of domestic water supplies, especially in urban areas.[81] Rural areas throughout East and Central Europe rely on rainwater harvesting systems.[82] Rainwater also is harvested extensively in India.[83]

'The construction of over 10 million 1–2 cubic metre ferro-cement jars for rainwater storage in Thailand between 1985 and 1991 has demonstrated the potential and appropriateness of rainwater catchment systems as a primary rural water supply technology. The unprecedented success of the programme was a result of several favourable factors all encouraging the rapid spread of the technology. These include the following:

- relatively high rainfall, large impervious roofs at most households, low cement and labour prices;
- the availability of low-cost, skilled rural labour;
- the ongoing rapid rural development;
- the development of a durable and affordable tank design;
- the combination of a top down and bottom up approach;
- the combined public and private sector involvement;
- a willingness to adapt, modify and improve both the design and implementation strategies.

'Although national, regional and local governments sponsored the programme through rural job creation incentives to the tune of $64 million and some financial support was provided by both foreign and local donors, the recipients themselves contributed most of the cost estimated between $250–350 million. The price of 1.8 cubic meter jars sold by entrepreneurs fell to just $20, making outright purchase affordable to most people and making the use of revolving funds unnecessary. By the early 1990s, most households in North-east Thailand, a region previously dogged by inadequate rural water supplies, had year-round access to clean water.'[84]

Fog is composed of much smaller water droplets than rain. Because of their small size, fog droplets descend to the ground much more slowly than raindrops and are subject to influence by even very light winds. Fog therefore travels horizontally and can be trapped by vertical surfaces. A fog harvester is often built of a rectangular piece of polypropylene mesh suspended above the ground on vertical posts, perpendicular to the prevailing flow of fog and clouds. Drops of water collect on the mesh, coalesce, and flow by gravity along a plastic conduit at the bottom of the mesh to a container for storage, treatment (if needed), and distribution.

'The far north of Chile, between the cities of Arica (latitude 18 degrees South) and La Serena (latitude 29 degrees South), is classified as an arid or semi-arid zone depending on the rainfall. The Antofogasta (latitude 23 degrees South), on the eastern edge of the Pacific Anticline, is a desert climate with virtually no rainfall. In these areas, natural watercourses are few and highly seasonal. Hence, alternative sources of freshwater are required.

'Special atmospheric conditions occur along the arid coast of Chile and Southern Peru, where clouds settling on the Andean slops produce what is know locally as camanchacas (thick fog). The clouds that touch the land surface can be 'milked' or 'harvested' to obtain water....'[85]

Table 4.4 Fog Water Production at Three Sites

Country	Average water production (litres/m²/day)	Length of fog season (days/year)	Annual water production (litres/m²/year)
Chile	3	365	1,095
Peru	9	210	1,890
Oman	30	75	2,250

From: Schenmenauer, R.S. & P. Cereceda, 1994. 'Fog Collection's Role in Water Planning for Developing Countries.' *Natural Resources Forum*, 18: 91–100. United Nations, New York.

Existing systems have demonstrated that fog harvesters can produce substantial quantities of water (see Table 4.4) at costs well below other alternatives for water supply systems in remote areas. Researchers have identified more than 20 countries on 6 continents where research supports the idea that fog harvesters could produce a reliable, high-quality water supply for local communities. These include Angola, Ascension Island, the Canary Islands, the Cape Verde Islands, Kenya, Namibia, South Africa and the Sudan. Evaluation programmes would also be appropriate for parts of Eritrea, Ethiopia, Madagascar, Morocco, Somalia, Tanzania and others.[86]

Dew harvesting requires a horizontal surface to allow the dewdrops to settle. Such systems commonly employ a gravel layer because gravel cools in the evening and remains cool in early morning, when water vapour condenses onto the gravel, creating droplets that pass between the gravel to the soil surface.[87]

Snow is harvested in heavily compacted pits ranging from six to eight metres in diameter and up to ten metres in depth. Communities collect the snow and dump it into the pit to a depth of two or three metres. They then cover the compacted snow with earth to insulate it, and place a bamboo pipe about 50 centimetres above the base of the pit to provide an outlet for the melting snow. The water trickles through the pipe into a butt placed beneath the outlet. Such systems are commonly used in the Takhar province of Afghanistan and can provide drinking water for up to 14 families.[88] Snow harvesting is also common in rural areas of East and Central Europe.[89]

Alternative Sanitation Systems

Circularity is one of the key principles of sustainability. If a system is to be sustainable, matter and energy removed from the system cannot exceed matter and energy put into the system. To maximize the benefits or services derived from the system, inputs must remain in service until they are degraded to the point where they are no longer usable and at a rate which allows for replacement on a continuing basis. While these concepts seem obvious to many people, a virtual taboo continues to apply to their application in the management of many natural resources, including human waste.

'In Sweden, only about 20 percent of the phosphorus and less than 5 percent of the nitrogen that leave agriculture as plant and animal products are returned to agriculture. Most of the nutrients are found in sewage where the major part is discharged to receiving waters or found in sewage sludge which is deposited in landfills or incinerated. The reason being that sewage treatment plants often have difficulties in retaining the sludge unpolluted, especially in large cities. Organic persistent chemicals and metals from households, industry and stormwater contribute to the contamination of sludge and reduce its quality and the possibilities for use as agricultural fertilisers. Wastewater must be collected and treated in order to promote human health but in a sustainable society the nutrients originated from agriculture should be returned.'[90]

Human excreta contain large quantities of nutrients, water, organic matter and pathogens. With the obvious exception of pathogens, all of these components have potential beneficial uses. Nitrogen and phosphorus from human waste can be used to fertilize crops, for example, replacing commercial fertilizers.[91] The organic matter found in faeces is also useful in building soil structure.

For more than one third of a century, composting toilets have been serving the function of breaking down pathogens and producing biologically useful material. Composting toilets are well-ventilated containers that provide the optimum environment for unsaturated, but moist, human excreta for biological and physical decomposition under sanitary and controlled aerobic conditions. The composting process transforms organic matter into an oxified, humus-like end-product using naturally occurring bacteria and fungi. Large units may require a space the size of a basement to install, but others are designed as self-contained appliances that need no more than a small space on a bathroom floor.[92] In dense settlement areas in hot climates, the best systems for wastewater treatment are those involving a combination of aerobic and anaerobic systems and dry deposition of solids – low-energy, low-technology systems that also profit from high ambient temperatures.[93]

A composting toilet system contains and processes excrement, toilet paper, carbon additives and sometimes food waste. Unlike septic systems, composting toilets rely on unsaturated conditions that allow naturally occurring aerobic bacteria to break down waste in a process similar to that of a yard waste composter. A properly sized and maintained composting toilet can reduce waste to between 10 and 30 percent of its original volume.[94]

Although composting toilets reduce human exposure to pathogens, communities can make additional progress in this regard by separating faecal material from urine. Most pathogens abide in faecal material and most nutrients are found in urine. Pathogens need nutrients and water to survive and reproduce. It is necessary to keep faeces and urine separated if human waste is to be used safely.[95] It is also important to keep human wastes free of contaminants from other sources, including not only household chemicals but the contaminated waste streams that industrial wastewater and stormwater often add to modern sewage treatment systems.

'The emerging recycling lesson is this: the more that re-use of human waste relies on conventional disposal technologies, the less likely that such re-use will be benign recycling. This is bad news for cities with heavy investments in disposal systems; they may require extensive adjustments to achieve environmentally benign recycling. It is good news, however, for cities that have not yet committed to a particular system of sanitation, and for cities that face extensive rehabilitation of old systems. These later-developing cities have a chance to leapfrog ahead to alternative technologies designed for recycling – and to save scarce investment funds in the process.'[96]

One set of technologies that permits the safe collection of human wastes, known as ecological or dry sanitation systems, is already in use in many parts of the world. These systems collect faeces and urine in separate compartments of toilets, composting the faeces so that it is useful as a soil additive. These toilets look very much like standard flush models, without a water tank (because most models use no water), and can hold up to several years' worth of excreta. Some maintenance is required, including periodic additions of bulking agents, such as popcorn, to create the air pockets needed to support microbes, and periodic inspections of the compost itself.[97]

There are two additional benefits to the water cycle of ecological sanitation systems. First, these systems conserve water, since it is unnecessary to use water to flush and transport human waste away from households, and the water content of excreta is put to use. Second, ecological sanitation systems can reduce discharges of pollutants into waterways, since human waste is no longer discharged directly into the environment and the systems eliminate the possibility of contaminating sewage effluent with industrial discharges and stormwater runoff.

'"Ecological sanitation" practices are now being applied in Asia, Africa, Latin America and Europe. In El Salvador, a peri-urban community discovered that diversion of urine eliminated flies and smells, and ecosanitation units have been installed in homes. In Mexico, people are experimenting with urine in urban agriculture as well as for growing traditional foods. In Kenya and Zimbabwe, 'arbor loos' are being developed to plant trees for household use. In the Pacific, livelihoods were threatened by dumping into coastal waters. 'Ecological sanitation' solutions were implemented to reduce contamination and restore fish populations. In Sweden, eco-communities are selling urine to farmers to apply to cropland.'[98]

Alternative Sewage and Wastewater Treatment Systems

Conventional sewage treatment plants are extremely consumptive of energy and chemicals, and may generate as many environmental problems as they solve. Wastewater treatment technology is getting more advanced. It is possible to reach stringent effluent standards for BOD_5 (biological oxygen demand, or the amount of oxygen consumed in the process of breaking down biological materials present in water), bacteria, phosphorus, and nitrogen. However, the upgrading of treatment plants to achieve a higher removal requires an input of chemicals such as aluminium or ferrous salts, while BOD_5 and nitrogen removal are energy-intensive. Higher treatment standards will increase the amount of resources that must be put into the treatment, and will generate environmental effects in other parts of an expanded system.[99]

Natural biological treatment systems provide additional alternatives to conventional sewage treatment plants. Such systems are generally less expensive and less sophisticated to operate and maintain than conventional treatment plants, if also more land-intensive – characteristics that render them suitable for use in many developing countries, where land is relatively more plentiful than capital.

Natural systems are often better at removing pathogens than are conventional systems. With the exception of disinfection – a high level of treatment that is unaffordable in many developing countries – conventional sewage treatment methods do not reduce pathogens sufficiently to render sewage effluent safe for re-use in applications such as agriculture. For example, a conventional sewage treatment plant can reduce the number of faecal coliform bacteria in a millilitre of water from one hundred million to one million.[100] While a 99 percent reduction may seem impressive, it is 100,000 times the World Health Organization's recommended faecal coliform maximum level of 1,000/100 millilitres (10 per millilitre) for irrigation of row crops likely to be eaten raw, public parks, and landscape irrigation with public access. In contrast, biological systems can remove more pathogens reliably and continuously if properly designed and not overloaded.[101] Natural systems benefit from containing a variety of species, including bacteria, invertebrates, detritavores, algae and plants. This polyculture renders natural systems more stable and effective than conventional systems.[102]

Oxidation ponds are shallow, artificial ponds or lagoons that purify sewage through the natural action of sun, wind, bacteria, algae, snails and other detritavores feeding on decomposing wastes. Sludge settles to the bottom where it decomposes anaerobically. Sewage must remain in residence for about a month to provide the equivalent of secondary treatment.[103]

The Solar Aquacell System consists of rectangular ponds (aquacells) covered with greenhouses to retain heat; artificial habitats to increase the biologically active surface area in ponds; channels to control water flow; aeration systems; and sand filtration. As raw sewage flows through the aquacells, water hyacinths and aquatic animals absorb nutrients and toxins. Water hyacinths from the first cell, which receives the most concentrated doses of toxins, are used for fuel in a methane digester that provides heat and power for the operation. After initial treatment in the first cell, the wastewater enters cells that are occupied by fish and giant freshwater prawns.[104]

A system called the 'neighbourhood sewage wall' has also been designed to counter the disadvantages of conventional sewage treatment plants. A sewage wall would run the length of a city block, separating the street from the sidewalk. Wide, low walls would slope toward the sidewalk and contain four glass-covered terraces. Each terrace would contain the plants and bacteria best suited for the various stages of sewage treatment. Wastewater from the houses lining the street would be filtered progressively through the terraces until it is sufficiently purified for use in gardens or other applications. The plants could be harvested and used for compost.[105] While as of 1998 these systems had yet to be put into operation, the design itself points the way towards aesthetically pleasing treatment methods that produce useful outputs because they keep human wastes separated from toxic contaminants common in discharges of household chemicals, industrial effluents, and stormwater runoff.

Wastewater Recycling and Re-use

Greywater, which includes all dirty water from a household except water from a toilet, can be safely used for many purposes ranging from flushing toilets to watering gardens. Although greywater is free of urine faecal material, it may contain grease, suspended solids, phosphorus compounds, large quantities of organic material in the form of food particles, and other residues. Untreated, greywater can be used to irrigate orchards, vineyards, and seed, fibre and pasture fodder crops. Greywater treated with simple sand filters can also be used for irrigating non-edible garden plants or applied to the soil around plants of which only the top part is eaten (for example, corn or tomatoes).[106] Treatment for other uses generally requires a combination of settling, filtering, and disinfection.[107]

Sewage water that has passed through a treatment facility can also be re-used. Rather than simply discharging treated wastewater into surface water systems, water managers around the world are increasingly using it in a wide range of applications. These include industrial applications, agriculture, groundwater recharge, landscape maintenance (including, for example, watering golf courses, cemeteries, parks and campuses), ecosystem restoration, non-potable household uses (such as flushing toilets and washing cars), and even potable water supplies. Of course, the purity of the treated water determines its acceptability for various uses.

'Wastewater is used in Japan for a variety of purposes. Over 40 percent goes to meet industrial water needs, and over 30 percent is used to supplement natural flows in rivers and streams.' [108]

'In Israel, treated wastewater has been used for irrigating a variety of field crops, orchards, and edible vegetables. Some analysts expect that because of Israel's severe water constraints, agricultural water demands there will increasingly be supplied solely from wastewater. In Portugal, the volume of treated wastewater discharged in 2000 is estimated to be enough to cover about 10 percent of irrigation water needs in a dry year.... In Tunisia, about 35 million m³/year of reclaimed water go to irrigation. Wastewater from Tunis has been used since the 1960s to irrigate citrus and olive orchards near the city. More recently, wastewater re-use has been expanded in Tunisia to other commercial and industrial crops, golf courses, and hotel gardens.' [109]

'One example of a company recapturing its own wastewater for re-use in its process is the Borden food company in Costa Rica. Borden uses water for cooling, cleaning and moving food in the production process. The wastewater resulting from many of these processes is clean enough to be re-used. The Borden Company invested $5,000 to purchase and install equipment to capture wastewater from the system and re-use it for cooling processes and building cleaning activities. The company was able to contain, immobilize, or destroy pathogens, thereby reducing the risk of human infection.' [110]

CONCLUSION

As with most of the water subsectors that are stricken with anxiety over the looming global water crisis, the alternative approaches that the world needs to provide water and sanitation services to its people while maintaining the water cycle are with us already. And, as with many water-related economic sectors, the developing world is strategically poised to take advantage of new and resurrected sustainable technologies. The key to successfully providing all of the world's people with affordable water supply and sanitation options is to look at a wide range of alternatives and determine which alternatives work best in which settings.

In much of the developed world, for example, there exist ample opportunities to increase water-use efficiency by repairing antiquated water supply and sewer systems, installing water-efficient plumbing fixtures, and re-using greywater for purposes such as flushing toilets and washing cars. The developing world, in contrast, suffers more from want than from waste. There is virtually no compelling reason for these populations to follow the infrastructure- and energy-intensive models of their industrialized neighbours, however. It is possible for communities in developing countries to adopt lower-cost, lower-maintenance and more efficient technologies while achieving an equivalent or better quality of service.[111]

The next two chapters will continue to reflect these themes, respectively discussing the flood damage reduction and commercial navigation subsectors.

Notes

1 Water Supply and Sanitation Collaborative Council, 2000. *Vision 21: A Shared Vision for Hygiene, Sanitation & Water Supply and a Framework for Action.* Geneva. p. 29.
2 World Health Organization and United Nations Children's Fund, 2000. *Global Water Supply and Sanitation Assessment.* p. 1.
3 Water Supply and Sanitation Collaborative Council, 2000. *Vision 21.* p. 1.
4 World Health Organization and United Nations Children's Fund, 2000. *Global Water Supply and Sanitation Assessment.* p. 1.
5 Water Supply and Sanitation Collaborative Council, 2000. *Vision 21.* p. 49.
6 James, K., S.L. Campbell & C.E. Godlove, 2002. *Watergy: Taking Advantage of Untapped Energy Efficiency. Opportunities in Municipal Water Systems.* Alliance to Save Energy, Washington. p. 1.
7 Saghir, J., M. Schiffler & M. Woldu, 2000. *Urban Water and Sanitation in the Middle East and North Africa Region: The Way Forward.* The World Bank Middle East and North Africa Region Infrastructure Development Group, Washington. p. 7.
8 Costantini, G. & A. Declich, 1996. *Operation, Maintenance and Management of Urban Water Supply and Sanitation Systems.* CERFE Group, Rome. p. 9.
9 World Health Organization and United Nations Childrens Fund, 2000. *Global Water Supply and Sanitation Assessment.* p. 25.
10 Saghir, J., M. Schiffler & M. Woldu. 2000. *Urban Water and Sanitation.* p. 7.
11 Rothert, S. & P. Macy, undated. 'The Potential of Water Conservation and Demand Management in Southern Africa: An Untapped River.' Submission to the World Commission on Dams. p. 17.
12 Richards, A., 2001. 'Coping with Water Scarcity: The Governance Challenge.' CGIRS Working Paper Series WP No. 01–4. Center For Global International and Regional Studies, University of California, Santa Cruz. p. 24.
13 Falkenmark, M. & G. Lindh, 1993. 'Water and Economic Development.' In P.H. Gleick (ed.), *Water in Crisis: A Guide to the World's Freshwater Resources.* Oxford University Press, New York. p. 86.
14 Saghir, J., M. Schiffler & M. Woldu, 2000. *Urban Water and Sanitation.* p. 4.
15 World Bank, 1994. *Making Development Sustainable: The World Bank Group and the Environment.* Washington. 270 pp.
16 Richards, A., 2001. 'Coping with Water Scarcity'. p. 23.
17 Lundin, M., S. Molander & G.M. Morrison, 1997. 'Indications for the Development of Sustainable Water and Wastewater Systems.' Paper presented at Sustainable Development Research Conference, Manchester. p. 2.
18 Gardner, G., 1998. 'Human Waste: Fertile Ground or Toxic Legacy?' *Worldwatch,* January/February. p. 34.
19 Nigam, A., B. Gujja, J. Bandyopadhyay & R. Talbot, 1998. *Freshwater for India's Children and Nature.* United Nations Children's Fund and World Wide Fund for Nature, New Delhi. pp. 41–2.
20 Wenger, D., 2002. *A Report on Evaporation and Groundwater Seepage.* Glen Canyon Institute, Flagstaff, Arizona.

21 Murakami, M. 1995. *Managing Water for Peace in the Middle East: Alternative Strategies.* United Nations University Press. Tokyo, New York & Paris.

22 Neal, B., P. Erlanger, R. Evans, A. Kollmorgen, J. Ball, M, Shirley & L. Donnelly, 2001. *Inland Waters. Australia State of the Environment.* CSIRO Publishing, Collingwood, Victoria. p. 5.

23 Sutherland, D.C. & C.R. Fenn, 2000. 'Assessment of Water Supply Options.' World Commission on Dams Thematic Review Options Assessment IV. 3. World Commission on Dams, Cape Town, South Africa. p. 20.

24 UN Conference on Desertification, Nairobi, 1997.

25 United Nations Environment Programme, 1999. 'The State of the Environment.' Chapter 2 in *UNEP Global Environment Outlook 2000.* Nairobi.

26 Smith, D., 2000. 'When Green Earth Turns into Sand.' *National Geographic News*, 19 December.

27 Mabbutt, J.A. 1984. 'A New Global Assessment of the Status and Trends of Desertification.' *Environmental Conservation*, 11 (2): 103–13.

28 United Nations Environment Programme, 1999. *UNEP Global Environment Outlook 2000.*

29 Smith, D., 2000. 'When Green Earth Turns into Sand.'

30 Zebidi, H., 1993. 'Effects of Desertification and Dessication on Ground and Surface Hydrologic Systems, Water Availability and Water Quality.' Paper presented at the United Nations Convention to Combat Desertification, Nairobi, 24–28 May.

31 United Nations Environment Programme, 1999. *UNEP Global Environment Outlook 2000.*

32 Zebidi, H., 1993. 'Effects of Desertification.'

33 Ibid.

34 Ibid.

35 D.S.G. Thomas & N.J. Middleton, 1994. *Desertification: Exploding the Myth.* John Wiley and Sons, Chichester, England. p. 116.

36 Chouhan, T.S., 1992. *Desertification in the World and its Control.* Scientific Publishers, Jodhpur, India. p. 9.

37 United Nations Environment Programme, 1999. *UNEP Global Environment Outlook 2000.*

38 Zebidi, H., 1993. 'Effects of Desertification.'

39 Harrison, P., 1992. *The Third Revolution: Environment, Population and a Sustainable World.* I.B. Tauris/Penguin Books, London.

40 A distinction is made here between the term 'pollutant,' which refers to substances added by humans or human activities which primarily alter the chemical composition of a water body, and the broader term 'pollution', which means the alteration, under human agency or pressure, of the chemical, physical, biological and radiological integrity of water. According to the National Research Council, the US Clean Water Act includes pollutants as well as other stressors such as habitat destruction, hydrological modifications, etcetera under the broader heading of pollution (National Research Council 2001. *Assessing the TMDL Approach to Water Pollution Reduction.* Committee to Assess the Scientific Basis of the Total Maximum Daily Load Approach to Water Pollution Reduction. Water Science and Technology Board, Division of Earth and Life Sciences. National Academy Press, Washington. p. 14).

41 Khanna, G. & F. Sheng, unpublished. 'Towards Full-cost Pricing of Water.' Paper prepared for the Second World Water Forum and Ministerial Conference. World Wide Fund for Nature. 13 pp.

42 Harrison, P., 1992. *The Third Revolution.*

43 World Bank, 1993. *Water Resources Management: A World Bank Policy Paper.* Washington. p. 93.

44 Nash, L. 'Water Quality and Health.' In P.H. Gleick (ed.), *Water in Crisis.* p. 35.

45 Rolpin, D.W., E.T. Furloy, M.T. Meyer, E.M. Thurman, S.D. Zaugg, L.B. Barber & H.T. Burton, 2002. 'Pharmaceuticals, Hormones and Other Organic Wastewater Contaminants in U.S. Streams, 1999–2000: A National Reconnaissance.' *Environmental Science and Technology*, 36 (6): 1202–11. This study found that the majority of streams surveyed contained small amounts of commonly used chemicals, including, for example, caffeine, fire retardants, insect repellants and antimicrobial disinfectants. While few of the contaminants exceeded established water quality standards, no standards have been set for some of the substances identified. In addition, multiple contaminants were frequently identified from one sample station (median of 7 different substances and maximum of 38). Little is known about the potential interactive effects of such complex combinations of chemicals on human health and the environment.

46 United Nations Children's Fund and World Health Organization, 2000. *Global Water Supply and Sanitation Assessment: 2000 Report*. Geneva and New York. p. 19.

47 Lovins, H. & W. Link, 2001. *Insurmountable Opportunities – Steps and Barriers to Implementing Sustainable Development*. Rocky Mountain Institute, Vail, Colorado. pp. 220–1.

48 Harrison, P., 1992. *The Third Revolution*.

49 Hoffman, D., 1998. 'Radioactive Materials Threaten Mighty River.' *Washington Post*, 17 August 1998.

50 Samphat, P., 2000. 'Groundwater Shock.' *Worldwatch*, January/February. p. 15.

51 Ibid., p. 16.

52 Ibid., p. 15.

53 Ibid., p. 13.

54 World Bank, 1999. 'Identifying Opportunities to Address Malaria through Infrastructure Projects. Workshop report, 9–10 June.' Washington. 11 pp.

55 Horowitz, M.M. 1999. 'An Alternative for Managing Tropical Floodplain Rivers.' Basis Brief No. 1, December 1999. 8 pp.

56 Lovins, H. & W. Link, 2001. *Insurmountable Opportunities*. p. 216.

57 Sutherland, D.C. & C.R. Fenn, 2000. 'Assessment of Water Supply Options.' p. 27.

58 US Environmental Protection Agency, 1998. *Water Conservation Plan Guidelines*. EPA-832-D-98-001. Washington. p. 38.

59 German Advisory Council on Global Change, 1999. *World in Transition: Ways Towards Sustainable Management of Freshwater Resources*. Springer-Verlag, Berlin & Heidelberg. p. 296.

60 Blockland, M. & K. Schwartz, 2000. 'Privatization and Public–Private Partnerships in Water Supply in Developing Countries: Impact on Children and Nature. A Note on the Forthcoming UNICEF–WWF Study.' UNICEF, New York, and WWF, Gland, Switzerland. 7 pp.

61 Sutherland, D.C. & C.R. Fenn, 2000. 'Assessment of Water Supply Options.' pp. 18–19.

62 Osann, E.R. & J.E. Young, 1998. *Saving Water, Saving Dollars: Efficient Plumbing Products and the Protection of America's Waters*. Potomac Resources, Inc., Washington. pp. 13–14.

63 US Environmental Protection Agency, 1998. *Water Conservation Plan Guidelines*. p. 97.

64 California Urban Water Conservation Council, 1998. *Memorandum of Understanding Regarding Urban Water Conservation in California. Best Management Practices Summary Report, 1996–1997*. Sacramento.

65 US Environmental Protection Agency, 1998. *Water Conservation Plan Guidelines*.

66 Costanza, R., 1996. 'Designing Sustainable Ecological Economic Systems.' In Schulze, P.C. (ed.), *Engineering with Ecological Constraints*. National Academy Press, Washington. pp. 81–2.

67 US Environmental Protection Agency 1997. *Pollution Prevention 1997: A National Progress Report*. EPA 742-5-97-001. Office of Pollution Prevention, Washington.

68 Ibid.

69 World Bank, 1994. *Making Development Sustainable*.

70 U.S. Environmental Protection Agency 1997. *Pollution Prevention 1997*.

71 *In vitro* approaches to water quality monitoring also miss the physical and biological aspects covered by the term 'pollution.'

72 Plafkin, J.L., M.T. Narbour, K.D. Porter. S.K. Gross & R.M. Hughes, 1989. *Rapid Bioassessment Protocols for Use in Streams and Rivers: Benthic Invertebrates and Fish*. EPA 440/4-89/001. US Environmental Protection Agency, Washington.

73 Conversely, sedimentation of a river can raise the bed so that a river that was once fed by aquifer discharge becomes a source of water. This does not necessarily affect the availability of water supply, but can cause waterlogging and loss of productive crop land in areas adjacent to the river.

74 Adapted from Hunt, C.E., 2000. 'New Approaches to River Management in the United States.' In Smits, A.J.M., R.H. Nienhuis & R.S.E.W. Leuven (eds.), *New Approaches to River Management*. Backhuys Publishers, Leiden, The Netherlands. pp. 119–40.

75 Broward County Staff, 2000. 'A Rationale for Supporting the Comprehensive Everglades Restoration Plan (Central and South Florida Restudy).' Broward County Staff Report to the Water Advisory Board through the Technical Advisory Committee. p. 4.

76 Mogensen, U. (ed.), 1998. *Sourcebook of Alternative Technologies for Freshwater Augmentation in Small Island Developing States*. United Nations Environment Programme, Division of

Technology, Industry and Economics, International Environmental Technology Centre, Nairobi. No. 8b. Section 3.10.

77 Van der Ryn, S. 1995. *The Toilet Papers: Recycling Waste and Conserving Water.* Ecological Design Press, Sausalito, California. Introduction.

78 United Nations Children's Fund and World Health Organization, 2000. *Global Water Supply and Sanitation Assessment: 2000 Report.* p. 4.

79 United Nations Environment Programme, 1998. *Sourcebook of Alternative Technologies for Freshwater Augmentation in Latin America and the Caribbean.* Division of Technology, Industry and Economics, International Environmental Technology Centre, Nairobi. No. 8c. Section 1.1.

80 Mogensen, U. (ed.), 1998. *Sourcebook of Alternative Technologies.* Section 1.5.

81 United Nations Environment Programme, 1998. *Sourcebook of Alternative Technologies for Freshwater Augmentation in Latin America and the Caribbean.* No. 8d. Section 1.1.1. Nairobi.

82 Janikowski, R. (ed.), 1998. *Sourcebook of Alternative Technologies for Freshwater Augmentation in East and Central Europe.* United Nations Environment Programme, Division of Technology, Industry and Economics, International Environmental Technology Centre, Nairobi. No. 8b. Section 1.5.

83 United Nations Environment Programme, 1998. *Sourcebook of Alternative Technologies for Freshwater Augmentation in Some Countries in Asia.* Division of Technology, Industry and Economics, International Environmental Technology Centre, Nairobi. No. 8e.

84 Sutherland, D.C. & C.R. Fenn, 2000. 'Assessment of Water Supply Options.' p. 89.

85 United Nations Environment Programme, 1998. *Sourcebook of Alternative Technologies for Freshwater Augmentation in Latin America and the Caribbean.* Section 5.2.

86 Gleick, P.H., 2000. *The World's Water 2000–2001: The Biennial Report of Freshwater Resources.* Island Press, Washington. p. 175.

87 United Nations Environment Programme, 1998. *Sourcebook of Alternative Technologies for Freshwater Augmentation in Some Countries in Asia.* Section 3.11.

88 Ibid., Section 3.11.

89 Ibid., Section 1.5.

90 Lundin, M., S. Molander & G.M. Morrison, 1997. 'Indications.' pp. 2–3.

91 Ibid., p. 2. Lunden *et al.* point out that the Earth's supply of mineral phosphorus is limited (with projections of a shortage in about 150 years) and frequently contaminated with cadmium and that nitrogen, while abundant, requires significant quantities of energy to be processed into fertilizer.

92 US Environmental Protection Agency, 1999. *Water Efficiency Technology Fact Sheet: Composting Toilets.* EPA 832-F-99-066. Washington. p. 1.

93 German Advisory Council on Global Change, 1999. *World in Transition.* p. 201.

94 US Environmental Protection Agency, 1999. *Water Efficiency Technology Fact Sheet: Composting Toilets.* p. 1.

95 Water Supply and Sanitation Collaborative Council, 2000. *Vision 21.* p. 21.

96 Gardner, G., 1998. 'Human Waste.' pp. 32–3.

97 Ibid., p. 34.

98 Water Supply and Sanitation Collaborative Council, 2000. *Vision 21.* p. 21.

99 Lundin, M., S. Molander & G.M. Morrison, 1997. 'Indications.' p. 2.

100 Gardner, G., 1998. 'Human Waste.' p. 32.

101 Pescod, M.B., 1992. 'Wastewater Treatment and Use in Agriculture.' Food and Agriculture Organization of the United Nations. FAO Irrigation and Drainage Paper 47. Section 3.3.

102 Van der Ryn, S. 1995. *The Toilet Papers.* p. 104.

103 Ibid., pp. 103–4.

104 Ibid., pp. 107–8.

105 Gardner, G., 1998. 'Human Waste.' p. 33.

106 Van der Ryn, S. 1995. *The Toilet Papers.* p. 86.

107 Ibid., pp. 81–2.

108 Gleick, P.H., 2000. *The World's Water 2000–2001.* p. 141.

109 Ibid., p. 142.

110 James, K., S.L. Campbell & C.E. Godlove, 2002. *Watergy: Taking Advantage of Untapped Energy Efficiency.* p. 55.

111 The conservation-minded options discussed in this chapter for water supply and sanitation may provide superior service for their very simplicity. Fog and rainwater harvesters, for example, might provide chlorine-free drinking water. Composting toilets can generate fertilizer. Plant-based sewage treatment systems can provide vegetative material that might be used as animal feed or for energy production.

5 When It Rains, It Pours

Water Management for Flood Damage Reduction

'One central problem is that many of the accepted methods for coping with hazards have been based on the idea that people can use technology to control nature to make themselves safe. What's more, most strategies for managing hazards have followed a traditional planning model: study the problem, implement one solution, and move on to the next problem. This approach casts hazards as static and mitigation as an upward, positive, linear trend.

'But events during the past quarter-century have shown that natural disasters and the technological hazards that may accompany them are not problems that can be solved in isolation. Rather, they are symptoms of broader and more basic problems. Losses from hazards – and the fact that the nation cannot seem to reduce them – result from shortsighted and narrow conceptions of the human relationship to the natural environment.'[1]

THE NATURE AND HISTORY OF FLOODS

In general terms, the inundation of land that is usually dry is considered a flood. The term 'normally dry' is open to interpretation, but in the case of rivers might generously include any inundation of land outside the banks of the river. The banks are defined by 'channel-forming' or 'dominant discharge' flows, which occur once every year or two on average for perennial streams in humid climates and every ten years on average in arid climates.[2] Flows that overtop the bank are only slightly less frequent than channel-forming flows.

Floods are natural events that usually result from heavy rainfall or snowmelt over a watershed. Most of the large rivers in the world have slightly to extremely periodic flows, with pronounced high flows once or twice a year. Monsoons are caused by wind systems that reverse their direction because of the seasonal change from high pressure to low pressure over large continental areas. The Indian subcontinent, where the monsoon is particularly strong, becomes very hot in the summer, allowing a strong low-pressure cell to develop. Humid air moving in from the ocean carries high rainfall with it. The southward-shifting Inter-Tropical Convergence Zone has a similar effect during the summer in the Southern Hemisphere, causing seasonal rains in subtropical southern Africa. The development of destructive hurricanes and typhoons is connected with extreme cases of convective rains that develop in sub-tropical areas when low-pressure convective cells form over sea surfaces warmer than 26 degrees centigrade. Regional deviations in global precipitation patterns also result from orographic effects. High rainfall usually occurs on the side of the cell where air is forced upward and low rainfall where the air mass moves down.[3]

The flooding process generally begins when rain or snowmelt saturates the soil and excess water begins to run off the landscape surface. Gravity propels this runoff to the lowest part of the landscape, where it enters surface water drainages such as small streams. The small streams contribute their flows to larger streams and so on until the exaggerated tributary flows reach the main river channel. If a number of tributaries discharge their peak flows into the main river at the same time, the resulting flood peak will be high, but of short duration.

Under natural conditions, characteristics of the watershed substantially moderate these accumulating flows through a process known as attenuation. Watersheds contain numerous types of temporary storage areas for water. Examples of these include interception (temporary trapping of water behind vegetation stems or other objects), soil pores, aquifers, surface depressions such as wetlands, floodplains and channels. All of these temporary storage areas delay the rate of runoff, so the peak of the flood in the main river channel occurs some time after the peak rate of the rainfall or snowmelt event that produced the flood flow. In very small watersheds, this delay may be a matter of minutes or hours. In larger watersheds, the delay may be several weeks to months.[4]

Many natural factors determine the severity of flood events. One factor is the state of the soils in the drainage basin prior to the triggering event. Runoff rates, and therefore flooding, increase if the soil is frozen or highly compacted, or if previous precipitation has filled soil pore spaces and other water storage areas to capacity. Vegetative cover also plays a role, since dense vegetation can block runoff and allow it to infiltrate into the ground or take up water through root systems and release it to the atmosphere through the process of evapotranspiration.

Another, very important, factor is watershed topography; steep slopes will shed water more quickly than flatter areas. Severe flooding in mountainous areas can have particularly devastating effects because the high-velocity runoff can sweep virtually everything along with it. The mixture of fast water and large debris can destroy bridges and roads, dig deep erosion channels in flooded areas and leave behind a landscape strewn with debris.[5]

Floods serve many purposes in nature. They signal to migratory fish that it is time to commence the seasonal movements essential to their life histories. They clear vegetation from floodplains, setting back plant community succession along portions of the river and providing a mosaic of different habitats for the plants and animals that live by the river. They deposit new beds of silt on which vegetation – whether wild plants or cultivated crops – can take root and flourish. They create pools on the floodplain in which young fish can find refuge from large predators until they are big enough to hold their own in a bigger river environment.

> **'In some circumstances, even those floods which seem to have brought disaster may in many respects be beneficial. This is the situation in Bangladesh, for example, where the usual shortage of water for crop growth in the winter may be resolved by the increased soil moisture following summer flooding. Also, the increased rainfall over higher ground, even while lower areas are inundated, may increase yields considerably, resulting in a net increase in grain output compared with non-flood years. These two factors resulted in Bangladesh having bumper harvests in both 1987 and 1988, despite these being the worst flood years on record.'**[6]

Floods become disasters when they conflict with desired human land uses or are exacerbated by human activities. A flood hazard is the threat to life, property and other valued resources presented by a body of water when it rises and flows over land that is not normally submerged. A flood is not hazardous unless people are somehow adversely affected by it.[7] In cases where floods result in the loss of lives, land and property, the key characteristics of the flood event that determine the extent of the damage are the depth, areal extent and duration of inundation; the rate at which the flood waters rise; and the velocity of the flow.[8] Especially in farmed land, seasonality is also an important variable. A flood before harvest may spell poverty and hunger for the farmer, while a flood after the harvest might increase crop productivity in the following growing season by laying down fertile soil and increasing soil moisture.

The exposure of a community or enterprise in a specific area to flood risk is a combination of the presence of a hazard in that area and the vulnerability of the area to damage, including the loss of life and property, if a flood occurs.[9] Choices made by communities and societies also have a great deal of influence on the extent of the flood risk they face.

Floods have thwarted humans for many centuries. After 800 years of occupation, citizens abandoned the city of Mohenjo-Daro along the Indus River in what is now Pakistan around 1700 BC, at least partly because of devastating floods. In 689 BC, the Assyrians dammed the Tigris River to build up a reservoir of water. They then breached the dam to send an extremely destructive flood downstream to destroy the city of Babylon. Historical flood records carved in stone tell the history of 5,000 years of Nile flood levels in Egypt. In India, historical flood records extend back to 1291 AD, but sedimentary deposits produced by floods indirectly record flood magnitude and frequency over the past 5,000 years.[10]

As human populations expand, and as our use of land and water increasingly dominates natural ecosystems, flood damage is increasing rapidly. Around the world, losses of life and property from floods increased substantially over the latter half of the twentieth century (see Table 5.1). Floods were the most common type of geophysical disaster, generating more than 30 percent of all disasters between 1945 and 1986.[11] Flood damage levels are mounting most quickly in Asia and the Pacific as a consequence of increasing populations, denser occupancy of flood-prone areas, and the expansion of destructive land uses in watersheds. Within this region, floods are the most frequently occurring and the most destructive form of natural disaster, although tropical cyclones have caused higher death tolls.[12]

Table 5.1 Great Flood Disasters, 1950–98

	1950–9	1960–9	1970–9	1980–9	1989–98
No. of events	7	7	9	20	34
Losses (US$ bn, adjusted for inflation)	27.9	20.2	19.2	25.5	199.6

From: Loster, T., 1999. 'Flood Trends and Global Change.' Paper presented at the EuroConference on Global Change and Risk Management: Flood Rises in Europe. Laxenburg, Austria, 6–9 June. International Institute of Applied Systems Analysis, Vienna. p. 5.[13]

The geographical distribution of the unwelcome impacts of geophysical disasters in general is uneven. Economic losses from such events are relatively evenly split between developing and developed nations, despite the overwhelming concentration of capital assets in developed countries. Because of the enormous differences in the gross domestic product (GDP), the per capita cost of natural disasters in relation to GDP is 20 times higher in the developing world than in industrialized nations.[14] At least one-third of all economic losses caused by geophysical disasters in the world were caused by floods.[15]

'The 1998 floods in north-eastern China affected 16.1 million people, killing 3,600 and destroying 1.3 million houses. They also degraded 8.5 million hectares of land and reduced the incomes of wide sections of the regional economy. The annual per capita incomes in the affected parts of one province – where incomes already averaged only 56 percent of urban incomes – fell by some 15 percent as a result of the floods.'[16]

A comparison of floods with other geophysical disasters between 1988 and 1997 shows that floods cause more than half of all fatalities due to geophysical disasters throughout the world.[17] The largest numbers of deaths due to floods occur in the poor and heavily populated portions of the world (see Table 5.2).[18]

Table 5.2 Deaths from Major Flood Events, 1990–8

Country(ies)	Date	Number of deaths
India, Bangladesh, Nepal	June–September 1998	4,750
China	May–September 1998	3,656
China	June–September 1993	3,300
China	May–September 1991	3,074
China	June–August 1996	3,048
Somalia	October–December 1997	1,800
India	September–October 1992	1,500

From: Loster, T., 1999. 'Flood Trends and Global Change.' Paper presented at the EuroConference on Global Change and Risk Management: Flood Rises in Europe. Laxenburg, Austria, 6–9 June. International Institute of Applied Systems Analysis, Vienna. p. 3.

Flood-related damage levels have been increasing in recent decades in relation to two factors: increases in flood hazards and increases in the vulnerability of people, property and ecosystems to floods.

Increasing Flood Hazards

People exacerbate the hazardous nature of floods by changing the ecology and hydrology of the river channel, floodplains and watershed. Such disruptions of the natural water cycle can create unwelcome repercussions for people and for nature.

Watershed alterations, for example, can greatly increase the rate of flooding, accentuating flood peaks. The process of deforestation is infamous for increasing downstream flood hazards. In agricultural areas, the removal of natural, perennial vegetation and the construction of drainage ditches and tiles can substantially increase the rate of rainwater runoff compared to natural conditions. In urban areas, over 80 percent of the volume of rainfall can contribute to direct runoff to watercourses, compared to 15 to 20 percent under natural conditions.[19] Wetland destruction can also influence the frequency and severity of floods by removing natural retention areas from the landscape.

In addition, land laid bare by ploughing or in preparation for building construction can become a significant source of sediment to a river. Increased sediment loads magnify floods for two reasons. First, sediments that settle on the bottom of the river channel reduce the capacity of the channel to convey flood flows and raise the level of the river bed relative to the floodplain, increasing the probability of inundation. Second, heavy sediment loads contribute to the sheer volume of material conveyed by the river channel. The flow volume of a severely altered watershed may exceed the capacity of a river channel formed under more natural conditions.

Alterations of a river for the purpose of reducing flooding can actually increase flood hazards for many people, as discussed below. Global warming is also expected to increase flood hazard in the coming decades. This topic is covered in Chapter 7.

Increasing Vulnerability

Historically floodplains have been attractive places for people to settle. They tend to be level and stable, compared to steeply sloping land. Because they receive regular replenishment from the rise of river flows, they frequently contain soils that are more moist and rich than surrounding uplands, ideal for crop production. Floodplains provide easy access to rivers, which are important sources of water for a wide variety of uses and often serve as arteries of transport and commerce.

For a large part of human history, people have relied on the concept of reducing or eliminating floods by structurally altering waterbodies to keep water within the banks. In the Middle Loire valley, for example, some major flood embankments are over 200 years old. The Rhine and Danube rivers were straightened for flood control and navigation purposes before 1900. In Hungary, there is documentary evidence of flood defence works as early as the thirteenth century. The United Kingdom has had flood defence legislation since at least 1531.[20]

Flood control structures are typically designed to protect a specific land area surface from flood events of specific magnitudes. Their design usually corresponds to the statistical probability of the occurrence of a flood of a given magnitude. For example, a levee that is designed to protect a land area against a '100-year flood' is designed to protect that area from floods that have a one percent chance of occurring each year. Such a levee would also protect against floods that occur more frequently, because more frequent floods are smaller in magnitude. The levee, however, would not protect the land against a '200-year flood,' which has only a 0.5 percent chance of occurring in any given year. Flood-control structures are virtually certain to fail when their design capacity is exceeded.

Unfortunately, the statistical estimates of flood probability on which most flood-control structures are designed frequently underestimate the true risk faced by floodplain inhabitants. Most estimates of the magnitude of a '100-year' flood are based on less than 100 years of hydrological data, and are therefore inherently inaccurate. Even where good hydrological records exist, changes in the landscape and the climate of the river basin in question often ensure that future hydrological conditions will be quite different from the past. In most cases, these changes (deforestation, urbanization, wetland destruction and stream channelization, for example) increase the frequency and severity of flood events.[21]

When the capacity of flood control structures is exceeded and they fail, the damage to life, land and property is often far greater than it would have been without the structures. This is because, under unaltered conditions, floodplain land is subject to gradual inundation as the flood event reaches a peak and then recedes. In contrast, flood-control structures are most likely to fail during the flood peak. The sudden torrent of water that is released when a dam or a dyke fails can be much more destructive than a more natural flood event.

The presence of flood control structures often leads to intensified land use in flood-prone areas by creating a false sense of security for floodplain inhabitants. Many people who take up residence on a floodplain protected from the 100-year flood believe that such an event will only occur once a century. Thus, if a 100-year flood was recorded five years ago, they might think that the next similar event

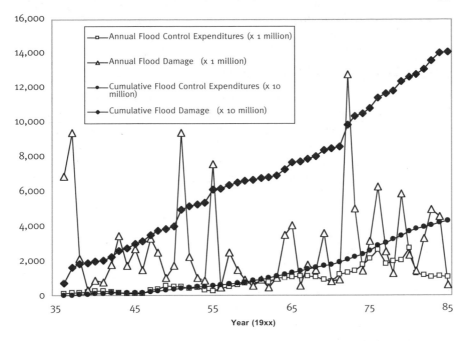

Figure 5.1 Flood Control Expenditure and Costs of Flood Damage in the US, 1935–85 (1993 dollars)

Data sources: US Army Corps of Engineers and US Weather Service.

won't happen for nearly five generations. Statistically, however, the probability of a 100-year flood is one percent every year and is not influenced by past flood events.

Structures built and alterations made for the purpose of controlling floods sometimes directly increase the risk of flood damage by interfering with the water cycle. The following subsections give examples of these structures and how they may exacerbate flood risks. It is primarily for these reasons, and possibly for others such as global warming and population growth, that flood damage levels around the world are increasing despite increasing expenditures on flood control. The US, for example, witnessed a steady increase in spending on flood control structures while experiencing an almost exponential rise in flood damage levels during much of the twentieth century (see Figure 5.1). Over the last 25 years, the federal government has spent nearly US$140 billion in federal tax revenue preparing for, and recovering from, natural disasters. Over the same period of time, the US Army Corps of Engineers spent more than US$25 billion building and operating flood control projects.[22]

In fact, the increase in US government expenditures on flood control structures between 1936 and 1985 was 103 percent in real dollars, but was surpassed by the rise in flood damage, which increased by 268 percent in real dollars in the same period.[23] These data do not include the frequent and often massive floods which the US experienced in the 1990s, such as the 1993 events in the Mississippi Basin that caused damage put at over US$16 billion. They also do not include the floods that continue to plague the country in the twenty-first century, including disasters in Minnesota and Texas in 2002.

THE FLOOD CONTROL CONCEPT

Flood risk can be reduced through the management of either the flood hazard or the vulnerability of communities and enterprises, or both. For centuries, the preferred approach to both of these objectives has been an attempt to constrain floodwaters using increasingly sophisticated structures. Yet, as Figure 5.1 illustrates, increased spending on structural constraints has not always led to decreases in flood damage – and, in some cases, the opposite is true. Different control structures are associated with distinct benefits and detriments, and some of the most common structures are discussed below.

Levees and Polders

Levees, also known as embankments, dykes or bunds, are barriers erected parallel to the river channel to prevent high-water levels from overflowing the river banks and flooding areas adjacent to the river. Polders, sometimes called ring levees, are barriers erected around parts of the floodplain to protect the areas they encircle.[24]

These structures have many drawbacks. First, they interfere with natural drainage patterns and can actually cause or exacerbate flooding in the areas they are designed to protect. Levee- or polder-induced flooding occurs when the levees are overtopped during a flood and then block the return of the water into the river channel after the flood recedes. Levees and polders can also trap water from local precipitation events, preventing the natural drainage of runoff into a receiving water body. In parts of Bangladesh, for example, river embankments and polders have prevented rainfall and river overspill water from draining back into river systems, leading to drainage congestion, waterlogging, and flooding. The areas behind the Brahmaputra Right Embankment in the north and west parts of the country have often suffered from backwater flooding and have been deliberately breached by affected people so that the water could drain back into the river.[25] Engineers sometimes add special structures such as pumps or gates to levees to minimize backwater flooding. The former alternative is costly and energy-consumptive and the latter will not work while the flood stage is high enough to prevent water from draining into the river from behind the levee.

Levees along river channels separate the river from portions of the floodplain that, under natural conditions, would serve as additional storage and conveyance areas for high flows. By reducing the amount of storage available on a river's floodplain, the constriction of a river between levees can increase flooding downstream by effectively increasing flood peaks over natural conditions. Upstream embankments that protected farmland worsened flooding of cities along the Rhine River in 1994, for example.[26]

Levees can also exacerbate flooding upstream by creating a bottleneck in the river channel below. This bottleneck raises the stage of the flood, increasing the probability that the levees themselves will be breached or overtopped and the degree of risk faced by communities that are not protected from floods. Many levees are planned and constructed by specific communities rather than by larger units of government. As a result, the levee units are not well coordinated. If a levee along the west bank of a river is higher than the levee on the east bank, for example, the areas on the eastern floodplain are more subject to flooding. Motivated by the uneven distribution of flood risk, people during floods may attempt to redistribute the risk by either raising their own levees or destroying those of other communities.

'It is becoming more difficult to protect the Chinese people from floods. Since 1954, the population has more than doubled, from 582 million to 1.2 billion, with most of it concentrated along riverbeds. Farmers with no other place to till crops have turned floodplains near major waterways into farmland, inhabiting flood channels, man-made flood diversion zones and natural runoff areas.

'Land reclamation by farmers, along with accumulated silt deposits, have shrunk Hunan Province's Dongting Lake from an area of nearly 600,000 hectares in 1825 to 270,000 hectares today.... In the 1950s, there were 1,332 lakes in Hubei Province; by the 1980s, there were 843. Local embankments built by farmers inside the dikes are also hemming in – and thus raising – the Yangtze's level.

'Those individual decisions – most in contravention of China's Flood Control Law – are affecting the entire Yangtze region. This year, flood crests have actually been higher than the massive floods of 1954, even though the volume of water rushing down the Yangtze was greater then.'[27]

Levees also prevent rivers from depositing sediment on floodplains. In many instances of engineered rivers, sediment instead accumulates on the bottom of the channel itself, with the result that the elevation of the bed of the river may actually exceed the elevation of adjacent floodplains.

'A second factor in the increase in flood severity and in flood frequency in unprotected areas is the constriction of the floodplain and channels of the Upper Mississippi River and tributaries by levees and other structures. Historical and scientific literature reflects that these concerns are not new. The Illinois Department of Purchases and Construction stated in 1930 that the floods of 1844, 1904, 1913, 1926, and 1927 were reaching successively higher stages because of floodplain constriction by levees.'[28] Belt compared the 1844 and 1973 Mississippi River floods and concluded that, in 1973, the river crested at St Louis

60 cm (2 feet) above the 1844 level, despite the fact that the flow in the river was 35 percent less. He attributed the difference to the loss of about one-third of the original channel volume.[29] The American Society of Civil Engineers supported the conclusion that levees contribute to the increase in Mississippi River flood stages.[30] According to R.E. Sparks, although the 1993 flow was about 20 percent less than the 1844 flood, the 1993 flood was 20 percent higher.[31]

'The most remarkable thing about [the Dutch water management system] is the fact that the rivers and canals in the western part of the Netherlands are higher above sea level than is the land—found practically nowhere else in the world. This difference in height is maintained artificially and will only become greater in the future because, the more we pump the South and North Holland polders the more we sink. Water administrators say that we live in a technologized country.'[32]

The deposition of sediment and resulting elevation of the riverbed and reduction of channel carrying capacity are exaggerated in places where a steep, headwater tributary joins a shallower mainstem river. In the North China Plain, for example, where the Yellow River emerges from its mountainous regions near Kaifeng, it is said that floods have claimed more lives and caused more human suffering than any other single natural feature on the planet. The lower reaches of the river are contained within a high embankment and the river itself is raised above the level of the surrounding land. As a result, breaches in the dykes lead to virtual flash floods instead of the slow-onset floods that would occur under natural conditions. Despite the massive flood hazard, this area is one of the most densely settled parts of China because of the land's high agricultural potential.[33]

Channelization

River channels are expressions of equilibrium between the flow rate and volume of water transported by the river, the river's sediment load, and the steepness of the gradient from the river's headwaters to its outlet. The width, depth and meander wavelength of an alluvial river channel, for example, are directly proportional to stream flow, which is inversely proportional to channel gradient. Similarly, alluvial channel width, meander wavelength and channel gradient are directly proportional to sediment discharge, which is inversely proportional to depth and sinuosity (the tendency to meander).[34] Physical alterations to the river channel for flood control and other purposes disrupt this equilibrium, resulting in somewhat unpredictable and often destructive changes in flow and sediment transport patterns.

Many of the world's rivers have been channelized partly to speed the conveyance rate of floodwaters to the ocean or other receiving body. Channelization can include the straightening of a river by removing meanders; widening or deepening the channel; and removing friction by altering the channel shape, paving the channel or removing vegetation from the river banks. The shortening of the channel in an attempt to speed the delivery of floodwater to some outlet often removes many hectares of floodplain land that would, under natural conditions, provide areas for storing and conveying high flows. Thus, the concentration of the flood volume into a single, straightened channel can result in increased flood peaks.

In addition, channelization projects remove some of the natural mechanisms that desynchronize flood peaks throughout a river basin. During a rainfall or snowmelt event over a river basin, different characteristics of the tributaries to the river – including meander patterns and the extent of floodplain wetlands – help to determine the rate at which water entering the tributary channels is passed downstream. If the rates of flow differ among the tributaries, flood peaks from each tributary will arrive in the mainstem at different times, creating a flood peak in the mainstem with a long duration but small crest. When the tributaries are channelized, water passes downstream at a more rapid and uniform rate, creating a shorter but more severe flood peak in the mainstem.

'As a result of channelization projects on the Rhine River, the river was shortened in the braided section by 14 percent and in the meander zone by 37 percent. The loss of 130 km² of inundation area through the damming up of the Rhine has caused a rise of the extreme flood discharge as well as an increase in flow velocity. Before 1955, the flood peak took a period of 65 hours from Basel to Karlsruhe; since the end of Rhine development in 1977, it takes only 30 hours.

'Today, because of the accelerated flows in the Rhine, the flood peaks of the Rhine and those of the tributaries meet, increasing flood danger immensely. According to the statistics, catastrophic floods measuring more than 5,000 m³ per second at the gauge Karlsruhe-Maxau, which used to occur every 200 years, now can occur every 50 to 60 years. The larger cities along the Rhine, such as Karlsruhe, Mannheim-Ludwigshafen, Mainz, Koblenz, Bonn and Cologne are in serious danger.'[35]

Other aspects of channelization cause significant disruptions of the water cycle. Paving a stream channel with concrete to increase the flow rate eliminates the exchange of water between the river and aquifer. The result is a reduction in aquifer recharge and groundwater availability if the river discharges into the aquifer, or a reduction in critical low flows if the river receives water from the aquifer.

The removal of riparian vegetation accelerates the rate at which runoff enters a river, and can therefore increase flood peaks. In addition, vegetation next to a waterbody can provide an effective filter for many pollutants. Conversely, removal of this vegetation can result in increased levels of contaminants in the river. While many conventional engineers view the removal of riparian vegetation as essential for reducing channel 'roughness' (the degree of resistance to water flow that slows down the rate at which floods are conveyed downstream), others argue that floodplain vegetation, and forests in particular, reduce downstream damage by slowing and spreading floodwaters.

By-pass channels are often constructed to increase the conveyance capacity of a river and to carry flood flows around densely populated areas. These systems can be designed to be relatively benign environmentally if they are gated and used only during extreme events. If water from a river is diverted into an artificial channel on a regular basis, however, the natural flow regime of the river will be disrupted with damaging consequences to the river's ecology and ultimately to the water cycle. In recent years, multi-stage channels that mimic natural river forms are more frequently used.[36]

'Near its mouth the Manawatu River [New Zealand] turns to run parallel to the shore for several kilometres before reaching the sea. This extra length of channel restricts the river's ability to evacuate flood flows. To ease this bottleneck a flood diversion channel, carrying the river directly to the sea, was built. A permanent diversion would have changed the river gradients too much, with possible deleterious consequences upstream, so gates were erected at the top end of the diversion channel to enable flood flows to be diverted while the original channel continued in use for normal flows. The diversion channel is contained by means of dykes and as it is used only rarely, the land is leased for grazing on the understanding that the farmers will remove their stock when required.'[37]

Dams

Large dams have been successful in flood mitigation and prevention.[38] On the Damodar River in Bihar and West Bengal in India, for example, dams are credited with greatly reducing damage to West Bengal during the floods of 1978. Dams in the upland tributaries of China's Yellow River may have prevented serious flooding in 1981, despite an unprecedented peak discharge.[39] A federal panel investigating the Mississippi River floods of 1993 estimated that dams reduced the average discharge of the Missouri River, one of the largest Mississippi tributaries, by 211,000 cubic feet per second (nearly 6,000 m^3 per second) during the month of July. As a result, the panel concluded, the peak stage of the Mississippi River at St Louis was five feet (more than one and a half metres) lower than it would otherwise have been.[40]

However, dams also cause or contribute to flood disasters. Many dams fail when their design capacity is exceeded, unleashing a sudden, violent torrent of water on downstream communities and ecosystems. At other dams, operators make emergency releases in order to prevent the dam from failing. Most dam failures occur because of lack of understanding of the geological properties beneath and adjacent to the dam; underestimation of the magnitude and frequency of possible extreme floods in the reservoir basin; or improper design/construction of the dam.[41]

Dams are frequently constructed with spillways that are unable to withstand major floods. For example, in a 1995 World Bank study of 25 Indian dams, engineers calculated the amount of water that the dams should have been able to release at the height of a flood. They found that in every case the expected floods were greater than those the dams had been designed to discharge over their spillways.[42]

Design-related failures of embankment dams may result from several factors. Often, flood events simply overtop the dams or overpower inadequate spillways. Water seepage through the dam's fill material may lead to cracking and deformation or settlement of the dam, weakening the structure sufficiently to cause failure during a flood event. Engineers sometimes build dams on faulty foundations with defects (uneven settlement, weathered and fractured rock, seepage, excessive pressure) that can weaken the structure to the point of failure. Finally, surface erosion of the embankment or slope failure on embankments that were too steep may sometimes undermine dams and lead to their failure.[43] Concrete dams generally fail because of foundation defects; overtopping or inadequate spillways; improper design; substandard construction material; or poor maintenance.[44]

Less than 3 percent of existing dams failed between 1831 and 1965 (see Table 5.3). A census of serious dam failures between 1964 and 1985 lists 43 failures of large dams. Fifteen of those failures resulted in the cumulative deaths of 2,572 people, although one incident – the 1979 overtopping of the 26-metre-high Machau II earthen dam in India – accounted for 2,000 of these deaths. Approximately one-fourth of these failures occurred during construction and another one-fourth occurred on first filling or during the first five years of service. Overtopping of a dam by a flood was the most common cause of failure. A full 83 percent of failures were of earth or rockfill dams. Overtopping of these dams leads to rapid erosion and a progressive collapse of the structure.[45]

Table 5.3 Percentage Failure Rate of Dam Types, 1831–1965

Dam type	No. of dams built	No. that failed	Failure rate (%)
Embankment			
Earth	4,551	121	2.66
Rock	285	13	4.56
Total	4,836	134	2.77
Concrete			
Arch	566	7	1.24
Buttress	373	7	1.88
Gravity	2,271	40	1.76
Total	3,210	54	1.68
Combined total	8,046	188	2.34

From: Cenderelli, D.A., 2000. 'Floods from Natural and Artificial Dam Failures.' In Wohl, E.E. (ed.), *Inland Flood Hazards: Human, Riparian and Aquatic Communities*. Cambridge University Press, Cambridge. p. 85.[46]

May 1998: Thawing snow pours down hillsides in the Suzah district of southern Kyrgyzstan, bursting a 100-metre wide dam on the River Kugart. More than a thousand homes are swept away by the frozen river (BBC).

July 1998: Water from melting glaciers smashes through a dam on the Kuban-Kel Lake in the mountains of central Asia. As the lake empties, water levels rise by four metres in the river below. Forty-three people in Uzbekistan are killed and six villages are destroyed (AP).

August 1998: Ten people die and 100,000 are evacuated after heavy rains topple the Benanga dam near Samarinda in the Indonesian state of East Kalimantan (DPA).

October 1998: A series of dam bursts and overflows in the hills around the Honduran capital Tegucigalpa adds significantly to the death toll from Hurricane Mitch (USGS).

September 1999: At least 48 people die during floods in northern Ghana after engineers in neighbouring Burkina Faso open spillways to relieve water pressure on the Bagre dam. Local reports say three other dams burst their banks. Forty villages are reported completely submerged (BBC).

September 1999: Thirty-nine die and 80,000 are made homeless in floods in the Mexican state of Hidalgo. A significant cause is water released from the Esperanza dam, which floods two rivers (CINDI).

March 2000: Rushed water releases from the Kariba dam on the River Zambezi in Southern Africa flood a district occupied after the dam's construction made it 'safe' (*New Scientist*).

July 2000: Floodwaters swamp towns in central Luzon, Philippines. Parts of Manila are submerged after power authorities open the gates of four hydro-electric dams north of the capital to prevent water overflowing (Dartmouth floods register).

August 2000: Monsoon floods in the Indian state of Andhra Pradesh crack the Roxsagar dam near the state capital Hyderabad. Thousands of workers rush to mend the breach, but are forced to retreat as water gushes towards the capital. Nearly 40,000 people are evacuated from their flooded homes (BBC).

September 2000: Emergency releases from at least four dams in West Bengal add to floods that cross the border into Bangladesh, killing more than a thousand (BBC).[47]

It is important to note that most of the world's existing dams were constructed in the latter half of the twentieth century. Thus our dams are aging even as the pace of watershed alteration, and disruptions of the water cycle, are accelerating.

The operation of dams for uses in addition to flood control can also cause or exacerbate flooding. The desire of dam operators to maintain high water levels in reservoirs for later use in energy production, navigation or irrigation, for example, is contrary to the objective of leaving ample storage capacity empty for flood damage reduction purposes.

'Under normal circumstances, dams are built to control floods and the flood-plains along the lower Niger do experience an annual flooding of a low magnitude. The annual white floods event usually sets in July and peaks in September. And it does not re-air with the same frequency as almost every four years the flood sets in with greater ferocity.

'The story is, however different this year. September 14, 1999. The National Electric Power Authority (NEPA), Kainji Regional Headquarters, New Bussa sent an urgent message to communities and establishments around Jebba, downstream of River Niger. The message: a possible flooding of River Niger with damaging consequences. It was directed to the communities through the traditional rulers. It said that 'most of the tributaries from the measurement of current inflow were already flooding.' States like Zamfara, Katsina, Sokoto and Kebbi experienced the effect of the flood despite the fact that the dam is not within the area. Inhabitants were warned rather too late to safeguard lives and properties. Before they could digest the message another letter came from the same source; it also bore the same message but it directed downstream users to move to safe grounds. Most of them woke up the following day to see their houses and farmlands overtaken by the water. The dam had overflowed its banks as authorities of NEPA decided to open dams letting out torrents of water which in all overran an estimated 200 communities, killing over 1,000 people, submerged 1,500 houses while 52 primary schools were rendered uninhabitable, rendering thousands jobless and homeless in Niger, Kwara and Kogi states. NEPA took the action to save the Kainji dam from collapse (which could result in great catastrophe).'[48]

SHIFTS TOWARDS A HOLISTIC APPROACH TO FLOOD MANAGEMENT

'The required logical approach is to begin by analyzing the nature of the flood problem in the area, identify the available options, compare these in terms of their contributions to society's objectives, and finally to select the best available option. A second key principle in this report is the need for an appropriate strategy for the local problem; floods differ very widely in their nature as do the characteristics of the floodplains affected. What is an appropriate flood management strategy in the context of one catchment may not be so in another catchment. In particular, a problem for the developing countries has been the parochialism of the approaches proposed as the solution of those countries' problems. There has been a tendency to propose that the approach adopted for the Rhine, Mississippi or Thames should be applied to the Yangtze or Bramaputra although conditions are quite different in the five countries [involved].'[49]

Adaptation to periodic flooding, non-structural flood damage reduction, and ecosystem restoration processes with flood damage reduction as an objective have the same characteristics as most sustainable resource management strategies. They are far more dependent on knowledge and far less dependent on large inputs of energy and material than were the large-scale, structural approaches that characterized the last century.

The reduction of flood damage using these approaches is most successfully implemented when all the processes and components that support the water cycle within a given drainage basin are treated as an integrated whole. Successful flood damage reduction results from identifying the root causes of the flooding problem (for instance, poor land-use management in the headwaters of a river, or inappropriately dense development of the floodplain), rather than treating only the symptoms of flooding by structurally altering the aquatic ecosystem. Finally, flood damage reduction strategies maximize their potential for success when they are designed to adapt to environmental changes or social preferences.

Adaptation

Communities have occupied floodplain land for many centuries, accepting and adapting to the risk of flooding. In the traditional floodplain villages of Malaysia, for example, houses are constructed on stilts to raise them above anticipated flood levels. Villagers commonly use small boats to conduct their affairs. Along rivers, estuaries and coastlines in South-east Asia, similar adaptations to flooding are abundant. The Cajun or Acadian population that joined the native American communities in the coastal swamps and marshes of Louisiana in the eighteenth century also adapted their dwellings to floods by placing the base floor on cypress pilings or stilts sunk into the silt deposited by spring or summer floods. In Bangladesh, floodplain occupants sometimes dismantle their dwellings during floods and move them to the tops of earthen embankments. These communities also adapt to frequent flooding through their use of flood-tolerant rice crops and the use of boats instead of roads, since the bridges are sometimes washed away.[50]

These traditional responses are often constrained by class and ethnic position in society, however, all of which determine the proximity of their domestic and livelihood resources in time and place to a flood hazard. In flood-prone villages of the Gangetic plain of North India, for example, the more substantially built houses of wealthier groups are often near the centre, where the land is usually slightly higher. Poorer classes, including lower classes and untouchables, for the most part live around the edges of the settlements in low-lying sites.[51]

Elevation of buildings and other structures located in the floodplain can be an effective means of reducing flood damage without altering ecosystem functions. Some communities opt to elevate structures in place, so that the lowest floor is above specific flood levels. Buildings can be raised on soil mounds, concrete foundations, piers, posts or columns.[52]

Flood proofing is the process of making a building resistant to flood damage. Wet flood proofing refers to the design of a building that is intended to be flooded in the basement and ground floor or higher, depending on the flood level, but also to sustain minimal damage during flood events. Wet flood proofing requires that the contents of the inundated floors can be moved to higher levels during a flood and that building construction materials are able to withstand immersion without damage. Buildings must be strong enough to resist the pressure of the floodwaters on the walls and floors. Flood-proofed buildings must be able to withstand the drag forces due to the flow of water around the building and the potential for scouring underneath. They must also be sufficiently heavy to avoid being swept away by the floods.[53]

Dry flood proofing involves making a building watertight up to the flood level. Windows and doors can be sealed easily, but water can still enter a building through various conduits. The ventilation holes for underfloor spaces can allow the entry of water that can then rise up through the floorboards. A watertight building must be designed to withstand the stresses imposed by the flood. Like wet-flood-proofed buildings, dry-flood-proofed buildings must be able to withstand the drag and scour effects of floodwaters.[54]

Non-structural Flood Damage Reduction

The basic principle underlying non-structural flood damage reduction approaches is that the most effective way to prevent flood damages is to avoid unwise use of the floodplain. Reducing flood damage by altering human behaviour rather than by altering freshwater ecosystems brings four distinct advantages. First, non-structural strategies allow the natural hydrological processes of the ecosystem to continue to function, thus ensuring a steady flow of goods and services such as fish and clean water. Second, non-structural strategies don't inflate the amount of damage that communities are likely to experience should flood risk be underestimated, compared to communities that experience a dam or dyke failure during a flood. Third, non-structural strategies are generally much less expensive to implement, operate and maintain than structural ecosystem alterations. Finally, non-structural measures are extremely adaptable to changing conditions, because they are based on information rather than on infrastructure.

Non-structural flood damage reduction approaches can address flood risk and damage in three time periods: before the flood, during the flood, and after the flood.

Before the Flood: Floodplain Planning and Management

'Despite clear evidence that prevention of disaster-related expenditures are aimed at preventing or mitigating disaster before it happens, individuals, industries and governments find it difficult to justify expenditures in response to events that may happen at some unspecified time in the future. Rarely do individuals or organizations consider the full range of costs that may result from disaster or consider the benefits derived from disaster prevention and mitigation over a sufficiently long time horizon. Complex and far-reaching linkages make it difficult to calculate the true cost of disaster even in its aftermath. Economic impacts may be extensive and severe, but obscured. The value of family and community feelings of comfort, security, independence and control cannot be measured in economic terms.'[55]

Floodplain management requires identifying a community's flood risks on a spatial and temporal basis, and planning land use in flood-prone areas to reduce the risk of severe flood damage. Effective floodplain management requires a sound understanding of the physical, biological, and chemical processes that affect flood hazards and the natural functions of floodplains. An understanding of the social processes involved in human interaction with flood hazards and natural flood plain functions is also critical.[56]

The information requirements for successful floodplain planning and management can be substantial and complex. Minimal requirements include short-term weather forecasts, detailed stream flow data, and an understanding of long-term climate conditions and topographical details.[57] Local knowledge of the history and extent of flood damages can be extremely helpful in discerning trends and identifying flood-prone areas where long-term data have not been compiled by water resource management organizations.

Once a community has collected, organized, and mapped the necessary information about floodplain hazards and natural resources, it chooses management approaches that will reduce the risk of flood damage while maintaining natural and beneficial floodplain functions. Strategies that address flood risks by isolating human communities from the floodplain can lead to impoverishment for people who depend on these fertile zones for fish, recession agriculture and grazing land, for example. In urban areas, it is often important to maintain a relationship between human communities and the floodplain for recreational and commercial benefits.

Communities should consider the past history of flooding and the historical and current uses of the floodplain in floodplain management processes. Communities should also consider whether future development may increase risk of flood damage by inducing greater population density in flood-prone areas or by extending the area of impervious surfaces, and therefore runoff rates, in the watershed. Development and redevelopment policies are particularly important in this regard.

The design and location of services and utilities, for example, can have both direct and indirect effects on flood losses. If roads, bridges, sewer lines and other utilities are constructed in flood-prone areas without adequate consideration of flood hazards, they will be susceptible to flood damage. In addition, services and utilities installed in and passing through flood-prone areas (a sewer line, for instance), can catalyse pressure for more intensive development on the floodplain.[58]

Disaster preparedness encompasses a broad spectrum of activities, including plans and programmes for pre-disaster warning and emergency operations, training, public information activities, testing of disaster preparedness plans and readiness evaluations. Preparedness plans are often developed in concert with flood forecast, warning and emergency plans, as described in the following section.[59]

Flood managers make use of remote sensing to create land-use maps and show changes over time, feed information to Geographic Information System (GIS) models and gather information after a flood event. Decision support systems assist flood damage reduction strategies by analysing information from a core database, including data on building inventories, infrastructure demographics and risk.[60]

During the Flood: Warning, Emergency Response and Evacuation Systems

Flood warnings and emergency response have long been recognized as effective ways to reduce flood damage and save lives. Over the past fifty years, the death toll from floods, excluding storm surges, has decreased substantially, largely because of early warning systems based on improved storm forecast models, together with the availability of elevated shelter that allowed people on low land to escape the floodwaters.[61]

In riverine flooding, the opportunities for effective flood warning and response depend on the nature of the flood threat. Flood forecasting procedures rely on real-time hydrological and meteorological data, accessible to a user almost immediately after an event occurs. These data are analysed and transferred to downstream points by various methods.

'The Yorkshire region of the United Kingdom Environment Agency operates a comprehensive flood forecasting system for protection of life and properties in its region. The rivers of Yorkshire, dominated by the River Ouse and its tributaries rising in the Pennines to the west and the North Yorkshire moors to the north, drain an area of 13,500 km². Snowmelt from the Pennines has been an important cause of flooding in the past and there is a risk of storm surges in the tidal reaches of the Ouse. In the region there are about 5,000 houses on unprotected floodplains and it has been estimated that the potential annual benefits of timely warning exceed one million pounds (US$1.7 million).'[62]

Flood forecast and warning systems are extremely dependent on data and technology, characteristics that may place them temporarily out of reach for many developing nations. Meteorological data for floods and other natural hazard assessments need to be based on comprehensive systems of recording stations that are compatible with, and exchange information with, similar systems throughout a river basin regardless of national borders. This information can feed into hydrological models, which convert precipitation data into predictions of runoff, and hydraulic models, which track the fate of flood runoff once it enters the river channel. The general data needs include precipitation, wind, atmospheric pressure, flood discharges, water levels and flow velocities.[63]

In a large river basin, upstream flows in the river and its tributaries may produce an extremely accurate forecast of downstream flooding, with many hours or even days to prepare for the flood. In upstream areas, where the watersheds are generally smaller and more steeply sloped, the time between the causative event (usually rainfall) and the onset of flooding may be only a few hours or minutes.[64] With a minimum warning of 1.5 hours, fatalities during local flood events in smaller regions can be almost entirely prevented.[65]

Models of flood hazards fall into two general categories: single-event simulation models and continuous models. The latter models are concerned with the simulation of watershed processes during a period of time that encompasses more than one precipitation or flood-triggering event. Thus, continuous models are also concerned with evaporation and subsurface pore moisture redistribution during the inter-storm period.[66] Continuous models may provide more accurate predictions of a flood hydrograph because they take into account the natural processes occurring throughout the watershed that can alter runoff volume during a flood.

Flood warning systems have two key weaknesses. First, they don't significantly limit damage to land and structures on the floodplain, nor do they mitigate economic disruptions from floods.[67] Second, they are only useful if the warning actually reaches vulnerable people and communities, and if these communities are able to respond appropriately.

Flood damage reduction strategies in developing countries, and particularly in urban areas, need to take into account massive squatter settlements and refugee camps – so-called 'invisible communities.' Often, the poorest and most vulnerable members of society are concentrated in hazardous areas because it is the only land available to them.[68]

'The delivery and receipt of the warning messages cannot be taken for granted. There have been cases where warnings may be issued only for the most vulnerable sections of the rural people to become victims for lack of a transistor radio on which to hear the broadcast. In a report of the impact of exceptional flooding around Alice Springs in central Australia in 1985, it was clear that the ethnic bias was responsible for the lack of delivery of warnings to the aboriginal people, many of whom were living in flimsy accommodations in low-lying land. The radio broadcasts that alerted the white people were not on channels which were customarily used by the aborigines.'[69]

In addition to the technical difficulties involved in delivering flood warnings to invisible communities, there are often sociological barriers that prevent cooperative relationships with disaster-related agencies. Past mistreatment may fuel distrust of institutions, despite dependence on foreign and government aid. This frame of reference may generate a reluctance to accept official warnings and a greater dependence on the kin group as a source of advice and help.[70]

Flood warning systems are not static. They must be modified over time as more is learned about regional hydrology, as the needs of society change, and as technology advances. In addition, the institutional components of the warning system need to be maintained, tested and improved on a regular basis to ensure that warnings can be delivered and received in a timely manner, and that target communities can respond in a way that reduces flood damage.

Appropriate responses on the part of the affected communities, particularly in the case of preventative evacuation, are the result of appropriate attention to planning and to communications with potentially affected communities. It is essential that authorities clearly articulate the threat and the recommended or mandated response – including evacuation routes and the location of shelters. A study of pre-impact evacuation procedures in the Red River Basin in Manitoba, Canada, showed that the most important factors influencing a family's decision to evacuate their homes prior to a predicted, extreme flood event were the behaviour of others and the flooding of upstream communities. Other factors involved include the past experience of the recipients of evacuation advisories or orders (whether the authorities were 'crying wolf' or an actual flood threat existed) and the degree to which potentially affected communities trust the authorities issuing the evacuation advisory or order.[71] Continuing rehearsals and cooperation between the parties involved are also essential for successful emergency response.[72]

'Being at risk to floods is a very important condition of life in the Netherlands. About half the Netherlands is protected from flooding by dikes, and over half of the Dutch population is at risk....

'The situation in the UK is very much a contrast. Approximately five percent of the population are subject to flooding with about another five percent protected to varying levels by river and sea dikes....

'Many thousands of people were severely affected by the flooding of Easter 1998 [in the UK], particularly in Warwickshire, Northamptonshire and Oxfordshire. Five people lost their lives, 4,500 properties were flooded and many hundreds of people had to be evacuated from their homes. In some places, Easter 1998 flood levels exceeded those recorded in 1947, the benchmark event on many river systems in England and Wales. There was a public, media and political outcry. In most regions the primary reason for the outcry was the lack of warning and perceived inadequacies in emergency response....

'The effectiveness of early warning – do people and institutions receive the message and react appropriately – relies to a major extent on the credibility of the authority that disseminates. In the Netherlands, this authority is RIZA. RIZA relies on the timeliness and quality of information received from Germany (River

Rhine) or from Belgium and France (River Meuse) to be able to issue reliable warnings. In addition, because foreigners cannot always be trusted, RIZA uses meteorological observation and discharge models to double-check flood warnings, and even has some discharge monitors in Belgium. The Dutch public respects its public engineers and takes flood warnings very seriously....

'Contingency planning was put to the test in 1995, when the Rhine dikes almost broke and 250,000 people (from a population of 15 million, or 1 in 60) were evacuated as a precaution. This operation was executed rather smoothly.'[73]

After the Flood: Buyouts and Relocation

Depending on the extent of government subsidies to frequently damaged floodplain properties, it is often more cost-effective for the public sector to purchase land that experiences frequent flood than to restore and maintain it in its pre-flood condition. Figuring the cost-effectiveness of such action is merely a matter of comparing the chronic costs of flood-fighting, evacuations, temporary shelters and supplies for evacuees, restoration of pre-flood conditions and structures, and the potential costs of new flood control infrastructure. Moreover, the public acquisition of frequently flooded land, and its restoration to natural floodplain conditions, can provide additional benefits to society (for instance flood damage reduction, water quality enhancement, recreation, and wildlife observation).

'St Charles County, Missouri, which sits at the confluence of the Missouri and Mississippi Rivers, was hit hard by the 1993 flood. Total federal disaster assistance for the county topped $26 million. After the flood, the county purchased 1,374 flood-damaged properties in the 100-year floodplain, including 560 single-family homes and three mobile home parks with a combined total of 814 mobile home pads. When floodwaters rose again in 1995, about 1,000 families already had been moved to higher ground. This time, federal disaster assistance to the county totaled only $283,094, a 99 percent reduction compared to 1993. The difference can be attributed in large part to moving the vast majority of repetitively damaged properties out of flood prone areas.'[74]

When considering post-flood buyouts as an option for reducing future flood damages, it is important for decision makers to assess the financial capabilities of relocated households to afford mortgages and property taxes on higher ground. Often, the reason that families take up residency on floodplains is because they cannot afford to live in a safer environment. In other cases, floodplain residents assume the risk willingly, with the assumption that if a flood damages their properties, the public sector will make them whole.

Flood Damage Reduction through Ecosystem Restoration

Substantial gains in flood damage reduction can be achieved simply by restoring the natural hydrological characteristics of floodplains and watersheds.

Floodplain Restoration

Floodplain restoration to pre-development conditions is one of the most desirable landscape modifications to reduce flood damage, particularly if the restoration is designed to return the dynamics of a meandering river and the natural pulses of inundation and sediment distribution.[75]

The removal of economic activity that is unsustainable in the light of the natural or artificially restrained flood regime directly reduces the cost of flood damage to that activity. In many cases, the cumulative damage caused by floods exceeds the cost of removing the activity from the floodplain, making floodplain restoration cost-effective even ignoring other benefits such as flood damage reduction up-stream or downstream of the flood, enhanced water quality, and improved habitat for fish and wildlife.

Floodplain restoration results in reduced flood crests by reestablishing the availability of the floodplain for flood flow conveyance and temporary water storage. This potentially increases security for economic activities upstream, downstream and across the river from the property being restored.

'Several 100-year flood totals were recorded along the Flint River [during the floods of 1994]. At Albany [Georgia] the new record of 42.7 [feet] exceeded the old (37.5 – 1925) by almost 5 feet. The old record (41.3 – 1925) gave way to the new record of 45.2 at Newton GA. Bainbridge was far more fortunate than most in that the predicted heights did not occur and the old record (40.9 – 1925) still stands. The Flint rose to a level of 37.3 feet, several feet below the level forecast by flood officials as they did not take into account the drainage area north of Bainbridge known as the "Big Slough." The flood waters that were absorbed by the "Big Slough" prevented major damage to homes and businesses along the Flint and possibly an explosion at a nearby fertilizer plant.'[76]

Watershed management

Each watershed is a physically discrete hydrological unit in which surface water is channelled from upland areas to lower areas and eventually into rivers or lakes. The degree to which rainfall is captured by, and released from, the watershed affects the stage, frequency and duration of flooding in a freshwater ecosystem. Well-managed watersheds reduce downstream flood stages with resulting reductions in flood damages and increases in water quality and ecosystem benefits.[77]

Small watersheds in particular are highly sensitive to the effects of changes in land use and other overland flow factors; therefore, appropriate forms of land management can provide a particularly effective method of flood mitigation. As the size of the watershed increases, the effects of channel flow and basin storage become increasingly dominant and sensitivities to rainfall interception and infiltration become increasingly suppressed.[78] Thus in large watersheds land-use measures are less effective on the lower reaches of the basin, though they still help to attenuate flows and can therefore reduce flood peaks, particularly if they are broadly applied.

Watershed management strategies include components that may have multiple objectives, such as capturing rainfall, restoring wildlife habitat, or preventing erosion. These methods can provide flood damage reduction benefits. Wetland restoration, for example, has proved to be an effective flood reduction measure in the upper watershed areas where the localized effects of flooding are most pronounced.[79] Wetland restoration can provide other benefits such as improving water quality and providing habitat for wildlife. Similarly, contour ploughing can reduce flood damage and at the same time improve water quality and increase groundwater infiltration (and thereby soil moisture, groundwater storage, and river flows during the dry season).

'The government of Indonesia has placed emphasis on the development of a watershed conservation programme. The programme is based on four key activities: soil and water conservation; land management; development of appropriate farming systems; and development of the necessary physical and social infrastructure to support these approaches. These activities have contributed significantly to the improved sustainability of natural resources and a reduction in the frequency and intensity of natural disasters.'[80]

'Over the last few months, the State Council, China's cabinet, has issued stern notices, prompted in part by the catastrophe that left 3,656 people dead and doused 64 million acres of land. It has banned most logging in Sichuan Province to halt the massive soil erosion that contributed to the deluge. It has prohibited further land reclamation projects of the sort that squeezed the Yangtze's floodplain. It has earmarked $2 billion to reforest barren hills in the Yantgze's upper reaches. 'Sustainable development' is the new buzzword among Chinese economists and officials.'[81]

Adaptive Management

'Policies are the governing plan, the question set based on experience that sets the stage of further action.... In this light policies are not magic bullets that address the right mix of objectives to solve a problem, rather they are astute hypotheses about how the world works or "Questions masquerading as answers."'[82]

Traditional approaches to floods and other natural disasters treat such events as discrete phenomena that are external to the social or environmental systems with which they interact. They therefore tend to focus on the causes of, and appropriate mitigation actions for, individual flood events. The increasing frequency of floods and the mounting magnitude of the damage they cause indicate that floods are not isolated events but instead emerging properties of interactions within and between complex and dynamic systems.[83]

Basing flood protection systems on the '100-year flood' theory treats floods as isolated events. One can compare this theory to the idea of a jar full of 100 marbles, one of which is black. In any given year, the probability of a blindfolded person pulling the black marble from the jar is one percent. If the marble is put back into the jar and the game is repeated the following year, the chances of drawing the black marble are the same – one percent – a probability statistically unrelated to the fact that the black marble had been drawn the year before. In other words, the fact that a river stretch experienced a '100-year flood' this year does not affect the probability that a 100-year flood event will occur on the same river stretch next year. The probabilities are assumed to be the same.

An adaptive management approach would assume that our understanding of the causes and effects of floods changes over time as we learn about relationships between rivers and their environments. We make a set of predictions, manage accordingly, and monitor the results so that if reality manifests in a manner significantly different from our predictions, we change our future predictions so that they are in synch with our new, systemic understanding. We then change our management policies as a result.

Rising flood events and flood damage around the world are indeed not exclusively related to the statistical probability of isolated precipitation and river flow events. Ongoing environmental trends need to be considered, including alterations of watersheds, floodplains and river channels, as well as the increasing encroachment of human economic activities in flood-prone areas. Adaptive management requires recognition of the links between the incidence of damaging floods and trends towards increased vulnerability of communities, decreased buffering ability of ecosystems and global warming. Once people have acknowledged these links, the path is open to readjust behaviours in a manner that reduces future damages.

Flexibility is an important characteristic that allows for adaptation to changing environmental conditions, shifts in societal preferences and the development of new information. The adaptive management approach implies that we should have a preference for options that involve resilient natural systems, or flexible artificial systems, and enhance the coping capacity of individuals and communities.[84]

CONCLUSION

Flooding is a natural event that, under many circumstances, has benefits for humans and for nature. When flooding is exacerbated by human alterations of the landscape, and the location of economic activities in floodplain areas, flooding becomes a problem. Flooding has become such a problem in many areas in recent years that governments are willing to pump enormous amounts of money into structural flood control programmes. Despite these growing expenditures, each year the world seems to experience more disastrous floods. The flood control strategy must therefore be called into question.

It is illogical to expect that we can suppress raging floodwaters at the same time that we change the climate, denude watersheds and increase population density near flood-prone water bodies. The laws of nature are immutable, and humans are products, not generators, of natural law. The measures we take to eliminate natural flood pulses are more than overtaken by our undoing of the ecological processes that ensure floods are a net benefit for humanity. By our very attempts to control floods, we negate their positive value and render them ever more dangerous to our self-interest.

Safety from flooding requires that human society look at the linkages between our actions and the repercussions in terms of flood damage and other undesirable impacts. As we learn how natural ecosystems function, how they are resilient to and ultimately overcome periodic disturbances, we will come to accept the fact that it is the species *Homo sapiens* that needs to adapt; not Mother Nature. Natural resources management must use this knowledge as a template for future damage reduction strategies and continue to monitor, reflect and learn. Only a continuous flow of incoming knowledge, and our appropriate response, can reduce future catastrophic losses from future floods.

The theme of learning how to manage water resources for the good of humanity following natural models continues in the following chapter on commercial navigation.

Notes

1 Mileti, D.S., 1999. *Disasters by Design: A Reassessment of Natural Hazards in the United States.* Joseph Henry Press, Washington. p. 2.

2 Shields, F.D., 1996. 'Hydraulic and Hydrologic Stability.' In Brookes, A. & F.D. Shields (eds.), *River Channel Restoration: Guiding Principles for Sustainable Projects.* John Wiley & Sons, Chichester, England. p. 30.

3 Mook, W.G. (ed.), 2000. *United Nations Educational, Scientific and Cultural Organization/ International Atomic Energy Agency Series on Environmental Isotopes in the Hydrological Cycle: Principles and Application.* Volume I. p. 11.

4 Whitehouse, G. & J.R. Burton, 1999. 'Water Hazards, Resources and Management for Disaster Prevention: A Review of the Asian Conditions.' Paper prepared for the United Nations Economic and Social Commission for Asia and the Pacific and the International Decade for Natural Disaster Reduction Secretariat. Section 2.

5 German Advisory Council on Global Change, 1999. *World in Transition: Ways Towards Sustainable Management of Freshwater Resources.* Springer-Verlag, Berlin & Heidelberg. p. 99.

6 Cannon, T., 1990. 'Rural People, Vulnerability and Flood Disasters in the Third World.' Working Paper Series No. 90. Institute of Social Studies, The Hague. p. 18.

7 Green, C.H., D.J. Parker & S.M. Tunstall, 2000. 'Assessment of Flood Control and Management Options. World Commission on Dams Thematic Review: Options Assessment IV. 4.' Cape Town. p. 2.

8 Whitehouse, G. & J.R. Burton, 1999. 'Water Hazards,' Section 2.

9 White, W.R., undated. *Water in Rivers: Flooding. A Submission to the World Water Vision.* World Water Council, Marseille. p. 10.

10 Wohl, E.E., 2000. 'Inland Flood Hazards.' In Wohl, E.E. (ed.), *Inland Flood Hazards: Human,*

Riparian and Aquatic Communities. Cambridge University Press, Cambrige. p. 10.

11 Glickman, T.S., D. Golding & E.D. Silverman, 1992. 'Acts of God or Acts of Man: Recent Trends in Natural Disasters and Major Industrial Accidents. Center for Risk Management,' Discussion Paper 92–02, Resources for the Future, Washington.

12 United Nations Economic and Social Commission for Asia and the Pacific, 1997. *Guidelines and Manual on Land-use Planning and Practices in Watershed Management and Disaster Reduction*. ST/ESCAP/1781. United Nations, New York. 133 pp.

13 In this context, floods are classified as great if the ability of the region to help itself is distinctly overtaxed, making interregional or international assistance necessary. This is usually the case when thousands of people are killed, hundreds of thousands are made homeless, or when a country suffers substantial economic losses (depending on the economic circumstances generally prevailing in that country).

14 International Institute for Applied Systems Analysis, 1999. 'Natural Catastrophes, Infrastructure, and Poverty in Developing Countries.' *Options,* Fall/Winter. Vienna. p. 6.

15 Loster, T., 1999. 'Flood Trends and Global Change.' Paper presented at the EuroConference on Global Change and Risk Management: Flood Rises in Europe. Laxenburg, Austria, 6–9 June. International Institute of Applied Systems Analysis, Vienna. p. 1.

16 International Institute for Applied Systems Analysis, 1999. 'Natural Catastrophes, Infrastructure, and Poverty in Developing Countries.' p. 8.

17 Loster, T., 1999. 'Flood Trends.' p. 2.

18 Ibid., p. 4.

19 P. Martin et al,, 1999. *Sustainable Urban Drainage Systems Design Manual for England and Wales*. C522, Construction Industry Research and Information Association (CIRIA), London.

20 White, W.R., undated. *Water in Rivers*. p. 8.

21 Hunt, C., 1999. 'A Twenty-first Century Approach to Managing Floods.' *Environments* 27 (1): 97–114.

22 National Wildlife Federation 1998. *Higher Ground: A Report on Voluntary Property Buy-outs in the Nation's Floodplains. A Common Ground Solution Serving People at Risk, Taxpayers, and the Environment*. Washington.

23 Hunt, C.E. 1997. *A Natural Approach for Flood Damage Reduction and Environmental Enhancement*. Long Term Resource Monitoring Program Special Report 97-S005. US Geological Survey Environmental Management Technical Center, Onalaska, Wisconsin. p. 1.

24 In some cases, such as along the Rhine River in Germany, the term 'polder' is applied to excavated areas adjacent to the river channel which are normally dry but which, during flood events, store overflow from the river.

25 Hughes, R., A. Adnan & B. Dalal-Clayton, 1994. *Floodplains or Flood Plans? A Review of Approaches to Water Management in Bangladesh*. Russell Press, Nottingham, UK. 94 pp.

26 Acreman, M., 2000. *Wetlands and Hydrology*. Conservation of Mediterranean Wetlands No. 10. Tour du Valat, Arles, France. p. 51.

27 Laris, M., 1998. 'China's Rivers of Death'. *Washington Post*, 17 August .

28 Mulvihill, W.F. & L.D. Cornish, 1930. *Flood Control Report. An Engineering Study of the Flood Situation in the State of Illinois*. Illinois Department of Purchase and Construction, Division of Waterways. Journal Printing Company, Springfield. 402 pp.

29 Belt, C.B. Jr., 1975. 'The 1973 Flood and Man's Constriction of the Mississippi River.' *Science*, 189: 681–4.

30 Stevens, M.A., D.B. Simons & S.A. Schumm, 1975. 'Man-induced Changes of the Middle Mississippi River.' *Journal of the Waterways, Harbors and Coastal Engineering Division of the American Society of Civil Engineers*.

31 Sparks, R.E., 1993. Unpublished testimony before the US House of Representatives Subcommittee on Water Resources and the Environment, Washington. See also Hunt, C.E. 1997. *A Natural Approach*.

32 Kers, M. & M. Kers, 1998. *Holland Land of Water: Water Management in the Netherlands*. Terra Publishing, Warnsveld, The Netherlands. 144 pp.

33 Cannon, T., 1990. 'Rural People.' pp. 3–4.

34 Federal Interagency Stream Restoration Working Group, 1998. *Stream Corridor Restoration:*

Principles. Processes and Practices. Washington. pp. 2–21.

35 Dister, E. & P. Obrdlik, undated. *The Renaturalization of Alluvial Floodplains as a Part of Flood Control on the Upper Rhine.* WWF Institute for Floodplains Ecology, Rastatt, Germany.

36 Green, C.H., D.J. Parker & S.M. Tunstall, 2000. 'Assessment of Flood Control.' p. 61.

37 Miller, J.B., 1997. *Floods: People at Risk, Strategies for Prevention.* United Nations Department of Humanitarian Affairs DHA/97/107. New York and Geneva. p. 48.

38 The information in this section refers to artificial dams. Natural dams made of ice, earth or vegetation can also fail and unleash destructive water flows.

39 Cannon T., 1990. 'Rural People,' p. 19.

40 Interagency Floodplain Management Review Committee, 1994. 'Sharing the Challenge: Floodplain Management into the 21st Century. Report of the Interagency Floodplain Management Review Committee to the Administration Floodplain Management Task Force, Executive Office of the President,' Washington. p. 48.

41 Cenderelli, D.A., 2000. 'Floods from Natural and Artificial Dam Failures.' In Wohl, E.E. (ed.), *Inland Flood Hazards: Human, Riparian and Aquatic Communities.* Cambridge University Press, Cambridge. p. 99.

42 Pearce, F., 2001. ''Dams and Floods.' WWF International Research Paper. Gland, Switzerland. p. 3.

43 Cenderelli, D.A., 2000. 'Floods from Natural and Artificial Dam Failures.' p. 86.

44 Ibid., p. 87.

45 Miller, J.B., 1997. *Floods: People at Risk,* p. 64.

46 Gravity dams depend on weight for stability. Arch dams are thin, curved structures made of concrete reinforced with steel rods, designed to distribute horizontal stresses within the dam towards abutments for stability and usually built in narrow valleys. Buttress dams consist of a thick slab of concrete resting on a succession of upright buttresses that hold the dam in place.

47 Pearce, F., 2001. 'Dams and Floods.' p. 1.

48 African Network for Environmental and Economic Justice, 1999. 'Large Dams, Food Security and Livelihood: Understanding the Nigerian Experience.' Paper presented at the Third WCD Regional Consultation on Large Dams and their Alternatives in Africa and the Middle East in Cairo, Egypt, 8–9 December 1999.

49 Green, C.H., D.J. Parker & S.M. Tunstall, 2000. 'Assessment of Flood Control.' p. iii.

50 Ibid., p. 4.

51 Cannon, T., 1990. 'Rural People,' p. 19.

52 Riley, A.L., 1998. *Restoring Streams in Cities: A Guide for Planners, Policymakers, and Citizens.* Island Press, Covelo, California. p. 285.

53 Miller, J.B., 1997. *Floods: People at Risk,* pp. 55–6.

54 Ibid. pp. 55–6.

55 Warmington, V., undated. *Prevention Pays: The Socio-Economic Benefits of Preventing Disaster.* Canadian National Committee for the International Decade for Natural Disaster Reduction.

56 L.R. Johnston Associates, 1992. *Floodplain Management in the United States: An Assessment Report.* Volume 2: Full Report. Prepared for the Federal Interagency Floodplain Management Task Force. Washington.

57 Ibid.

58 Ibid.

59 Ibid.

60 Mileti, D.S., 1999. *Disasters by Design.* p. 9.

61 Loster, T., 1999. 'Flood Trends.' pp. 1–2.

62 Miller, J.B., 1997. *Floods: People at Risk,* p. 60.

63 Whitehouse, G. & J.R. Burton, 1999. 'Water Hazards,' Section 2.

64 L.R. Johnston Associates, 1992. *Floodplain Management.*

65 German Advisory Council on Global Change, 1999. *World in Transition.* p. 109.

66 Ramirez, J.A., 2000. 'Prediction and Modeling of Flood Hydrology and Hydraulics.' In Wohl, E.E. (ed.), *Inland Flood Hazards: Human, Riparian and Aquatic Communities.* p. 322.

67 Mileti, D.S., 1999. *Disasters by Design.* p. 8.

68 Cannon T., 1990. 'Rural People,' p. 22.

69 Ibid., pp. 22–3.

70 Laituri, M.J., 2000. 'Cultural Perspectives on Flooding.' In Wohl, E.E. (ed.), *Inland Flood Hazards: Human, Riparian and Aquatic Communities.* p. 461.

71 Ahmad, S. & S.P. Simonovic, 2001. 'Modeling Human Behavior for Evacuation Planning: A System Dynamics Approach.' In Phelps, D. & G. Sehlke (eds.), *Bridging the Gap. Proceedings of the American Society of Civil Engineers World Water and Environmental Resources Congress.* Orlando, Florida. p. 8.

72 Green, C.H., D.J. Parker & S.M. Tunstall, 2000. 'Assessment of Flood Control.' p. ix.

73 Handmer, J., E. Crook, N.M. van der Grijp, A.A. Osthoorn, R.S.J. Tol & P.E. van der Werff, 2001. *Flood Hazard Management in Britain and the Netherlands: History, Risk, Governance and Adaptation to Climate Change. Social and Institutional Responses to Climate Change and Climatic Hazards.* Oxford. pp. 3–8.

74 Salvesen, D., 2001. 'Incorporating Disaster Resilience into Disaster Recovery.' Chapter 8 in Natural Hazards Research and Applications Information Center, *Disaster Recovery: Ideas for Building Local Sustainability after a Natural Disaster.* University of Colorado, Boulder. pp. 3–8.

75 Riley, A.L., 1998. *Restoring Streams in Cities.* pp. 287–9.

76 Bainbridge Bass Club Lake Seminole, undated. The Flood of 1994. http://bassangler.com/bbc/flood-94.htm.

77 Interagency Floodplain Management Review Committee, 1994. 'Sharing the Challenge.' p. 94.

78 Whitehouse, G. & J.R. Burton, 1999. 'Water Hazards,' Section 7.

79 US Army Corps of Engineers, 1995. *Floodplain Management Assessment of the Upper Mississippi River and Lower Missouri Rivers and Tributaries.* St Paul. pp. 8–30.

80 United Nations Economic and Social Commission for Asia and the Pacific, 1997. *Guidelines and Manual.* pp. 66–7.

81 Pomfret, J. 1998. 'Yangtze Flood Jolts China's Land Policy.' *Washington Post,* 22 November.

82 Sendzimir, J., S. Light & K. Szymanowska, undated. 'Adaptive Understanding and Management of Floods.' Institute for Agriculture and Trade Policy, Institute for Adaptive Management Practitioners' Network. http://www.iatp.org/AEAM/abstracts.htm. Unpaginated.

83 Sarewitz, D. & R. Pielke, 2001. 'Extreme Events: A Research and Policy Framework for Disasters in Context.' *International Geology Review,* 43 (5): 406–7.

84 Green, C.H., D.J. Parker & S.M. Tunstall, 2000. 'Assessment of Flood Control.' p. viii.

6

Arteries of Commerce
Inland Waterways
and the Water Cycle

'Co-evolution is attractive from the perspective of continued activity of the [dredging] sector, but this requires a deeper understanding of ecological processes: how to interact with nature instead of how to beat nature should be the slogan.'[1]

'Overall, the key shift in development planning should be away from adapting the river to the ships, to adapting the ships to the river and current economic needs.'[2]

Inland waterway navigation poses a bit of a conundrum for water managers concerned about a looming, global water crisis. On one hand, inland navigation is much more fuel-efficient than road, rail or air transport of freight, which means that a substantial reliance on water transport in international trade could reduce the potential impacts of global warming (covered in Chapter 7). The growth in international trade has already led to a huge increase in the cross-continental movement of goods in container-bearing ships. Inland navigation around the world, which has not expanded as rapidly as road transport, is well positioned to take advantage of the increase in ocean shipping because rivers provide relatively low-cost transport from coastal ports to inland destinations. As modes of freight transport rapidly adapt to container freight, the potential for inland waterway transport to serve as a cost-effective and relatively environmentally friendly mode of transport between ocean and final transport (by road or rail) to terminal also increases.

On the other hand, a blind leap towards increased freight transport by inland waterways could also spell trouble for aquatic ecosystems and for the water cycle. Physical alterations of rivers to support ever-increasing bulks of barges and tows (groups of barges linked together and pushed up- or down-river by a tug or towboat) can substantially interfere with natural ecological processes. Win–win situations that result in increased efficiency, and thus economic competitiveness, of barge traffic are already available. They require sophisticated information systems to guide barge traffic, better environmental management of large areas of watershed (which is desirable also from food, water quality and supply, and flood damage reduction perspectives, as outlined in previous chapters), and more sensitive design of barges and tows. While it may seem simpler, over the short term, to enlarge river and stream channels to accommodate expanding inland waterway traffic, over the long term, more environmentally enlightened inland navigation is likely to provide an economic, as well as an environmental, boon.

BUILDING THE WATER HIGHWAYS

The convenience of water-borne transport, in combination with the need for water for other purposes, has always provided an incentive for human civilizations to settle in river valleys and near the shores of oceans and lakes. While roads and railways have put inland navigation in the backseat for intra-continental commerce, sea-borne ships provide enormous cost savings compared to the only alternative available for intercontinental shipping today: air. As roads become increasingly congested, and air pollution becomes an increasingly important concern for emerging economies, inland navigation is becoming more attractive even for shipments to destinations not separated from the source by a sea.

The Birth of Inland Navigation

Civilizations have modified rivers to serve transportation needs for thousands of years. During the sixth dynasty in Egypt (between 2300 and 2180 BC) Pepi I sent expeditions up the Nile and wanted to bypass the first cataract near Aswan. He ordered Uni, governor of upper Egypt, to build canals that would make this possible.[3]

The Grand Canal, one of the world's most famous waterways, developed out of the Pien Canal during the Sui dynasty in China (581–617 BC). The canal began near Hangzhou and then ran north across the Yangtze and Yellow rivers to end near Beijing. Its routes were made up partly of river courses and partly of canals running beside and fed by rivers. Along the canal in Shangdong, the Chinese cut a short section through slightly rising land, constructed single gates at either end of the cut, and diverted two small rivers to compensate for water loss at the gates.[4]

Navigable irrigation canals, and possibly other canals used only for transportation, date back at least to the Assyrians in the land between Tigris and Euphrates in what is now Iraq. Some of those that served Babylon on the Euphrates were navigable and used by the ships of Alexander the Great in 331 BC.[5]

By the last half of the first century BC, the Chinese had developed a more sophisticated lock-like system. They built short walls on either side of a narrowed section of canal and carved vertical grooves opposite to each other in the walls. They then slid logs into the grooves and raised and lowered the logs using ropes running over the pulleys of primitive cranes. Sometimes they would join the logs together to form a gate which they raised and lowered with the help of counterweights. By 984 AD, they had placed stanchions with vertically rising gates close together to create the world's first known navigation lock.[6]

Sea routes, mostly in the Mediterranean, linked the Roman Empire together.

The Romans navigated rivers for both military and commercial purposes as extensions of their sea routes. On smaller rivers, the Romans built the first 'flash-locks,' which released water from dams to help boats ascend shallow water.[7]

Shallow water, overland crossings and rock outcrops were not the only challenges faced by people travelling on inland waterways. Simply moving upstream against the river current was physically impossible under most circumstances without an external, driving energy input. In many cases, people or draft animals on towpaths adjacent to the waterways pulled boats upstream. During the nineteenth century, steam-powered riverboats were developed.

In the twentieth century the wartime deployment of goods and the expanding industrial revolution generated a demand for high-volume, commercial transport. The inland navigation industry discovered that it was possible to load a number of barges, flat-bottomed boats capable of transporting goods with a mass greatly exceeding their own, bind them together, and push them upriver with another, smaller boat under its own power.[8] The self-powered boat was labelled a 'towboat' or a 'tugboat' in reference to tug people, tow donkeys and the like. The term 'pushboat' would have been more accurate.

Current Status of Inland Navigation Systems

The importance of barge transport varies considerably between different continents. In Europe, barge transport has always been concentrated in the northwestern countries of the Netherlands, Belgium, Germany and France, although there is considerable potential for navigation expansion in eastern Europe.[9] Inland navigation trends in Europe exhibit a clear distinction between tonnage carried by inland waterways in domestic and international trade. Inland navigation has a very modest share in domestic inland transport operations, but a large chunk – 38.5 percent in weight – of international, inter-community traffic is carried on inland waterways. At 46.3 percent, the share of traffic between the European Union and non-member countries carried on inland waterways is even greater.[10]

The US also has an extensive inland waterway transportation system, anchored by the Mississippi River which serves as a sort of spinal cord up the middle of the country and links the ports at New Orleans and Baton Rouge with the nation's breadbasket upstream. Ports and waterways handle almost all US overseas traffic by weight and about half by value. Approximately 145 inland and coastal ports handled more than one million metric tons of cargo each in 1996. In 1997, water-borne transportation of all US commodities totalled more than two billion metric tons, comprising about half domestic and half international trade.[11]

Barge transport has been of lesser importance in Africa, Australia and Asia, where short sea shipping is dominant.[12] As always, continental summaries mask international differences. In Asia, for example, 48 percent of total freight in Myanmar (Burma) moves on inland waterways. This figure is 35 percent in Bangladesh and Laos.[13] Navigation on the Niger River is quite important in transport between Nigeria and Niger.

In its current incarnation, inland waterway transport is low-cost and low-speed. While these characteristics make it a desirable transport mode for low-cost, bulk goods such as coal and grain, the growth in the global market is in flexible and fast transport modes with the capacity to respond to the 'just-in-time' demands of today's corporate consumers. The switch from the inexpensive, bulk-transport needs of the industrial era to the smaller-quantity, faster transport needs of the technology/information-intensive era results in trend differences in inland waterway transport between developed and developing countries.

In Europe, the share of waterway transport has remained very stable in recent times. In contrast, the European transport market on the whole has almost doubled, with road haulage taking up most of the growth. The poor performance of Western European water transport is due largely to the industrial restructuring that is taking place in all developed countries. Drop-offs in the heavy industry and construction fields have affected the transport of raw materials, construction materials, and first-stage processing that have traditionally found advantages in water transport. This structural effect accounts for about 60 percent of waterway traffic losses in Germany, with the remaining 40 percent due to the lack of waterway competitiveness in traditional markets. In central and eastern Europe, the slump in industrial production has hammered waterway transport for over a decade.[14]

'In the Antwerp and Rotterdam hinterland, waterway transport has seen considerable growth backed up by the introduction of container terminals along the Rhine. Container transport is also a promising market. However, it should be pointed out that waterways are mainly used for the redeployment of empty containers, since the transport time for such containers is less penalising than for containers carrying goods with high specific value.'[15]

In China, on the other hand, the use of the Yangtze alone for freight transport is increasing by 40 percent per year.[16] In 2001, Indonesia's waterway system carried six to seven million tons of freight per year. This volume was expected to triple to about 20 million tons per year, largely as a result of natural resource development in South Kalimantan.[17]

Many countries are spending vast amounts of money to upgrade their inland navigation systems in order to stimulate an increase in their use. Motivations vary from a need to ease congestion on crowded highways to a desire to increase trade on the global market.

'European ports are beginning to deepen their access channels and berths again to maintain competitiveness, particularly in the container trade. Adding another 2 metres to an existing navigable depth frequently represents a sizeable dredging project; work which may be carried out by trailer, backhoe and bucket dredger. The deepened ports may also require additional maintenance. More work for trailers! If European container terminals are getting deeper, it is probable that container ports in the rest of the world will be developing in a similar fashion and that more capital dredging will occur.

'Some of the South American economies have seen formidable growth rates in the past five years. Although the west coast of South America is not likely to generate massive dredging works, there being few substantial rivers on that side of the continent and deep water relatively close inshore, the situation on the east coast is very different. Large rivers and estuaries exist and a considerable amount of trade depends on river transport, estuarine ports and dredged channels. It is likely that trailer dredgers could be gainfully employed in these areas for some time to come.'[18]

The desire to increase the depth of inland waterways is largely driven by an increase in the size of barges, which keeps the cost of barge transport low relative to truck and rail. The standard barge size throughout much of the twentieth century was approximately 8 x 58 metres. By the turn of the century, these watercraft had been all but phased out and replaced by jumbo barges of roughly 11 x 65 metres. One jumbo barge has the same capacity as 15 railroad cars or 58 semi-trucks.[19] Super jumbo barges, of approximately 22 x 100 metres, are now making their debut on the world's waterways.

'The Paraguay–Parana river system forms a 3,440-kilometre waterway from the mouth of La Plata Basin, on the Atlantic coast between Uruguay and Argentina, to Careces in the state of Mato Grosso, Brazil, in the heart of South America.

'In 1991, Argentina, Brazil, Paraguay and Uruguay formed MERCOSUR, the Southern Cone Common Market of South America. MERCORSUR represents Latin America's largest economic base, with a market of nearly 200 million people and a gross regional product of US$427 billion per year. Because the waterway passes through these countries, it has a high symbolic value for the integration of their economies.

'A major impediment to increased trade for Latin America, and hence economic growth, is the lack of transportation infrastructure....'[20]

'The proposed plan of the Hydrovia Project is to create and maintain a navigation channel in the Paraguay and Parana rivers that is sufficiently deep and wide to guarantee "round the clock" navigation for 90 percent of the year during the following 10 years. The size of the canal will be determined by the size of the barges.'[21]

'A main motive for past developments in barge transport has been its cost-effectiveness, which has been expressed by an increasing scale of operations. As increasing the scale of the vessels will lead to potential cost reductions, there still remains a strong motive for increasing vessel size....'[22]

'In the relationship between the vessel and the waterway, there has always been a tendency to build vessels as large, and to load them as deeply, as is just permitted by the dimensions of the waterway and safety regulations.'[23]

One reason that inland barge transport is inexpensive is that fuel consumption is low, since half the time the towboats are moving they are assisted by downstream-flowing river currents. This advantage also leads to reduced pollutant emissions from towboats compared to other modes of freight transport, and thus to the claim that inland navigation is an environmentally friendly transport mode (see Table 6.1).

Table 6.1 Emissions (Pounds [Kilograms]) Produced in Moving 1 Short Ton (0.91 Metric Tons) of Cargo 1,000 Miles (1,609.34 Kilometres)

	Towboat	Rail	Truck
Hydrocarbon	0.09 [0.04]	0.46 [0.21]	0.63 [0.29]
Carbon Monoxide	0.20 [0.09]	0.64 [0.29]	1.90 [0.86]
Nitrous Oxide	0.53 [0.24]	1.83 [0.83]	10.17 [4.61]

From: Arkansas River Historical Society Museum, undated. *McClellan–Kerr Arkansas River Navigation System Waterway Fact Sheet.*

The nature of freight transport is changing rapidly as more countries join the global market place. This trend may pose a threat to the barge system because the raw materials that have traditionally moved from coastal ports to markets over inland waterways are increasingly processed at the country of extraction while the market for end products becomes increasingly global. The 'just-in-time' require-ments of today's markets also place a higher premium on shipment speed. If barge transport is to remain competitive, it must become more rapid while maintaining its cost advantages.

These trends could erode the environmental benefits of barges compared to trucks, particularly if time-efficiency gains are to be met by an increase in energy consumption by tows. The barge industry is also attempting to improve time efficiency by increasing the size of barges and tows – an effort that is only success-ful on waterways equipped with the mega-locks and profoundly deep and wide channels that are necessary to avoid costly bottlenecks. The environmental effects of constructing, operating and maintaining inland navigation, which are already considerable, will grow as the size of navigation channels and other infrastructure increases to accommodate larger barges and larger tows. More environmentally friendly options for efficiency improvements are discussed below (see 'Navigating Gently,' p. 180).

Inland navigation comprises three different subsectors. One is the barge industry, which has an interest in moving as much commerce as possible in the shortest possible amount of time. Thus, the trends in the barge industry are towards larger tows and larger barges. The second subsector is the dredging industry. While companies perform waterway dredging for a variety of purposes ranging from mining to removing contaminated sediments from aquatic ecosystems, much of the dredging industry is fuelled by the demands of the barge industry. The result is a continuously expanding demand for deeper and wider channels, deeper ports, and more ports and waterways.

The third subsector is the construction, operation and maintenance of inland waterway infrastructure. These responsibilities are often publicly funded and may have a number of political objectives. One objective often is to generate economic multiplier effects in the jurisdictions of specific public officials by triggering expenditures on ports, waterways and other navigation infrastructure (locks, dams, aids to navigation, etcetera). Another is to stimulate commercial activity at inland and coastal ports, and associated development of services, such as hotels, bars and restaurants, along the waterway itself. As long as the construction and maintenance of inland waterways continue to receive public funding, a huge incentive exists for both the barge industry and the dredging industry to encourage bigger boats, bigger tows, and bigger waterways and ports.

EFFECTS OF INLAND WATERWAY CONSTRUCTION AND OPERATION ON THE WATER CYCLE

One can reasonably argue that inland navigation provides a more environmentally benign means of freight transport than trucking. When compared to rail, the comparison is a bit more difficult to make. Even if one could conclude that inland navigation is the environmentally preferable means for moving goods from source to market, it would be fatuous to argue that the environmental performance of waterways and barges could not be improved. In fact, given that a large proportion of funding for river alterations to accommodate today's heavy barge traffic comes from public coffers, it makes a great deal of sense to take stock of the damage to aquatic ecosystems and the water cycle attributable to inland waterway transport. After all, this damage in terms of degraded water quality, impaired fisheries, bank erosion, and the diversion of water from other public uses to support barge transport during dry periods is all ultimately borne by the public.

Inland Waterway Construction

People frequently alter rivers to improve conditions for navigation. Alterations may include channelization and the installation of locks and dams specifically to facilitate navigation. Additional training works, structures meant to channel water and sediments in a manner that maintains a navigable channel, are also quite common along inland navigation routes. Some inland navigation projects involve the construction of artificial channels to connect two natural rivers.

Alluvial rivers tend to establish equilibrium between the water flow volumes and sediment loads. Any substantial modifications to the system, including realignments, locks, dams, changes in sediment regimes, and so forth will disrupt this balance. Changes in the rates and locations of sediment erosion and deposition will occur as the river attempts to re-establish a new state of equilibrium, and these changes are often not anticipated by project engineers. The development of an inland navigation system typically involves many such modifications, the impacts of which can be assessed individually. The ultimate response of the river system, however, depends on how the system integrates these individual impacts in an effort to attain a new equilibrium state.[24]

Channelization Projects

The straightening of a river, or the artificial channelling of multiple branches of a river into a single channel, causes changes in the hydrology and geomorphology of the river that in turn influence the water cycle. River engineers use 'corrective dredging' to realign the channel bank lines; to develop cut-offs; and to remove obstructions such as gravel bars, rock outcrops, and clay plugs.[25] The removal of fallen trees and debris jams from the channel as well as the harvesting of timber from the banks and floodplains to increase hydraulic capacity and prevent hazards to bridges or navigation is termed 'clearing and snagging.'[26] Investigators have demonstrated that clearing and snagging cause bank erosion and channel widening.[27]

'Crossing 2,102 km and five states, ten protected areas – including the world's largest river island, the Ilha do Bananal – and 35 indigenous reserves, directly affecting 11 percent of Brazilian national territory, the Hydrovia project is an ambitious part of the federal government's Brazil in Action plan. $124 million will be spent in the first stage, and $110 million in a second phase which plans an artificial canal of 60 km to bypass the rapids of Santa Isabel, on the Araguaia River, Pará state....

'The greatest number of interventions will take place along a stretch of 279 km of the Araguaia River where there are natural dykes. The study says that 'most of these dykes will require use of explosives for rock removal'. The explosions, according to the study, will kill many fish and will destroy breeding areas....

'Dredging (removal of sand from the riverbed) will have even greater impacts. The study said that dredging could cause 'alteration and degradation of local scenery, erosion of the riverbanks, siltation and deepening of channels and disappearance of sand banks and natural islands. Environmentalists reject the project.'[28]

The separation of the river from its floodplain reduces the area around the river subject to regular inundation. The loss of floodplain area can lead to reduced groundwater recharge and increased flood peaks. In addition, the construction of a publicly funded channelization project sometimes induces upstream landowners to invest in drainage systems for their own land that discharge unwanted water into the larger system. This further interrupts the water cycle by increasing the rate of runoff and decreasing groundwater recharge.

Separating a river from its floodplain through channelization significantly alters floodplain ecology. The reduction in the extent of flooded areas that results from artificially lowering the bed of a river often eliminates special floodplain habitat features that support aquatic, wetland and terrestrial life.

'In Slovakia, the more than 1,800-kilometre free-flowing section of the middle and lower Danube up to the Black Sea is interrupted only by the large impounded section of the two hydropower dams at the Iron Gates....

'If the plans [for an expanded Danube River navigation system] go through, projected environmental threats include the cutting off of large natural areas from the river leading to a direct loss of diverse habitats and species, many of which are seriously threatened. Species such as sturgeon and beavers are already significantly threatened. Groundwater levels will decrease, threatening human drinking water supplies and the health of millions that depend on the rivers for clean water. This will be exacerbated by deterioration in the river's natural capacity for self-purification and curbing pollution.'[29]

The increase in stream gradient that results from the loss of total channel length as engineers straighten a river can cause erosion of the river's bed and banks. Deepening of the channel to accommodate loaded barges can change the river from a source of recharge water to local aquifers into a groundwater discharge conduit. Cutoffs of river channel meanders have also had unintentional results.

'Perhaps one of the earliest and most vivid descriptions of the effects of a man-made cutoff was that made of the River Dorback in Scotland by Lauder in 1830. Immediately after the cut had been executed, the onlookers:

"Heard the deadened roar of the river, as it poured over the clayey bank in a fall of fifteen feet, carrying everything before it... Huge stones were continually rolling down ... the banks of the cut, being undermined, rapidly gave way."[30]

'On the East and West Prairie rivers in Alberta [Canada], the straightening of a meandering stream increased the slope by providing a shorter channel path. This increase in slope enabled the transport of more sediment than was supplied at the upstream end of the channelized reach and the difference was obtained from the bed, causing degradation which progressed upstream as a nickpoint [headwater cutting]. An excess of load was then supplied to the downstream part of the channelized reach and because the flatter natural reach downstream could not transport this sediment, it was deposited on the bed. The excess may be deposited in gradually decreasing quantities downstream. Degradation within the straightened reach may also cause bank collapse.'[31]

'The Atchafalaya has been flirtatiously beckoning the Mississippi for more than 100 years, daring the mighty river to jump out of its channel and join the Atchafalaya in a matrimonial march to the sea. The Army Corps of Engineers was the matchmaker in this relationship, although, as happens in most strong attractions, the Mississippi may have tried to change course without outside help. In 1828, Henry Shreve, the Corps' superintendent of western river improvements, dredged a cutoff through a large, horseshoe-shaped meander formed by the Mississippi at its confluence with the Atchafalya. The cutoff caused an increase of the Mississippi's flow into the Atchafalya, and ever since, the Corps has been fighting to keep the river in its original channel.'[32]

If levees or dykes are constructed to constrain the stream channel, river-borne sediment that might once have deposited on the floodplain can accumulate in the channel. Dredged channels are often prone to sedimentation because currents within the deepened areas are weaker than the currents that existed prior to channel dredging and are often incapable of preventing sediments from depositing.[33] In-channel sediment accumulation raises the height of the riverbed, and can result in rivers that are higher than surrounding landscapes: the example of the Netherlands has been cited above (see p. 140). These constitute a considerable flood hazard.

Channelization projects cause losses of aquatic, and often riparian, habitat. Dredging out a deeper channel directly removes important instream structure, such as mussel beds and gravel used by fish for spawning. Channelization reduces riparian habitats by de-watering wetlands, eliminating natural flood pulses, and by using these areas as disposal sites for dredged material, as well as by intentionally clearing them to widen the river or to reduce hydraulic resistance in the channel. Many cases have been recorded of fish populations declining in response to this type of habitat alteration.[34] The elimination of riparian vegetation during a channelization project can remove both food sources for riverine biota and shading, which leads to increases in temperature. The temperature effect is especially important in determining what fish species can inhabit the water, since cooler water contains more oxygen than warmer water.

The alterations of river hydrology brought about by channelization projects also destabilize estuarine ecosystems. Dredging projects intended to deepen river channels in coastal areas very often improve the water exchange in these areas, causing the waterbody landward of the dredged site to become more marine because of increased salinity.[35]

'River Niger is the largest river system in West Africa and is the largest and longest in Nigeria, being central to the entire drainage system of the country. In order to improve navigability of the inland waterways, it has been proposed to dredge the lower part of the Niger River for a distance of about 600 km from the Warri bifurcation in Delta State (South) to Baro in Niger State (North)....

'It is very obvious that any other activity upstream of the Niger and especially that which affects the hydrology of the river system such as dredging shall have significant and major impacts on the distribution of various water regimes (which constitute the life-supporting medium) of the delta ecosystem, and also on the hydrology of the various river tributaries which drain into the Niger along its course up north....

'Dredging of the lower Niger will involve deepening its channel and thus increasing its cross-sectional area. The total annual flows ... reaching the Niger bifurcation at Onya/Samabri would remain unchanged while its flow area increases, thus decreasing the flow velocities at the entrance of the deltaic distributaries. In the current dredging proposal, the deltaic tributaries which transmit water through the delta communities are to remain undredged or unchannelized and to transmit the same volume of flow at reduced velocities; thus the pattern of channel flows and overland flows shall change and the frontiers of freshwater, brackish and saline water shall also be altered.

'With inflow velocities of freshwater to the delta reduced, other important questions which need to be assessed with hydrological modelling are:

- What are the possible impacts on the need for construction of anti-salinity weirs to protect water treatment works supplying potable water to millions of population upstream of the Niger?

- With the decreased base level of the Niger River bed, the associated upstream tributaries spanning three major hydrological areas ... shall have increased down-cutting attributes thus increasing their erosive powers and thus accentuating the erosion hazards [to] the adjoining [land].'[36]

Locks and Dams

Managers of inland water navigation systems often construct locks and dams to increase river navigability over steep river reaches and during seasons of medium or low river flows. The purpose of the dam is to impound water and increase channel depth. The locks are essentially a pair of gates used to equalize the water level upstream and downstream of the dam so that barges and other boats can pass safely in both directions. The system operates as an aquatic elevator.

Typically, a barge or several barges travelling upstream will enter the lock at the downstream end. The downstream gates close and the upstream gates open, so that the water level inside the lock rises to that of the impounded water behind the dam.

The increased water levels elevate the barges, which then move out of the upper end of the lock. The process is reversed going downstream. The barges enter the lock through the upstream gate, which is then closed. The downstream gate is then opened, allowing water levels inside the lock to drop to the water level of the river below the dam.

Navigation system managers may construct locks and dams in rivers with steep gradients and velocities too high to permit navigation, or where conditions make it impractical to develop the required depths by dredging or blasting because of the extent of rock outcrops or patterns of sediment movement. Navigation channels that pass through estuaries, bays or river mouths and, in some cases, sea-level canals may include locks to prevent salt water intrusion or to minimize the effects of tides and the difference in water levels with the connecting waterway. Artificial canals used to connect two natural bodies of water, to bypass rock outcrops and rapids, or to decrease the length or curvature of a navigable river may also require locks.[37]

When engineers construct a dam for navigation or other purposes, sediments typically deposit in the river reach immediately upstream of the dam. Consequently, river water passing downstream of the reservoir or navigation pool is 'sediment hungry' – that is, the water is carrying a smaller sediment load than the load dictated by the physics of balance between flow volume, gradient and sediment load. The result is often significant erosion of the riverbed directly below the dam. This erosion can endanger the structural integrity of the dam. If for no other purpose than to protect the existing dam, engineers may propose the construction of another dam downstream to trap sediment below the first dam and stop the down-cutting of the riverbed. This process can extend downstream over many river reaches, resulting in the transformation of a natural river into a string of artificially regulated reservoirs or navigation pools.

'The Wisla (or Vistula) River is one of Europe's largest, most important rivers, with a catchment area that covers more than half of Poland. Rising in Poland's Beskidi Mountains and winding its way northwards to the Bay of Gdansk, it serves as an important ecological corridor, linking the Baltic Sea to the Danube basin in the south, the Varta basin in the west and the Bug in the east. It supports great biodiversity in its sandy islands, steep banks, and riverine meadows and forests provide important breeding sites for many species of birds, including some which are now rare in Europe because of the impact of dams and diversions on the region's rivers and wetlands. The river has been crucial in human history, as well, and its valley includes many important cultural landmarks.

'Now the government is proposing to build a series of seven dams (called a "dam cascade") along the 394-km length of the lower Wisla, each reservoir extending back to the previous dam. There is already one dam on the river. The proposals also include an east–west waterway linking the [Wisla to the] River Odra in the west and several more new dams on the Odra. Project promoters claim the dams will solve Poland's water supply problems, reduce floods, supply electricity and improve navigation. But most of these claims are unrealistic or even contradictory.'[38]

'Environmentalists argue that a government plan to build eight dams (the first one went up in 1975 in Wloclawek) and dig a 300-kilometre canal to factories in the south would kill several species and raise the water table, making vast tracts of land unfarmable. [River activist Jacek] Bozek points to the Wloclawek dam as a warning sign – the catchment has gathered a sewage-laden sediment that has destroyed more than half of the riverside land and killed marketable fish like sturgeon and salmon.'[39]

Continuous strings of locks and dams have transformed some rivers into 'strings of pearls' or 'dam cascades' – aquatic systems that are essentially contiguous reservoirs and lack the hydrology of natural river systems throughout their courses. In addition to blocking the upstream and downstream movements of river biota, nutrients and sediments, such multi-dam developments disturb the lateral relationships between the river and its floodplain, with effects on both biological communities and transfers of water between the river, floodplain, and water table.

Training Works

River training refers to channel realignment techniques that involve the installation of structures to selectively create sediment deposition zones, maintain the depth and location of the navigation channel, and reduce unwanted erosion, especially of banks and bridges.[40]

There are several categories of river-training works, including bank armouring techniques, flow deflection techniques and energy reduction methods.

Bank armouring refers to the practice of lining river banks with resistant material to combat the increased erosive power of a channelized river. Engineers often armour the riverbanks with concrete, rip-rap (rocks or chunks of concrete deposited along the bank), gabions (wire cages filled with rock), bulkheads (vertical walls constructed of metal or concrete adjacent to the riverbank) or other structures. The rivers, in turn, gradually or suddenly readjust themselves to regain equilibrium by burrowing into the riverbed or eroding the bank protection. Adjustments in lined channels frequently occur where engineers have deepened, straightened or widened the channel prior to protection. When these adjustments happen during flood events, the structures may be destroyed.[41]

Flow deflection techniques include the use of structures to direct scouring flows away from the banks to reduce or eliminate erosion. These techniques are generally less expensive than bank armouring strategies. Engineers construct deflective structures approximately perpendicular to the river flow, thereby reducing the effective width of the river.[42]

Spur dykes – also called transverse dykes, cross dykes, wing dams or jetties – are structures extending from the riverbank channelward, perpendicular to the channel being developed.[43] These structures trap sediment and build up land between the river banks and the natural channel. The result is a narrower river channel, straight and essentially devoid of floodplain wetlands, where the flow of water is directed through the centre of the channel, maintaining navigable depths. In some instances, such as in the construction of wing dykes on the Missouri River in the midwestern US, farmers use the newly created land for crop production.

Energy reduction methods diminish the ability of the river to erode its bed and banks. Some examples are longitudinal dykes that extend from the bank parallel to the river. The purpose of these structures is to divert scouring flows away from the banks, thus preventing bank erosion while maintaining the depth of the navigation channel.[44] Fence revetments are also constructed parallel to the river flow, but are pervious because they are made of wood or wire. Flow velocity decreases behind these structures.[45] Vanes are structures placed within the channel at an angle to normal flow so that they reduce the secondary currents, thereby reducing the erosive capacity of the river.

Closure dykes are used to prevent water from going down secondary channels during low and medium flows, with the result that all of the water is concentrated in the main, navigable channel.[46] These structures can cause severe alterations of stream and wetland ecosystems in the secondary, or excluded, channels by eliminating their source of water.

The nature and extent of impacts of river-training structures depend on many factors determined by river engineers, including the materials used to build the structures and the season of construction. The effects of river-training structures also depend on the basic characteristics of the altered river reaches, such as substrate (for example, sand, silt, cobble, bedrock), channel form (pool and riffle, meandering or braided), and dominant processes (rain-fed or snowmelt-fed; dominated by bedload or suspended load; agrading bed, degrading bed or stable bed). Structures that may merely deflect flows in a bedload-dominated, cobble-bed stream might function to trap sediments and build sandbars in a sand-bed stream with a high suspended sediment load.[47]

River-training structures affect the hydraulics, sediment transport and geometry of the river channel, as well as many of the exchange processes between the river and its banks. These effects include changes in surface water elevation, in flow velocities and in erosion and deposition.[48] Most of the direct effects are physical in nature, but these physical changes affect the chemical and biological nature of the river system. These physical changes can also affect the processes, or pathways, between ecosystem components.[49] Such changes can drastically affect hydrological processes, such as the exchange of water between rivers and aquifers, and biological processes, such as the composition and density of aquatic biota.

'Downstream of Gavins Point Dam, the Missouri River has been channelized ...
from Sioux City, Iowa to its mouth to permit navigation by boats and barges and
its banks were stabilized to enhance utilization of the bankline adjacent to the
channel. In addition, chutes and side channels have been blocked and diverted,
converting the once structurally complex channels and instream islands into a
single thread of deep, fast-moving water....

'Engineering works on the river's main channel have resulted in significant
ecological changes in the channelized reaches. Construction of revetment has
greatly narrowed and deepened the channel and has fixed its location. This has
virtually eliminated shallow water habitat and greatly increased water depth and
velocity. Ecological impacts of these changes on native fish and on streamside
vegetation have been strongly negative.'[50]

Inland Waterway Operation and Maintenance

Operation and maintenance of inland waterways have repercussions for the water
cycle beyond the initial construction. Maintenance dredging and the disposal of
dredged material can lead to major ecological imbalances. The management of
reservoirs, which often serve multiple functions, may also be altered to provide
adequate depths for navigation in rivers. Finally, barge traffic has environmental
consequences for the physical, chemical and biological integrity of inland waters.

Maintenance Dredging and Disposal of Clean-dredged Material

Because alterations to river systems in support of inland waterway transportation
create imbalances between sediment loads and the river's capacity to transport
them, sediments deposit in parts of navigable waterways where they did not
deposit under natural conditions. In addition, over large portions of the globe,
deforestation, agricultural practices and urban development are contributing
sediment loads to rivers and lakes at rates that greatly exceed natural conditions. In
order to maintain water depths adequate to support inland navigation, therefore,
waterway managers periodically dredge these reaches. The process of dredging
stirs up sediments, increasing their concentration in the water column. The general
ecological repercussions of increased suspended sediment loads are addressed
below (see 'The Impacts of Boat Traffic,' p. 178).

To a large extent, the problem with dredging revolves around where to place the
dredged material. Assuming it is relatively clean, trucking it back to the farms and
forestlands from which most of it originally came seems the ideal solution, but is
too expensive to be feasible in most cases. Conventional options include open
water disposal, floodplain placement, confined disposal (see 'Dredging and Disposal of Contaminated Sediments' on p. 175) and beneficial use (discussed under
'Navigating Gently', p. 180).[51]

Open water disposal falls into two categories: dispersive and non-dispersive,
depending on whether the sediment is transported out of the site or remains within

designated boundaries.[52] This technique is often the least expensive, but is generally limited to lakes and marine or estuarine systems that are sufficiently deep to prevent surface currents and wind action continually resuspending the material. Even in these deeper ecosystems, many questions remain regarding the effect of foreign substrate on benthic life. From an ecological perspective, it is preferable to dispose of clean sediment in areas already dominated by sediments of similar grain size and chemistry, so that native fauna have a chance to re-establish themselves following the disturbance caused by the disposal operation.

Floodplain placement is also relatively inexpensive, although it may require the purchase of rights to use floodplain land for disposal. The primary drawback from an environmental perspective is the substantial alteration of floodplain hydrology with attendant effects on biodiversity and river/floodplain interactions. A secondary, though not insubstantial, drawback is the tendency of dredged materials deposited on floodplains to wash back into the river during the following flood season or high-water release from an upstream dam. The results of such incidences are the potential loss of aquatic life from sediment suspension and subsequent deposition, and the renewal of the dredging process that the deposit of previously dredged materials initiates.

Dredging and Disposal of Contaminated Sediments

Most persistent toxic compounds that make their way into navigable waterways are trace metals and organic compounds such as dioxins, polychlorinated biphenyls (PCBs), and polyaromatic hydrocarbons that do not remain suspended in the water column. The metals are often too heavy to remain suspended. Many of the organic compounds are 'hydrophobic,' which means that they adsorb to sediments, or cling to fat molecules in animals, rather than remaining in suspension in the water or passing through an animal body in the liquid waste stream. Most highly contaminated sediments, regardless of the source of contamination, tend to be fine-grained materials deposited in low-energy areas that serve as sinks. This is because fine sediments have a greater combined surface area than coarse sediments, onto which contaminants adsorb.[53]

Because they can resuspend materials sorbed to sediments, dredging operations can dramatically increase the exposure of aquatic animals to toxic contaminants. Acute effects from contaminated sediments may arise in the immediate vicinity of the actual dredging operation. The risk of acute effects occurring is related to the degree of water exchange, with the highest risks occurring in stagnant water.[54] The release of chemical substances, which might be consumed and concentrated in the aquatic (and, later, terrestrial) food chain, is the most severe ecological effect of dredging or reclamation projects in industrially contaminated areas. Some compounds, such as heavy metals, often do not degrade in nature, or degrade very slowly, and therefore tend to accumulate in the aquatic food chain. The effect on the ecosystem will often become evident in the form of reduced fertility, physical deformities, or reduced resistance to infectious diseases at the top of the food chain several years after the release of these substances.[55]

The risk of releasing contaminants into the food chain as a result of dredging operations has inspired many countries to regulate the management of contaminated dredged material and to ensure that they are safely disposed of. The cost of handling and treatment of contaminated dredge spoils may increase the overall cost of a dredging operation by a factor of 5 to 100 compared to the costs of working with clean material.[56] During the dredging operation itself, some sort of technology such as a silt curtain may be required to prevent the resuspended contaminants from drifting away from the dredging site. The safe disposal of contaminated sediments is often even more costly, as it requires that they be treated, confined, or both.

Dredging project managers may opt to treat contaminated sediments prior to disposing of them. Because dredged sediments may contain a highly variable mix of contaminants from a fairly wide range of sources, any treatment method is virtually guaranteed to leave behind untreated components.[57] In addition, treatment methods have their own environmental impacts, including the production of contaminated wastewater, toxic gases, or highly dangerous concentrated residues. Some processes require large allocations of energy or land.[58] Treatment processes include the use of solvents to concentrate contaminants into smaller volumes, immobilization techniques that fix the contaminants to solid matter, incineration at extremely high (1,200 degrees centigrade) temperatures, and solidification in a cement mixture for use as a building material. All of these measures carry the risk of cross-media contamination and accidental release.

Confined disposal facilities are designed to retain dredged material solids and allow the discharge of process water from the containment site. Sites receiving contaminated material must also provide sufficient isolation of contaminants from the surrounding environment, and thus require complex systems of control measures.[59]

Reservoir Operation

On the majority of the world's waterways, the travel plans of towboats and barges are unscheduled, as are their arrival times at locks. Governments that strive to support inland waterway transportation are therefore driven to provide predictable, if not constant, river conditions sufficient to support increasingly large and heavily loaded fleets of barges. On many rivers, including the Missouri River in the US, control of water levels adequate to sustain barge traffic throughout the year requires the virtual elimination of seasonal variations in water level. When natural water levels are high, such as during snowmelt or high rainfall seasons, navigation system managers want to store water behind dams so that it is available to float their boats during drier climatic periods. Such actions result in artificially low water levels during natural flood seasons, which can retard biological processes, and artificially high water levels during natural dry seasons, with similar results. The repercussions of these hydrological shifts extend beyond the fish and invertebrates that have evolved with natural flood processes. The elimination of seasonal flooding, for example, can substantially reduce groundwater recharge and affect water supplies for communities during the dry season. Politics, rather than science, frequently dictates the pattern of water flows on highly regulated water bodies.

As a result of dam operation to support inland navigation, hydrographs may become inverted in the river reaches between navigation dams, meaning that

'Caught between competing [court] rulings, the beleaguered [U.S. Army] Corps [of Engineers] finally succeeded last week in draining some water from Lake Sharpe and Lewis and Clark Lake, two medium-sized Missouri River reservoirs in South Dakota. But Corps officials are continuing their desperate search for more water to ship south amid a bitter regional battle.

'The upstream forces, led by Senate Majority Leader Thomas A. Daschle (Democrat, South Dakota), are fighting to protect the $85 million fishing and recreational industry that has grown up around Missouri River reservoirs and lakes. The downstream interests, led by Sen. Christopher S. Bond (Republican, Missouri) are determined to maintain sufficiently high river levels for the aging and far-less lucrative barge industry....

'Ironically, the controversy over the Corps' efforts to divert water from the upper North-west to the Midwest comes at a time when North Dakota and South Dakota are experiencing the third year of drought, and Missouri and other midwestern states downstream are being pounded by heavy rain and flooding. So far this month, flooding has been blamed for eight deaths in Missouri and a boy's drowning in Illinois.'[60]

'Following discussions with navigation users during and after the 1986 drought, the [US Army] Corps [of Engineers] developed a technique to provide for a planned period of navigation called a Navigation Window [on the Apalachicola River]. This technique involves temporarily storing water in West Point Lake, Walter F. George [reservoir], and Lake Seminole[61] that is released over a 10-day to two-week period at a rate to provide for economical navigation depths (at least 7.5-foot channel) [approximately 2.29 metres] in the Apalachicola River.... This technique was employed beginning in 1990 and continued throughout the decade. Beginning in the mid-1990s, Navigation Windows were scheduled in advance, approximately one per month during the low water months, in order to provide the waterway users a predictable reliable channel. Because channel conditions were also deteriorating, Navigation Windows were used with increasing frequency, as many as six per year, generally between May and December.'[62]

'[E]ffects on habitat as a result of flow regulations to create a navigation window for barge traffic in the fall of 1990 were examined. For 19 days during this period, there were approximately 590 fewer acres [approximately 239 hectares] of connected aquatic habitats than there would have been if the navigation window had not been implemented. Effects of reduced aquatic habitats on fishes include reduction in the amount of food, protective cover, and spawning sites. A hydrological event with flows similar to this period of reduced flows occurred once every 10 years on average (1922–95) and probably would not have occurred in 1990 if the navigation windows had not been implemented.'[63]

portions of the floodplain that are normally inundated by floods are dry during the rainy season and wet during the dry season. This inversion occurs because river managers attempting to maintain a constant depth upstream of the dam artificially raise water levels just above the dam. When the river flow increases, river managers release water at the dam and water levels at the dam decrease. Opening dam gates and lowering the surface elevation of a river increases the slope of the river between the upstream point (directly below the next upstream dam on 'chain of pearl' rivers) and the dam, thereby increasing the river's flow rate without raising the surface elevation at the upstream end of the reach between dams. This complicated operating procedure minimizes floodplain inundation and thus avoids the costs of floodplain acquisition from private landowners, which gives it an economic advantage over the simpler procedure of just trying to maintain the water level at the lower dam. Either procedure is capable of maintaining adequate water depths for boat traffic.[64]

These inversions, where water is low during the flood season and high during the dry season, are especially harmful because the timing is wrong for the biota. The floodplain is exposed when fish need access to shallow spawning areas, then inundated when moist-soil plants should be growing on mudflats. If the plants do germinate, they are drowned by rising water during what should be their normal growing season. The water level drops in the fall, just when migrating waterfowl need access to the summer's production of tubers and seeds.[65]

Altered flood pulses can initiate long-term changes in the ecosystem that are difficult to reverse. Because navigation dams don't allow river water levels to go as low as they did before the dams were built, sediments delivered by the annual floods into areas influenced by the dams don't dry and compact during the summer as they did under pre-dam conditions. In many countries, sediment loads are increasing because of deforestation and agricultural activities. Navigation dams trap sediment, and raise the bottoms of rivers. As the river bottom rises, sediments are more easily suspended by wind and wave action, making the water cloudy. The resulting high water level can kill and carry away the remaining riparian trees that had not been removed during the initial creation of the navigation channel. When these natural wave-breaks are gone, riverbanks erode at increasing rates, releasing even more sediment into the reservoirs between dams. As a result, more wind-breaks disappear as entire islands erode. When these processes expand the open water area along the channel the wind fetch increases, leading to the uprooting of aquatic plants. Aquatic plants naturally function as biotic mediators, reducing sediment resuspension and turbidity by reducing waves with their leaves and anchoring the river bottom with their roots.[66] Thus, the loss of aquatic plants results in an increase in resuspended sediment, a decrease in light penetration, and a decrease in photosynthesis that can make life impossible for some native river creatures. It is indeed a vicious cycle.

The Impacts of Boat Traffic

Tows cause intensified, transient changes in water quality. Unrestricted growth in commercial barge traffic over the long term can cause semi-permanent water quality degradation. The passage of the submerged hull of a barge, and the velocity of the propeller jets of its tow, increase the flow velocity of the surrounding water. The amount of acceleration depends on the proximity of the barge to the riverbed – decreased clearance increases the relative velocity. Increases in towboat speed also increase flow velocity. When the flow rate of the river is accelerated, the cutting of the riverbed and banks increases.

Diverging waves from the bow, stern and side of a barge also amplify a river's natural currents, thus further increasing erosion. Wave amplitudes can be significant even when waves originate a long way away from the shore relative to the width of the channel. In narrow sections of a channel, where a towboat and its barges pass close to the bank, waves lose very little energy before reaching the shore and can cause substantial shoreline damage. The increased flow velocities and the propeller motion associated with towboats and barges also resuspend bottom sediments. A plume of suspended sediment may stretch as far as three to five kilometres behind a tow.[67]

The combination of increased channel erosion and sediment resuspension can have a number of effects on riverine ecology. First, increasing the sediment suspended in the water column reduces light penetration in the water. This can cause a decrease in instream photosynthesis and reduced levels of dissolved oxygen, which can shift aquatic habitat characteristics so severely that species of fish and invertebrates disappear from the river completely. The heavier the barge traffic, the greater the reduction in light penetration will be. In the Illinois River, a Mississippi River tributary, on a date when 15 towboats pushing 151 barges were present, water clarity decreased by nearly half compared to a day when only 3 towboats pushing 25 barges were present.[68]

Second, increased bank and channel erosion and sediment resuspension can have direct impacts on fish. Fish adapted to clear water foraging, such as trout and salmon, may experience a decrease in their ability to locate their prey as visibility declines. Sediment may also clog fish gills, impairing the ability to breathe. When the sediment finally settles out of suspension, it may smother fish eggs and choke colonies of invertebrates, such as mussels.

Third, sediments resuspended by boat and barge traffic or other forces settle out in more slowly moving water. On a river that maintains backwater and floodplain wetlands, sediments can build up to the point where aquatic habitat no longer exists in previously wet environments. The repercussions can be significant both for ecological communities and for the exchange of water between the river and water table.

Finally, if the sediments contain toxic materials, resuspension can increase the availability of these materials to the food chain. Pore water containing dissolved contaminants may escape during dredging or sediment transport. This tendency is exacerbated by the low settling rates of small particles released in the water during handling; they can remain suspended in the water column, where they are subject to wide dispersion.[69]

In a world simultaneously confronted by a rapid increase in international trade, global warming resulting from the combustion of fossil fuels, and a freshwater crisis, it would not be prudent to turn away from inland navigation completely as a mode of freight transport. We do have the ability to make inland navigation much more compatible with the protection of the global water cycle than it presently is, however.

NAVIGATING GENTLY

Inland waterway transport is forced to compete in a world that is rapidly integrating economically and in which inexpensive, industrial commodities are becoming less lucrative than pricy, specialized goods. To succeed in this highly competitive environment, inland waterway operators will need to increase the speed of delivery while maintaining their current cost advantage over other modes of freight transport. The strategy of upsizing barges, tows and waterways may not ultimately increase the competitiveness of inland navigation because such options are expensive and becoming more so as space for additional infrastructure and dredged material disposal becomes scarcer. A better strategy for the inland navigation industry would be to increase its efficiency substantially. Enormous strides towards increased efficiency can be made through better use of information. By relying more on information and less on the physical alteration of waterways, the inland navigation industry can also maintain its environmental competitiveness.

Further gains in protecting the aquatic environment and the water cycle can also be realized through altering the physical features of barges and tows to fit the waterways on which they operate, rather than altering the waterways to fit increasingly obese generations of barges and tows. Societies can reduce the costs of maintaining inland waterways through better watershed management. Finally, when dredging is necessary to maintain a navigable channel, creative uses of the dredged material may decrease the costs and environmental effects relative to more conventional disposal methods.

Making Better Use of Information

One way to minimize the costs of inland navigation is to ensure that tow navigators have access to accurate, up-to-date bathymetric data and real-time information on water depths.[70] In the last few decades, substantial progress has been made in the development of the hardware needed to transmit this information. Such systems can alleviate the need for the construction of new infrastructure by improving the efficiency of use of existing locks; reducing costly delays caused by bottlenecks at locks; and minimizing the need for dredging by providing current information on water depths.

A radiotelephone service, which allows communications both from boat to shore and from boat to boat for agreement on passing manoeuvres, has been established in recent years for inland waterways. The development of high-resolution radar for inland navigation and the equipment of the waterways with radar reflectors on buoys and beacons have recently enabled navigation during periods of poor visibility. Control centres for Vessel Traffic Services have been established to aid navigation in difficult traffic situations by using shore-based radar to monitor tow movements. On-board electronic navigable charts can contain depth information in narrow or shallow river stretches related to a reference water level or to the current water level, optimizing the draught of vessels.[71] Many towboats now carry on-board computers that connect to the Internet and can share databases with shore radar systems and with the reporting systems of other tows.[72]

In some countries, the Internet is used to exchange information about water levels, traffic regulations and other navigation conditions.[73]

Electronic systems that communicate information about the position and speed of tows can also be combined with policy options aimed at reducing congestion and improving traffic flows – two characteristics that can help waterways support a smooth and regular flow of commerce. In many of today's markets, such reliability matters more than speed. When a container ship from the Far East has spent more than twenty days at sea, an additional transport time of one or two days makes little difference.[74]

'Extra throughput [on the Upper Mississippi River] could be squeezed out of the current locks by improving congestion management. Although scheduling tows to arrive at locks is difficult, valuable steps can be taken. The level of traffic on the Upper Mississippi River is not uniform over the navigation system. Smoothing traffic would significantly reduce congestion and delays. Non-structural measures such as a scheduling system, congestion pricing, and tradable permits will also initiate smaller and far fewer environmental impacts than structural measures such as lock extensions. They are therefore more consistent with strategies for sustainable development (promoting improved traffic flow and environmental restoration) of the Upper Mississippi and Tributary system.'[75]

Improving Intermodal Interfaces

For much of the past two centuries, modes of freight shipment have operated largely in isolation from each other. Waterways have carried low-value, high-weight shipments of goods that, in general, were not particularly time-sensitive. In recent decades, as globalization has blossomed and the information age shifted commerce towards high-value, high technology and time-sensitive goods, the niche for expensive air freight has expanded. Rail and road shipments maintain comfortable shares of in-between goods, and shorter-haul, intra-continental commerce.

By the dawn of the twenty-first century, however, the lines between these genres of freight transport were blurring as increasing amounts of goods were travelling in containers. These truck-trailer-sized boxes were carrying 95 percent of general cargoes moving between continents by the year 2000.[76] Millions of containers crossed the oceans in ships, loaded onto barges to continue their journey inland, and/or finally shifted onto trucks or trains for delivery to a terminal.

The use of two or more modes to move a shipment from the point of origin to its final destination is known as 'intermodal' transport.[77] The challenges of choosing the most cost-effective means of transport and minimizing the time and expense involved in shifting containers from one mode to another has begun to force integration of freight transport modes. These challenges have also forced the shipping industry to focus more attention on improving the efficiency of the entire supply chain, which is defined as the network of organizations that are involved in the different processes and activities that create products and services of value to the ultimate consumer. Supply chain management is the management of the relationships between the organizations in the supply chain to deliver superior customer value at a reduced cost to the supply chain as a whole.[78] Intermodal transport, as it moves from a focus on infrastructure components to a holistic focus on process and systems, will have more viability and applicability in the world of global supply chain management than an obsolete and isolated approach to each individual mode of freight transport.[79]

Inland waterway navigation, strategically positioned as a node in a supply chain and prepared with the most up-to-date, information-based technology, could reap major rewards from the growth in intermodal freight transport. Strategic positioning comes naturally to inland waterway freight transport because rivers end in many of the same estuaries that house commercial ocean ports, making them easily accessible to trans-oceanic shipments. Once containers and other freight are transferred from ships to barges, a tow can transport the goods many kilometres upstream before there is a need to transfer them again to trucks or trains to reach their final destinations.

Improving Barge Design for Environmental Compatibility

Largely because the construction, operation and maintenance of inland waterways is a public responsibility in many countries, and because inland navigation must move more product to remain competitive, barge design is driven far more by the 'bigger is better' principle than by environmental considerations.

On the other hand, the increasing environmental costs of global freight transport are certain to catch up with those companies that do business on the world's inland waterways. In particular, the costs of dredged material disposal could force switches to shallow-draft tows and barges.

'The growth of navigation on the Rhine has been a strong incentive for the economic development of Europe and the Rhine River states in particular. To improve the inland water navigation system, a large number of river regulation and canalization projects have been implemented. In view of the large impacts that these interventions have had on the natural water system, and the high costs involved in compensating the negative effects, it is meaningful to consider navigation concepts which do not require such major interventions in the river system. An example is the so-called 'River Snake'. The principle is simple. The River Snake involves a new type of flat-bottomed vessel in the form of a snake. The Snake consists of container carriers joined with large ball joints and interspersed with 'power units.' These units are the propelling and navigating 'vertebrae' of the floating river train. They also ensure that the Snake easily adapts to bends in the river. A central computer located at the front end of the vessel controls the power units. We realize that this concept will be of limited use for the Rhine system, because this water system is already almost completely regulated and canalized. However, such vessels could be highly useful for the protection of natural river systems elsewhere. They could be tailor-made for any riverbed and provide economic potential while regulation and canalization measures could be kept to a minimum. There is a good chance that various countries will be interested in this concept. For instance, along the Elbe River, attempts are being made to construct a navigation vessel with less draught, making further canalization of this river unnecessary (so-called 'Elbe-schiff').'[80]

'Today, new shipbuilding technologies as well as new information and communication systems offer the possibility of increasing both the productivity and the interest of inland navigation without needing massive interventions in the river landscape. A reorientation to other groups of goods also changes the requirements for inland navigation: i.e. flexible, regular and frequent offers.'[81]

Watershed and Channel Management to Reduce Siltation

Increased deposition of sediments originating in artificially destabilized watersheds and stream channels decreases channel depth and flow conveyance capacity. As a result, frequent dredging of rivers that receive artificially heavy sediment loads is necessary both to maintain navigation and to avoid flood hazards. In North America, excessive sediment erosion, transport and deposition cause economic damages estimated at US$16 billion each year. The US alone spends about US$700 million per year on dredging. Sediment overloading from land and stream erosion causes significant environmental and economic challenges – excessive sedimentation in rivers, reservoirs and estuaries may contribute to high turbidity and loss of flood carrying capacity as well as sediment deposition in navigable waterways.[82]

Integrated river basin management strategies can potentially reduce the environmental and economic costs of inland waterway maintenance by reducing the volumes of sediment that are transported from the watershed and degraded tributary streams to navigable river channels. While such a strategy makes intuitive sense, it runs up against two real-world problems. First, sediments that have accumulated in tributary streams to inland waterways are likely to blow out during a large storm, resulting in downstream channel siltation regardless of watershed treatments. Second, in many cases river channels have already adjusted their contours to accommodate both increased silt loads and channel straightening. Therefore, the reduction in sediment loads into the river channels may only trigger increased erosion of the river's bed and banks as the river attempts to regain equilibrium by recruiting more sediment.

Perhaps the best method to offset the reduction of sediment input as a watershed approaches a pre-disturbance condition is to adjust the channel configuration to support the pre-disturbance ratios of sediment, flow and gradient. One way to accomplish this is to move away from a straight channel concept and instead mimic the pre-disturbance meander patterns of the waterway.

'The Nemadji River Basin covers an area of about 433 square miles of land in Carlton and Pine Counties in Minnesota and Douglas County in Wisconsin. Flows from the Nemadji River enter Superior Bay at Superior, Wisconsin, then enter Lake Superior through the Superior Entry navigation channel. Because the soils in the Nemadji River Basin are mostly sand or clay, erosion has been a sizeable and visible problem....

'The loose, well-drained sand makes it difficult for vegetation to grow, especially on slopes. Without vegetation to hold the sand in place, it is easily washed away by runoff from melting snow or heavy rain events. The clay is also susceptible to erosion, which can be seen in the red clay area of the watershed as slumping along hillsides and streams the colour of chocolate milk. Human activities, such as clear-cutting the mature red pine forests, clearing the land for agriculture, draining wetlands and building roads have all caused hydrological changes.

'These changes result in higher volumes of runoff and higher peak flows following storms and snowmelt, which in turn cause increased stream bank erosion and bluff slumping.

'In Carlton and Pine Counties, this accelerated soil erosion and hillside slumping result in degradation of trout streams and damage to roads. Further downstream, the extra sediment carried by the Nemadji River fills Duluth-Superior harbours, requiring costly dredging to keep shipping canals open....

'Since 1999 the Carlton County Soil and Water Conservation District and its partner have accomplished these actions:

- Used NASA LANDSAT satellite remote sensing data to define land-use changes over the past 15 years and begun to work with landowners as they develop forest harvesting zones;

- Set a goal that 40 percent of the watershed be maintained in mature forest land-uses to minimize clay slumping and erosion zones;

- Stabilized Spring Creek banks;

- Revegetated and stabilized Harding's Hill on the Blackhoof River;

- Offered cost-share tree plantings, the largest involving 30 acres of private land, 9 acres of which had severe slopes;

- Inventoried bluff and streambank erosion zones;

- Initiated riparian buffer projects....'[83]

'Where the location of a channel has to be moved then meandering alignments may be more expensive to construct than straight channels because of increased excavation costs. However, environmental benefits and reduced maintenance costs may offset increased construction costs over the life of the project. Well-designed meandering channels are more stable, provide a greater variety of flow conditions and aquatic habitat diversity, and are aesthetically more pleasing.'[84]

Maintaining Natural Flow Regimes in Navigable Rivers

A number of modifications to natural river systems to improve their utility as navigation routes can disrupt natural flow regimes and thus interfere with the life cycles of aquatic species and diminish overall ecosystem productivity. At the most extreme, the capture of high flows behind dams during the wet season and release during the dry season can reverse natural hydrological patterns downstream of the dam by generating high flows during the dry season and eliminating wet season floods. More subtle effects of navigation works on flow regimes include reversal of flood patterns in river reaches between navigation locks on a river.[85]

With knowledge of the pre-disturbance flow regimes on the river, or measurements of flow patterns on similar, relatively undisturbed reference rivers, scientists can deduce the flows that will be most likely to restore ecosystem resilience and protect native river species. Dam re-operation is the process of modifying releases to mimic a river's natural hydrological and temperature regimes. Re-operation for river restoration often involves restoring peak flows needed to reconnect and reconfigure channel and floodplain habitats, stabilizing baseflows to revitalize food webs in shallow-water habitats, reconstituting seasonal temperature patterns (by construction of depth-selective withdrawal systems on storage dams, for example), and maximizing dam passage to allow recovery of fish population structures.[86]

A return to more natural flow conditions can often be negotiated with navigation interests where sufficient information exists regarding river hydrology, the dynamics of traffic flow on the river, and the flow conditions necessary to maintain a vibrant aquatic ecosystem. In other cases, society will need to favour one or more objectives over others. This may prove to be the case on the Missouri River in the US, where continued (and arguably economically inefficient) navigation and floodplain farming interests are debating reservoir operation procedures with proponents of upper river recreation and biodiversity conservation.

'[According to the US Fish and Wildlife Service a] revision to the current Missouri River dam operation plans, which optimize river regulation for navigation, are necessary to maintain viable populations of the [endangered] pallid sturgeon, interior least tern, and piping plover. The recommended changes include an increase in spring flow rates on an average of every 3 years between May 1 and June 15, as conditions allow. A potential starting point for the spring rise is

15 thousand cubic feet per second [15 kcfs] above full navigation service releases. The amount of the spring rise would be adjusted upwards to 20 kcfs if monitoring and data analysis indicated this measure is necessary for the species. The rise is intended to provide a spawning cue for the pallid sturgeon.

'Summer flows would be lower every year as conditions allow. The low summer flows would expose more sandbar acres for the interior least tern and piping plover nesting and create shallow water habitat for young pallid sturgeon. A potential starting point for lower summer releases would provide minimum service to navigation by June 21. The lower releases would be held steady until September 1 when releases would be increased back to full navigation service. Summer releases could be stepped downward toward a combination of 25 kcfs to September 1 if monitoring and data analysis indicate that this is necessary for the species. These releases would normally not be adequate to provide even minimum service to navigation.

'When system inflows are above or below normal, the amount of water in the upper three, largest lakes is balanced so that the effects are shared equally among these lakes. To preclude jeopardy [of extinction] for listed [endangered] species, the FWS [Fish and Wildlife Service] recommends unbalancing the amount of water in these lakes as long as an extended drought (more than one year long) or an extended high runoff into the system is not occurring. Unbalancing also provides benefits to young fish in these three lakes.

'Unbalancing consists of purposely lowering one of the three lakes approximately 3 feet (1 meter) to allow vegetation to grow around the rim and then refilling the lake to inundate the vegetation. The unbalancing would rotate among the 3 lakes on a 3-year cycle. Higher spring releases in some years are intended to trigger spawning of the pallid sturgeon and scour vegetation on sandbars so that more suitable habitat is available for nesting terns and plovers.'[87]

Maintaining 'Environmental Windows'

When society makes use of an inland waterway to provide the most environmentally benign and economically reasonable mode of freight transport, planning of both spatial and temporal aspects of the work can reduce undesirable effects on aquatic ecosystems and the water cycle.

Engineers can, for example, plan fairways to avoid major changes to groundwater/surface water interactions and to critical spawning habitat for fish and invertebrates. River navigators can select fleeting areas (overnight on-river parking lots) for barges where there is minimal potential for the destruction of riparian trees or submerged mussel beds.

Some of the adverse impacts of altering waterways and performing maintenance dredging on rivers can be avoided by timing the work to avoid crucial ecological processes. Maintenance dredging can, for example, be timed to avoid the breeding seasons of aquatic organisms.

Making Beneficial Use of Dredged Material

While the concept of making beneficial use of dredged material is rooted in the idea of mitigating the environmental impacts of dredging and spoil disposal, the concept does not imply an environmentally benign process. The dredging industry defines the term 'beneficial use of dredged material' as 'any use which does not regard the material as waste.' This definition allows for uses that are beneficial for one purpose but harmful for another, such as the construction of an offshore berm using dredged material that will reduce coastal erosion but may simultaneously destroy an important fishing ground.[88] Beneficial uses are generally driven by the need to do something with the material rather than by a demand for it.[89] Beneficial use of dredged material can lessen the net negative effects of dredging on the environment. However, from the perspective of conserving the intact, aquatic ecosystems that, in turn, maintain the planet's water cycle, beneficial use offers a poor alternative to avoiding dredging in the first place.

This caution noted, there are many potential uses for dredged material that can reduce the harm caused by dredging operations to aquatic ecosystems. Aquatic habitat can be re-established on dredged material, though the creation of any new habitat means replacing an existing one.[90] In addition, the type of substrate provided by dredged material may differ substantially from the original substrate – a distinction that is an extremely important determinant of the invertebrates and fish that are able to live in the altered ecosystem. Ideally, any dredged material used to re-establish aquatic habitat should derive from the original substrate. This can be accomplished by stockpiling the original substrate and reinstating it after the excavation is complete.[91]

Dredged material has also been used to create or restore wetland habitats. The drawback to this approach is that most of the aquatic and semi-aquatic plant communities that make wetlands unique, and make their most valuable functions (such as denitrification) possible, only grow on hydric (anaerobic, or oxygen-deprived) soils. Dredged material may require 15 years or more to achieve this state. In the interim, project success may dictate the importation of hydric soils and wetland plants to the site, raising the overall costs of the process.[92] The same issue of habitat trade-offs applies to wetlands as to aquatic habitats. For example, the creation of coastal wetlands using dredged material in the Netherlands involves filling near-shore marine zones.

Other beneficial uses of dredged material that do not have a direct impact on aquatic ecosystems and which, therefore, have little implication for the water cycle include beach nourishment, island creation, land creation or improvement, replacing farmland topsoil, use as construction material, and capping of mines and landfills.[93]

CONCLUSION

From an environmental perspective, inland waterway navigation may already provide the least-damaging alternative for transport of international freight from ocean to ultimate transport mode compared to road and rail. However, this distinction is not sufficient for barge transport to win an environmental 'gold medal,' when better ways of managing waterway transport exist and in an era where the world is striving to avoid a water crisis. Inland waterway freight transport can and must include environmental sustainability as an objective of its continued operation.

The demands on the inland transport industry in this regard must not be trivialized. To be successful, such an effort must be able to rely on improved information about channel morphology and river flows, to design boats that can better navigate shallow or narrow river reaches, and to time arrivals at locks and ports to avoid traffic congestion and interface with ocean-going and land-based freight transport modes.

On the brighter side, in most cases these changes will ultimately reduce the costs of inland waterway freight transport. Aid to developing countries to construct the necessary information systems will ultimately result in the reduced cost of goods to the world economy. And the costs imposed on the global community by environmental degradation will be reduced substantially.

As with all of the world water resource issues addressed in preceding chapters, inland navigation may suffer severe consequences as a result of global warming. The likely impacts of global warming, as well as proposed solutions, are addressed in the next chapter.

Notes

1 Vellinga, P., 2002. 'Dredging in a Changing Environment.' *Terra et Aqua*, 87: 13–14.
2 Csagoly, P. 2002. 'WWF Backgrounder: New Shipping Canals will Destroy Last Chance for Blue Danube.' Vienna, Austria. p. 3.
3 Hadfield, C., 1996. *World Canals: Inland Navigation, Past and Present*. Facts on File Publications, New York. p. 16.
4 Ibid., p. 22.
5 Ibid., p. 16.
6 Ibid., p. 22.
7 Ibid., pp. 18–19.
8 Some barges have engines and are self-propelled; others, called 'sail-barges', are propelled by the wind.
9 Nederveen, A.A.J., J.W. Konings & J.A. Stoop, 1999. *Transport Innovations: An Inventory of Future Developments in Transportation*. Dutch National Research Project on Global Energy and Climate Change, Delft.
10 Economic Commission for Europe, Inland Transport Committee, 1996. *White Paper on Trends in and Development of Inland Navigation and its Infrastructure*. United Nations, New York and Geneva, p. 5.
11 National Research Council, 1999. *Applying Advanced Information Systems to Ports and Waterway Management*. Committee on Maritime Advanced Information Systems, Marine Board, Commission on Engineering and Technical Systems. National Academy Press, Washington. p. 6.
12 Nederveen, A.A.J., J.W. Konings & J.A. Stoop, 1999. *Transport Innovations*. p. 231.
13 Economic and Social Commission for Asia and the Pacific, 2001. *Review of Developments in Transport and Communications in the ESCAP Region, 1996–2001*. United Nations, New York. p. 103.
14 European Conference of Ministers of Transport, 1997. 'What Markets Are There for Inland Waterways? Conclusions of Round Table 108, Paris, 13–14 November.' CEMT/CS/RE (97) 8 p 1
15 Ibid., p. 1.
16 Economic and Social Commission for Asia and the Pacific, 2001. *Review of Developments*. p. 103.
17 Ibid., p. 107.

18 Bray, N.R.,1998. 'A Review of the Past and a Look to the Future.' *Terra et Aqua, the International Journal on Public Works, Ports, and Waterways Development*, 70: 3–11. International Association of Dredging Companies, The Hague.

19 Arkansas River Historical Society Museum, undated. *McClellan-Kerr Arkansas River Navigation System Waterway Fact Sheet*. Catoosa, Oklahoma.

20 Leite, A. (report coordinator), 1999. *Fact or Fiction: A Review of the Hydrovia Paraguay–Parana Official Studies*. World Wildlife Fund, Toronto. p. 1.

21 Ibid., p. 6.

22 Nederveen, A.A.J., J.W. Konings & J.A. Stoop, 1999. *Transport Innovations*. p. 6.2.1.

23 International Navigation Association, 2002. *Vessel Traffic and Transport Management in the Inland Waterways and Modern Information Systems*. Inland Navigation Commission Working Group 24. p. 7.

24 McCartney., B.L., J. George, B.K. Lee, M. Lindgren & F. Neilson, 1998. *Inland Navigation: Locks, Dams and Channels*. American Society of Civil Engineers Manuals and Reports on Engineering Practice No. 94. American Society of Civil Engineers. p. 21.

25 Ibid., p. 59.

26 Brookes, A., 1988. *Channelized Rivers: Perspectives for Environmental Management*. John Wiley & Sons, Ltd., Chichester. p. 39.

27 Ibid., p. 109.

28 Valente, R., 1999. 'Environmental Study is Suspect.' *Jornal do Brasil*, 22 August. Rio de Janeiro.

29 Csagoly, P., 2002. 'WWF Backgrounder.' p. 2.

30 Brookes, A., 1988. *Channelized Rivers*. p. 84.

31 Ibid., p. 85.

32 Hunt, C.E., 1988. *Down by the River: The Impact of Federal Water Projects and Policies on Biological Diversity*. Island Press, Covelo, California. p. 172.

33 Headland, G., P. Kotulak & S. Alfageme, 2000. 'Maintenance Dredging in Channels and Harbors.' Chapter 9 in Herbich, J.B. (ed.), *Handbook on Dredging Engineering*. McGraw-Hill, New York. Section 9.2.

34 Welcomme, R.L., 1995. 'Relationships between Fisheries and the Integrity of River Systems.' *Regulated Rivers Research & Management*, 11 (1): 121–36.

35 Jensen, A. & B. Mogensen, 2000. *Effects, Ecology and Economy. Environmental Aspects of Dredging*. Technical Report No. 6. International Association of Dredging Companies, and Central Dredging Association, The Hague, The Netherlands. pp. 29–30.

36 Triple E/Global Joint Venture, 1999. *Environmental Impact Assessment of the Proposed Dredging of the Lower Niger Waterway*. Lagos, Nigeria. pp. 375–9.

37 McCartney, B.L., J. George, B.K. Lee, M. Lindgren & F. Neilson, 1998. *Inland Navigation*. p. 9.

38 Bozek, J. & S. Naylor, 1998.' River Activist's Notebook: Vistula River Faces Seven New Dams.' *World Rivers Review*, 13 (3).

39 Oward, S., 2000. 'Saving the Vistula: Water Management in Poland.' Changemakers.net/ journal/ 00march/owad.cfmi.

40 As with channelization and dam construction, the objective of river training works is not only or exclusively to enhance navigation capacity. Other objectives, such as flood damage reduction, are often the primary purpose of such works, or co-objectives along with navigation enhancement.

41 Brookes, A., 1988. *Channelized Rivers*. p. 105.

42 Fischenich, C., 2000. *Impacts of Streambank Stabilization Structures*. Wetlands Regulatory Assistance Program (WRAP). Report prepared for US Army Corps of Engineers, Omaha District. Omaha. Nebraska. p. 4.

43 McCartney, B.L., J. George, B.K. Lee, M. Lindgren, & F. Neilson, 1998. *Inland Navigation*. p. 62.

44 Ibid., p. 64.

45 Fischenich, C., 2000. *Impacts*. p. 8.

46 McCartney, B.L., J. George, B.K. Lee, M. Lindgren, & F. Neilson, 1998. *Inland Navigation*. p. 64.

47 Fischenich, C., 2000. *Impacts*. p. 16.

48 Ibid., pp. 27–31.

49 Ibid., p. 16.

50 National Research Council, 2002. *The Missouri River Ecosystem: Exploring the Prospect for*

Recovery. Committee on Missouri River Ecosystem Science, Water Science and Technology Board, Division on Earth and Life Sciences. p. 61.
51 Headland, G., P. Kotulak & S. Alfageme, 2000. 'Maintenance Dredging.' Section 11.1.
52 Csiti, A. & T.N. Burt, 1999. *Reuse, Recycle or Relocate. Environmental Aspects of Dredging*, Technical Report No. 5. International Association of Dredging Companies, and Central Dredging Association, The Hague, The Netherlands. p. 54.
53 National Research Council, 1997. *Contaminated Sediments in Ports and Waterways: Cleanup Strategies and Technologies.* Committee on Contaminated Marine Sediments, Marine Board, Commission on Engineering and Technical Systems. National Academy Press, Washington. p. 23.
54 Jensen, A. & B. Mogensen, 2000. *Effects, Ecology and Economy.* p. 29.
55 Ibid.
56 Permanent International Association of Navigation Congresses, 1996. *Handling and Treatment of Contaminated Dredged Material from Ports and Inland Waterways: Volume 1.* Report of Working Group No. 17 of the Permanent Committee 1. Brussels. p. 10.
57 National Research Council, 1997. *Contaminated Sediments.* p. 23.
58 Csiti, A.. & T.N. Burt, 1999. *Reuse, Recycle or Relocate.* p. 90.
59 Ibid., p. 68.
60 Pianin, E., 2002. 'Water War Engulfs the Missouri River: Bid to Divert Flow for Barges Under Fire.' *Washington Post*, 20 May.
61 Corps policy dictates that reservoirs be named 'lakes.'
62 US Army Corps of Engineers, Mobile District, undated. *Information Paper: Navigation on the Apalachicola.* Mobile, Alabama. p. 2.
63 Light, H.M., M.R. Darst & J.W. Grubbs, 1998. *Aquatic Habitats in Relation to River Flow in the Apalachicola River Floodplain, Florida.* US Geological Survey Professional Paper 1594. p. 1.
64 Sparks, R.E., 1995. 'Need for Ecosystem Management of Large Rivers and Their Floodplains.' *BioScience*, 45: 168–82.
65 Ibid.
66 Ibid.
67 Hunt, C.E., 1988. *Down by the River.* p. 146.
68 Butts, T.A. & D.B. Shackleford, 1992. *Impacts of Commercial Navigation on Water Quality in the Illinois River Channel.* Illinois State Water Survey. Department of Energy and Natural Resources Research Report 122. Champaign, Illinois. p. 27.
69 National Research Council, 1997. *Contaminated Sediments.* p. 24.
70 National Research Council, 1999. *Applying Advanced Information Systems.* p. 11.
71 International Navigation Association, 2002. *Vessel Traffic.* p. 7.
72 Ibid.
73 Ibid., p. 9.
74 European Conference of Ministers of Transport, 1997. 'What Markets Are There?' p. 1.
75 National Research Council, 2001. *Inland Navigation Systems Planning: The Upper Mississippi– Illinois System.* Transportation Research Board. National Academy Press, Washington. p. 62.
76 Donovan, A., 2000. 'Intermodal Transportation in Historical Perspective.' *Transportation Law Journal*, 27 (3): 1.
77 DeWitt, W. & J. Clinger, 2002. *Intermodal Freight Transportation. Transportation in the New Millennium.* National Research Council, Committee on Intermodal Freight Transport, A1B05. National Academy Press, Washington. p. 1.
78 Economic and Social Commission for Asia and the Pacific, 2000. *Major Issues in Transport, Communications, Tourism and Infrastructure Developments in Multimodal Transport and Logistics.* Committee on Transport, Communication, Tourism and Infrastructure Development. E/ESCAP/CTCTID(3)/3. Bangkok. p. 2.
79 DeWitt, W. & J. Clinger, 2002. *Intermodal Freight Transportation.* p. 2.
80 Smits, A.J.M., H. Havinga & E.C.L. Marteijn, 2000. 'New Concepts in River and Water Management in the Rhine River Basin: How to Live with the Unexpected?' In Smits, A.J.M., P.H. Nienhuis & R.S.E.W. Leuven (eds), *New Approaches to River Management.* Backhuys Publishers, Leiden, The Netherlands. pp. 276–7.
81 Csagoly, P., 2002. 'WWF Backgrounder.' p. 3.

82 US Army Corps of Engineers, 2002. 'Regional Sediment Management Research Program. Draft – 1 January.' Coastal and Hydraulics Laboratory, Waterways Experiment Station, Vicksburg, Mississippi. p. 1.

83 Minnesota Pollution Control Agency, 2002. 'Nemadji River Basin Clean Water Partnership Project. Water Quality/Clean Water Partnership/No. 1.05.' St Paul, Minnesota. pp. 1–2.

84 Brookes, A., 1988. *Channelized Rivers*. p. 195.

85 Wlosinski, J.H. & L. Hill, 1995. 'Analysis of Water Level Management on the Upper Mississippi River (1980–1990).' *Regulated Rivers*, 11 (2): 239–48.

86 Abell, R., M. Thieme, E. Dinerstein & D. Olson, 2002. A *Sourcebook for Conducting Biological Assessments and Developing Biological Visions for Ecoregion Conservation. Volume II: Freshwater Ecosystems*. World Wildlife Fund, Washington, p. 157.

87 US Army Corps of Engineers, 2001. 'Missouri River Master Water Control Manual Review and Update. Revised Draft Environmental Impact Statement Review and Update. Summary.' Northwestern Division, Portland, Oregon. pp. 10–11.

88 Csiti, A.. & T.N. Burt, 1999. *Reuse, Recycle or Relocate*. p. 11.

89 Ibid., p. 33.

90 Ibid., p.. 45.

91 Brookes, A., 1988. *Channelized Rivers*. p. 196.

92 Csiti, A.. & T.N. Burt, 1999. *Reuse, Recycle or Relocate*. p. 50.

93 Landin, M., 2000. 'Beneficial Uses of Dredged Material.' Chapter 16 in Herbich, J.B. (ed.), *Handbook on Dredging Engineering*.

7 A Warmer World
The Interrelationships between Global Warming and the Water Cycle

'Most of the scientific and media attention given to the impacts of climate change on society has focused on a very limited aspect of those changes – the increase in temperature. Even the colloquial names given to the problem – 'global warming' and 'the greenhouse effect' – reflect this bias. Yet some of the most severe impacts of climate change on society are likely to result not from the expected increases in temperature *per se* but from changes in precipitation, evapotranspiration, runoff, and soil moisture: in short, from changes in the most important variables for water planning and management.'[1]

Scientists attribute unusual climatic events in many parts of the globe, such as flooding in Poland and East Africa and freak snowstorms in eastern Canada and the central United States, in part to long-term climate change triggered by the accumulation of 'greenhouse gases' in the Earth's atmosphere. While our planet's atmosphere has always contained high concentrations of greenhouse gases, human activities have added vast quantities of substances such as carbon dioxide, methane and chlorofluorocarbons to the atmosphere, quantities that skyrocket as economies industrialize. Should humankind's economic endeavours continue to emit such onerous streams of gases, global warming will be, by far, the greatest anthropogenic destabilizer of the water cycle that the world has ever seen.

THE NATURE OF THE GREENHOUSE EFFECT

The greenhouse effect is generally natural and beneficial. It is caused by the presence of trace amounts of gases such as water vapour, carbon dioxide, nitrous oxide and methane that permit incoming solar radiation to pass through to the planet's surface but trap outgoing infrared radiation that would otherwise pass into outer space. Without this trapping of radiation, the Earth would be much colder than it is and potentially unable to sustain life as we know it.

Over the past two and a half centuries, however, the concentration of these gases in the atmosphere has substantially increased, greatly exacerbating the greenhouse effect. The atmospheric concentrations of carbon dioxide, methane and nitrous oxide have grown by about 30, 145 and 15 percent, respectively, since pre-industrial times.[2] In the last century, industry added new synthetic chlorofluoro-carbons, with the capacity to trap huge amounts of heat, to the mix.

Global warming potential differs for different gases. Methane absorbs more infrared radiation than carbon dioxide. As a result, each additional kilogram of methane introduced into the atmosphere blocks more of the planet's transmitted heat than one kilogram of carbon dioxide. The concentration of carbon dioxide in the atmosphere is naturally much higher than the concentration of methane, so the incremental effect of the addition of a kilogram of carbon dioxide is less important than the addition of a kilogram of methane. On the other hand, methane only resides in the atmosphere for 15 to 20 years, after which it oxidizes into carbon dioxide and water. Carbon dioxide has a residence time ten times as long.[3]

Natural ecosystems exert a variety of effects on the concentrations of green-house gases in the atmosphere (see Table 7.1). For example, most forests absorb carbon dioxide and methane, while natural lakes are sources of these gases. Northern peatlands are carbon dioxide sinks but important sources of methane.[4]

Table 7.1 Fluxes of Greenhouse Gases from Ecosystems

Ecosystem	Areal flux (mg/m²/day)	
	Carbon dioxide	**Methane**
Boreal/temperate forests	−2100	−1.0
Tropical forests	−710	−0.2
Northern peatlands	−230	+51
Lakes (world-wide)	+700	+9
Temperate reservoirs	+1500	+20
Tropical reservoirs	+3000	+100

Note: Minus signs = net sinks; plus signs = net sources.
From: McCulley, P., 2002. *Flooding the Land, Warming the Earth: Greenhouse Gas Emissions from Dams.* International Rivers Network, Berkeley, California.

Most greenhouse gas emission results from human activities such as fossil fuel combustion, biomass burning, the use of nitrogen fertilizer, and actions that eliminate natural sinks for greenhouse gases, such as deforestation.

'Greenhouse gases are pollutants, and pollutants – by definition – arise from so-called market failures, which means that the standard neoclassical assumption of perfect markets and perfect competition has no place for them. Perhaps that helps to explain why the Bush administration acts – despite the recent lip service to climate change – as though those gases don't really exist.'[5]

Carbon dioxide, the atmospheric form of carbon, is the most important green-house gas emitted as a result of human activity. Fossil fuels, including coal, oil and natural gas, provide 90 percent or more of the energy in most industrial countries and 75 percent of energy world-wide.[6] In the twentieth century, humanity used more energy than in all of preceding history – ten times as much as in the 1,000 years before 1900.[7] Global emissions of carbon from the burning of fossil fuels reached a record 6.2 billion tons in 1996, a nearly four-fold increase since 1950. Current levels of atmospheric carbon dioxide are higher than at any time in the last 160,000 years.[8] Current projections are that, without additional policy initiatives, global carbon emissions from fossil fuels will exceed 1990 levels by 40 percent in 2010 at a level of 9 billion tons per year.[9]

Industrial countries have emitted 76 percent of the world's cumulative carbon emissions since 1950. In 1996, carbon emissions in the US, Australia and Japan were, respectively, 8.8, 9.6 and 12.5 percent above 1990 levels.[10] Augmentation of the world's automobile fleet, which has surged from 50 million to 500 million since 1950 and is projected to double over the next quarter-century, accounts for a great deal of the increase in carbon emissions. Expected increases in car ownership in the developing world are not the only factor that adds to the projected escalation of carbon emissions. Larger vehicle sizes and greater driving distances are augmenting carbon releases at the same time as the popularity of big houses with lots of electrical appliances is spreading as a status symbol.[11]

'A world of 10 billion people, with as many cars per person as in the United States, would be overrun with 5 billion cars – ten times more than today's already problematic stock. Despite the folly of stuffing cities with cars, the automobile continues to receive special treatment that helps it maintain its dominant position in many countries.'[12]

The fastest growth in greenhouse gas emissions in recent years has been in developing countries, where industrialization is still picking up momentum. In 1994, energy consumption in the developing world accounted for 27 percent of the world total and was projected to increase to 40 percent of the total by 2010.[13] Energy use in developing countries expanded an average of 28 percent faster than their economies between 1973 and 1991.[14] Carbon dioxide emissions in developing countries in 1996 were 71 percent above 1986 levels and 44 percent up on 1990. The rising trend in emissions corresponds with rapid economic growth, particularly in East Asia and Latin America, where increasing numbers of people are able to buy home appliances, motorcycles, cars and the other energy-intensive amenities that have come to symbolize a modern lifestyle.[15]

The effects of increases in atmospheric concentrations of greenhouse gases on temperature are already measurable. Since the late 1800s, average global surface air temperature has increased by between 0.3 degrees and 0.6 degrees centigrade. The final decade of the twentieth century was the warmest decade in the period of instrumental records. The rise in the Earth's temperature has possibly increased evaporation by about 10 percent over the last 20 years, causing more intense episodes of both precipitation and drought.

Precipitation over land increased by 2.4 millimetres per decade between 1900 and 1988. This increase has been most marked during the winter in high latitudes. During the same period, average global rainfall increased by more than two percent. Consistent with the upward trend in global precipitation, the average interval between two drier-than-average months increased by about 28 percent between the periods 1900–44 and 1945–88. Total annual snowfall in the far northern latitudes appears to be increasing, consistent with the observed increases in northern latitude precipitation.[16]

At the same time, snow and ice cover seem to be decreasing and melting earlier in the year. Snow cover over the land surface of the northern hemisphere has been consistently below the 21-year average (1974–94) since 1980. The decrease in snow cover over North America and Asia has been about 10 percent. Scientists have observed lake ice melting earlier, earlier snowmelt-related flooding in western Canada and the US, and earlier warming of northern hemisphere land areas in the spring.[17] Glaciers in Latin America have receded in the past decade. Half of Europe's alpine glaciers could disappear by the end of the twenty-first century.[18] The Antarctica peninsula has recently experienced spectacular collapses of ice shelves.[19] The extent of sea ice decreased and remaining sea ice thinned in the last two decades of the twentieth century.[20] As frozen water melts, it contributes to the volume of water in our planet's swelling oceans. Global sea levels have risen by between 10 and 25 centimetres over the past century.[21]

'[S]ea level rise is going to be an urban planner's worst nightmare. In many coastal cities, the problem is compounded by the fact that the land underneath them is sinking. Excessive groundwater pumping is the primary cause of the subsidence, but urban sprawl is a factor, too, since buildings and pavement cause rainfall to run off instead of seeping back into the earth to recharge the groundwater. In addition to lowering the ground level, this overpumping makes the cities vulnerable to a kind of underground flooding: as the freshwater is pumped out of coastal aquifers, saltwater tends to seep in. Underground salt-water intrusion is a serious problem for Manila, Dhaka, Bangkok and Jakarta. Obviously, continued sea level rise will tend to make the aquifers under these cities even saltier. Most of Manila's wells, for instance, might very well turn too saline to use at all if the sea level rises by a meter or so. That would force officials to spend billions of dollars that the Philippines doesn't have on desalination plants. The money would have to be borrowed from abroad, saddling the country with more foreign debt.'[22]

In the future, depending on the model used and the amount of carbon dioxide emitted into the atmosphere, average global temperatures are expected to increase by 1.5–5.5 degrees centigrade. This figure is as high as 4–8 degrees centigrade when the effect of water vapour is included. The highest temperatures relate to a doubling of carbon dioxide in the atmosphere.[23] These changes in average temperature may seem small in comparison with seasonal and annual fluctuations. However, a reduction of only 1 percent in mean global temperature would bring the planet back to the climate of the Little Ice Age that dominated the Earth's climate from the fourteenth to the seventeenth centuries. An increase of two degrees centigrade would push average global temperatures beyond anything the planet has experienced in the past 10,000 years. An average warming of five degrees centigrade from present conditions would make the Earth warmer than it has been since three million years ago, when there was no ice cap, tropical and subtropical regions existed in Canada and England, and the sea level was 75 metres higher than at present.[24] Scientists expect the central parts of the continents to become warmer and drier in the summer and wetter in the winter. According to predictions, polar regions would warm up more than those at the equator.[25]

Climate change alters a wide range of environmental conditions and thus could have severe consequences for aquatic ecosystems. The planet can expect direct effects as specific physical, chemical and biological characteristics of ecosystems change, as well as indirect effects brought about by human alteration of ecosystems in an attempt to compensate for the increasingly erratic nature of the climate.

EFFECTS OF GLOBAL WARMING ON THE WATER CYCLE, AQUATIC ECOSYSTEMS AND PEOPLE

The complex and interacting effects of an increasing concentration of greenhouse gases on the hydrological system are shown in Figure 7.1. These interactions are generalized to the global scale.

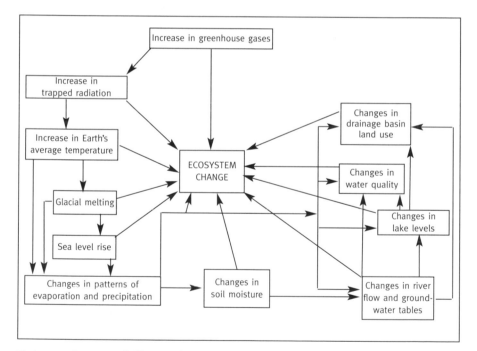

Figure 7.1 Impacts of Climate Change on the Hydrological System
Modified from Arnell, N.W., 1994. 'Hydrological Impacts of Climate Change'. In: P. Calow and G.E. Petts (eds.), *The Rivers Handbook*, vol. 2. Blackwell, Oxford. pp. 173–85.

Climatic Changes

The most immediate effects of global warming, which are already being identified and measured in many parts of the globe, are shifts in climatic patterns. These same patterns – the timing, distribution and quantity of precipitation, evapotranspiration, river flow and soil moisture – form the mechanics of the water cycle. Therefore, changing the patterns will result in largely unpredictable changes in the availability of water.

Changes in Precipitation

Climate models consistently predict an increase in average global precipitation of between 3 and 15 percent for a temperature increase of 1.5 to 3.5 centigrade.[26] The global average, however, masks geographical and temporal variations in precipitation. Many models project slight decreases in summer rainfall over much of the northern, mid-latitude continents while winter precipitation increases. Winter precipitation over eastern and southern Australia is expected to decrease by 10 to 20 percent by the year 2070.[27] The Intergovernmental Panel on Climate Change predicts that possible decreases in rainfall combined with increased evaporation could adversely affect water supply, agriculture and the survival and reproduction of key species in parts of Australia and New Zealand.[28]

Changes in seasonal precipitation patterns could cause important shifts in the timing of water availability. Where global warming leads to a decreased amount of precipitation falling as snow, for example, there would be a widespread shift from spring to winter runoff. Changes in the seasonal distribution and amounts of precipitation might modify this effect.[29]

Many scientists expect global warming to produce changes in the frequency of intense rainfall in a catchment for two reasons. First, the paths and intensities of depressions and storms may change and, second, convective activity is likely to increase. A working group of the Intergovernmental Panel on Climate Change concluded from the analysis of several climate model experiments that rainfall intensity is likely to increase with greater greenhouse gas concentrations and that there may be an increasing concentration of rainfall on fewer days. Studies of river basins in Belgium, Switzerland, the US, China and Australia all predicted increased frequency and/or severity of floods as a result of global warming.[30] Increased precipitation intensity, particularly during the summer monsoon, could increase flood-prone areas in temperate and tropical Asia. Arid and semi-arid parts of Asia could become drier and subject to more severe drought during the summer. Scientists predict more frequent flooding in parts of India, Nepal and Bangladesh as a result of decreased return periods for extreme precipitation events.[31]

Changes in Evapotranspiration

Evaporation is a function of the climatic demand for water and the supply of water. It is driven by energy availability, particularly net radiation. An increase in net radiation increases the demand for evaporation. This effect is complicated by changes in atmospheric humidity, which alter the capacity of the air to accept more water, and by changes in the rate of air movement across evaporating surfaces. The humidity of air masses is also tightly linked to evaporation over land and water bodies, including the ocean. Higher temperatures will increase the capacity of the atmosphere to hold water, thus enhancing the effects of increased net radiation where air humidity currently imposes a constraint on the rate of evaporation, as in humid areas. A temperature rise of about two degrees centigrade could cause an increase in potential evaporation of up to 40 percent in a humid temperate region, but less in a drier environment, where changes in humidity are not as important in determining evapotranspiration rates.[32]

Plant properties such as albedo, roughness, root depth and stomatal character-istics influence the rate of transpiration. Shifts in plant communities could result in changes in all of these properties, and changes in growing season could also alter transpiration rates. Concentrations of carbon dioxide in the atmosphere also affect transpiration rates, because some plants use water more efficiently and transpire less when carbon dioxide levels are high, and because many plants grow more when carbon dioxide rates are higher. The addition of leaves might cancel any reductions in transpiration from increased efficiency.[33]

Changes in River Flow

In most regions of the Earth, climate change is likely to result in increases of flood magnitude and frequency, while simultaneously lowering flows during dry periods. These trends are broadly consistent among scientific predictions, although con-fidence in the magnitude or even direction of change in any particular catchment is low. In general, increases in the frequency of heavy precipitation events will lead to concentrations of river flows, although the effect of a given change in pre-cipitation depends on catchment characteristics. Both precipitation and evaporation patterns are responsible for changes in low flows. Scientists generally predict that evaporation will increase, with the result that rivers will carry less water at low flow than under current circumstances, even in regions where precipitation increases or shows little change.[34]

Changes in Soil Moisture

In the highest northern latitudes, scientists expect increases in precipitation to greatly exceed increases in evapotranspiration, with a resulting increase in soil moisture levels. However, most models predict that the Earth's surface will experience large-scale drying over northern, mid-latitude continents in the northern summer because of higher temperatures and insufficient or diminished precipita-tion. Soil moisture reductions could also be extensive throughout south-central Asia and Latin America, where increases in temperature also exceed increases in precipitation. One consequence of this general drying trend is likely to be an increase in droughts, as measured by soil moisture conditions, even in some regions where precipitation increases, because of heightened evaporation rates.[35]

'Africa is the continent with the lowest conversion factor of precipitation to runoff, averaging 15 percent. Although the equatorial region and coastal areas of eastern and southern Africa are humid, the rest of the continent is subhumid to arid. The dominant impact of global warming will be a reduction in soil moisture in subhumid zones and a reduction in runoff. Current trends in major river basins indicate decreasing runoff of about 17 percent over the past decade.'[36]

The models used by scientists to predict specific changes in the hydrological cycle as a result of global warming are generally too clumsy to predict changes in specific drainage basins accurately. Even the most complex models, the general circulation models, have serious limitations when it comes to incorporating and reproducing important hydrological processes such as the formation and dis-tribution of rain-generating storms.[37]

'I caught up with [US Army Corps of Engineers official Eugene Stakhiv] at a coffee break at the same UNESCO conference where I had met Peter Gleick. I had found Stakhiv's own paper a model of clarity and logic, and wanted to tell him so, since neither logic nor clarity was necessarily a hallmark of the papers thus far presented, Gleick's excepted. I asked him what he thought was happening to the global climate.

'"Have you read all the studies?" he demanded, peering at me owlishly. Before I could confess that, no, I hadn't read them all, he patted the air at around waist height, about a metre off the ground. "Pile them on each other, you'd have this much paper," he said. "I've read 'em all, and I can tell you, many are useless, some are useful, the data are ambiguous, and some of them are simply outrageous." Since I'd identified myself as a Canadian, he bored in on what he perceived to be Canada's shortcomings. "The Canadian GCM [General Circulation Model] on climate change is the worst of the lot," he said happily, grinning at me. "Hopeless. Apocalyptic. Which is why so many people like it...." '[38]

Changes in Aquatic Ecosystems

Freshwater and wetland ecosystem responses to climate change depend on complex interactions of physical, chemical and biological processes. As a class of ecosystems, freshwater ecosystems are vulnerable to global warming and other pressures because of their position downstream from many human activities and because of their relatively small size. Changes in runoff, groundwater inputs and direct precipitation inputs could modify the chemistry of lakes and streams, for example, altering the input of nutrients and dissolved organic carbon. Such changes would alter the clarity and productivity of these ecosystems.[39] Other effects, including the reduction and loss of ice cover on lakes and streams, the loss of cold water habitat, increases in extinctions of native species, invasions of alien species, and the potential exacerbation of existing pollution problems such as eutrophication, toxic pollution, acid rain and ultraviolet-beta radiation.[40]

Habitats for cool and cold water organisms will decrease and warm water habitat will increase. Many species of plants and animals will attempt to adapt to a warming climate through poleward dispersal to cooler climates. Barriers to dispersal (such as mountains, highways, and cities) will be considerable for terrestrial organisms, and may be unsurpassable for many aquatic organisms. Most of these plants and animals can only move through waterways, and will be limited by a lack of suitable dispersal routes north or south. In addition, reduced streamflow may eliminate small streams that connect freshwater lakes, further limiting dispersal opportunities for lentic organisms. Organisms that do manage to move into new ranges may compete with the organisms that currently inhabit these spaces.[41]

Ecological impacts of climate change will probably be linked to other human impacts. In many cases, if coastal marshland disappears, human settlements or agriculture will leave little room for migration of the habitat. Eutrophication from fertilizer and sewage pollution could produce particularly severe algae blooms if the temperature rises. Increased drought will also boost irrigation requirements, further stressing freshwater ecosystems. Perhaps most damaging of all, the fragmentation of wetland habitats as a result of human disturbance means that natural systems are already under severe stress and thus many do not have the capacity to buffer further changes.[42]

Changes in Rivers

In rivers, changes in the quantity and timing of precipitation can influence the relationship between sediment, streamflow and channel shape. Shifts in climate can also change the composition of watershed vegetation, resulting in changes in runoff characteristics, stream shading and other factors.[43] Rivers may expand or contract with substantial effects on the quantity and timing of water available to people and ecosystems. In arid and semi-arid regions, these changes can be especially pronounced as runoff responds dramatically to slight variations in precipitation amount, variability and seasonality.[44] Small changes in average precipitation across a dry region can therefore produce large changes in streamflow.[45]

Current predictions of changes in river flow are extremely variable, reflecting substantial differences in the assumptions behind the various models. Many scientists predict that river flows in general will decrease, with the greatest effects realized in relatively arid basins. Examples are predictions that the Colorado River may see its water flow halved in the future, while some rivers in western Australia might have a 45 percent flow reduction.[46]

Some predictions seem somewhat counter-intuitive at face value, such as one that forecasts a 3 percent increase in precipitation in the Niger River basin coincident with a 31 percent decrease in runoff. As discussed above, increased rates of evapotranspiration could make this possible. Other changes predicted seem grossly out of proportion to their proposed triggers, such as the forecast that a 29 percent increase in precipitation in the Orinoco River basin may yield a 96 percent increase in runoff.[47] Still other predictions directly contradict each other: for example, one estimates a 50 percent or greater increase in flows in the Ganges and Brahmaputra rivers in Bangladesh,[48] while another predicts that increased precipitation in these same river basins would be accompanied by a decrease in runoff.

Despite the considerable uncertainty in predictions of the effects of global warming on flow regimes in specific river basins, some conclusions about the general effects of warming on riverine biota can be drawn based on relationships between climatic variables and freshwater ecology. Changes in river flow regime can affect fish migration and spawning, the extent and duration of floodplain inundation, the availability and distribution of nutrients, and sediment dynamics, along with other processes. In general, a warmer climate is likely to lead to overall reductions in aquatic biodiversity and in fisheries production.[49]

Under a warmer climate, habitat available to cool-water species will likely decrease and the distribution of these species will become more fragmented; in some instances cool-water species may be pushed beyond their upper lethal temperature limits. Temperature strongly influences the life history characteristics, biogeography and productivity of aquatic insects. It is logical, therefore, to expect that the temporal and spatial patterns of abundance and productivity of riverine insects will shift as the climate warms. In general, scientists expect to see an increase in insect productivity that could benefit fisheries, but shorter life cycles and lower average biomass may prevent fish from effectively exploiting this increased productivity.[50]

Global warming will also produce longer periods of low flow in many of the world's rivers. Warm water temperatures and accumulations of biomass, resulting from longer periods between scouring episodes, will increase respiration rates in aquatic biological communities and therefore lower concentrations of dissolved oxygen. In addition, in rivers polluted by anthropogenic sources, a decrease in flows will result in an increase in pollutant concentrations.[51]

Changes in Lakes

In lakes, changes in the temperature of the atmosphere lead to changes in water temperature, which can trigger profound alterations of water chemistry and the availability of habitats for specific organisms. Shifts in the depth and extent of winter ice cover would result in altered mixing patterns and dissolved oxygen concentrations, potentially causing imbalances in species composition.[52] Changes in the length of ice cover on Arctic lakes can also modify the acidity of the lakes through a complex process involving the carbon dioxide content of the water.[53]

'Scores of mountain lakes may burst their banks in the next 10 years because of global warming, sending millions of gallons of floodwaters swirling down valleys and endangering tens of thousands of lives, scientists warned Tuesday [16 April 2002].

'Research released today by the United Nations Environment Program (UNEP) shows that lakes in the Himalayas are rapidly filling with icy water as rising temperatures accelerate the melting of glaciers and snowfields.'[54]

African Great Lakes are sensitive to climate variation on time scales of decades to millennia. Lake Victoria, which is the world's second-largest freshwater lake by area, Lake Tanganyika, the world's second-deepest lake, and Lake Malawi were closed basins (with no inlets or outlets) for much of the Pleistocene and Holocene. Lakes Malawi and Tanganyika were hundreds of metres below their current levels; Lake Victoria dried out completely. These lakes presently maintain a very delicate hydrological balance and are nearly closed. Only six percent of water input into Tanganyika leaves at its riverine outflow, which was completely blocked when Europeans explored the lake. Global warming has created a barrier to vertical circulation in these lakes. Additional warming could strengthen this barrier and reduce the mixing of deep, nutrient-rich bottom waters and nutrient-depleted, but better oxygenated, surface water, undercutting one of the world's most productive freshwater fisheries in the process.[55]

Global warming may also substantially influence the water quality in lakes. Warming could increase the occurrence of methyl mercury (biologically available mercury) in lakes and the accumulation of mercury in fish because methylation is positively related to water temperature. Heavy metals and pesticide accumulations are also greater at higher water temperatures.[56] Summer warming of surface waters and dissolved oxygen depletion in deep water force cool-water species into a habitat 'squeeze' as areas with suitable temperatures and adequate dissolved oxygen contract. The constriction of suitable habitat will increase the vulnerability of cool-water fisheries to food depletion, over-harvest and disease.[57]

Changes in water levels can also endanger nearshore biological communities. In South America's Lake Titcaca, submerged macrophytes experience significant mortality when water levels change more rapidly than they can adapt. In the Middle East, Lake Kinneret experiences changes in inshore ecosystems when water level fluctuations are rapid. A decline in water level of four metres reduces the stony belt around the lake by 30 to 94 percent. This results in a switch in the fish community from dominance by fish that spawn on stone to dominance by fish that spawn on sand, which may affect year-class strength of the primary planktivorous fish and eventually the entire food chain. A warmer and drier climate would exacerbate such changes.[58]

Changes in Wetlands

Wetlands may simply dry out or they may undergo more subtle transformations. In the northern wetlands of Alberta, Canada, for example, seasonally flooded vegetation zones may shift from a flood-driven ecosystem to a drought- and fire-driven ecosystem given a warmer and drier climate, leading to invasion by exotic plant species. In New Zealand, several freshwater wetlands are likely to be inundated by a rising sea level, thus altering the saline balance and destroying the unique vegetation patterns.[59]

Most wetland processes are dependent on catchment-level hydrology, and thus adaptations for projected climate change may be practically impossible. Arctic and subarctic ombotrophic bog communities on permafrost, as well as more southern depressional wetlands with small catchment areas, are likely to be most vulnerable to climate change. The increasing speed of peatland conversion in Asia is likely to place these areas at a greatly increased risk of fire and affect the viability of tropical wetlands.[60]

In an interesting twist, wetlands may exacerbate the warming trend that is destined to disrupt or destroy them. Global warming is correlated with increased fluxes of carbon dioxide and methane from wetland soils to the atmosphere at seasonal time scales, with higher atmospheric concentrations at geologic time scales. The most likely initial responses to warming will be enhanced methane fluxes from tundra and boreal wetland ecosystems during summer months. On time scales of decades or more, permafrost depths will increase in the tundra, further increasing the flux of methane into the atmosphere in regions of saturated peat.[61]

Hydrological changes in wetlands can provide advantages to alien species over native species. In most cases, alien species are cosmopolitan in nature, meaning that they have the ability to survive under a very broad range of ecological conditions.

'Increasing winter minimum temperatures (or more probably reduction in frequency and severity of freezing conditions) will likely produce a northward shift in the range of subtropical species. Range shifts would be expected for several recently introduced invasive species, such as the tree *Melalueca quinquenervia* (Cajeput) and the shrub *Schinus terebinthifolius* (Brazilian pepper), that can quickly suppress native species. In central and northern portions of [Florida], freshwater marshes may become dominated by *Melalueca* and hardwood swamps by *Schinus* as has occurred in the south. General climatic warming would also favour the spread northward of the subtropical/tropical exotic fishes, such as *Clarias batrachnus* (walking catfish), as native species become stressed by higher water temperatures and reduced dissolved oxygen concentrations, the factors generally controlling their distributions. The high connectivity of lakes, streams, and wetlands further enhances the potential for rapid spread of invasive subtropical aquatic species northward as climate becomes warmer.'[62]

Likely Effects of Global Warming on Human Water Uses

People, so far, have proved highly adaptable to changes in their environments. Keen intellects and opposable thumbs combine to give humans the knowledge and capacity to alter vital practices in order to proliferate under changing conditions. The question remains, however, whether actions taken today to adapt to the conditions of tomorrow might adversely alter the longer-term prospects of human survival by further undercutting the ecological processes that support human life.

Agriculture

Because several feedback mechanisms exist between climate and productivity levels of plants and animals, global warming is likely to create a variety of changes in agricultural productivity around the world, depending on location and type of crop, livestock or fish produced. For example, plant water use is sensitive to changes in temperature, but even more so to changes in stomatal resistance (the tendency of a plant to close its pores to reduce water loss through transpiration).[63] Therefore, the increased efficiency of water use by crops can outweigh the increased evaporative potential of a warmer climate.

Irrigated agriculture outstrips dryland farming in both yields and profitability as climate conditions become hotter and drier. In areas where water supplies are available and affordable, therefore, hotter and drier conditions resulting from global warming would tend to increase both the amount of land under irrigation and the amount of water consumed per irrigated acre.[64] As we have seen in previous chapters, however, the growing competition between economic sectors for water is unlikely to place irrigated agriculture in an economically dominant position when compared with more lucrative applications of water. Therefore, the amount of water applied to irrigation may remain steady or decrease, as more urgent uses predominate.

In Asia, acute water shortages combined with thermal stress are likely to adversely affect wheat and, more severely, rice production in India even under the positive effects of elevated carbon dioxide.[65] Likewise, a two-degree centigrade increase in air temperature accompanied by a 5–10 percent decline in precipitation during summer would cause substantial reductions in surface runoff in Kazakhstan, with serious implications for agriculture and livestock.[66]

In Africa, a continent that already experiences enormous food production deficits, declines in soil moisture could further exacerbate food insecurity. In addition, water stress and land degradation are likely to render fisheries, which provide the major source of animal protein for many Africans, more vulnerable to episodic drought and habitat destruction.[67]

Water Supply and Sanitation

Global warming will exacerbate regional differences in water supply, and could very well increase the range of vector- and water-borne disease. Water resource differences between northern and southern Europe, for example, will increase in a changing climate, resulting in more severe water shortages in the southern parts of the continent.[68] Water-borne diseases such as cholera and the suite of diseases caused by organisms such as *girardia*, *salmonella* and *cryptosporidium* could become more common in South Asia and Africa, particularly in areas that lack adequate water supply and sanitation infrastructure.[69]

While global warming may not significantly alter the net quantities of freshwater used domestically, it may change the temporal distribution of demand in a way that increases the conflict between household and other water uses. This trend is likely to aggravate the problems of balancing water supplies with demands during droughts, because they are likely to be greatest during seasons and years when supplies are under the most stress.[70]

Industrial Use

Rising water temperatures would reduce the efficiency of industrial and electrical cooling systems, thereby contributing to an increase in water demand. Nearly all water used for cooling, 95 percent, is not consumed but instead returns to water sources. As a result, the effect of global warming on the quantity of water available for other uses may not change much. The danger is that releases of warmer water into aquatic ecosystems will raise water temperatures even further, with devastating effects on fish and other aquatic life forms.[71]

Inland Navigation

During an era when inland shippers are trending towards larger barges with deeper draughts that require deeper channels, the flows needed to float these barges will become less reliable and more erratic. While navigation channels in high latitudes will benefit from longer ice-free seasons, both low flows and floods could pose problems in many waterways. Low flows can ground boats, and floods render river conditions too hazardous for navigation. On channels with navigation locks, the locks may be incapacitated as river managers keep dams open to allow free flows of floodwaters downstream.

PSEUDO-SOLUTIONS

Naturally, industries of many stripes, including hydropower and nuclear energy companies as well as agriculture and forestry concerns, have attempted to pitch their various products as the solution to the very grave threat of global warming.

On close examination, however, these sectors of the economy have little to offer. The replacement of fossil fuel plants with hydropower projects may not lead to a net reduction in greenhouse gas emissions. Replacing fossil fuel plants with nuclear energy could reduce greenhouse gas emissions, but would contribute to the already problematic issues regarding security, plant decommissioning, and the disposal of radioactive wastes. Carbon sequestration through agriculture or forestry can become a shell-game, producing economic windfalls for actions that would have taken place in any case, and which are justifiable for their own sake.

Hydropower: No Net Loss of Greenhouse Gases

'There is no justification for claiming that hydro[power] does not contribute significantly to global warming and climate change.'[72]

Hydroelectric generation has long been promoted as an environmentally benign power source compared with fossil fuels and nuclear energy. Global concern about climate change increases support for hydropower in many circles because hydropower is thought to be a relatively clean source of energy. Recent studies have shown that this is an assumption that must be investigated on a case-by-case basis, particularly for hydropower projects with large reservoirs, as many reservoirs emit substantial quantities of greenhouse gases (see Table 7.2). Some reservoirs emit a larger quantity of greenhouse gases per unit energy produced than were avoided by not building a fossil fuel plant of similar capacity.[73]

Table 7.2 Greenhouse Gas Emissions from Reservoirs in Brazil and Canada Compared with Fossil Fuel Emission

Project	Reservoir area at operating level (km²)	Average annual generation (GWh/year)	Annual CO_2 emissions (tons/km²/year)	Annual methane emissions per km² (tons/km²/year)	Emissions per gigawatt-hour (10^6 tons CO_2 equivalent/GWh)
Balbina Dam (Brazil)	3,147	970	7,550	45	26,200
Tucurui Dam (Brazil)	2,247	18,030	4,210	40	580
Grand Rapids Dam (Canada)	1,200	1,700	190–200	4-8	300–500
Conventional coal-fired generation					1,000
Combined-cycle natural gas generation					400

From: McCully, P., 1996. *Silent Rivers: The Ecology and Politics of Large Dams.* Zed Books, London. p. 143.

Scientists estimate that the world's reservoirs cumulatively release 70 million tons of methane and approximately 1 billion tons of carbon dioxide each year[74] –

an amount equal to about 20 percent of estimated methane emissions from all anthropogenic sources and 4 percent of known anthropogenic carbon dioxide emissions. Combined releases of these two gases from reservoirs account for roughly 7 percent of the human-related global warming impact calculated over a 100-year period.[75]

In contrast to the combustion of coal, oil or natural gas in thermal power plants, which produces mainly carbon dioxide through combustion-related chemical reactions, reservoirs are the sites of bacterial decomposition of organic matter, which produces both carbon dioxide and methane. Other gas-producing processes also operate, particularly in tropical reservoirs, where anaerobic decomposition of flooded biomass generates nitrous oxide in addition to carbon dioxide and methane.[76]

Estimating greenhouse gas emissions from reservoirs is complex: more factors must be considered than when thermal power plants are assessed. These factors include the gross emissions from the reservoir; the net emissions, taking into account natural emissions prior to dam construction; carbon sequestration from the atmosphere by reservoir water; and nitrous oxide emissions from the submerged soils.[77] Characteristics of the river basin – including land use, climate, types of ecosystems flooded, reservoir depth and shape, and dam operation – all influence emission levels.[78] Some researchers now believe that releases of dissolved methane from water being discharged from the dam may prove to be the largest component of the warming impact of tropical hydropower. This degassing occurs because the water pressure that holds these gases in a dissolved state while in the reservoir is suddenly released when the water is discharged through turbines or over a spillway.[79]

Patterns of gas emission from fossil-fuel plants and hydroelectric reservoirs are also quite different. Thermal power plants emit carbon dioxide uniformly over the entire period of operation, unless changes are made to the physical infrastructure of the plant or to operating procedures or fuels. In contrast, conventional wisdom assumes that the emissions of such gases from a reservoir will peak after the initial inundation and gradually decrease afterwards, often becoming insignificant in a period of time much shorter than the lifespan of the reservoir.[80]

Studies have found, however, that most reservoirs will actually continue to emit carbon dioxide and methane at lower levels over a long time horizon, because of the decomposition of residual stored biomass remaining in the reservoir after the initial, intense, degradation. In addition, new biomass produced over time inside the reservoir and from organic matter washed in from the watershed can extend the period of greenhouse gas emissions from reservoirs.[81]

'Results obtained by Hydro Quebec for reservoirs in boreal regions have indicated that there is no statistical evidence of significant decrease of GHG [greenhouse gas] emission for a given reservoir or for reservoirs of various ages.... In the case of tropical reservoirs in Brazil, the apparent decrease in GHG emissions between past and new measurements is not confirmed by recently obtained data for CO_2.'[82]

The relative value of hydroelectricity in reducing greenhouse gas emissions resulting from power generation varies regionally. Emissions from tropical reservoirs are typically between 5 and 20 times higher per unit of flooded area than those from reservoirs in temperate and boreal regions. The climate change impact of hydropower in Canada and the northern US appears to be well under half that of natural gas power plants.[83] The greatest reservoir emitters of greenhouse gases, generally located in the tropics, can contribute many times more to global warming than coal plants generating the same amount of power.[84]

The production of hydroelectricity is itself particularly vulnerable to climate change. A river suffering a drought will not produce much power, especially when energy generation must compete with consumptive uses of water for irrigation and water supply. In addition, in the hot and arid parts of the world where global warming will lead to the greatest reductions in streamflow, the demand for electricity is highest in the summer months, driven by the demand for refrigeration and air conditioning. Thus, the season of highest demand corresponds with the season of lowest generation capacity, rendering hydropower a less than ideal energy alternative for countries with hot climates.

'**Most of Africa has invested significantly in hydroelectric power facilities to underpin economic development. Reservoir storage and major dams have reached critical levels, threatening industrial activity.**'[85]

Nuclear Energy: No Net Gain of Environmental Protection

Advocates of nuclear energy argue that society should shift more of its energy generation capacity to this non-carbon-based source in an effort to curb global warming. Nuclear plants provided 7 percent of world total primary energy and one quarter of input energy into electricity at the end of the twentieth century.[86] At the dawn of the twenty-first century, however, the prospects for a major role for nuclear plants in providing energy to the world were rapidly fading. It is unlikely that nuclear energy can overcome the current barriers of poor public perception and escalating costs that are restricting its expansion.

Nuclear energy poses enormous problems involving the safe disposal of highly dangerous and long-lived radioactive waste and the eventual decommissioning of contaminated power plants. Recent concerns over possible terrorist attacks on nuclear plants and acquisition of nuclear materials for the production of nuclear weapons or 'dirty bombs' have created additional public pressure for heightened security at nuclear facilities. Nuclear energy also poses risks to the water cycle, particularly the potential for eventual seepage of radioactive wastes into groundwater.

Accidents at the Three Mile Island plant in the US and the Chernobyl plant in the former USSR in 1979 and 1986, respectively, demonstrated the dangers of nuclear power in a very public way. Since these accidents, costs for security and additional government regulation in many countries have considerably increased the cost of nuclear energy. At the same time, the costs of alternative energy sources, including combined-cycle natural gas plants and wind turbines, have been steadily dropping, providing fierce competition to nuclear sources. As a result of these trends, at the turn of the century only three of the Organization for Economic Cooperation and Development (OECD) countries – France, Japan, and Korea – expected to construct new plants after 2000.[87]

'Recently the nuclear industry has been upbeat. Gerald Doucet of the World Energy Council claimed here that nuclear will play "an essential role in electricity production and strategies against global warming.... Create a level playing field by taxing carbon emissions and the market might decide to buy nuclear."

'Or not. Energy policy in the developed world is driven by market liberalisation and the need to tackle climate change. But liberalised markets do not favour nuclear. Despite decades of public support for nuclear research and development, it is still too expensive.... Carbon taxes would need to double and possibly quadruple the current price of fossil fuels to level the playing field. Alternatively each new nuclear power station would require 2 billion [pounds sterling] of public subsidy. Neither is on....

'The private sector is unlikely to step back into the breach. The technological breakthrough that would [be needed] to attract investment is unlikely after 40 years of intensive research and development. The long-term nature and political uncertainties of storing nuclear waste create huge financial risk for private investors. Reprocessing of waste is worse, as it combines high cost and the problem of plutonium proliferation – a threat so severe that most governments, including the US, want to end reprocessing of nuclear waste.... The state should encourage new energy technologies by means of tax incentives and support for demonstration projects and dissemination. Definite targets could kick-start an important new industry – something Denmark and the Netherlands clearly recognize for offshore wind power, for example. Providing the revenues for these should be a key short term role for a fairly modest carbon tax.

'As for nuclear, it needs to focus on the enormous technical and financial problems of decommissioning and radioactive clean-up.'[88]

'Given time and technological advances, renewables might be in a better economic position than nuclear power to "receive the baton" from fossil fuels.'[89]

Carbon Sequestration: Breaking Even and Paying for it

In addition to preventing the release of greenhouse gases into the atmosphere, it is possible to reduce the potential for global warming by removing greenhouse gases from the air. The term carbon sequestration refers to the removal of carbon, usually in the form of carbon dioxide, from the atmosphere and storing it for indefinite lengths of time in various sinks. Carbon sequestration can be accomplished with various degrees of success and for varying lengths of time through a number of processes, including injecting carbon dioxide into oceans or deep, underground strata and binding up more carbon dioxide in vegetation by changing management practices on farm, range, and forest land. Valid reasons for caution exist regarding both these approaches. Injection technologies have uncertain results and unpredictable ecological side effects. Sequestration in vegetation, by increasing vegetative cover and soil organic matter while reducing soil erosion, brings a plethora of benefits both to landowners and societies, and therefore deserves more attention in the absence of an international subsidy in the form of carbon credits (discussed below). The use of biotic carbon sequestration as an economic commodity would open the door for all sorts of accounting shenanigans.

Injection technologies – whether into deep saline formations, depleted oil and gas reservoirs, unminable coal seams, or the ocean – involve complex geophysical, chemical and biological interactions and therefore require relatively pristine sources of carbon dioxide. Such technologies face a number of unanswered questions regarding their effects on the environment and their longevity. For example, oceans exchange carbon dioxide with the atmosphere. This exchange can reach 90 billion metric tons (90 gigatons) per year, with a net ocean uptake of about 2 gigatons. Scientists remain unsure about how effective ocean sequestration would be at keeping carbon out of the atmosphere. If the injections of carbon dioxide occur below the thermocline, that is, the ocean depth that more or less permanently separates the upper strata from the lower strata and prevents mixing, an estimated 80 percent of the carbon injected can be expected to remain sequestered over the long term. The remaining 20 percent will outgas to the atmosphere on a time scale ranging from 300 to 1,000 years.[90]

The most significant anticipated environmental impact would be lowered pH resulting from the reaction of carbon dioxide with seawater.[91] Caution is required in implementing this approach because the oceans play a key role in the global carbon cycle and in climate regulation. Phytoplankton are central to this function, since they convert carbon dioxide into organic carbon in our ocean's surfaces. Even though phytoplankton account for less than one percent of the Earth's photosynthetic biomass, they are responsible for roughly half of the planet's carbon fixation. The organic carbon produced by marine phytoplankton is mostly eaten by other organisms in the surface waters. Phytoplankton also regenerate the carbon dioxide as these organisms sink into the deep ocean, thus reducing carbon dioxide in the surface layer and elevating it in the deep sea. This biological pump maintains the carbon dioxide concentration gradient, removing carbon dioxide from the atmosphere by storing it in the ocean interior.[92]

The available data indicate that deep-sea organisms are highly sensitive to even modest changes in pH. Small perturbations in carbon dioxide or pH may have important consequences for the ecology of the deep sea and for the global biogeochemical cycles that depend on deep-sea ecosystems.[93] The injection of carbon dioxide into deep earth strata also raises a number of complex environmental issues. Perhaps the most important of these regards the potential for increased underground pressure, triggering heightened seismicity, with unpredictable consequences.

Changes in land management techniques can also lead to substantial increases or decreases in biological carbon sequestration. The potential for reducing atmospheric carbon levels through forest management is tremendous, according to the Intergovernmental Panel on Climate Change. During the period 1995–2050, slowing deforestation, promoting natural forest regeneration and encouraging global reforestation could offset between 220 and 320 billion metric tons of carbon, an amount equal to 12 to 15 percent of fossil fuel emissions.[94] Farming removes carbon from the soil through ploughing, which increases the rate of microbe respiration, and through erosion. Soils typically lose up to half their original carbon content in the first few decades following cultivation.[95] Retiring farmland can increase carbon uptake rates to 80 grams per square metre per year during the first decade or two after retirement, after which the uptake rate declines. If the land is brought back into cultivation the stored carbon may be released back into the atmosphere, resulting in no net atmospheric carbon removal in the long term.[96]

'[C]urrent hypotheses concerned with the fate of biotic carbon suggest that as the world warms, carbon sequestered now may re-enter the atmosphere at a later time. Compared to avoiding the use of carbon sequestered in fossil fuel form, biotic sequestration may be inherently unstable and require long-term accounting and tracking of biotic resources.'[97]

Changes in land management that use natural processes, such as conservation tillage, no-till, reduction of grazing pressure, and reforestation are valuable investments in their own right, regardless of their beneficial contributions to climate stabilization. These practices enhance land fertility and ultimately increase productivity. In addition, they improve the functioning of the global water cycle by reducing excess sediment and pollutant inputs to aquatic ecosystems and enhancing water infiltration into the soil.

The ongoing drive to increase carbon sequestration is due not solely to the fear of catastrophic consequences arising from global warming, but also to economic incentives created under the umbrella of the 1992 United Nations Framework Convention on Climate Change. The adoption of the Kyoto Protocol to this convention in 1997 created legally binding emission reduction targets for industrialized countries and countries with economies in transition (the convention refers to these as Annex 1 countries). During the first commitment period of 2008–2012, the Annex 1 countries must collectively reduce emissions of greenhouse gases by 5 percent below 1990 levels. Targets for the second commitment period are to be negotiated no later than 2005.

The Conference of Parties to the convention negotiated individual targets for each country, with the 15-member European Union allowed to distribute its target 8 percent reduction amongst its members. The Kyoto Protocol specifies that Annex 1 countries may offset emissions by increasing the removal of carbon from the atmosphere through carbon sequestration. The protocol also allows emissions trading among Annex 1 countries, allowing them to sell the unused portion of their emissions quotas to countries that are unable to meet their targets economically.

While the long-term benefits of carbon sequestration in reducing atmospheric concentrations of greenhouse gases, as well as the potentially unwelcome side effects of injection technologies, are largely unpredictable, the potential for exploitation of the sequestration concept is tremendous. As a commodity, carbon sequestration credits are an attractive investment. Because of time discounting, policy uncertainty and limited current demand for offsets, carbon dioxide offsets can be acquired today for roughly US$1 per ton. By 2010, based on predictions of future economic impacts of limits on greenhouse gas emissions, the implied carbon dioxide price will exceed US$20 per ton.[98]

The creation of such a lucrative market in carbon credits invites all sorts of mischief, however. In placing a tangible price tag on atmospheric carbon reductions that may or may not really exist and whose lifespan is also questionable, society generates opportunities for countries to sidestep international law. Clever sequestration claims might allow the world's biggest polluters to avoid weaning themselves off fossil fuels as they struggle to meet the greenhouse gas reduction levels mandated by the Kyoto Protocol. Sequestration claims could change reduction targets into allowances for continued increases in emissions.[99] Canada could possibly meet over 250 percent of the 6 percent reduction target negotiated in Kyoto, changing the Canadian target from a 6 percent emissions reduction to a 17 percent emissions increase. The United States could meet approximately 140 percent of the 7 percent reduction target negotiated in Kyoto and about 30 percent of the needed reductions in 2005. The credits for this sequestration would change the US target from a 7 percent reduction to an 11 percent increase in emissions.[100]

The legitimacy of carbon reductions through sequestration would need to be carefully policed for the world to benefit from the commodification of carbon credits. Otherwise, countries could easily engage in double-dipping and free-rider strategies, claiming credits for carbon emission reductions which either do not exist or which would have taken place in the absence of assignment of value to credits.

'Australian federal and state government forestry policies call for the establishment of 2 million hectares of new plantations in Australia by 2020. A complementary federal/state initiative, the "Regional Forest Agreements," also channels taxpayer's money to fund this.

'Both state forest and private land is being earmarked for conversion to plantations, mixed between land uses currently in native forests and agricultural production.

'The native forest destruction for plantations agenda in Australia is inextricably linked to the "carbon credits" game. The system is already being exploited for potential commercial gain, and investments are going into various corporate plantation share offers due in part to the belief that money will be made by selling carbon rights via joint ventures later on.

'When examined holistically, the economics of developing carbon sequestration markets is becoming an additional economic driver for projects also clearing native forests, further enhancing their profitability. In the case of the TEPCO [Tokyo Electric Power Company] joint venture, the power utility paid $10 million for the Australian partner to establish "offset" plantations within the larger joint venture worth $90 million. In turn, this money will have been used by NFP [North Forest Products, an Australian company] for logging and wood chipping of forests elsewhere in Tasmania.'[101]

A number of global trends suggest that carbon sequestration as a method of absorbing greenhouse gas emissions may soon be obsolete. Among these are trends towards improved land management as an investment in future productivity in the absence of saleable carbon credits, and the world's emergence from a fossil-fuel economy to a post-petroleum economy. Both of these trends are good news for the global water cycle and the creatures that depend on it.

NEW GENERATION

'In the near term, the greatest opportunities for cleaner energy lie in energy efficiency on the demand side and switching to less polluting fuels and energy conversion technologies on the supply side.... [T]his conclusion is equally true for other countries throughout the world. The remarkable achievement of China in reducing coal production of 250 million tonnes per year in the past two years is an example of the ability of international capabilities to reduce local pollutant and green house gas emissions in the near term.'[102]

The real outputs of the energy sector that are valued by society are energy services, such as transport, travel, lighting, heating and cooling, rather than energy output *per se*. The energy industry, which ultimately supplies these services, loses large amounts of energy, particularly in the production of electricity by burning fuels.[103] At the global level, just 37 percent of primary energy is converted to useful energy, meaning that nearly two-thirds is lost.[104]

Humanity has the option to provide itself with the same valued outputs by different means, such as different fuels, different transformation systems, and updated end-use technologies. As each fuel and each technology has different social, economic and environmental consequences, strategic mixing of the different components of energy services allows societies the flexibility needed to respond to a wide variety of demands.[105]

The avoidance of global warming is only one incentive – although it is certainly one of the most compelling – for modern society to shift its energy strategies away from fossil-fuel-based and demand-driven philosophies towards strategies that optimize the service derived from each unit of energy input. Fossil fuel and nuclear dependency not only threaten our water resources, but also have the potential to create, and have created, significant risks for human and environmental health and security. Fortunately, like a cavalry galloping over a hill at the last minute, a new generation of safer and more sustainable energy alternatives are on the horizon, and the cost of these alternatives relative to conventional sources is dropping every day.

Foremost among these alternatives is increasing energy efficiency and conservation – or simply cutting down on our consumption. Besides relieving some of the serious problems related to conventional sources, including global warming, pollution and economic reliance on politically unstable parts of the world, these solutions will help to maintain the water cycle in excellent working order.

Increasing Energy Efficiency

An energy efficiency project is an initiative undertaken to improve the quantity of energy services per unit of energy consumed in commercial, industrial, institutional or residential facilities. The incremental costs of high-efficiency equipment and related engineering services are recovered from savings on energy bills. Examples of energy efficiency projects include replacing standard equipment with high-efficiency equipment, applying energy-efficient design principles in a new facility or renovation, and improving operations and maintenance to better manage and track energy use.[106]

Energy efficiency improvements are important factors in predicting and managing future world environmental and economic trends. Since the 1970s, more efficient energy use in the member countries of the OECD has weakened or eliminated the link between economic growth and energy use. The next generation is likely to experience energy efficiency gains of 25 to 35 percent in most industrialized countries and more than 40 percent in transition economies.[107] Because of declining energy consumption, China's carbon dioxide emissions have fallen by 17 percent since the mid-1990s, from just over 800 million metric tons of carbon in 1996 to about 670 million metric tons in 2000. A complex combination of forces – including energy efficiency programmes, energy price and market reforms, household fuel switching, and systemic economic reforms that closed inefficient factories and shifted production to more efficient ones – brought about this reduction. During the same time period, China's gross domestic product grew by 36 percent.[108]

Energy productivity is particularly important in developing countries. They have far greater scope to use more efficient processes and products as they are still in the early stages of building an industrial infrastructure. Developing countries have a golden opportunity to leapfrog the fossil-fuel dependence of industrialized countries by adopting energy-efficient design and technology, just as many consumers in developing countries have jumped to cellular phones in the absence of more traditional telecommunications infrastructure. Because developing countries are still at the beginning of the market saturation curve for most energy-consuming technologies, energy efficiency companies have an opportunity to enter these markets offering higher value-added, energy-efficient technologies.[109]

Developing countries are taking advantage of this opportunity at an increasing rate. International financial and development institutions are gradually beginning to accept energy efficiency as critical to future sustainable development throughout the world. The Global Environment Facility has made millions of dollars available to support energy efficiency in developing countries. The European Bank for Reconstruction and Development has established an Energy Efficiency Unit to finance energy-saving retrofits in central and eastern Europe. The World Bank's International Financial Corporation has capitalized the Renewable Energy and Energy Efficiency Fund to finance private sector sustainable energy projects throughout the developing world. Even large commercial banks are beginning to make financing available for certain energy-efficiency investments. The International Institute for Energy Conservation (IIEC) estimates that development and environment-related financial sources currently make at least US$500 million per year available to finance energy efficiency projects in emerging markets. The remaining challenge, according to the IIEC, is to create a pipeline of 'bankable' energy efficiency projects to exploit these new funding sources.[110]

Many countries are already responding to this opportunity to reduce their dependence on foreign fuel sources, avoid the cost of constructing new power plants, and modernize their economies. South Africa's national utility is planning to achieve a peak demand reduction of around 2,500 megawatts from end-use energy efficiency improvements in the commercial, industrial and residential sectors by 2015. Thailand projects a peak demand reduction of more than 700 megawatts during the first five years of its national demand-side management programme. The Philippines' Energy Regulatory Board directed all utilities to prepare and submit demand-side management plans by the end of 1997, identifying motors, lighting and air conditioning as high-priority areas for efficiency improvement. Brazil's government and utilities sponsor a range of effective energy efficiency programmes targeted at reducing electricity consumption for lighting, motors, air conditioning and industrial processes. Mexico is promoting energy efficiency in the commercial, industrial and residential sectors. India has established demand-side management programmes for several states and cities. The overhaul of polluting industries and district heating systems in eastern and central European countries with the end of central planning could also lead to the adoption of energy-efficient replacements.[111]

'The "Energy Efficiency Management System in South Korea – Standards and Labelling" programme was started in 1992. The programme dictates minimum efficiency standards for a range of energy-consuming technologies including air conditioners, refrigerators and lighting equipment. (Target efficiency levels were established for passenger vehicles.) The labelling component of the programme also covers commercial and industrial equipment such as boilers. Key to the programme has been its focus on manufacturers, retailers and consumers to ensure that energy-efficient equipment is available and properly labelled.**

'The Standards and Labelling programme has achieved remarkable results in a short period of time. Over the past three years, the energy efficiency of common appliances In South Korea has dramatically increased. For example, refrigerators' energy efficiency have increased by 11 percent, while air conditioners' efficiency levels have increased by an average of 24 percent. These gains point to the success of the programme in transforming markets of common household appliances to high efficiency equipment.'[112]

Within the past decade, the world has witnessed the emergence of a host of energy-efficient technologies. From light bulbs to refrigerators, many new energy-using technologies are at least 75 percent more efficient than the current standard technologies. Even in the power industry, which has sought to improve the efficiency of its equipment for a century, the plants that opened in the early 1990s were 50 percent more efficient than those that opened a decade earlier.[113]

Co-generation (the combined production of heat and power) is likely to become widespread. Many factories may generate their own power with biomass, using the waste heat for industrial processes as well as heating and cooling. Such systems are in wide use in some parts of the world already, and can raise total plant efficiency from 50 to 90 percent. Excess power can be transferred to the electric grid and used by other consumers.[114]

When disposable income increases in lower-income developing countries, energy consumption shifts from traditional fuels, such as biomass, to commercial fuels. The efficiency of cooking appliances that use commercial fuels is higher than that of those that use biomass, so household energy consumption tends to fall as a result. The move from a fuelwood stove with a technical efficiency of 12 to 18 percent to a kerosene stove with an efficiency of 48 percent, or to a liquified petroleum gas stove with a efficiency of 60 percent, proves the point.[115]

'The most important new light source may be compact fluorescent bulbs that, for example, use 18 watts instead of 75 to produce the same amount of light as an incandescent bulb. Energy saving technologies are particularly attractive in developing countries, where (despite the fact that many homes still depend on kerosene lights) electric lighting accounts for a large fraction of residential power use.

'In India, for example, some 300 million incandescent bulbs are responsible for nearly one-third of the country's peak electrical demand. If India replaced just 20 percent of these with compact fluorescents, it could avoid building 8,000 megawatts of generating capacity, saving US$430 million annually, and significantly cutting the cost of village electrification. This is an example of leap-frogging – going right from kerosene to high-tech. Already, in 1991, a prototype factory to produce compact fluorescents was being considered near Bombay.'[116]

'It may be possible to virtually eliminate space heating in many climates by means of building shells with very high resistance to heat loss or gain involving high insulation walls, ceilings and floors and triple pane windows with transparent heat-reflecting films, wide use of passive designs and mass-produced components (walls, ceilings) with very low infiltration rates.'[117]

Investing in Renewable Resources

The growth of renewable energy technologies is providing humanity with opportunities to address several pressing issues in the energy sector. Concern about global warming is driving much of the current expansion of renewable energy's market share, but these technologies can also reduce air pollution, improve energy system efficiency, cut the economic costs of new energy supplies, and provide electricity to rural populations that are out of reach of energy grids. The following text discusses some of the most promising renewable energy sources. While renewables provide only a small fraction of world energy demands today, the growth in use of these resources is far outpacing growth in fossil fuels and nuclear energy (see Table 7.3).

Economies of scale associated with water and steam turbines shaped the large-scale electricity systems of the late twentieth century. Large, remote, central stations based on these machines generate electricity in the form of synchronized, alternating currents and deliver it to users over a network using long, high-voltage transmission lines. Yet traditional electricity systems have failed to reach more than 2 billion people, or one-third of humanity.

The most important new energy technologies are relatively small devices that can be mass-produced in factories – a stark contrast to the huge oil refineries and power plants that dominated the energy economy of the last century. The economics of mass manufacturing will quickly bring down the cost of the new technologies, and ongoing innovations will rapidly be incorporated into new products in much the same way as today's consumer electronics industry operates.[118]

Table 7.3 Trends in Energy Use, by Source, 1990–7

Energy source	Average annual growth rate (%)
Wind power	25.7
Solar photovoltaics	16.8
Geothermal power	3.0
Natural gas	2.1
Hydroelectric power	1.6
Oil	1.4
Coal	1.2
Nuclear Power	0.6

From: Brown, L.R. (project director). *State of the World 1999: A Worldwatch Institute Report on Progress Towards a Sustainable Society.* W.W. Norton & Company, New York. p. 36.

In addition, the small size of energy-producing units will generate a number of other advantages. By decentralizing energy production, these technologies will provide the flexibility needed to encourage the development of local power sources. The ability to harness solar energy in sunny climates and geothermal power where it is available will allow communities to generate energy at or close to the point of consumption, cutting down on massive losses of electricity in transmission over power lines. The creation of a mosaic of energy sources also provides a number of back-ups in case one source fails.

'One aspect that detracts from [the value of renewable energy resources] to an electricity grid is the intermittent generation potential of solar and wind sources. Absent a technology such as hydroelectric pumped storage or batteries to store electricity and/or potential energy, the energy from the sun and the wind are only available a portion of each day. Often, the availability corresponds with periods of peak energy demand, but not always. The possible unavailability of these resources, especially at peak periods, detracts from their potential contribution to a system grid.

'Yet, these technologies have an offsetting virtue associated with their relatively small scale and independence from fuel supply. These attributes make siting easier and especially practical in remote areas not served by the electricity grid. This feature enhances the "niche market" appeal of renewable technologies, particularly in remote areas of the Third World. Hence, renewable energy will often compete not on the cost of energy, but on the basis of value provided to the customer. In addition, the distributed nature of these generation resources can be used to ease congestion and loop-flow problems on the electricity grid, thereby adding to their value within an electric system.'[119]

'The conditions for an energy transition are particularly ripe in developing countries, most of which are far better endowed with renewable energy sources than with fossil fuels. Most of these countries have embryonic energy systems and massively underserved populations and therefore represent a potentially far larger market for innovative technologies.'[120]

Solar Energy

Direct sunshine is the most abundant energy source of all. Each year, 2.5 million exajoules reach the Earth's surface, more than 6,000 times the amount of energy used by all human beings world-wide in 1990. The entire exploitable resource of fossil fuels in place when civilization began – oil, coal, natural gas, and tar sands – is equivalent to less than 30 days of sunshine striking the Earth.[121]

Photovoltaic solar energy conversion is the direct conversion of sunlight into electricity. The energy of light particles in a solar cell generates free electrons which produce electricity. The net conversion efficiency of sunlight to electricity is typically 10 to 15 percent,[122] but maximum efficiencies of around 30 percent are achievable.[123]

The world market for solar cells more than doubled from annual sales of about 70 megawatts in 1994 to 160 megawatts in 1998.[124] In 1998, cumulative solar electricity production was around 800 megawatts. Although still tiny by energy industry standards, recently the solar market has grown at ten times the rate of world oil production. If annual production were to grow at 25 percent per year from 2003, solar capacity would reach 106,000 megawatts by 2020, generating as much power as 30 to 40 large nuclear plants. Researchers at the US Department of Energy have estimated that if photovoltaic panels were mounted on top of 5,000 km^2 of roof space, they could generate 25 percent of the electricity used in the United States.[125]

As technical advances drive down the cost of solar photovoltaic systems,[126] governments around the world are embracing them. Japan plans to install 4,600 megawatts of mainly residential, grid-connected photovoltaic systems by 2010. The US intends to build one million solar hot water heaters and photovoltaic systems by 2010. Italy aims to generate 50 megawatts of solar energy by 2005. The European Union has made a commitment to install 500,000 grid-connected photovoltaic systems on roofs and walls in the Union and to export another 500,000 village systems for decentralized electrification in developing countries. India's five-year national plan (1997–2002) envisaged a deployment of 58 megawatts in addition to the 28 megawatts installed as of 1997, plus the export of 12 megawatts.[127]

'Government support for solar home systems – led by the government of Japan, which provides generous subsidies for rooftop solar power – has triggered the current solar boom. Japan requires electric utilities to purchase electricity produced by these systems at the same price they charge consumers – a price that is currently more than 20 cents per kilowatt-hour. The transaction is determined by "net metering," meaning that the rooftop's output is subtracted from the consumer's use of power from the grid. At the end of the month, the consumer pays a utility bill that covers the "net" electricity used. Some 9,400 solar home systems were installed under this arrangement in 1997, and 13,800 are expected in 1998. Japanese officials say they hope to have solar power systems in 70,000 homes by 2000, and to be able to eliminate direct subsidies by the year after that, as the market continues to grow.'[128]

Solar cells have long been the most economical power source in remote parts of the developing world. By the mid-1990s, solar photovoltaic systems were powering village and domestic lighting systems, water pumps, battery rechargers, and rural health clinics in developing countries. In 2001, developing countries had installed over one million solar home systems, including around 150,000 in Kenya, more than 100,000 in China, 85,000 in Zimbabwe, 60,000 in Indonesia and 40,000 in Mexico.[129]

'Since 1985, Kenya has nurtured a healthy solar PV [photovoltaic] market. Today, equipment worth between $2 million and $4 million is sold each year. The market is driven by strong rural demand and has grown exponentially. PV dealers now operate in almost every town across the country. There are now more PV systems installed in rural Kenya (approximately 150,000) than there are connections under the Kenya Power and Lighting company's Rural Electrification Programme (just over 60,000). Roughly 4% of rural households now own solar home systems.

'Most of the growth in the commercial PV market in Kenya has been in straight cash sales of systems to rural customers. But some customers have made partial payment on signing the contract with the remaining amount paid upon completion of installation....

'In general, formal credit is not available to the great majority on low incomes in rural areas, but informal credit agreements have been used successfully to expand the market to those who cannot afford the up-front costs....

'In the mid-1980s several small-scale demonstration and training initiatives, supported by relief agencies, NGOs and church organizations, stimulated interest in the technology among potential customers. Local technicians were trained to install systems for higher income customers. Local electricians and merchants were quick to realize that PV could fill a niche which at that time was dominated by diesel generators. The cost of a PV system – between $500 and $1000 – was often less than the initial cost of a generator. Demand for PV increased rapidly and there are now 15 distributors of systems in Nairobi.'[130]

Because of the lack of radiation during the night and because of cloud cover and other weather-related effects, solar photovoltaic systems on Earth provide an intermittent energy source. Most existing, stand-alone systems use batteries to store solar energy, and grid-connected systems use the grid as virtual storage. Another interesting alternative that addresses problems of intermittence involves deploying space-based solar satellites to provide reliable, base-load electricity. The maximum power density, or irradience, in space – 1,360 watts per m^2 – is much higher than on Earth and is nearly constant.[131] Concepts for space-based solar energy systems include satellite-to-Earth transmission of energy via radio waves or laser beams.

Environmental concerns about solar photovoltaic systems centre on the release of toxic pollutants during the manufacturing process. These worries should diminish as life-cycle analyses of photovoltaic systems and components lead to the development of more benign materials and processes.[132]

Wind Power

Wind power has generated mechanical energy to serve humanity for many centuries. In recent decades, technicians have made tremendous progress in the development of wind energy for electricity production. The first grid-connected wind turbines came on-line in the early 1980s.[133] By the 1990s, wind power was the world's fastest growing energy source.[134] In many areas, wind power is already less expensive than electricity from coal-fired plants.[135]

The world had roughly 20,000 wind turbines in operation by the end of 1993, producing about 3,000 megawatts of electricity, 30 times as much as a decade earlier.[136] Between 1994 and 1999, the annual growth of installed operating capacity varied between 27 and 33 percent. By the end of the twentieth century, over 5,400 megawatts had been installed in the European Union alone, followed by 1,700 megawatts in the United States and just under 1,000 megawatts in India. At the beginning of 2000, approximately 13,500 megawatts of wind power were in operation.[137] In 2001, over 50,000 small wind turbines were providing electricity in remote rural areas around the world.[138]

China's wind potential is estimated to exceed its total current electricity use. A huge stretch of Inner Mongolia could, by itself, provide most of the power needed in Beijing and the rest of northern China.[139] The states of North Dakota, South Dakota and Texas alone have sufficient wind capacity to provide all of the electricity consumed in the United States.[140] Many other countries, including Argentina, Canada, Chile, Russia, and the United Kingdom, could theoretically provide all of their energy with wind power. Other countries, including Egypt, India, Mexico, Tunisia and South Africa, should easily be able to push their reliance on wind power to 20 percent or more. Europe as a whole could obtain between 7 and 26 percent of its power from the wind, depending on how much land is excluded for environmental and aesthetic reasons.[141] At the turn of the century, 29 countries had developed actives wind energy programmes.[142]

'On the plains of Mongolia ... where the wind blows steadily, nomadic herdspeople use portable wind generators for powering lights, radio and other appliances.'[143]

State-of-the-art wind turbines are highly automated and reliable. Their downtime for maintenance averages under five percent, less than for fossil fuel plants. Maintenance costs are minimal. Landowners can either install their own wind turbines or lease their property to wind companies, with the bulk of the land still available for other uses such as farming or ranching.[144]

Critics cite several drawbacks associated with wind energy. One is that, like solar power, wind sources are inherently intermittent. This problem can be overcome through the use of batteries in combination with wind turbines. Other drawbacks are aesthetic and environmental in nature. Some people find the sound emitted from wind turbines disturbing and the turbines themselves unsightly. Others are concerned that birds will collide with the turbines. A research project in the Netherlands found the bird problem to be negligible, however, demonstrating that bird casualties from collisions with rotating rotor blades on a wind farm of 1,000 megawatts are a small fraction of the casualties from hunting, high voltage lines, and vehicular traffic over a similar area of land.[145]

Geothermal Power

Geothermal energy, which is derived from the Earth's heated core – the same energy source that powers earthquakes and volcanoes – was first harnessed to generate electricity in Italy in 1904. Today, geothermal resources provide energy both directly and through electricity generation. Direct applications include space heating and cooling, industry, greenhouses, fish farms and health spas.[146]

By 1993, world-wide geothermal generating capacity was estimated at 7,000 megawatts, providing 28 percent of the power in Nicaragua, 26 percent in the Philippines, and 9 percent in Kenya.[147] Geothermal resources have been identified in more than 80 countries, with quantified records of geothermal use in 46 of these.[148] The growth of total geothermal electricity generation capacity was around 40 percent between 1990 and 1998. The largest additions during this period were realized in the Philippines (957 megawatts), Indonesia (445 megawatts), Japan (315 megawatts), Italy (224 megawatts), Costa Rica (120 megawatts), Iceland (95 megawatts), the US (75 megawatts), New Zealand (62 megawatts), and Mexico (43 megawatts).[149]

'Renewable energy resources show promise. This year the [World] Bank funded two projects in the Philippines: the Lyte-Cebu Geothermal and the Leyte-Luzon Geothermal (also supported by the Global Environment Facility), which added a combined 640 megawatts to the country's existing 1,000 megawatts of installed geothermal capacity. Geothermal energy production has much lower carbon dioxide, sulfur dioxide, and nitrogen oxide emissions than fossil fuels, and it helps reduce the country's dependence on imported oil.'[150]

'Geothermal heat pumps are rated among the most energy-efficient space conditioning equipment available in the United States. Reducing the need for new generating capacity, they perform at greater efficiencies than conventional air source heat pumps used for air conditioning. Several electric utilities have introduced financial incentive schemes by encouraging house owners to use groundwater heat pumps for space cooling and heating purposes, and thus reducing the peak loads on their electric systems. The Geothermal Heat Pump Consortium has established a $100 million, 6-year programme to increase the geothermal heat pump unit sales from 40,000 to 400,000 annually, which will reduce greenhouse gas emission by 1.5 million metric tonnes of carbon equivalent annually.'[151]

Although geothermal reserves can be depleted if managed incorrectly, world-wide resources are sufficiently large for this energy resource to be treated as renewable. In the United States, for example, the Department of Energy estimates that hydrothermal reservoirs (hot water or steam trapped in rock much the way oil and gas are) could theoretically provide 30 times current energy use indefinitely.[152]

Other concerns about geothermal energy include the potential for release of toxic materials and gases that are currently stored deep underground. Geothermal fluids do contain a variable quantity of gas, largely nitrogen and carbon dioxide with some hydrogen sulphide and smaller amounts of ammonia, mercury, radon and boron. The amounts depend on the geological conditions of different fields. Most of the chemicals are concentrated in the disposal water, which is routinely re-injected into drill holes and therefore not released into the environment. The concentrations of gases are usually not harmful, and the removal of such gases as hydrogen sulphide from geothermal steam is a routine matter in geothermal power stations where the gas content is high. The range of carbon dioxide emissions from the high-temperature fields used to generate electricity is 13 to 380 grams per kilowatt-hour, less than for fossil fuel power stations. Sulphur emissions are also significantly less for geothermal than fossil fuel electric stations. The gas emissions from low-temperature geothermal resources are normally only a fraction of the emissions from high-temperature fields.[153]

Hydrogen Fuel Cells

Fuel cells do the reverse of electrolysis, combining hydrogen with oxygen and using the release of chemical energy to create an electric voltage. Hydrogen (H_2) is the most abundant element in the universe, but almost all of it is found in combination with other elements in substances such as water (H_2O) or methane (CH_4). Therefore, it is necessary to manufacture hydrogen from either water or fossil fuels before it can be used to generate electricity in a fuel cell.

Approximately 95 percent of all hydrogen in use at the end of the twentieth century was produced by the conversion of methane,[154] which can be derived from composting toilets (see Chapter 4), landfills, and other sources. While this process emits carbon dioxide, the process is cleaner than burning fossil fuels in internal combustion engines or fossil fuel plants.[155] Fuel cells are also two to three times more efficient than internal combustion engines in turning fuel into power. Using fuel cells for utility operations can improve energy efficiency by 60 percent.[156] This is largely because fuel cells convert chemical energy directly into electrical energy, unlike combustion, which involves the conversion of heat into mechanical energy.[157]

The most promising technologies under development today, from an environ-mental perspective, will use renewable energy sources – including solar, wind and geothermal energy – to split water molecules into hydrogen and oxygen.[158] Com-bined into stacks, fuel cells can power cars, boats, houses, factories and even portable electronics such as radios, compact disk players and mobile phones.[159] At the beginning of the twenty-first century, over 200 fuel cell units of 200 kilowatts each were already in use as utility plants around the world, and small-scale technologies for home heating and utility applications were under development.[160]

'Fuel cells are not just laboratory curiosities. While there is much work that needs to be done to optimize the fuel cell system (remember, the gasoline internal combustion engine is nearly 120 years old and still being improved), hydrogen fuel cell vehicles are on the road – *now*. Commuters living in Chicago and Vancouver ride on fuel cell buses. You can take a ride around London in a fuel cell taxi and even compete in the American Tour de Sol on a fuel cell bicycle. Every major automobile manufacturer in the world is developing fuel cell vehicles.'[161]

CONCLUSION

With regard to the continued operation of the water cycle, global warming could turn out to be the straw that breaks the camel's back. While greenhouse gases occur naturally in our atmosphere, and even make life on Earth possible, the gigantic amounts of additional gases that human economic activity are contributing may be causing a potentially catastrophic warming trend. The shifts in climate and changes in ecosystem functions that result from global warming will have profound effects on the quality, quantity and timing of water availability over huge swaths of our planet.

Some industries are rallying to take advantage of this looming crisis, arguing that their products, be they hydropower, nuclear energy or crops and timber, provide the pathway to mitigation of the problem. Each of these pseudo-solutions to global warming has serious weaknesses. In the end, if we are still able to avoid a major ecological disruption as a result of global warming, the solution lies in changing global energy strategies. It is imperative that people switch from a supply-side, fossil-fuel-based energy sector to one that relies on efficiency and non-hydropower renewables.

The first five chapters of this book have described how conventional approaches to generating energy, transporting goods over inland waterways, reducing flood damage, managing water supply and sanitation services, and growing our food place the water cycle and the aquatic ecosystems that support it in peril. These chapters have also suggested alternative technologies to which humanity must quickly turn to avoid a true water crisis. The following two chapters will address additional measures that we can take as insurance policies against future water-related catastrophes. Chapter 8 discusses the restoration of aquatic ecosystems, while Chapter 9 analyses ongoing global policy debates that will surely affect the way we manage water in the future.

Notes

1 Gleick, P.H., 1998. *The World's Water: 1998–1999*. Island Press, Covelo, California. p. 140.

2 Ibid., p. 138.

3 Rosa, L.P. & M.A. dos Santos, 2000. *Certainty and Uncertainty in the Science of Greenhouse Gas Emissions from Hydroelectric Reservoirs: Part 2*. Report prepared for the World Commission on Dams, final version. World Commission on Dams, Cape Town. p. 2.

4 McCully, P., 2002. *Flooding the Land, Warming the Earth: Greenhouse Gas Emissions from Dams*. International Rivers Network, Berkeley, California.

5 Ayers, R.U., 2001. 'How Economists Have Misjudged Global Warming.' Worldwatch, Washington, September/ October. p. 24.

6 Flavin, C. & S. Dunn, 1999. 'Reinventing the Energy System.' In Brown, L.R. (project director),

State of the World 1999: A Worldwatch Institute Report on Progress Toward a Sustainable Society. W.W. Norton & Co., New York. p. 23.

7 International Energy Agency, 2001. *Highlights: Toward a Sustainable Energy Future.* Organization for Economic Cooperation and Development, Paris. p. 22.

8 Flavin, C. & S. Dunn, 1998.' Responding to the Threat of Climate Change.' Chapter 7 in Brown, L.R. (project director), *State of the World 1998: A Worldwatch Institute Report on Progress Towards a Sustainable Society.* W.W. Norton & Company, New York.

9 Ibid., p. 3.

10 Ibid., pp. 2–3.

11 Ibid., p. 3.

12 Gardiner, G., 1998. 'When Cities Take Bicycles Seriously.' *Worldwatch,* September/October. pp. 17–18.

13 World Bank, 1994. *Making Development Sustainable: The World Bank Group and the Environment.* The World Bank, Washington. p. 115.

14 Flavin, C, & N. Lenssen, 1994. *Power Surge: Guide to the Coming Energy Revolution.* Worldwatch, Washington.

15 Flavin, C. & S. Dunn, 1998. 'Responding to the Threat.' p. 3.

16 Frederick, K.D. & P.H. Gleick, 1999. *Global Climate Change: Potential for Impacts on US Water Resources.* Pew Center on Global Climate Change, Philadelphia. pp. 14–15.

17 Ibid., pp. 14–15.

18 Manning, M. & C. Nobre, 2001. *Technical Summary. Climate Change 2000: Impacts, Adaptation, and Vulnerability. A Report of Working Group II of the Intergovernmental Panel on Climate Change.* Geneva. pp. 53–4.

19 Ibid., p. 59.

20 Ibid.

21 Gleick, P.H., 1998. *The World's Water: 1998–1999.* pp. 138–9.

22 Hinrichson, P., 2000. 'The Oceans are Coming Ashore.' *Worldwatch,* November/December. p. 31.

23 Minshall, G.W., 1991. 'Troubled Waters of Greenhouse Earth: Summary and Synthesis.' In Firth, P. & S.G. Fisher (eds), *Global Climate Change and Freshwater Ecosystems.* Springer-Verlag, New York. p. 310.

24 Gleick, P.H., 1998. *The World's Water: 1998–1999.* p. 138.

25 Minshall, G.W., 1991. 'Troubled Waters.' p. 310.

26 Arnell, N., B. Bates, H. Lang, J.J. Magnunson, & P. Mulholland, 1996. 'Hydrology and Freshwater Ecology.' In Watson, R.T., M.C. Zinyowera & R.H. Moss (eds.), *Second Assessment Report of the Intergovernmental Panel on Climate Change.* Cambridge University Press, New York. p. 333.

27 Gleick, P.H., 1998. *The World's Water: 1998–1999.* pp. 140–1.

28 Manning, M. & C. Nobre, 2001. *Technical Summary.* p. 50.

29 Arnell, N., B. Bates, H. Lang, J.J. Magnunson, & P. Mulholland, 1996. 'Hydrology and Freshwater Ecology.'

30 Ibid., p. 338.

31 Manning, M. & C. Nobre, 2001. *Technical Summary.* p. 49.

32 Arnell, N., B. Bates, H. Lang, J.J. Magnunson, & P. Mulholland, 1996. 'Hydrology and Freshwater Ecology.' p. 333.

33 Ibid., p. 335.

34 Manning, M. & C. Nobre, 2001. *Technical Summary.* p. 31.

35 Gleick, P.H., 1998. *The World's Water: 1998–1999.* p. 142.

36 Manning, M. & C. Nobre, 2001. *Technical Summary.* p. 45.

37 Gleick, P.H., 1998. *The World's Water: 1998–1999.* p. 140.

38 De Villiers, M., 2001. *Water: The Fate of Our Most Precious Resource.* Mariner Books, Boston and New York. p. 82.

39 Arnell, N., B. Bates, H. Lang, J.J. Magnunson, & P. Mulholland, 1996. 'Hydrology and Freshwater Ecology.'

40 Manning, M. & C. Nobre, 2001. *Technical Summary.* p. 34.

41 Arnell, N., B. Bates, H. Lang, J.J. Magnunson, & P. Mulholland, 1996. 'Hydrology and Freshwater Ecology.'

42 Markham, A., N. Dudley & S. Stolten, 1993. *Some Like it Hot: Climate Change, Biodiversity, and the Survival of Species.* WWF-International, Gland, Switzerland. 144 pp.

43 Poff, N.L., 1991. 'Regional Hydrologic Responses to Climate Change: An Ecological Perspective.' In Firth, P. & S.G. Fisher (eds), *Global Climate Change and Freshwater Ecosystems.* Springer-Verlag, New York. pp. 88–115.

44 Grimm, N.B. & S.G. Fisher, 1991. 'Responses of Arid Land Streams to Changing Climate.' In Firth, P. & S.G. Fisher (eds), *Global Climate Change and Freshwater Ecosystems.* Springer-Verlag, New York. p. 211.

45 Dahm, C.N. & M.C. Molles, 1991. 'Streams in Semi-arid Regions as Sensitive Indicators of Global Climate Change.' In Firth, P. & S.G. Fisher (eds), *Global Climate Change and Freshwater Ecosystems.* Springer-Verlag, New York. p. 251.

46 Markham, A., N. Dudley & S. Stolten, 1993. *Some Like it Hot.*

47 Miller, J.R. & G.L. Russell, 1992. 'The Impact of Global Warming on River Runoff.' *Journal of Geophysical Research*, 97 (D3): 2759.

48 Markham, A., N. Dudley & S. Stolten, 1993. *Some Like it Hot.*

49 Arnell, N., B. Bates, H. Lang, J.J. Magnunson, & P. Mulholland, 1996. 'Hydrology and Freshwater Ecology.'

50 Mulholland, P.J., G.R. Best, C.C. Coutant, G.M. Hornberger, J.L. Meyer, P.J. Robinson, J.R. Stenberg, R.E. Turner, F. Vera-Herrera & R.G. Wetzel, undated. 'Effects of Climate Change on Freshwater Ecosystems of the Southeastern United States and the Gulf Coast of Mexico.' *Hydrologic Processes*, 11: 949–70.

51 Ibid.

52 Arnell, N., B. Bates, H. Lang, J.J. Magnunson, & P. Mulholland, 1996. 'Hydrology and Freshwater Ecology.'

53 Wolfe, A.P., 2002. 'Climate Modulates the Acidity of Arctic Lakes on Millennial Time Scales.' *Geology*, 30 (3): 215–18.

54 Nelson, D., 2002. '"Catastrophic Threat" from World's Mountain Lakes, Warns UN.' Oneworld-news on Yahoo http://www.oneworld.net, 16 April 2002.

55 Arnell, N., B. Bates, H. Lang, J.J. Magnunson, & P. Mulholland, 1996. 'Hydrology and Freshwater Ecology.' p. 341.

56 Ibid., pp. 347–8.

57 Mulholland, P.J., G.R. Best, C.C. Coutant, G.M. Hornberger, J.L. Meyer, P.J. Robinson, J.R. Stenberg, R.E. Turner, F. Vera-Herrera & R.G. Wetzel, undated. 'Effects of Climate Change.'

58 Arnell, N., B. Bates, H. Lang, J.J. Magnunson, & P. Mulholland, 1996. 'Hydrology and Freshwater Ecology.' p. 350.

59 Markham, A., N. Dudley & S. Stolten, 1993. *Some Like it Hot.*

60 Manning, M. & C. Nobre, 2001. *Technical Summary.* p. 34.

61 Minshall, G.W., 1991. Troubled Waters.' p. 311.

62 Mulholland, P.J., G.R. Best, C.C. Coutant, G.M. Hornberger, J.L. Meyer, P.J. Robinson, J.R. Stenberg, R.E. Turner, F. Vera-Herrera & R.G. Wetzel, undated. 'Effects of Climate Change.'

63 Frederick, K., 1997. *Water Resources and Climate Change.* Climate Issues Brief No. 3. Resources for the Future, Washington. p. 6.

64 Frederick, K., 1997. *Water Resources and Climate Change.* p. 6.

65 Manning, M. & C. Nobre, 2001. *Technical Summary.* p. 48.

66 Ibid.

67 Ibid., p. 45.
68 Ibid., p. 53.
69 Ibid., pp. 45 & 50.
70 Frederick, K., 1997. *Water Resources and Climate Change*. p. 6.
71 Ibid.
72 Rosa, L.P. & M.A. dos Santos, 2000. *Certainty and Uncertainty*. p. 1.
73 Ibid., p. 47.
74 St Louis, V.L., C.A. Kelly, E. Ducheman, J.W.M. Rudd & D.M. Rosenberg, 2000. 'Reservoir Surfaces as Sources of Greenhouse Gases to the Atmosphere: A Global Estimate.' *BioScience*, 5 (9): 766–75.
75 McCully, P., 2002. *Flooding the Land*. p. 2.
76 Rosa, L.P. & M.A. dos Santos, 2000. *Certainty and Uncertainty*. p. 22.
77 Ibid., p. 2.
78 McCully, P., 2002. *Flooding the Land*, p. 3.
79 Ibid., p. 5.
80 Manning, M. & C. Nobre, 2001. *Technical Summary*. p. 3.
81 Ibid.
82 Rosa, L.P. & M.A. dos Santos, 2000. *Certainty and Uncertainty*. p. 3.
83 This advantage to hydropower would be much less if compared to the most environmentally friendly fossil fuel option: gas co-generation plants that make use of the waste heat from fuel combustion.
84 McCully, P., 2002. *Flooding the Land*. p. 1.
85 Arnell, N., B. Bates, H. Lang, J.J. Magnunson, & P. Mulholland, 1996. 'Hydrology and Freshwater Ecology.' p. 45.
86 Poffenberger, J., 1998. *Nuclear Power: Sustainability, Competition, Climate Change*. International Energy Agency, Organization for Economic Cooperation and Development, Paris. p. 45.
87 Ibid.
88 Cavendish, W. & R. Gross, 2000. 'Fuel Fallout.' *The Guardian*, 22 February.
89 Poffenberger, J., 1998. *Nuclear Power*. p. 24.
90 Herzog, H.J., K. Caldreira & E. Adams, 2001. 'Carbon Sequestration via Direct Injection.' pp. 408–14 in Steele, J.H., S.A. Thorpe & K.K. Turekian (eds.), *Encyclopedia of Ocean Sciences, Volume 1*. Academic Press, London.
91 Ibid.
92 Chisholm, S.W., P.G. Falkowski & J.J. Cullen, 2001. 'Dis-crediting Ocean Fertilization.' *Science*, 294: 309.
93 Seible, B.A. & P.J. Walsh, 2001. 'Potential Impacts of CO_2 Injecton on Deep-Sea Biota.' *Science*, 294: 320.
94 Dayal, P., 2000. 'Carbon Trading and Sequestration Projects Offer Global Warming Solutions.' *EM*, March: 17.
95 Gurney, K. & J. Neff, 2000. *Carbon Sequestration Potential in Canada, Russia and the United States under Article 3.4 of the Kyoto Protocol*. WWF paper, 12 August, p. 2.
96 Ibid., p. 3.
97 Ibid., p. 16.
98 Dayal, P., 2000.' Carbon Trading.' p. 17.
99 Gurney, K. & J. Neff, 2000. *Carbon Sequestration*. p. 15. Under the Kyoto Protocol, Russia would have surplus carbon credits to sell. This is because emissions of greenhouse gases are lower in Russia now than they were in 1990, a result of the country's economic decline following the break-up of the Soviet Union.
100 Ibid.
101 Cadman, T., 2000. *The Kyoto Effect: How the Push for Carbon Sinks by Industry and Government*

Has Become a Driver for Deforestation. Study commissioned and published by Greenpeace International and the WWF Climate Change Campaign. p. 16.

102 Interlaboratory Working Group, 2000. *Scenarios for a Clean Energy Future.* ORNL/CON-476 & LBNL-44029. US Department of Energy, Washington. p. 8.1.

103 Wulfinghoff, D.R., 2000. 'The Modern History of Energy Conservation: An Overview for Information Professionals.' *Electronic Green Journal,* 13 (http://egj.lib.uidaho.edu/egj13/wulfinghoff1. html). Unpaginated document.

104 Jochem, E. (ed.), 2000. 'Energy End-Use Efficiency.' Chapter 6 in United Nations Development Programme, United Nations Department of Economic and Social Affairs and World Energy Council. *World Energy Assessment: Energy and the Challenge of Sustainability.* United Nations Development Programme, New York. p. 174.

105 International Energy Agency, 2001. *Highlights.* p. 15.

106 International Institute for Energy Conservation & Export Council for Energy Efficiency, 1998. *Developing and Financing Energy Efficiency Projects and Ventures in Emerging Markets.* International Institute for Energy Conservation, Washington. p. 2.

107 Jochem, E. (ed.), 2000. 'Energy End-Use Efficiency.' p. 174.

108 Sinton, J.E. & D.G. Fridley, 2001. 'Growth in China's Carbon Dioxide Emissions is Slower than Expected.' *Sinosphere,* 4 (1): 3.

109 International Institute for Energy Conservation & Export Council for Energy Efficiency, 1998. *Developing and Financing Energy Efficiency Projects and Ventures in Emerging Markets.* p. 4.

110 Ibid., p. 1.

111 Ibid., p. 5.

112 Rumsey, P. & T. Flanigan, 1995. *Compendium: Asian Energy Efficiency Success Stories.* International Institute for Energy Conservation, Washington. p. 16.

113 Flavin, C, & N. Lenssen, 1994. *Power Surge.*

114 Brown, K.R., C. Flavin & S. Postel, 1991. *Saving the Planet: How to Shape an Environmentally Sustainable Global Economy.* W.W. Norton & Co., New York. p. 39.

115 Jochem, E. (ed.), 2000. 'Energy End-Use Efficiency.' p. 181.

116 Brown, K.R., C. Flavin & S. Postel, 1991. *Saving the Planet.* pp. 37–8.

117 Interlaboratory Working Group, 2000. *Scenarios for a Clean Energy Future.* p. 8.6.

118 Flavin, C, & N. Lenssen, 1994. *Power Surge.*

119 McVeigh, J., D. Burtraw, J. Darmstadter & K. Palmer, 1999. 'Winner, Loser, or Innocent Victim? Has Renewable Energy Performed as Expected?' Discussion Paper 99–28. Resources for the Future, Washington. p. 4.

120 Flavin, C. & S. Dunn, 1999. 'Reinventing the Energy System.' p. 36.

121 Flavin, C, & N. Lenssen, 1994. *Power Surge.*

122 Turkenburg, W.C. (ed.), 2000. 'Renewable Energy Technologies.' Chapter 7 in United Nations Development Programme, United Nations Department of Economic and Social Affairs & World Energy Council. *World Energy Assessment: Energy and the Challenge of Sustainability.* p. 236.

123 Ibid., p. 231.

124 O'Meara, M. 1999. 'Solar Power.' *People and the Planet,* 8 (2).

125 Flavin, C. & M. O'Meara, 1998. 'Solar Power Markets Boom.' Worldwatch, September/October. p. 25.

126 Between 1980 and 1999, these costs plunged by 80 percent. O'Meara, M. 1999. 'Solar Power.'

127 Turkenburg, W.C. (ed.), 2000. 'Renewable Energy Technologies.' p. 242.

128 Flavin, C. & M. O'Meara, 1998. 'Solar Power Markets Boom.' p. 25.

129 Derrick, A. 2001. *Power to Tackle Poverty: Getting Renewable Energy to the Poor.* A background report produced for Greenpeace and the Body Shop by IT Power, Sussex, UK, p. 9.

130 Ibid.§

131 Turkenburg, W.C. (ed.), 2000. 'Renewable Energy Technologies.' p. 242.

132 Ibid., p. 239.
133 Ibid.
134 Flavin, C., 1999. 'Bull Market for Wind Energy.' *Worldwatch*, March/April 1999. p. 25.
135 Ibid., p. 27.
136 Flavin, C, & N. Lenssen, 1994. *Power Surge*.
137 Turkenburg, W.C. (ed.), 2000. 'Renewable Energy Technologies.' p. 230.
138 Greenpeace and the Body Shop, 2001. *Power to Tackle Poverty*. p. 9.
139 Flavin, C., 1999. 'Bull Market.' pp. 26–7.
140 Ibid., p. 27.
141 Flavin, C, & N. Lenssen, 1994. *Power Surge*.
142 Turkenburg, W.C. (ed.), 2000. 'Renewable Energy Technologies.' p. 231.
143 Greenpeace and the Body Shop, 2001. *Power to Tackle Poverty*. p. 9.
144 Flavin, C., 1999. 'Bull Market.' p. 27.
145 Turkenburg, W.C. (ed.), 2000. 'Renewable Energy Technologies.' p. 233.
146 Ibid., p. 255.
147 Flavin, C, & N. Lenssen, 1994. *Power Surge*.
148 Turkenburg, W.C. (ed.), 2000. 'Renewable Energy Technologies.' p. 255.
149 Ibid.
150 World Bank, 1994. *Making Development Sustainable: The World Bank Group and the Environment*. World Bank, Washington. p. 119.
151 Turkenburg, W.C. (ed.), 2000. 'Renewable Energy Technologies.' p. 257.
152 Flavin, C, & N. Lenssen, 1994. *Power Surge*.
153 Turkenburg, W.C. (ed.), 2000. 'Renewable Energy Technologies.' p. 258.
154 Thomas, S. & M. Zalbowitz, 1999. *Fuel Cells: Green Power*. Los Alamos National Laboratory, US Department of Energy, Los Alamos, New Mexico. p. 24.
155 Dunn, S., 2000. 'The Hydrogen Experiment.' *Worldwatch,* November/December. p. 18.
156 Thomas, S. & M. Zalbowitz, 1999. *Fuel Cells: Green Power*. p. 21.
157 Ibid., p. 4.
158 Dunn, S., 2000. 'The Hydrogen Experiment.' p. 18.
159 Ibid.
160 Thomas, S. & M. Zalbowitz, 1999. *Fuel Cells: Green Power*. p. 21.
161 Ibid., p. 3.

8 When the Water Cycle Breaks Down
The Potential for Restoration

'We learnt by trial and error that the resilience of our rivers needs attention. Rivers are like living creatures. They are dynamic and need space. It is in the nature of rivers that they refuse to stay straight. If you try to cage a river by building dikes too close to the main stream and by excessive normalization and canalization, it will struggle to break out like a wild beast. Eventually it will increase its pressure upon dikes, dams and artificial banks, look for their weak spots, and break through them. The usual response is of course to strengthen our dikes. But this will increase the water's pressure even further! It will get us into a spiral which will only make us more vulnerable. Therefore, we have opted for another approach: "giving rivers more space."'[1]

Given that the gap between freshwater needs and availability on Spaceship Earth is growing like a population of suburban deer, the world can ill afford breakdowns in the ecological processes that ensure a steady supply of clean water. Like an automobile, freshwater ecosystems require regular maintenance to ensure that a critical function is not about to break down. Many car owners have learned too late that a simple repair could have avoided the meltdown of a transmission. Once the meltdown happens, often the only economically feasible option is to replace the vehicle. Humanity has not yet learned how to replace the vital functions of aquatic ecosystems in the water cycle. In fact, as the following pages explain, we're not really even good at repairing them. These facts make maintenance all the more important.

But what happens if we do break the back of an important river, lake, wetland or estuarine ecosystem? Can it be repaired? At best, efforts to date have brought aquatic ecosystems back from a critical to a (temporarily) stable condition. The following pages discuss the importance of preventative health care for the world's aquatic ecosystems, and the best approaches to take when continued deterioration, in spite of our best efforts, becomes obvious. The concepts discussed under the headings of protection and restoration may be viewed as the flip sides of the same coin. The concepts of maintaining habitat diversity and connectivity are presented under the heading of protection, for example, but the reestablishment of diversity and connectivity is a legitimate restoration goal. On the other hand, the reinstatement of natural flow regimes is discussed as a component of a river restoration strategy, but the maintenance of flow regimes is an important part of river conservation efforts.

FRESHWATER ECOSYSTEMS ON THE BRINK

The vital functions of freshwater ecosystems in providing man and beast with clean and reliable sources of water were described in Chapter 1. Throughout the preceding chapters, the effects of prevailing human uses of these ecosystems on the ability of the Earth's water cycle to function have been discussed. One might summarize the histories of various uses and abuses of these ecosystems as growing at a virtually exponential rate. The rapid augmentation of the planet's human population adds a factor of magnitude to humanity's effects on aquatic ecosystems. Multiply this factor several-fold to reflect swelling consumption of land and water by an increasingly affluent upper class and you have the shadow of a looming crisis.

Over the past century, the world has experienced a virtually cancerous expansion of alterations to freshwater ecosystems through deforestation, industrialization of agriculture, the spread in use of synthetic chemicals, the increase in human waste entering waterways, acid rain and atmospheric deposition of pollutants, and many other factors. Dams and channelization projects cause the most direct impacts.[2] Other rapidly growing pressures on aquatic ecosystems include pollution, especially as developing countries industrialize without adequate environmental regulation, the introduction of alien species, sedimentation from poor land use management, overexploitation of native species, excessive water withdrawals, substantial alterations to flow patterns, and encroachment by human domestic and economic activity.

'Dams and channelization remain the two most pervasive threats to freshwater ecosystems today, with dramatic effects on species abundance and diversity. Since 1970, when Egypt's Aswan Dam came into operation, the number of commercially harvested fish species on the Nile has dropped by almost two-thirds, and the sardine catch in the Mediterranean has fallen by more than 80 percent. On the Rhine River, more than 100 years of channelization and riverside development have cut the river off from 90 percent of its original floodplains, and the native salmon run has nearly disappeared.'[3]

As discussed in Chapter 4, trends in the population structure and dynamics of aquatic biota often serve as the most sensitive, and therefore the most accurate, gauge of ecosystem health. The species composition and population structure of an ecosystem are also terrific integrators of a multitude of stresses. When a species disappears, or one species proliferates as the previously dominant species disappear, scientists know that some relevant environmental condition has changed. For example, sunfish (*Centrarchidae* family) may become dominant in a stream previously populated by trout because of reductions in the dissolved oxygen concentration resulting from pollution, or alewives (*Alosa pseudoharengus*) may flourish in Lake Michigan because over-fishing has diminished populations of their predators.

When one compares the status of aquatic species to those of marine and terrestrial species, the trend towards aquatic ecosystem degradation stands out like a skyscraper on a Hopi mesa (see Figure 8.1). The Living Planet Index for 2002, a joint project of the World Wide Fund for Nature, the United Nations Environment Programme's World Conservation Monitoring Centre, and the non-profit organization Redefining Progress, analysed trends in the Earth's biota over the 30-year period from 1970 to 2000. During this period, populations of forest species fell by about 15 percent on average. Marine species populations fell by about 35 percent. Populations of freshwater species declined by about 54 percent.[4] According to the World Conservation Union, by 1998, approximately 34 percent of fish species around the world were threatened with extinction.[5]

PROTECTION

Beyond the technological shifts recommended in earlier chapters, there is much that can be done simply to prevent the aquatic ecosystems that provide the machinery that drives the water cycle from breaking down.

Maintaining Ecological Processes

Strategies for the conservation of aquatic habitats, in comparison to those strategies intended to protect terrestrial habitats, must focus on processes as much or more than on area. Aquatic systems are much more dynamic than their terrestrial counterparts, with habitat components that shift frequently and are dependent on all of the terrestrial ecosystems that drain into them, as well as the air masses that flow over them and, to a certain extent, the marine systems that border them. Among the processes that must be considered in an aquatic ecosystem conservation programme are flow regimes in lotic systems (discussed in more detail under the restoration heading below), nutrient and sediment cycles, the mixing cycles of lakes, and the life histories and migratory patterns of aquatic and semi-aquatic biota.

Protecting Key Habitats

While it would be impracticable to set aside entire drainage basins from development to protect aquatic ecosystems, it is possible to target key ecosystem components for protection in an effort to maintain ecological viability. Scientists have identified the following key habitats for rivers, lakes and wetlands.

Rivers are clearly important as migration routes for both marine and aquatic life forms, for transporting nutrients to estuaries, and for maintaining the salinity

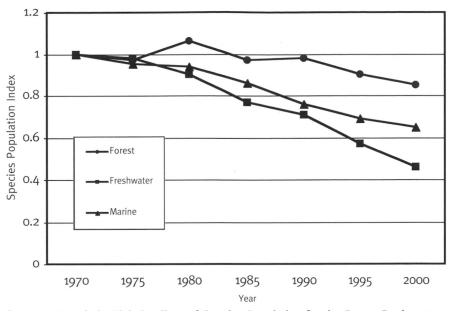

Figure 8.1 Trends in Global Indices of Species Population for the Forest, Freshwater and Marine Biomes, 1970–2000

From: Loh, J. (ed.), 2002. *Living Planet Report 2002*. World Wide Fund for Nature, Gland, Switzerland. p. 30.

balance in nearshore waters. Large, alluvial (sand or silt-bottomed) river reaches serve as habitat for core populations of fish. When there is a major disturbance in peripheral habitat for important fish species, these reaches can act as reservoirs for re-population.[6]

Riparian zones provide many regulatory functions and deserve to be protected. Riparian vegetation exerts control over the mass movement of materials into the river channel and thus is important in the regulation of channel morphology and nutrient loads.[7]

The headwater systems of river are often underestimated in terms of their ecological importance. Small streams in the upper reaches of river basins are often the only places that certain fish will spawn or where rare species of fish, invertebrates and amphibians can be found. Headwater streams also provide high levels of water quality and quantity regulation, sediment control, nutrients and woody debris that benefit downstream communities.[8] Unfortunately, as international opposition to large dams on major rivers grows, many hydropower advocates are arguing for placing smaller dams on fragile headwater streams.

Lakes are vital reservoirs of freshwater and aquatic life. When attempting to conserve a lacustrine ecosystem, it is essential to manage steep slopes draining into it to prevent soil erosion and premature sedimentation. Near-shore areas that are known to provide important nursery or feeding areas for fish or other animals should also be protected. As in the case of river systems, riparian areas have an impact on lacustrine ecosystems in providing additional wetland habitat and filtering sediments and nutrients from terrestrial landscapes.[9] The ecological health of tributary rivers to lakes is also fundamental to the continued survival of many species. Where the rivers are acceptable habitat for lacustrine fish, they serve as refuges for these species during major disturbances, such as the sudden influx of pollutants or the advent of a powerful storm.[10]

Beyond these key habitat types, it is extremely important to maintain a general diversity of habitats within aquatic ecosystems. Maintenance of habitat diversity is an important principle for several reasons. First, as described in Chapter 1, biota in downstream reaches of a river, or in the deeper strata of a lake, may rely on upstream or upper-layer plants and animals as sources of food. Second, the same species may rely on different habitat types during temporal cycles, whether diurnal, seasonal, or over the course of an organism's lifetime. Freshwater mussels, for example, spend their infancy as free-floating larvae until they hitch a ride on the gills of a passing fish. The open water habitat that the fish depends on may contrast starkly with the clean gravel that many mussels prefer as sedentary adults. Fish typically make use of different habitats for their life-cycle activities. An individual fish may chose one habitat for feeding, such as the open water or surface of a stream or lake, but a quite different habitat for spawning, such as a shallow gravel bar or a floodplain wetland. The same fish may rely on a third habitat type for taking refuge from predators and ecological disturbances, such as a rocky, under-water crevice, deep pool or tributary stream.

Wetland is such a catch-all category that it is difficult to devise guidelines to key types deserving of protection. Different sorts of wetlands are important for different purposes. Wet meadows and prairies and vernal pools, for example, are generally quite high in biological diversity and rich with endemic species. Coastal wetlands are important shellfish habitats and nurseries for marine fish, and protect on-shore ecosystems (as well as human developments) from the ravages of tropical storms and hurricanes. Riparian forests and wetlands provide important functions for their adjacent rivers and lakes, including filtering pollutants, regulating ground-water interactions, and providing spawning habitat. Small, isolated wetlands, such as prairie potholes, are important breeding habitats for waterfowl. Wetlands in urban areas, even if degraded, can provide important islands of wildlife habitat, as well as stormwater regulation and water purification functions. Several formulaic assessments have been devised to predict the relative importance of individual wetlands in serving specific functions,[11] but it is very much an evolving art.

Preserving Connectivity

While conservationists recommend the preservation of migratory corridors for terrestrial wildlife, particularly in landscapes slated for development, connectivity between blocks of habitat is even more important for obligate aquatic species (those organisms that can't move through the air or overland). Connectivity is essential for species that rely on different habitats during different segments of their life cycles. When dams and reservoirs interrupt their routes from headwater spawning habitats to the sea, for example, salmon may develop the ability to respire in saltwater before they leave the freshwater behind, with lethal results. The construction of levees between a river channel and its floodplain may prevent spawning fish from accessing nursery wetlands.

Habitat connectivity is also important in maintaining the potential for recolonization of habitats that temporarily lose their fauna as a result of disturbance. A river reservoir that backs water up into the mouths of smaller tributaries can present a substantial barrier to the recolonization of the river's headwaters. A chemical accident or heavy siltation from road construction, for example, may decimate the fauna of a headwater stream. Other tributaries to the same river might contain the same or very similar faunas. Under normal circumstances, these generally small organisms might be able to enter the mainstream of the river during the low flow season and migrate up the mouth of the depopulated tributary. With a reservoir in place, the water level in the main river channel behind the dam may never be low enough to permit migration by such diminutive denizens of headwater streams.

Proponents of dams often recommend the construction of fish passages to facilitate the movement of fish through the structures. Types of fish passages include ladders, pools, baffles, locks, elevators, nature-like channels, and capture and trucking. Fish passages of different types have met with varying degrees of success in facilitating the vertical migration of target species, but are virtually useless in providing the other ecological functions of connectivity, such as the movement of invertebrates and food and energy sources. In addition, the types and designs of fish passes that enable the movement of one species of fish may be unusable by other species. For example, a short, steep pass might work well for strong swimmers, such as salmon, while presenting a barrier to smaller, weaker fish. Similarly, passes that require a fish to leap to a higher level, such as a pool or ladder system, might fail in the conservation of bottom-dwelling fish such as the carp and catfish that dominate many Asian river systems.

From an ecological perspective, the most promising type of fish passage is the nature-like channel. These channels, which function much like riverine side channels, have a very low gradient – generally 1–5 percent, but often less in lowland rivers. In contrast to the distinct and systematic drops that characterize many other fish pass designs, the nature-like channel typically descends in a series of riffles or cascades positioned at roughly regular intervals as in natural watercourses. Nature-like fish passages present design challenges to engineers, however. They require a great deal of space in the vicinity of the dam. They are also unable to adapt to the upstream changes in water levels that are typical in reservoir operation without the addition of special devices such as gates or sluices. The construction of these devices might negate the natural attractiveness of the artificial channel, create hydraulic conditions that make fish passage difficult, and render the passes virtually useless in transporting invertebrates and vegetation up- or down-stream.[12]

RESTORATION

Aquatic ecosystem restoration involves the return of a degraded ecosystem to a level that can be permanently sustained through protection and conservation. Rather than reverting to some unspecified level of nascent chemical, physical and biological status, contemporary restoration of aquatic ecosystems more often attempts to mitigate the effects of anthropogenic practices that have degraded these systems. 'Restored' aquatic ecosystems may not mirror the pristine rivers and lakes of bygone days, but they often exhibit a higher order of ecological sustainability than ecosystems in degraded condition.[13] Restoration processes may also aim to deliver ecosystem services of value to people, such as renewed vitality of recession farming and fisheries or improved water quality.

Restoration is almost always a more expensive option for sustainable water resource management than conservation of natural ecosystems. In addition, the science of ecosystem restoration is young, and the relatively few restoration projects so far attempted throughout the world have met with varying degrees of success. Some ecosystem functions, such as floodwater storage and the removal of nutrients from surface water, are relatively well understood and can be restored in many cases. Other functions, particularly the support of biodiversity, depend on specific and often delicate ecosystem characteristics such as water chemistry, the specific timing of hydrological events, or the specific location of the wetland in a catchment or along a migratory flight path. These characteristics are much more difficult to restore or replace once they have been altered. The barriers to successful restoration efforts can increase exponentially when an entire river system or lake basin is involved, because the complications of cumulative and indirect effects, as well as cross-boundary-political issues, may need to be addressed. It is wise in general to consider restoration as a secondary option for maintaining freshwater ecosystems; it is less desirable than conserving the natural functions of these ecosystems in the first place.

Despite the relative expense and difficulty involved in ecosystem restoration, many countries, particularly in the industrialized world, are discovering that the most cost-effective way to meet their water management objectives is through restoration of freshwater ecosystems. An extreme example is the intention of the United States government and the State of Florida to spend upwards of US$7 billion on restoration of the wetland system that provides freshwater to the Everglades ecosystem and to Florida Bay. The South Florida/Everglades restoration process is striving to restore the biological diversity and hydrological functions of these systems, but economic concerns are paramount in the design of the process. The restoration of the South Florida ecosystem has been promoted as a way to provide major benefits in the form of secure water supplies for the Miami metropolitan area, improved tourism opportunities in Everglades National Park, and improved production of fish and shellfish in Florida Bay, among others. This project has no guarantee of success, however, and squabbling over issues from gravel mining in the ecosystem to how much water should be allocated to the ecosystem and how much to urban use is beginning to erode political support.

Restoration is usually described as the reestablishment of pre-disturbance aquatic processes and related physical, chemical and biological characteristics. Most attempts at aquatic ecosystem restoration to date have involved relatively simple projects on tiny segments of a drainage basin. Examples include the reconnection of a segment of river to its floodplain and the placement of logs in a stretch of a stream both to provide habitat and to channel water so that deep pools form from scour action. Such efforts are often worthwhile, but they frequently fail to address the root causes of ecosystem degradation and thus serve as only short-term solutions.

Restoring Processes

Ensuring the sustainability of a restored ecosystem requires a focus on the reestablishment of the dynamic processes that maintain the ecosystem, rather than merely direct interventions in the chemical, physical and biological components. While the latter may be necessary to begin the healing process, the recreation of a self-sustaining system can be invoked by the old adage: if you give a man a fish, he eats for a day; but if you teach a man to fish, he eats for a lifetime. Important processes to consider include the gradual, such as ecological community succession; the dramatic, such as floods and fires; and the basic, such as flow regimes and sediment transport. These processes are often interrelated.

The Gradual

Ecological succession is the process by which one 'pioneer' ecological community creates the conditions that facilitate its replacement by a more mature community, which in turn sets the stage for its successor and so on until the theoretical 'climax' community emerges. Human intervention can either halt or stimulate succession. Ploughing farmland provides an example of halting or reversing succession in areas where, if grassland were not artificially maintained, forest would take over.

Human activities most often accelerate succession in aquatic ecosystems. The use of fertilizers and discharge of sewage, for example, increase the nutrient loads entering lakes, setting off a process of accelerated eutrophication that causes lakes to fill in and become terrestrial habitats faster than they would under natural conditions. The removal of animals such as muskrats, nutria and alligators from marshes eliminates the workforce that maintains open water areas, speeding the succession of wetland ecosystems to wet prairie or forest and then to terrestrial systems. In many cases, natural succession processes that help to maintain aquatic ecosystems in our landscapes can be re-established simply by removing the human intervention.

With the exception of the inevitable in-filling of lakes, which can also be temporarily offset by heavy precipitation or flooding events, ecological community succession is not a straight-line process involving the maturation of pioneer communities to climax communities that dominate into the hereafter. Disturbances abound that set back succession to earlier stages, as in the muskrat/nutria/alligator example. To the extent that biological diversity relies on a range of habitat types, these disturbances constitute valuable assets, as described below.

The Dramatic

Among the processes that set back succession and maintain a variety of habitats in our world are the sometimes violent and often unexpected incidents of fire and floods. Fires help maintain herbaceous vegetation in prairie and grassland ecosystems by eliminating the woody shrubs and trees that would otherwise become dominant. Because rivers serve as firebreaks, it is not unusual to find rivers that are lined with wet prairie vegetation and floodplain wetlands on one bank, and terrestrial forest on the other bank, where the river protected the trees from fire. Some rivers in prairie areas never had defined, open-water channels before the advent of human fire suppression. These systems have changed from marshy swales to incised, tree-lined channels, partly because root systems remove water from the soil surface and help to lock a channel in place.

As discussed in Chapter 1, floods set back succession by scouring saplings from river banks and floodplains while depositing silt in other reaches of a river. Floods thus help to maintain a mix of early and late succession communities along river reaches that would otherwise succeed to forest. Flooding in a sediment-starved river, however, results in the erosion of the river channel, islands and floodplains and, therefore, in diminution of habitat diversity.

The Basic

The long-term sustainability of aquatic ecosystems is built on the bedrock of essential processes such as flow regimes and sediment transport.

Flow Regimes, the diurnal, weekly, seasonal and annual variation in the quantity of river flow is a key factor in determining what sorts of habitats will be available within a river and where and when they will occur. Natural river ecology is determined as much by the timing of flows as by their quantity and quality. A clear priority for almost any river restoration project is therefore the maintenance or reestablishment of natural (or near-natural) flow regimes. River managers have developed several approaches to producing recommendations for instream flows.

Hydrological index methodologies rely primarily on historical flow records for making flow recommendations.[14] Where there is no reliable, long-term hydrological record, the flow regime can be reconstructed using a post-disturbance record. In this case, modellers reconstruct flow regimes using models that estimate what the flow regime would be if the anthropogenic influences on hydrology were absent. The model is designed to negate hydrological changes resulting from dam operations or water diversions. Where no adequate hydrological record exists, estimations of flow regimes can be made based on a 'reference' stream or river, which is a near-natural river with hydrological and ecological characteristics similar to the river that is being restored prior to the disturbance of the river.[15]

Hydraulic rating methodologies use the relationship between simple hydraulic variables, such as wetted perimeter or maximum depth, and stream discharge to develop environmental flow recommendations. River managers typically measure these variables along a single cross-section. Habitat simulation methodologies are also based on the relationship between discharge and hydraulic response, but entail a more detailed analysis of the quantity and quality of physical, instream habitat available to target biota under different flow regimes. These analyses are drawn from the integration of hydrological, hydraulic and biological response data. Hydraulic rating and habitat simulation methodologies are generally designed to achieve specific objectives, such as boosting the reproductive success of certain species.[16]

In a distinctive departure from the methods listed above, holistic methodologies attempt to optimize flow regimes to benefit the ecology of an entire river system. Such methodologies can also provide a basis for improving ecosystem functions that find particular favour, such as maintenance of aesthetic quality, system productivity, protection of features of cultural or scientific interest, and recreational use.[17]

'In the late 1960s the Pongolapoort dam was constructed on the Phongolo River in north-east South Africa near its borders with Swaziland and Mozambique. The reservoir was filled in 1970 with a view towards irrigating 40,000 hectares of agricultural land for white settlers, with no provision for hydropower generation. No assessments were undertaken of the impacts of the impoundment on the floodplain, where 70,000 Tembe-Thonga people were dependent on recession agriculture, fishing and other wetland resources, nor on the biodiversity of the Ndumu game reserve. In the event no settlers came to use the irrigation scheme. The dam changed the whole flooding regime of the river, which had significant negative impacts on agriculture and fisheries.

'In 1978 a workshop was held on the Phongolo floodplain to review the future of irrigation and how to minimize negative impact on the floodplain. This led to a plan for controlled releases to rehabilitate the indigenous agricultural system and wildlife. However, initial releases of water from the dam were made at the wrong time of year and crops were either washed away or rotted. In 1987, the Department of Water Affairs and the tribal authorities agreed to experiment with community participation. As a result, water committees were established, representing five user groups: [farmers], fishermen, livestock keepers, women and health workers.... They were given the mandate to decide when flood waters should be released. These committees were very successful at implementing people's views and have led to management of the river basin to the benefit of floodplain users. Indeed, they have been so successful that attempts have been made to disband them by the KwaZulu government as they were seen as a threat to power.'[18]

'As an example of demonstrating practical solutions, the Waza-Logone project, a multi-partner initiative in northern Cameroon, has achieved impressive results in pilot releases of dammed water, in order to rehabilitate a floodplain which had largely dried up, as a result of an ill-conceived dam and rice-irrigation scheme. The reflooding trials, carried out in close collaboration with local communities, have resulted in rapid and beneficial ecological and socio-economic changes: regrowth of floodplain vegetation, improved fisheries, livestock and rice production, as well as improved conditions for wildlife and waterfowl – a win–win situation for humans and nature.'[19]

One holistic method for establishing instream flows is the 'range of variability' approach. This method is based on the assumption that no single management regime based on the needs of a single species or ecological function can optimize habitat conditions for the full suite of biota in a river. Natural flow regimes favour some species during some periods of time and others during other periods. Over time, the theory goes, the natural variability will optimize conditions for all of the river's native biota, even though populations of certain species will wax and wane as flows increase and decrease.

The range of variability in a river is reconstructed from the actual or simulated hydrological record of the pre-disturbance river, with a focus on a set of statistics that describe flow patterns established on the basis of five main characteristics. First, the magnitude of flow at any given period of time (maxima and minima) defines such habitat attributes as wetted habitat and position of the water table. Second, the timing of occurrence of specific flows can determine whether certain life cycle requirements are met and can influence the degree of stress or mortality associated with extreme flow events. Third, the frequency of occurrence of certain flows influences population dynamics. Fourth, the duration of specific flows determines whether a certain life cycle phase can be completed and the degree to which the effects of stressful effects such as inundation and desiccation accumulate. Finally, the rate of change of flows can influence the degree of stranding of certain organisms along the water's edge or in ponded depressions, or the ability of plant roots to maintain contact with groundwater tables.[20]

'The biotic composition, structure and function of aquatic, wetland and riparian ecosystems depend largely on the hydrological regime. Intra-annual variation in hydrological conditions is essential to successful life-cycle completion for many species that depend on these ecosystems and often plays a major role in the population dynamics of these species through influences on reproductive success, natural disturbance, and competition. The full range of natural intra- and inter-annual variation of hydrological regimes is necessary to sustain the native biodiversity and evolutionary potential of freshwater ecosystems.'[21]

Sediment Transport is also important in determining water quality and the nature of aquatic habitat within aquatic ecosystems. River, lake and wetland ecology can easily be turned upside-down by extreme changes in sediment regimes. In the cases of lentic ecosystems, reductions in sediment loads are rarely of consequence unless unusual erosive forces are at work. Increases in sediment loads, on the other hand, may lead to premature filling. The effects of shifts in sediment transport are more complex in river systems. Increases in sediment loads can lead to the burial of important habitats, such as mussel beds and spawning gravel. Large rivers with large dams more often lead to sediment-deprived reaches, with resulting deltaic deterioration and channel erosion.

The restoration of natural sediment dynamics requires an analysis of the source of the disruption and the locations where undesirable results are likely to occur. Sediment transport models can assist in this assessment. Several approaches are available to address the imbalance in sediment loads depending on the source of the disturbance and the areas most vulnerable to untoward erosion or deposition. These include watershed treatments (reforestation or the implementation of soil and water conservation practices, for example), channel stabilization (preferably using native plant species, since concrete and other artificial materials can exacerbate erosion upstream and downstream of the treatment site), and, at the extreme, artificial sediment transport.

'Only thirty years ago the Colorado River was as young and athletic as any river in the world.... Today she lies sedate with many of her resources, beaches, fish, aquatic communities, struggling for survival.... We should step back from the [Grand] Canyon and consider ways to restore the blood and circulation to the Colorado before it reaches [the head of the Grand Canyon at] Lees Ferry.

'Warm, muddy water was the lifeblood of the Colorado. While we cannot (and may not want to) restore the pre-dam floods, we can partially restore the warm, muddy waters. We should seriously consider structural means of warming the water and adding the sediment.

'[Addition of sediment could be accomplished by construction of] a sediment slurry line to transport Colorado River mud from the base of Cataract Canyon to the head of the Grand Canyon.... The pipe need not be blasted into the solid rock surrounding Lake Powell, but could be brought to the Colorado at the mouth of the Paria River. Operated seasonally such a pipeline may add enough sediment to rejuvenate the natural processes in the Canyon.

'Blasphemy you say. The engineers have done enough damage! It's true that [these solutions] will cost money to build and operate. But these costs should be weighed against the alternative costs of maintaining a close and constant vigil over our patient. It may be that these solutions are not needed and that's fine. But they should be considered as we search for long-term solutions to the effects of Glen Canyon Dam on the Colorado River through Grand Canyon.'[22]

Contemporary Principles of Aquatic Ecosystem Restoration

As societies have tried and failed and tried again to restore aquatic ecosystems, we have learned a lot about the complexity of such undertakings. Small-scale, short-term solutions can be found in the classic approaches of George Palmiter, who triangulates like a billiards buff and finds exactly the right spot and angle to throw a log in a stream to correct a localized sedimentation or erosion problem. These solutions are inadequate to cope with the magnitude and multitude of insults facing large-scale ecosystems. In response to the scale and complexity of today's environmental problems, restoration professionals are increasing the scale, depth, and temporal span of their approaches. These changes include the shift from site-specific to basin-scale analysis, a search for the social and economic root causes of disturbances instead of a superficial assessment of immediate causes, and a long-term, adaptive process of monitoring and response.

Basin-Scale Analysis

Success requires that restoration projects be conceived and implemented at a spatial scale that is appropriate to the scale of the disturbance. Regardless of where the ecosystem or site targeted for restoration is situated within a drainage basin, an assessment of an entire drainage basin will usually aid in the long-term success of the process. Drainage basins are nested entities. The basin of a large river such as the Amazon comprises many smaller, tributary basins, which again are aggregates of even smaller basins, and so on. Projects at small scales are usually effective only when the disturbance is also at a small scale. Restoration of even an individual freshwater site is a complicated undertaking because it almost always requires attention to processes within a larger catchment.[23]

'Loktak Lake is the largest wetland in the north-eastern region of India and has been referred to as the lifeline of the people of Manipur [State] due to its important role in the ecological and economic security of the region. The lake has been the source of water for generation of hydroelectric power, irrigation and water supply. A large population living around the lake depends upon the lake resources for their sustenance.[24]

'The staple food of Manipur is directly linked to Loktak Lake. The lake is rich in biodiversity and has been designated as a wetland of international importance under the Ramsar Convention in 1990. The Keibul Lamjo National Park, in the southern part of the lake, is home to the endangered Manipur Brow Antlered Deer, locally called Sangai. The lake has also been the breeding ground of a number of riverine fishes and continues to be a vital fisheries resource. It supports a significant population of migratory and resident waterfowl....[25]

'The hill areas of Manipur which constitute the catchment areas of important rivers, including Loktak Lake, are under pressure mainly due to deforestation, prolonged practice of *Jhum* [swidden, or slash-and-burn] cultivation and overall exploitation of resources. These factors have mainly contributed to the rapid siltation of the lake and consequently have reduced its carrying capacity....[26]

'A preliminary survey was undertaken to identify the critical areas, which contribute to soil erosion leading to sedimentation of the lake. Based on this

survey, five sub-catchments have been identified which constitute the catchments for the major river entering the lake. Two broad land-use categories, i.e. fallow land ... and degraded forest ... have been delineated for soil and water conservation treatment purposes. Treatment for these areas has to be addressed separately with specific modifications at the different locations.'[27]

Every millimetre of land and water that drains into ecosystems located in the lower portions of a drainage basin influences the health, productivity and sustainability of the downstream systems. The effects of downstream portions of the drainage on ecosystems in the headwaters are not so obvious, but may also be important. These may include erosive headcutting, backwater flooding, and barriers to dispersal that prevent migratory biota that cannot travel overland from reaching upper portions of the basin which once supported part or all of their life cycles.

On the other hand, it is important not to confine the analysis of ecosystem degradation to drainage basins. The delineation of a drainage basin isn't a hard line, but is pervious in many ways. Groundwater tables often occupy different geographical spaces than the surface systems with which they interact. Pollutants may enter aquatic ecosystems from airsheds many kilometres removed from the relevant drainage basin. Alien species such as zebra mussels and Asian snakeheads may enter aquatic ecosystems by various means, such as attached to the hulls of ocean liners or by squirming over land, respectively. Invasive plant species can enter aquatic systems by adhering to the feet of migrating ducks. Conversely, reductions of populations of semi-aquatic animals, such as waterfowl, may occur outside the limits of the drainage basin.

Analysis of Root Causes

It is possible to address a problem in a simplistic way – for example, one might attempt to remedy channel siltation by dredging out the accumulated silt. Unless one addresses the driving forces behind the problem, however, the solution will only be temporary, will need to be repeated, and may eventually become ineffective (for example, if the dredging company runs out of feasible disposal sites for the silt it removes). A longer-term solution, involving an investigation of the causes of excessive sediment loads in the stream, may be more expensive to implement initially but more cost-effective over time. Suppose, for example, that the reason for the siltation is that communities in the drainage basin are cutting down the woody vegetation for use in cooking fires. In addition to removing the sediments that have already accumulated in the stream, a sustainable solution would include providing the community with more efficient cooking stoves and investing in reforestation. In addition to being more cost-effective over the long run, attention to root causes can provide multiple benefits for human communities and ecosystems.

'On the island of Cyprus, there are real water shortages. As a result, a number of water supply investments and interventions, including surface water dams and groundwater exploitation, have been made. The most significant investment has been the Southern Conveyor Project that transfers water across southern Cyprus. However, even with these schemes the possibility of further exploitation of surface water has largely been exhausted and this has led to the consideration/use of more costly unconventional sources such as desalinization, recycling and evaporation suppression.

'The current water shortages were not a result of water scarcity, but of an inadequate property rights structure and the lack of consideration of all interest groups within the watersheds. This has led to a system of first come first served and the diversion of water by predominantly agricultural users in the upper reaches of the watershed. This in turn has reduced the surface flows downstream along the Southern Conveyor belt. Downstream, much of the water is diverted to storage dams for distribution to the main urban centres, which reduces the freshwater resources reaching the coast and feeding wetlands. There is concern that this has damaged habitats important for migratory bird species. The result of a lack of planning and management on the watershed is an uncoordinated, unregulated interplay of water users and a highly inefficient use of the island's scarce and dwindling water resources.

'A study of the Kouris watershed in south-west Cyprus examined the distribution of water resources among different users. Based on this information, it proposed more efficient, equitable and sustainable alternatives. Taking the watershed as the unit of analysis, the study comprised two stages. In Stage 1, economic valuation techniques were used to establish the economic value of the competing demands for surface and ground water and therefore to determine the most economically efficient distribution between users. In Stage 2, a policy impact analysis was carried out, incorporating issues of social equity. It also examined the value of water for environmental and ecological purposes.

'Some of the policy recommendations emerging from the analysis included:

- new management structures at the watershed level are needed to cope with the complex integration of water users under a limited water supply;

- pricing schemes could be effectively used to create incentives for more efficient, as well as equitable and sustainable, uses of the water. For example, there needs to be a reduced appropriation for agriculture and a switch away from water-intensive crops, e.g. watermelons, into other uses;

- individuals' willingness to pay for wetland protection is £15 per household

per year, implying that a greater amount of freshwater resources should be diverted to the wetlands; and

- **the timing of water uses also needs to be considered in policy choices (for example, the highest demand for water for agriculture and tourism occur at the same time).**

'This study highlighted the need for integrated watershed management and planning at the level of the watershed. The information generated brought greater transparency to the planning and management process, allowing the balancing of conflicting demands on limited water resources in a more sustainable and equitable manner.'[28]

Adaptive Management

Like most strategies that aim to alleviate problems related to changes in the abundance and/or behaviour of natural resources (strategies to reduce flood damage, as discussed in Chapter 7, for example), restoration processes are ideally adaptive in nature. Successful processes must be equipped with monitoring programmes that provide resource managers with feedback on how well the process is performing relative to the achievement of the goals. If the monitoring programme reveals that the restoration process is not performing as well as anticipated, or if resource managers decide to adjust the goals of the process in response to changing environmental conditions or social preferences, then the process can be adjusted and changes in performance monitored again. The restoration process can be viewed as an ongoing cycle of adaptive experimentation and adjustment, rather than as a linear process with a defined end point.

In its most effective form, active adaptive management uses management programmes designed to compare selected policies or practices experimentally by evaluating alternative hypotheses about the system being managed. A typical adaptive management approach includes a number of key components. First, managers commit to making adjustments based in part on scientific experimentation. Second, managers shift from a 'trial and error' operational mode to formal experimentation with management actions and alternatives. Third, managers abandon fragmented scientific investigations and adopt integrated ecosystem science, with, for example, hydrologists, engineers, microbiologists and ichthyologists working in teams and sharing knowledge. Fourth, managers pay explicit attention to scientific uncertainties in ecosystem processes and to the effects of management alternatives. Fifth, managers employ formal experimental design and hypothesis testing to reduce scientific uncertainties and help guide management adjustments. Sixth, managers ensure careful monitoring of responses to their operations and of ecological and social effects. Seventh, managers analyse experimental outcomes in ways that guide future management decisions. Finally, adaptive management requires collaboration among stakeholders, managers and scientists in all phases of these processes.[29] For management approaches to be truly adaptable, they must also be reversible and avoid permanent and rigid changes to the ecosystem.

'Here, two examples of DRM [Dynamic River Management, a Dutch variation of the adaptive management concept] are given that are currently realized along the Waal River [in the Netherlands]. In order to increase the economic attractiveness of shipping as the most environmentally sound method of transport, enlargement of the draught and a wider fairway in the Waal River would be required. In the traditional management approach, a smaller normal width [gained] by extending the present groynes would solve this problem. This measure permanently increases the flow velocity, causing a scouring of the riverbed that would lead to the desired fairway dimensions. DRM prefers locally effective and reversible measures. A pilot project is now investigating aspects of systematically dredging shoals and re-allocating the dredged material in troughs, as an alternative to extending groynes. Another example of DRM concerns the Waal River bends, where the fairway width is limited by the shallow inner bend, caused by the so-called 'spiral flow.' At present various forms of river bend improvement are being tested that have only [local] and reversible effects. A most promising technique [is] the so-called 'bottom vanes' which cause degradation of the inner bend. DRM means that measures will be applied that are able to cope with dynamic river reactions and that are flexible in view of future demands. Instead of large rigid constructions, small-sized measures to correct river responses will be used. To restore riverine habitats, in the floodplains more vegetation will be allowed. In practice, the river will show more dynamic changes, in water levels as well as in bed geometry, complicating river management. To be prepared to take action, information regarding these changes is essential. For this purpose an extensive monitoring and impact assessment programme (including forecasting) has to be available....'[30]

Restoration of Specific Aquatic Ecosystem Types

Restoration strategies may be predominantly active or passive. Active approaches may be essentially negative (the removal or attenuation of chronic disturbance activities, such as excessive phosphorus loading to a lake); positive, (the reconnection of a river with its floodplain); or a combination of both. Restoration frequently requires one or more of the following processes: reconstruction of antecedent physical conditions; chemical adjustment of the soil and water; and biological manipulation, including the reintroduction of absent native flora and fauna.[31]

The appropriate processes involved in restoration differ by ecosystem type, by the principal problems or disturbances addressed, by the specific goals of each restoration endeavour, and by the degree of degradation and the degree of recuperation desired. In general, however, restoration involves the articulation of goals, the identification and characterization of problems and disturbances, an assessment of alternative approaches for addressing the disturbances, the selection of a preferred set of alternatives, implementation of the selected alternatives, and monitoring of the results. These processes come full circle under an adaptive management regime, since the findings from the monitoring programme will most likely entail some changes to the implementation plan. The results of such changes will then be recorded and modified in response to ecosystem feedback, and adaptation will continue until the ecosystem has achieved a state of dynamic equilibrium.

Rivers

The changes that have stressed flowing water systems have impaired their value for both human use and environmental services. Stresses arise from water quantity or flow mistiming, morphological modifications of the channel and riparian zone, excessive erosion and sedimentation, deterioration of substrate quality, deterioration of water quality, decline of native species, and introduction of exotic species. The locus of the problem can be in the watershed, along the riparian or floodplain zone, or in the channels and pools.[32]

The most extreme form of stress is the complete appropriation of water flowing on the surface, either by direct withdrawal or by pumping water from the riparian zone. Only slightly less extreme is the conversion of reaches of free-flowing river to a series of lake-like impoundments. In these cases, the free-flowing river no longer exists, and restoration of some semblance of the natural system would require drastic measures such as the reduction of water withdrawals or the removal of dams. Riverine ecology is also dramatically altered when the connection between the river and its floodplain, or riparian zone, is severed – directly, by channelization and the construction of levees or dykes, or indirectly, by regulating the flood regime with dams for uses such as navigation and hydroelectricity generation.

Scientific evidence increasingly indicates that the most successful way to restore the river environment is to encourage the river to restore itself through natural processes, rather than to re-engineer the ecosystem. This self-healing is best accomplished by removing or reducing human interventions.[33]

Surface water, groundwater, floodplains, wetlands and other features do not function as separate and isolated components of the watershed, but rather as a single, integrated, natural system. Disruption of any one part of this system can have long-term and far-reaching consequences for the functioning of the entire system.[34] For restoration purposes, the main components of riverine ecosystems can be divided into channels, floodplains, flow regimes and watersheds.

Channels occur in four distinct types: alluvial, meandering channels; straight bedrock channels; channels armoured with rocks and cobbles; and braided channels. Factors that can distinguish different stream types include the geology or soils making up the streambed, the gradient or steepness of the stream slope, and the degree to which a stream meanders. Additional factors that distinguish stream types include the ratio of the widths and depths of channels that are full to the bank; whether streams have wide or narrow floodplains; and the width of the meander belt (the boundary of the stream meander pattern).[35]

Floodplains can generally be restored simply by letting them flood. The trick is to accomplish the flooding with no significant loss of revenue from the land, which, if public subsidies for floodplain development are eliminated, can be accomplished in many ways. The restoration of floodplains and associated riparian habitats can be accomplished on a small or large scale, using simple techniques such as grazing management and tree planting or more complex techniques such as dam removal. The reinstatement of natural flow regimes is potentially the most important factor in sustainable floodplain ecosystem restoration.[36]

Successful floodplain restoration projects are based on extensive local knowledge of hydrology and ecology, including the range of natural variability, disturbance regimes, soils and landforms, and vegetation; on understanding the history of resource development; and on identifying reference sites. Because restoration is not a deterministic process for which the outcome can be predicted with high temporal or spatial resolution, it might appropriately be considered a journey involving floodplain ecosystems and societal goals, with both evolving over time.[37]

'Many of the world's most valuable natural and cultural resources, including wetlands, fertile soils, rare and endangered plants and animals, and sites of archaeological and historical significance, are associated with floodplains. Floodplains are shaped by dynamic physical and biological processes driven by climate, the water cycle, erosion and deposition, extreme natural events, and other forces. The movement of water through ground and surface waters, floodplains, wetlands, and watersheds is perhaps the greatest indicator of the interaction of natural processes in the environment.'[38]

The alteration, setback, or removal of levees may be more important in restoring floodplain ecosystems than in other aquatic systems. Moving levees back from the river channel reinstates contact between the river and a portion of its floodplain. Gaps can also be constructed to allow periodic inundation of former floodplains and the re-establishment of riparian vegetation. If gap construction is undertaken in conjunction with setback levees, the system could be re-designed to provide flood protection to target communities or developments. The complete removal of existing levees or their replacement by levees further from the river can be expensive, involving not only costly earth-moving activity but potentially major changes in existing land uses.[39]

However simple or complex the restoration effort, monitoring the work after it is installed is an essential part of the programme. The relatively small effort required to visit a project site once a week for several months after planting, for example, and perhaps less frequently as the project matures, can prevent disasters from insect predation, flood-related scouring, drought or other unforeseen events.[40]

Watersheds are important because they help to determine the quality, quantity and timing of water flows into rivers, lakes and estuaries. The success of a river restoration process is often highly dependent on the integrity of the watershed, because much of the movement of material, energy, and organisms between the river itself and its interdependent, external environments (such as floodplains, wetlands, and estuaries) is dependent on the movement of water.

Knowledge of land uses alone is not sufficient in describing watershed processes. How lands are managed can dramatically affect these processes. The use of fertilizers and management of wastes from livestock operations can significantly influence the nutrient loads of runoff from an agricultural watershed, for example. Urbanization is another global trend that will play a major role in determining the status of river systems in the twenty-first century.[41]

Dam decommissioning, or the removal of obsolete and/or unsafe dams, is increasing as a more economical alternative to repair. Many aging dams are considered a safety hazard with a high risk of failure. Other dams were constructed to serve purposes that are now obsolete, such as providing mechanical power for mills or factories that no longer exist. In some cases, economic analyses indicate that the ecological benefits of removing the dam are greater than the benefits generated by the dam, and/or that the costs of removing the dam pale in comparison to those of maintaining it in a safe condition.

'A record number of dams – 63 dams in 15 states and the District of Columbia – are scheduled for removal in 2002, says the conservation group American Rivers....

'Another milestone was reached in October of 2001, when conservationists celebrated the completion of a series of dam removals that restored 115 miles of Wisconsin's Baraboo River, the longest stretch of river ever returned to free-flowing condition in America....

'"In Wisconsin, dam removal is, on average, three to five times less expensive than dam repair. And if you're a small town or an individual owner, that price difference can be the straw that breaks the dam's back," explained Helen Sarakinas, small dams programme manager for the River Alliance of Wisconsin.'[42]

'Surrounded by a small crowd of Central Valley citizens, [former US] Secretary of the Interior Bruce Babbitt stood atop McPherrin dam, on Butte Creek, not far from Chico, California, in the hundred-degree heat of the Sacramento Valley. The constituencies this crowd represented – farmers, wildlife conservationists, state fish and game officials, irrigation managers – had been at one another's throats for the better part of a century, wrangling over every trickle of water that flows through this naturally arid basin. On this day, however, amity reigned. At the appointed moment, with CNN cameras rolling and a *New York Times* photographer framing the scene, Babbitt hoisted a sledgehammer above his head and – "with evident glee," as one reporter later noted – brought his tool of destruction down upon the dam. Golf claps all around. "That's one small blow for salmon!" Babbitt told the crowd.'[43]

'The Masions-Rouges and Saint-Etienne-du-Vigan dams are located on tributaries of the Loire River in France. Between September 1998 and early 1999, the Masions-Rouges dam was torn down. Maisons-Rouges dam was 5 metres high and eliminated all 700 hectares of spawning grounds of the Atlantic Salmon on the Vienne River, the second-most important tributary of the Loire River. This dam also blocked other migratory fish, such as eel and shad, from roughly a fifth of the entire Loire basin. An earlier unsuccessful traditional restoration project was launched in the mid-1970s. This effort included fish ladders and other infrastructures. The latest fish-restoration programme now includes the removal of this dam and the Saint-Etienne-du-Vigan dam and the construction of an improved fish ladder on a third dam in the watershed. Costs of demolition were about $1.6 million. Demolition was supervised by Electricité de France.

'Saint-Etienne-du-Vigan was a small hydro dam on the upper Allier River. This dam was also removed in 1998. The dam had an installed capacity of 35 MW, was 13 metres high, and blocked or flooded 30 hectares of prime spawning habitat. Prior to the construction of the dam, this area produced 10 tons of salmon a year for nearby villages. The Allier River is the only tributary in the Loire Basin where the Atlantic salmon still return to spawn, and only 67 returning salmon were counted in 1996. The Atlantic salmon have disappeared from all the large rivers on the European Atlantic coast. The regional managers of the rivers in the area stated that the dam "representait une menace pour la sécurité publique et constituait un obstacle infranchissable pour numbreuses espèces de poisson migrateur" (the dam represented a menace to public safety and constituted an impassable obstacle for numerous species of migratory fish).'[44]

'Scotts Peak Dam on the Gordon River in Tasmania has been proposed for removal. The dam created a reservoir that flooded Lake Pedder, a lake in Tasmania famous for the beauty of its pink quartzite beach. Local environmentalists have proposed draining the reservoir and restoring Lake Pedder to its natural state. Scotts Peak Dam produces hydropower, but local activists believe that the hydropower from the dam can be replaced or simply eliminated because Tasmania has a substantial surplus of generating capacity. The Tasmanian government and the Opposition Party oppose the proposed removal. Further research and planning are needed before a final decision is made.'[45]

There are, of course, difficulties associated with dam decommissioning. The primary concern is usually the fate of the sediment stored in the reservoir behind the dam and the subsequent physical changes in the river channel that follow dam removal. Although there has been relatively little scientific study of this essentially contemporary event, most changes seem to have occurred immediately following dam removal. Modelling results from studies of dam removals suggest that it may take decades or centuries for the fish and riparian plant communities to recover from the ecological disturbances caused by the dam. Ecosystems upstream of the dam may also require many years before they recover from inundation. Surveys and soil cores indicate that in 80 percent of cases, post-dam removal channels don't follow the pre-dam channel alignment, but rather develop a new course, Furthermore, plant communities in former impoundment sites may not resemble naturally occurring plant assemblages. The extreme habitat alteration, such as the sudden availability of extensive amounts of nutrient-rich sediments, means that plants that initially colonize the exposed sediments are able to persist for several years and prevent other species from becoming established. The difficulties and uncertainties involved in dam removal increase in magnitude with the size of the dam.

Because ecosystems are naturally dynamic, it is not possible, or necessarily desirable, to replicate completely the structure and function of an ecosystem at a particular moment in time. The key to successful restoration is the reinvigoration of the ecosystem so that it can self-regulate. Thus, specific habitat features may disappear from one stretch of a stream or portion of a lakebed, only to be recreated elsewhere within the system – a state known as 'dynamic equilibrium.' The restoration process re-establishes the general structure, function, and dynamic but self-sustaining behaviour of the ecosystem. The constantly changing nature of ecological communities requires that restoration processes be monitored once they are set in motion. Continued vigilance will ensure that opportunities for course corrections are maximized.

The essence of a lotic ecosystem is the dynamic equilibrium of the physical system, which in turn establishes a dynamic equilibrium in the biological components. The goal of restoration, therefore, should be to restore the river or stream to dynamic equilibrium, not to 'stabilize' a channel or bank. The objectives under this broad goal are as follows: restoration of the natural sediment and flow regimes, the natural channel geometry, the natural riparian plant community, and the restoration of native plants and animals. In many cases, the restoration of the sediment transport and flow regimes will provide adequate stimulus for the natural (unaided) restoration of the other components.[46]

Wetlands

A wetland is an ecosystem that depends on constant or recurrent shallow inundation or saturation at or near the surface of the substrate (usually soil or sand). Wetlands are characterized by the presence of physical, chemical, and biological features that reflect recurrent, sustained inundation or saturation.[47]

Because wetlands are neither fully aquatic nor terrestrial, they have not been easily assimilated by the well-established scientific disciplines of terrestrial and aquatic ecology. Wetlands have some of the features of deepwater systems, frequently including anoxic (oxygen-depleted) substrate and some species of algae, vertebrates and invertebrates. Most wetlands share with terrestrial ecosystems a flora dominated by vascular plants, although the species composition of wetlands generally differs from that of uplands. Wetlands often are found at the interface of terrestrial ecosystems (such as upland forests and grasslands) and aquatic systems (such as lakes, rivers, and estuaries). Some are isolated from deepwater habitats, and are maintained entirely by groundwater and/or precipitation. Even though they show structural and functional overlap and physical interface with terrestrial and aquatic systems, wetlands are different from these other ecosystems in so many respects that they must be considered a distinctive class.[48]

Techniques for restoring wetlands fall into three broad categories: reestablishing or managing wetland hydrology; eliminating or controlling chemical or other contaminants affecting wetlands; and reestablishing and managing native biota, which may entail the eradication of exotic species. The restoration technique required depends on the type of disturbance. At the simplest level, restoration may involve elimination or control of overgrazing, allowing for the ultimate reestablishment of native wetland vegetation. At a more complex level, restoration may require a combination of techniques such as removing fill material, reestablishing proper hydrology, reintroducing native flora and fauna, and controlling exotic species.[49] Examples of wetland restoration approaches also include establishing river flow and re-establishing topography.

The reestablishment of a frequent fire regime may also be necessary in restoring endemic wetland vegetation. In the wet prairie ecosystems of the midwestern United States, for example, fires frequently set back succession by removing woody vegetation that was encroaching on the highly diverse, native herbacious plants. Such brilliant foliage as white-fringed prairie orchids (*Habernaria virides* var. *bracteata*), shooting stars (*Dodecatheon meadia*) and marsh marigold (*Caltha palustris*) might have been doomed to extinction by thirsty, shadowy, woody competitors were it not for annual or biannual burns.

For wetlands that have been modified by the diversion of water, the first step in restoration is reestablishing flow into the wetland. Initial restoration techniques may consist of installing structures to redivert flow back into old river channels and adjacent marsh.[50] Alteration of surface wetland hydrology occurs in several forms, ranging from excessive flooding to excessive draining. Excessive flooding of wetlands often occurs in dammed and dyked rivers, streams, lakes and wetlands. Providing control structures, or removing the structures that cause flooding, is the first step in restoration. If sedimentation in the flooded area has altered the original bottom elevation, sediment removal may be required.

'The Danube Delta is one of the world's largest wetlands areas and among Europe's last largely natural landscapes. In the interests of navigation and agriculture, a development strategy that involved cutting floodplain islands in the delta off from river flows was implemented over several decades. Two of these, Balbina and Cernovca, are being restored.

'Before they were dyked, both islands provided valuable natural resources to the local population and the regional economy, including fish, reeds, and game. The elimination of the natural hydrological regime arrested all traditional land uses. A combination of inadequate labour reserves and soil degradation (resulting primarily from changes in the flow regime) doomed agricultural efforts in the reclaimed islands to failure. Restoration efforts, which began in 1994, involved breaching dykes, reestablishing overland flows.

'Following restoration activities, the flora and fauna of the islands have already demonstrated substantial recovery. People are also benefiting. Only four years after restoration of Balbina, 15 fishermen are making a living on the island once more. Additional prospects of sustainable grazing, reed cutting, sustainable hunting and ecotourism will also benefit the local economy.'[51]

Subsurface drainage, or lowering of the groundwater table, usually results in the loss of surface water provided to wetlands. The use of ditches to de-water the landscape (even if wetlands and streams themselves are not directly affected), groundwater pumping and subsurface tile drainage systems can lead to the desiccation of wetlands. In these cases, the first step in the restoration process is to address the cause of subsurface drainage. In wetlands that have accumulated sediments and have therefore experienced an increase in bottom elevation relative to the rest of the landscape, it may be necessary to remove sediment or build a small berm to impound water in the wetland.[52]

When wetlands have been altered through filling or substrate removal (dredging), re-establishing the landscape contour concomitant with surface and subsurface hydrology is an essential first step in restoration.[53]

When wetlands are degraded by heavy contaminant loadings, the simplest restoration technique is the removal of contaminant inflow. Depending on the type and concentration of contaminants, removal of material that has already settled to the bottom of the wetland may be necessary. In these cases, it may be difficult to find a proper disposal site for the contaminated sediments.

The final step in restoration is often an effort to reintroduce native biological communities. The level of effort required to accomplish this objective depends on the ability of surrounding wetlands to provide a natural source of plants and animals to the restored wetland, the size of the area being restored, and the potential for invasion by exotic species. Although the ultimate goal of restoration should be a self-sustaining ecosystem, some management may be necessary in the initial phase of restoration (for example, stabilizing hydrology to assist in the establishment of plant communities). Introduction of animal life and replanting or additional planting may also be necessary.

Lakes

Many of the approaches used in restoring wetlands are also applicable to the restoration of rivers and lakes. Lake specialists have applied the term restoration rather broadly to actions designed to alleviate degraded conditions in lakes. There are also some important differences between lakes and other surface waters relative to the ease of restoration, and a number of methods used to restore lakes that are not applicable to the restoration of wetlands and streams. Rivers and streams can, for example, be restored in many cases by simply removing the source of contamination and relying on the self-purification functions of the ecosystems. This approach is seldom sufficient for lakes, which tend to have long water and substance residence times and behave more as closed systems. In-lake treatments are often necessary in addition to source controls to restore lakes. Streams most commonly need restoration because of loss of habitat through physical alterations (for example, channelization or dam construction). In contrast, most degraded lakes suffer from chemical contamination by excess nutrients, organic matter, toxic substances or acidity.

Successful lake restoration often depends upon the restoration of watershed components. The restoration of influent streams is likely to affect the input of sediment, solutes (including nutrients and contaminants) and water to the lake. The wetlands surrounding a lake partially control water and solute fluxes and the availability of appropriate habitats for fish spawning. Conversely, lake restoration exerts effects on the ecological health of wetlands by influencing the distribution of aquatic and emergent vegetation, water levels, and wave and ice impacts on littoral areas. Lake and stream ecosystems also interact through the life cycles of migratory fish.

A major determinant of lake and reservoir productivity is the steady-state, long-term average concentration of nutrients, especially those (such as phosphorus, nitrogen, and silica) that can limit or trigger biological productivity. The natural water chemistry of a lake is heavily influenced by the characteristics of its watershed, so a great range of base chemical conditions can be expected in different landscapes (deserts with salty, highly erosive soils and boreal regions with peat-based soils and high acidity, for example). Increased loading of nutrients and organic matter, usually from cultural sources such as wastewater treatment plants and runoff from urban or agricultural land, often leads to sharply increased nutrient concentrations in the water and ultimately to algal blooms, oxygen depletion and other indicators of premature eutrophication. In these cases, elimination or reduction of pollutant loadings is a necessary, but often insufficient, step towards restoration.

Various in-lake activities can be used in combination with reductions in pollutant loads. Dredging the lake bottom can remove contaminated sediments or restore the depth of a lake that is prematurely filling in as result of excessive erosion in the watershed. Alum treatment can draw excess phosphorus from the water and prevent it recycling to the water from the sediments by forming an aluminium hydroxide barrier at the sediment–water interface. Aeration, the continuous artificial supply of oxygen, can improve the quality of hypoxic waters. Repeated applications of lime can buffer acidity in lakes affected by acid rain. Herbicide treatments are sometimes needed to eradicate excessive growth of aquatic weeds triggered either by excess nutrient loads or because the weeds are non-native to the ecosystem and thus lack natural control mechanisms.

Estuaries

Estuaries are unique waterways where freshwater drained from the land mixes with salt water from the ocean. This blend of salt and freshwater makes estuaries biologically productive, sustaining certain fish, shellfish, marshes, underwater grasses and microscopic marine life.[54] Although estuaries are not freshwater ecosystems, and thus are not discussed extensively here, they are extremely dependent on the healthy functioning of the ecosystems that provide them with freshwater.

Because of their economic, aesthetic and recreational value, estuaries are increasingly attracting people and commerce to their shores. Aquatic life is affected by these growing populations, which use water for services and for commercial and industrial activity.[55] These ecosystems are also affected by activities that take place many kilometres upstream in their watersheds.

Often, the need for estuary restoration is recognized when a community notices declines in specific living resources, such as fish or shellfish, or other drastic changes in the ecology of the system: red tides and algae blooms, for example. Declines in living estuarine resources usually indicate a greater underlying disturbance. Poor water quality, lack of adequate freshwater flows, and changes in the timing of freshwater inflows are potential causes of estuarine degradation that must usually be addressed at the watershed scale. Other causes of declines, including the destruction of habitat; modification of spawning, nursery, or forage areas; and over-fishing may originate within the boundaries of the estuarine ecosystem itself. Finally, large-scale or global influences on marine systems, such as the expansion inland of a wedge of salt water caused by global sea-level rise, can also be the source of estuarine disturbances.

The design of restoration plans should be appropriate to the scale of the root causes of the ecological disturbance. In many cases, this will mean restoring the wetlands, streams and watershed functions that support the estuary.

Understanding the Limits

Restoration of freshwater systems to a previous state of equilibrium will be prevented in an absolute sense by such irreversible human-caused changes as species extinction and urban expansion. In addition, humans and human settlements are now an integral part of the environmental systems that are in need of restoration and rehabilitation. In most cases, watersheds and their freshwater ecosystems have been altered for decades or even centuries. Functional rehabilitation (restoring a system or creating a system similar but not equivalent to the natural one) may be the only realistic alternative if the presence of people is to be accommodated. System rehabilitation requires reduction of degradation, coupled with active restoration and enhancement to recreate displaced functions.[56] Restoration can also mean knowing when not to act. Nature is resilient and often adjusts to changes in the watershed. A critical part of a restorationist's role is to know when to allow nature to make adjustments on its own.[57]

In an age of increasing water stress, the major barrier to successful restoration projects will be the lack of the key ingredient – water. Because most uses of water are not consumptive and return flows to river channels and lakes, in many cases sufficient water remains in the target drainage basins to support restoration. Often, however, the perception of scarcity motivates current water users to dig in their heels and deny water for restorative purposes. In the long run, such attitudes help to ensure future water shortages by contributing to the decimation of aquatic ecosystems.

'Interest in the ecological values of the Colorado River delta [in Mexico], and opportunities for preserving and enhancing these values, have grown markedly in the past decade. This is partly attributable to the diversity and abundance of habitat types and species found in the delta, and partly because the delta has demonstrated a remarkable resilience. Both the riparian corridor and the emergent wetlands areas have regenerated in response to releases of fresh and brackish water, with no outside intervention of management. Simply adding water to the system apparently is sufficient to prompt such growth....

'Despite the small volumes of water required to preserve this remnant habitat – less than 1 percent of the river's mean annual flow – identifying and allocating such water to the delta is far from simple. Water users in the United States have strongly resisted efforts to date to dedicate Colorado River flows for delta preservation and enhancement.... This resistance reflects the tension between growing support for environmental protection and restoration, and the water development legal framework developed almost a century ago.'[58]

CONCLUSION

With the dawning of the understanding of the importance of aquatic ecosystems in maintaining the water cycle and providing goods and services to people, more attention is now being paid to the practicality of restoring degraded ecosystems than ever before. Restoring ecosystems generally involves inputs of time, money and energy that greatly exceed the costs associated with protecting them in the first place. In addition, the success of restoration projects is hampered by lack of understanding of the complex interactions between components of the environment. In addition, even if we had perfect knowledge of these interactions as they relate to the pre-disturbance ecosystem, some of the conditions that facilitated the existence of pristine ecosystems have changed virtually irrevocably. Human claims to water rights can stand in the way of re-establishing sufficient flows for restoration. Developments in reclaimed wetlands, on the shores of lakes and on river flood-plains can shrink the potential area of a restored ecosystem substantially, forcing managers to attempt to recreate sustainable ecological processes and populations of biota in a space that is only a fraction of the ecosystem's original extent.

Because of the difficulties, uncertainties and expense involved in ecosystem restoration, it is highly advisable to keep aquatic ecosystems from breaking down in the first place. The previous chapters have presented examples of the technologies that can protect aquatic ecosystems while maintaining a steady flow of goods and services to human communities. The following, final chapter will look at the broader, international policy frameworks that can help or hinder shifts to sustainable water management.

Notes

1 Crown Prince Willem-Alexander of Orange, 2000. 'The Value of Sustainable River Management.' In A. J.M. Smits, P.H. Nienhuis & R.S.E.W. Leuven (eds.), *New Approaches to River Management*. Backhuys Publishers, the Netherlands. pp. 3–6.

2 Johnson, N., C. Revenga & J. Echeverria, 2001. "Ecology: Managing Water for People and Nature.' *Science*, 292 (5519): 1071.

3 World Resources Institute, United Nations Development Programme, United Nations Environment Programme & the World Bank, 1998. *World Resources: 1998–1999. A Guide to the Global Environment*. Oxford University Press, Oxford.

4 Loh, J. (ed.), 2002. *Living Planet Report 2002*. World Wide Fund for Nature, Gland, Switzerland. p. 3. The trends discussed here and depicted in Figure 8.1 are based on species indices for the three biomes. The forest species index is the average of two indices – one each for temperate and tropical forests. The marine species index is the average of six indices, one for each major ocean. The freshwater species index is the average of six indices, one for each major terrestrial region. The species tracked in the freshwater index include 195 species of birds, mammals, reptiles, amphibians and fish from the world's lakes, rivers and wetlands. The indices for all biomes were set to one in 1970.

5 World Resources Institute, United Nations Development Programme, United Nations Environment Programme & the World Bank, 1998. *World Resources*.

6 Abell, R., M. Thiene, E. Dinerstein & D. Olson, 2002. *A Sourcebook for Conducting Biological Assessments and Developing Biodiversity Visions for Ecosystem Conservation, Volume II: Freshwater Ecosystems*.World Wildlife Fund, Washington. p. 45.

7 Ibid., p. 46.

8 Ibid.

9 Ibid., pp. 46–7.

10 Ibid., p. 47.

11 Within the US, functional assessment methods have ranged from the US Army Corps of Engineers' 1979 wetlands evaluation manual to the more recent formulations based on hydrogeomorphic classification and reference wetlands. For additional references, see National Research Council, 1995. *Wetlands: Characteristics and Boundaries*. Committee on Characterization of Wetlands, Water Science and Technology Board, Board on Environmental Studies and Toxicology, Commission on Geosciences, Environment, and Resources. National Academy Press, Washington. Chapter 10: Functional Assessment of Wetlands. The Ramsar Convention on Wetlands of International Importance also has an ever-evolving system for identifying wetlands deserving of the protective Ramsar designation. For more information, go to http://www.ramsar.org.

12 Larinier, M., 2000. 'Dams and Fish Migration.' Paper prepared for Thematic Review II.1: Dams, Ecosystem Functions and Environmental Restoration. World Commission on Dams, Cape Town. p. 8.

13 Allan, R.J., 1997. 'What is Aquatic Ecosystem Restoration?' *Water Quality Research Journal of Canada,* 32 (2): 229.

14 King, J., R. Thume & C. Brown, 1999. 'Definition and Implementation of Instream Flows.' Paper prepared for Thematic Review II.1: Dams, Ecosystem Functions and Environmental Restoration. World Commission on Dams, Cape Town. p. 10.

15 Richter, B.D., J.V. Baumgartner, R. Wigington & D.P. Brown, 1997. 'How Much Water Does a River Need?' *Freshwater Biology,* 37: 238–9.

16 King, J., R. Thume & C. Brown, 1999. 'Definition and Implementation.' p. 10.

17 Ibid.

18 Acreman, M., 2000. 'Managed Flood Releases from Reservoirs: Issues and Guidance.' Paper prepared for Thematic Review II.1: Dams, Ecosystem Functions and Environmental Restoration. World Commission on Dams, Cape Town. p. 65.

19 Gawler, M. 1997. *WWF Strategy to Conserve Freshwater Ecosystems in the Africa and Madagascar Region.* WWF International, Gland, Switzerland. 48 pp.

20 Richter, B.D., J.V. Baumgerner; J. Powell, & D.P. Brown, 1996. 'A Method for Assessing Hydrologic Alterations within Ecosystems.' *Conservation Biology,* 10 (4): 1166–7.

21 Ibid., p. 1164.

22 Moody, T., 1993. 'A Coronary Bypass.' *Boatman's Quarterly Review,* 7 (1). Grand Canyon River Guides, Inc, Flagstaff, Arizona.

23 Abell, R., M. Thiene, E. Dinerstein & D. Olson, 2002. *A Sourcebook.* p. 156.

24 Wetlands International – South Asia, undated. *Integrated Wetland and River Basin Management – A Case Study of Loktak Lake.* Wetlands International-South Asia, New Delhi. p. 1.

25 Ibid., p. 2.

26 Ibid., p. 8.

27 Ibid., p. 9.

28 Swanson, T., P. Koundouri & B.Groom, 2002. 'Balancing Demand and Supply: Water Resources in Cypress, The Kouris Watershed.' Case Study 6 in McNally, R. & S. Tognetti (eds.), *Tackling Poverty and Promoting Sustainable Development: Key Lessons for Integrated River Basin Management.* A WWF discussion paper. WWF-UK, Surrey, UK. p. 22

29 National Research Council, 1999. *Downstream: Adaptive Management of Glen Canyon Dam and the Colorado River Ecosystem.* Committee on Grand Canyon Monitoring and Research, Water Science and Technology Board, Commission on Geosciences, Environment and Resources. National Academy Press, Washington. p. 53.

30 Havinga, A. & A.J.M. Smits, 2000. 'River Management along the Rhine: A Retrospective View.' In Smits, A.J.M., P.H. Nienhuis & R.S.E.W. Leuven (eds.), *New Approaches to River Management.* Backhuys Publishers, Leiden, The Netherlands. pp. 29–30.

31 National Research Council, 1992. *Restoration of Aquatic Ecosystems: Science, Technology and Public Policy.* National Academy Press, Washington. p. 18.

32 Ibid., p. 189.

33 Williams, P.B., 2001. *River Engineering v. River Restoration.* Philip Williams and Associates, Cortre Madera, California. p. 13.

34 L.R. Johnston Associates, 1992. *Floodplain Management in the United States: An Assessment Report. Volume 2: Full Report.* Prepared for the Federal Interagency Floodplain Management Task Force. Washington.

35 Riley, A.L., 1998. *Restoring Streams in Cities: A Guide for Planners, Policymakers, and Citizens.* Island Press, Covelo, California, p. 115.

36 National Research Council, 2002. *Riparian Areas: Function and Strategies for Management.* Pre-publication copy. Committee on Riparian Zone Functioning and Strategies for Management, Water Science and Technology Board and Board on Environmental Studies and Toxicology, Divison on Earth and Life Sciences. National Academy Press, Washington. p. 319.

37 Ibid.

38 L.R. Johnston Associates, 1992. *Floodplain Management.*

39 National Research Council, 2002. *Riparian Areas.* pp. 325–6.

40 Hunt, C.E., 1988. *Down by the River: The Impact of Federal Water Projects and Policies on Biological Diversity.* Island Press, Covelo, California. p. 234.

41 National Research Council. 1997. *Watershed Research in the U.S. Geological Survey.* National Academy Press, Washington. 86 pp.
42 Environmental News Service, 23 July 2002. Washington.
43 Barcott, B., 1999. 'Blow-up.' *Outside,* February 1999.
44 Gleick, P.H., 2000. *The World's Water 2000–2001: The Biennial Report on Freshwater Resources.* Island Press, Covelo, California. p. 125.
45 Ibid., p. 127.
46 National Research Council, 1992. *Restoration of Aquatic Ecosystems.*
47 Federal Interagency Stream Restoration Working Group, 1998. *Stream Corridor Restoration: Principles. Processes and Practices.* Washington.
48 National Research Council, 1995. *Wetlands: Characteristics and Boundaries.* National Academy Press, Washington. pp. 21–2.
49 National Research Council, 1992. *Restoration of Aquatic Ecosystems.*
50 Ibid.
51 Institutut de Cercetare si Proiectare Delta Dunarii & WWF Auen Institut, 1997. *Ecological Restoration in the Danube Delta Biosphere Reserve/Romania. Balnina and Cernovca Islands.* Danube Delta Biosphere Reserve Authority, Danube Delta Research and Design Institute, WWF-Germany Institute for Floodplains Ecology & WWF International Green Danube Programme. 120 pp.
52 National Research Council, 1992. *Restoration of Aquatic Ecosystems.*
53 Ibid.
54 US Environmental Protection Agency 1989. *Saving Bays and Estuaries: A Primer for Establishing and Managing Estuary Projects.* EPA/503/8-89-001, Washington, DC. 58 pp.
55 Ibid.
56 Naiman, R.J., J.J. Magnuson, D.M. McKnight & J.A. Standford (eds.), 1995. *The Freshwater Imperative: A Research Agenda.* Island Press, Covelo, California. pp. 53–4.
57 Riley, A.L., 1998. *Restoring Streams in Cities.* p. 31.
58 Cohen, M., 2002. 'Managing Across Boundaries: The Case of the Colorado River Delta.' In Gleick, P.H., W.C.G. Burns, E.L. Chalecki, M. Cohen, K.K. Cushing. A.S. Mann, R. Reyes, G.H. Wolff & A.K. Wong, *The World's Water 2002–2003: The Biennial Report on Freshwater Resources.* Island Press, Covelo, California. pp. 143–4.

9 Avenues of Governance
Institutional Options
for Protecting the Water Cycle

'"There is a tremendous gap between understanding and action," says [political water consultant Joyce] Starr. "It's not only the men and women who lead nations but the interests behind them. Even if officials understand that the people in their country will die [from water scarcity or water-borne diseases], they may be powerless to change the realities of the powerful forces in their countries. It takes a lot of energy and it's brutal. I think you have to throw yourselves up against the system. We have to be Don Quixote. We have to, because the alternative is...." She shrugs. The alternative is unthinkable.'[1]

As the previous six chapters have illustrated, the global community already has the tools it needs to provide for virtually universal access to critical water supplies and services without breaking down the water cycle. This realization begs the question of why we aren't collectively moving forward into a new era of truly sustainable water development and use. Just as the factors driving the water cycle reside in multiple, interacting and imbedded levels, the reasons for the tremendous resistance to the adoption of environmentally gentle technologies lie at many levels and in many of society's institutions.

The following pages contain an assessment of some of the institutions that have been established at the global level to provide governance over various aspects of international water management. The reader can use this material to assess the relative effectiveness of binding agreements, non-binding dialogues, and financial and trade institutions in implementing their water-related agendas. I believe that most readers will conclude that the financial and trade institutions are emerging as the most effective of the global governance bodies examined. These institutions, however, tend to promote economic activity, often in ways that are inimical to sustainable resource use. If the world is to realize sustainable water management, therefore, we must work together to create and strengthen institutions that work to protect our planet's water cycle and the ecosystems that support it.

BINDING AGREEMENTS: TREATIES

Binding international agreements, known as treaties or conventions, have provided the most common method for international environmental governance since the early 1970s. Such agreements generally come into effect through a series of steps. The first is adoption, the formal act that establishes the form and content of a proposed treaty. The expression of consent of the states participating in the creation of a treaty leads to adoption of the text of a treaty. However, the adoption of a treaty by a state doesn't mean that the state has agreed to be bound by it. States may support the general concept of a treaty, yet hold back on final approval to see whether critical allied or opponent states adopt the treaty as well.

The second step in treaty enactment is signature by the head of state. In some cases, such as most bilateral treaties, signature is sufficient to bind the state to adherence to the rules of the treaty. In the case of multilateral treaties, however, some sort of ratification process must follow the signature if the state is to be bound by the treaty and if the treaty is to enter into force. Although a signature doesn't indicate the willingness of a state to be bound to a treaty in such cases, it does authenticate and express the desire of the state to continue the process of creating the treaty: to proceed to ratification, acceptance or approval. Signature of a treaty also generates a goodwill obligation to refrain from actions that would defeat the objective or purpose of the treaty.

The third step in enacting a treaty, applicable in states where the signature of the head of state is necessary but not sufficient, is ratification. The provision in international law for a ratification process serves to allow signatory states to seek any domestic approval required and to pass any legislation deemed necessary to implement the treaty. In many democratic societies, ratification is achieved through an act of parliament or congress. In states where constitutional law doesn't require ratification of a treaty, acceptance and approval constitute acceptable vehicles for states to express willingness to be bound by a treaty. International organizations can express their consent to be bound through an act of formal confirmation.

Multilateral treaties often specify the number of parties that must express their consent to be governed by the principles of the treaty before the treaty enters into force. Some treaties require the satisfaction of additional conditions, such as a certain category of states (developed/developing; Latin American/African/Asian/European; democratic/communist or socialist). Treaties may also allow an additional time period to elapse after the required number of states have expressed their consent and have met any additional conditions. Treaties enter into force for those states that gave their required consent. Treaties also sometimes provide that they shall come into force provisionally if certain conditions have been met.

States may become parties to a treaty that has been signed by other states through the process of accession, which is legally equivalent to ratification but generally occurs after the treaty has entered into force. As with ratification, treaties may allow and encourage the accession of all states or specify conditions for a limited and defined number of states to accede.

Once in force, many treaties are administered by a secretariat conscripted by the contracting parties. At fixed intervals (usually a specified number of years), the secretariat may organize, in concert with the participants, a conference of contracting parties. Generally, the conference provides an opportunity for the parties to report on their progress in implementing the convention, attend to administrative matters such as strategic planning and budgeting, and direct the future course of the convention through the adoption of amendments, recommendations, resolutions and guidelines.

Treaties can be effective mechanisms for raising the profile of important environmental and natural resource-related issues. Especially in an age of international media, treaties and conventions of contracting parties provide citizens with opportunities to compare and contrast the performance of their governments with those of other countries. In addition, networks of non-governmental organizations (NGOs) may use these high-profile events to call attention to non-compliance on the part of individual countries that are party to a treaty. Treaties and other international agreements also provide avenues for nations to press each other on issues of international concern by employing incentives (such as aid or debt forgiveness) or disincentives (sanctions, public rebuke) for action.

The effectiveness of treaties in achieving international environmental goals is undermined by a series of factors. To attract the maximum number of contracting parties, for example, negotiations may tug treaty language towards the lowest common denominator – or express the duties of parties in the most permissive of rhetoric. Compliance monitoring is often lacking and enforcement virtually non-existent.

Treaty effectiveness is determined as much by the attitudes of contracting parties as by the language of the treaty and the number of contracting parties it attracts. Countries and international governmental organizations may join a treaty because they sincerely believe that the treaty is in their own best interest. For example, many speculate that the signatures of Japan and the European Union on the Kyoto climate change protocol signal their desire to finesse the global market in a new and potentially very profitable generation of alternative energy sources. On the other hand, countries may sign on to treaties because the international community pressures them to do so. In such cases, the countries may have no intention of changing current practices to comply with the treaty. The United States, for example, is a party to the Ramsar Convention on Wetlands of International Importance (discussed in more detail below), but has limited its designation of wetlands protected by the convention to those that are already legally protected by domestic law. The US also has wetland laws that are more stringent than the Ramsar Convention requirements, and so believes that additional policy reforms are not necessary to comply with the convention. On the other hand, the US provides roughly one-quarter of the total funding for implementation of the convention both at home and abroad – an obligation that it would not need to shoulder if it chose not to become a party. This situation stands in stark contrast to developing countries, which may join treaties to avoid international sanctions or enjoin aid even when they do not have the resources or the will to enforce compliance within their borders.

Measuring the effectiveness of a treaty is often difficult. The obligations of contracting parties may be so broad that any quantitative analysis of their implementation is virtually impossible. The provisions may not be mandatory and may be softened by language such as 'may' instead of 'shall' or requiring states to 'take into account' factors such as environmental quality rather than compelling them to document their environmental analyses and justify their decisions. And when an international environmental issue becomes so pressing that countries are willing to cede some of their sovereignty to an instrument of international law, it is probable that other unilateral, bilateral and/or multilateral solutions have already been launched to solve the problem. In such cases, it may be difficult to ascertain whether any improvement realized post-treaty was the result of the treaty or of other, independent measures.

'International treaties are generally weaker than national laws because no country can be bound to the former without its consent. Conservation treaties must involve many countries and so have to reflect the compromises necessary to accommodate widely disparate political systems and priorities. They therefore tend to be the weakest. Moreover, there is no effective legal method of enforcing international treaties. Recourse to international arbitration or to the International Court of Justice in the Hague can only be had by agreement with the Party accused of a transgression – and any ruling is difficult to enforce. The imposition of economic sanctions is not a realistic option.'[2]

Even when treaties are effective in achieving their stated objectives, they may not be effective in addressing the problems that elicited them. For example, compliance with a treaty may result in the cessation of an activity that contributes to pollution, but it may also lead to a net increase of pollution by encouraging other activities or substitutes with even worse consequences. A treaty prohibiting international trade in a rare plant or animal could successfully halt the export of the species from a country, while stimulating domestic markets for the same species.[3]

In the following sections the effectiveness of treaties in maintaining the integrity of the hydrological cycle is examined using two case studies: the Ramsar Convention on Wetlands of International Importance Especially as Waterfowl Habitat and the Convention on the Law of the Non-navigational Uses of International Watercourses.

The Ramsar Convention

The Ramsar Convention is named for the Iranian town where the first 18 nations signed on in February 1971, launching the world's first international, environmental conservation treaty. The Ramsar Convention's objectives were initially rather narrowly conceived and the provisions for its implementation narrow, but the broad language employed in the treaty and subsequent development of 'soft'[4] law have allowed the Convention to grow in scope and effectiveness over time.

Genesis and Key Provisions

Two NGOs interested in the conservation of migratory waterfowl – the International Council for Bird Preservation and the International Waterfowl Research Bureau – initially conceived and advocated the Ramsar Convention. Besides the heavy involvement of waterfowl interests in its design, Ramsar was heavily oriented towards the conservation of waterfowl because organizations of avid birdwatchers had been collecting information on waterfowl for decades.[5] In contrast, data on fish, reptiles, amphibians, invertebrates, and aquatic and semi-aquatic plants were lacking for most of the world's most spectacular wetlands. The perception that Ramsar was oriented almost exclusively towards the protection of waterfowl may have diminished the initial support of both conservationists and developing countries at the outset.[6]

Much of the convention's language, however, was so sweeping that it could be interpreted to encompass an enormous range of ecosystems and human actions. For example, the convention defines the term 'wetland' as 'areas of marsh, fen, peatland, or water, whether natural or artificial, static or flowing, fresh, brackish or salt, including areas of marine water the depth of which at low tide does not exceed six metres.' Article 2(1) broadens the definition of wetland even further by providing, in part, that 'the boundaries of each wetland ... may incorporate the riparian and coastal zones adjacent to the wetlands, and islands and bodies of marine waters deeper than six metres at low tide lying within the wetlands, especially where these have importance as waterfowl habitat.' The contrasting focus provided by the convention's initial emphasis on waterfowl may have eased the international community's acceptance of a convention embracing such a diverse variety of habitats.[7]

'The Director General of IUCN [the International Union for the Conservation of Nature], delivering the keynote address at the Fourth Meeting of the Conference of Contracting Parties in Montreux, Switzerland, joked that this very broad definition "suggests to me that only two conventions are really needed to cover the conservation of all the habitats in the world – the Ramsar Convention dealing with any land that can generally be termed 'wet', and a Drylands Convention dealing with everything else, with some useful agreement between the Bureaux and Standing Committees on how to handle the interface."'[8]

The obligations of the treaty, with the exception of naming wetland sites on a list of wetlands of international importance, are also quite broad and poorly defined. The treaty obligates contracting parties to designate at least one wetland site as internationally important and promote its conservation, including, where appropriate, its wise use. The convention doesn't define the terms 'conservation' or 'wise use.' The convention intends each contracting party to define the concept of conservation as appropriate in its own context and according to its own needs. Such definitions are to be illuminated in National Wetland Plans. The parties adopted a definition of wise use at their third convention, held in Regina, Canada, in 1987. Recommendation 3.3 states that 'the wise use of wetlands is their sustainable utilization for the benefit of mankind in a way compatible with the maintenance of the natural properties of the ecosystem.' Sustainable utilization is further defined as 'human use of a wetland so that it may yield the greatest continuous benefit to present generations while maintaining its potential to meet the needs and aspirations of future generations.' The criteria for selecting sites to be added to the Ramsar List are discussed below.

The Ramsar Convention also obligates parties to promote, as far as possible, the wise use of wetlands in their territory. Ramsar guidelines direct participating countries to implement wise use by adopting national wetland policies and developing appropriate programmes, including wetland inventories, monitoring, research, training, education and public awareness.

A third obligation imposed on parties by the Convention is the establishment of wetland reserves and training programmes. The fourth and broadest obligation is set forth by Article 5 of the Convention and involves international cooperation. Parties agree to consult with each other about the implementation of the Convention, especially in regard to transfrontier wetlands, shared water systems and shared species.

Expansion

Over the years, the parties have expanded the interpretation of these obligations substantially, so that today the Convention could play a vital role in the conservation of the Earth's water cycle and the ecosystems that support it. Changes in the criteria for placing a wetland on the Ramsar List strongly reflect this trend. The Convention itself states that 'wetlands should be selected for the List on account of their international significance in terms of ecology, botany, zoology, limnology or hydrology. In the first instance, wetlands of international importance to waterfowl at any season should be included.' By 1999, when the seventh conference of parties was convened in San Jose, Costa Rica, subsequent meetings of the contracting parties had adopted resolutions that greatly expanded and defined these criteria. Today, a wetland is considered internationally important if it:

- Contains a representative, rare or unique example of a natural or near-natural wetland type found within the appropriate biogeographical region;

- Supports vulnerable, endangered or critically endangered species or threatened ecological communities;

- Supports populations of plants and/or animal species important for maintaining the biological diversity of a particular biogeographic region;

- Supports plant and/or animal species at a critical stage in their life cycles or provides refuge during adverse conditions;

- Regularly supports 20,000 or more waterbirds;

- Regularly supports 1 percent of the individuals in a population of one species or subspecies of waterfowl;

- Supports a significant proportion of indigenous fish subspecies, species or families, life-history stages, species interactions and/or populations that are representative of wetland benefits and/or values and thereby contributes to global biodiversity; or

- Is an important source of food for fish, or a spawning ground, nursery, and/or migration path on which fish stocks, within the wetland or elsewhere, depend.

During their 1999 conference, the parties adopted guidelines for international cooperation to implement Article 5. These guidelines expand the obligations of the parties for coordinating the management of international (shared) wetlands beyond the narrower definition of these as wetlands that cross international boundaries. Article 5 is now interpreted to include those situations where a wetland in one contracting party is within the drainage basin of another contracting party, and where the actions of the parties within the drainage basin may result in changes to the ecological character of the wetland.

The 1999 conference also adopted Resolution 7.18, which contains guidelines for integrating wetland conservation into river basin management, launching the River Basin Initiative on Integrating Biological Diversity, Wetland and River Basin Management, in cooperation with the Convention on Biological Diversity. The resolution defines the River Basin Initiative as an incentive-based, participatory mechanism for solving conflicts and allocating water between competing uses, including ecosystems. The resolution states that the focus of land and water planning and management processes at the river basin scale is critical for the successful allocation of water to such uses. The resolution also finds that there is a need to consider the ecological requirements of marine and coastal systems that are influenced by discharges from the drainage basin.

'A water source that is reliable, in terms both of its quantity and quality, is a prerequisite for the survival of human civilization and socio-economic development.'[9]

Guidance for the River Basin Initiative encourages issuance of permits for water abstraction and use, rules and regulations regarding use and abstraction of groundwater, integration of water and wetland conservation within national socio-economic development agendas, and the maintenance of natural flow regimes.

Effectiveness

Because much of the Ramsar programme is so qualitative and broad, it is difficult to identify variables that might be of use in measuring its effectiveness. Generally, one can credit the Convention with changing the world opinion that wetlands are wastelands that must be filled in or drained to be useful to a view that wetlands are important and productive organs of our planet's biosphere.

A standard measure of the effectiveness of an international convention is the number of parties that have ratified or otherwise joined it. As the weight of the

Ramsar Convention has evolved, the number of parties has grown – but remains relatively unimpressive compared to other conservation treaties (see Table 9.1). As of September 2002, 133 countries were parties to Ramsar. The list of Ramsar-designated sites included 1,198 wetlands covering a total area of over 103 million hectares.

Table 9.1 Dates of Adoption of and Current Numbers of Contracting Parties to Major Environmental Treaties

Convention	Year of adoption	Most recent year of reporting	Number of contracting parties
UN Framework Convention on Climate Change	1992	2001	186
Convention on Biological Diversity	1992	2002	185
Convention to Combat Desertification	1994	2002	184
Vienna Convention for the Protection of the Ozone Layer	1985	2002	184
Convention on International Trade in Endangered Species of Wild Fauna and Flora	1973	2002	160
Ramsar Convention on Wetlands of International Importance	1971	2002	133
Stockholm Convention on Persistent Organic Pollutants	2001	2002	21

Data from the websites of the various conventions.

The Ramsar Bureau relies on the parties themselves to provide detailed information about the condition of their wetlands and the measures they have taken for the conservation of their listed sites in triennial, national reports. Despite exhortations at Ramsar conferences, the rate of timely submission of such reports has fallen over the years.[10]

One way to assess the Convention's effectiveness is to consider the status of listed sites. The Montreux protocol, adopted by the parties at their 1990 conference in Montreux, Canada, created a 'Montreux List' of Ramsar sites that were in danger of ecological degradation. The process of adding sites to the Montreux List is triggered whenever it comes to the attention of the Ramsar Bureau that the ecological character of a Ramsar site may have changed, may be changing, or may be likely to change. The contracting party whose territory contains the subject wetland must concur with the placement of the site on the Montreux List. The

Bureau generally relies on the parties themselves to report conditions that might qualify one or more of their Ramsar sites for the Montreux List, with the national reports supplied to the Bureau before a conference as the usual vehicle. While many contracting parties report degradation at Ramsar sites in order to qualify for technical and financial assistance from the Bureau for addressing the problem, developed countries that don't qualify for such assistance have also agreed to have their sites Montreux-listed. The number of Montreux-listed sites has generally crept upwards over the past decade, though it is still quite small compared to the total number of listed sites (see Figure 9.1). The Montreux record in all likelihood underestimates the number of Ramsar sites undergoing ecological change, however. According to the Ramsar Bureau's own estimates, about 10 percent of Ramsar sites are undergoing change. The environmental group Friends of the Earth estimates that fully 38 percent of listed sites are undergoing change.[11]

Article 6 (2) (d) of the Convention grants the conference of contracting parties the power to make specific recommendations to specific countries that are party to the Convention for the conservation of their wetlands. Beginning rather timidly at the Groningen conference (1984, the Netherlands), the advice to specific members from the conference has grown progressively bolder at each subsequent meeting. At Regina (1987, Canada), for example, the conference urged the government of Jordan to conduct a proper assessment of the environmental impact of the use of water from Azraq to supply the city of Amman with drinking water and to establish a long-term water resources plan for the site. The conference further suggested that pumping be reduced by at least half until the study had been completed. Another recommendation urged the parties generally not merely to take swift and effective action to restore the value of specific, degraded wetland sites, but also to report the action taken to the Ramsar Bureau. The Montreux and Kushiro (1993, Japan) meetings produced lengthy lists of recommendations regarding particular sites, with some calling for very specific remedial measures.[12] No record is available showing the degree of implementation of the recommended measures.

A second, measurable component of the Ramsar programme is the Small Grant Fund for Wetland Conservation and Wise Use. The conference at Montreux established this programme, then known as the Wetland Conservation Fund, to assist developing countries in meeting their obligations under the Convention. During the 1996 conference in Brisbane, Australia, countries with economies in transition became eligible for assistance under the fund. The Ramsar Bureau considers the fund a 'gap filler,' providing grants of up to 40,000 Swiss francs per project, a significantly smaller amount than the grants that can be accessed through the Global Environment Facility, for example.[13] Countries submit proposals to the Ramsar Bureau, which reviews them and passes its recommendations regarding their suitability for funding to the Standing Committee,[14] which makes the final decision. Recipient countries are required to submit final reports on their projects to the Bureau.

The Small Grant Fund has helped countries to prepare to join the Convention, conduct wetland inventories, compile lists of wetland species, develop site and national management plans, study and improve listed sites, train and equip staff, and conduct environmental impact assessments. Little information is available on

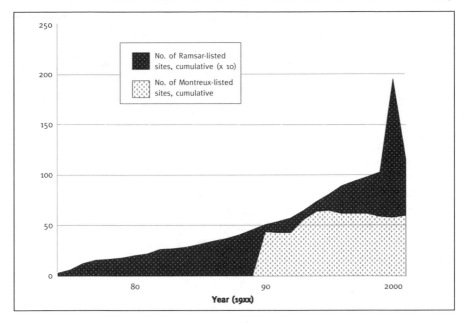

Figure 9.1 Trends in Numbers of Ramsar-listed Sites Compared with Montreux-listed Sites

Data from the Ramsar website, http://www.ramsar.org.

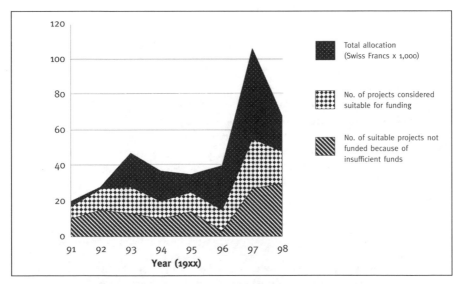

Figure 9.2 Suitable Projects Not Supported by the Small Grant Fund Due to Inadequate Funding

From: Ramsar Bureau, 1998. *Critical Evaluation of the Ramsar Small Grant Fund for Wetlands Conservation and Wise Use.* Gland, Switzerland. http://www.ramsar.org.

the effectiveness of the programme, however. The countries often submit final reports late and sometimes not at all. The Bureau rarely visits project sites to assess progress or success.[15]

A report produced by the Bureau, but lacking substantial evidence, found the Small Grant Fund to be 'highly cost-effective at the project scale,' stated that 'the results obtained are generally worthy of much larger budgets,' and concluded that 'the SGF constitutes a highly successful mechanism.' The report asserts that the Fund's major challenge is insufficient and inconsistent funding. The Bureau supported this finding with data comparing the number of projects deemed suitable for funding with the number of projects funded, stressing the inability to fund many worthy projects (see Figure 9.2).[16]

Overall, the Ramsar Convention has enhanced international understanding of the importance of conserving aquatic and semi-aquatic ecosystems and has provided incentives, in funding and technical assistance, to its parties to protect and restore these ecosystems while using them in a sustainable manner. The Convention could be strengthened by increased attention to its effectiveness. A review of the condition of wetlands on the Ramsar List, actions taken to restore wetlands on the Montreux List, and the projects undertaken with assistance from the Small Grants Fund, might reveal provisions of the Convention and its resolutions, recommendations and guidelines that could be strengthened to increase effectiveness.

The United Nations Convention on the Law of the Non-navigational Uses of International Watercourses

The perception of emerging water crises, and the possibility of regional conflicts over water, was the driving force behind the establishment of the UN Watercourse Convention. The Convention focuses on establishing collaborative relationships between countries sharing international rivers and lakes so that such water bodies can become catalysts for cooperation rather than catalysts for war.

'With the fall of the Berlin Wall in 1989 and the collapse of the Soviet Union, the traditional focus of the security agenda broadened: human security is understood as an absence of threat to human life, lifestyle or culture and ["threat" has come] to include other factors such as environmental and social threats, rather than just military. Subsequently, water resources conflicts have gained increasing attention and some international institutions have predicted "Water Wars."'[17]

In contrast to the Ramsar Convention, the UN Watercourse Convention is a very young treaty, adopted in 1997. With only 12 of the 35 parties necessary ratifying the treaty, it has not yet entered into force. There appears to be an interesting but disturbing pattern in the countries that have voted for/opposed adoption by the United Nations and those that have/have not signed and ratified the Convention.

During the General Assembly session in which the treaty was brought before delegates, for example, 103 countries voted in favour of the treaty and three opposed it. Among the three states expressing opposition were Turkey and China. Both of these states are upstream in major river basins (the Tigris–Euphrates and Mekong, respectively), and are developing plans that may threaten uses by downstream countries.[18] In addition, the territories of current parties and signatories to the treaty don't encompass any single, major river basin. For example, in the case of the Paraguay/Parana Basin, only Paraguay is a signatory. In the case of the Danube Basin, only Hungary has become a party to the convention. In the Jordan Basin, Jordan, Syria and Lebanon are parties but Israel is not. Further, Article 3 of the Convention specifies that 'nothing in the present Convention shall affect the rights or obligations of a watercourse state arising from agreements in force for it on the date on which it became a party to the present Convention.'

The Convention's definition of watercourse is key to the scope of its eventual implementation. The Convention defines a watercourse as 'a system of surface waters and groundwaters constituting by virtue of their physical relationship a unitary whole and normally flowing into a common terminus.' An international watercourse is defined as a watercourse, parts of which are situated in different states. The inclusion of groundwater was a bold step reflecting the realities of the hydrological cycle, but elicited the opposition of some countries who feared that such a broad definition might infringe on their internal sovereignty. The term 'common terminus' intends to prevent river basins that are connected by way of an artificial canal being understood as a single watercourse, thereby extending the reach of the treaty. The definition of 'watercourse state' includes only parties to the Convention, which substantially limits the Convention's effectiveness in shared watercourses where few countries have become parties. Regional economic organizations may also become party to the Convention if at least one of their member states contains part of an international watercourse.

The substantial provisions of the treaty include the entitlement of any watercourse state to participate in and become party to any watercourse agreement that applies to the entire international watercourse. In addition, watercourse states are entitled to participate in consultations involving only a portion of the watercourse if it might affect their use of the watercourse.

Another substantial provision, contained in Article 7, is the obligation of a watercourse state not to cause significant harm to other watercourse states. If significant harm does result from the actions of a watercourse state, that state is obligated to eliminate or mitigate the harm and, where appropriate, to discuss the question of compensation. This sort of provision is made more explicit in Articles 21, 22 and 23, which require watercourse states to avoid polluting and refrain from introducing alien species into shared watercourses, and to take measures necessary to protect marine and estuarine ecosystems.

Article 9 contains a striking provision of the Watercourse Convention: the requirement for watercourse states readily to exchange available data and information on the condition of the watercourse. Many states at present jealously guard their hydrological data as security-sensitive information, because vulnerability to drought or flood, as well as treaty abrogation, could very well be used against them. Article 31 weakens this provision, however, by stating that '[n]othing in the present Convention obliges a watercourse state to provide data or information vital to its national defence or security.' The phrase 'vital to its national security' is not defined.

Article 12 requires a watercourse state to provide timely notification to other watercourse states that may be affected by a planned action before the state implements the action. Article 13 requires the state contemplating the action to allow the notified states a period of six months to study and evaluate the possible effects of the planned measure, a period that the state must extend for a further six months if requested to do so by a notified state. The state contemplating the action is further required by Article 14 to provide any additional data requested by the notified states that is available and necessary for an accurate evaluation. Article 14 also prohibits the state contemplating the action from implementing the action without the consent of the notified states. Article 17 seems contradictory to this requirement, however, in that it only requires the state contemplating the action to refrain from implementing the action for six months after a notified state has objected to it, unless otherwise agreed. Article 19 provides another safety valve by allowing states to proceed to implementation without notifying other watercourse states in the case of 'utmost urgency in order to protect public health, public safety, or other equally important interests.'

Some of the other obligations listed in the convention are quite fuzzy and open to interpretation. For example, the convention requires watercourse states to use an international watercourse in an equitable and reasonable manner. Rather than defining the terms 'equitable' and 'reasonable,' however, the convention merely requires such states to 'take into account' a series of factors including natural factors, social and economic needs and the availability of alternatives to planned or existing uses. Article 8 establishes a general obligation for watercourse states to cooperate. In determining the manner of such cooperation, watercourse states 'may consider' the establishment of a joint mechanism to facilitate cooperation.

The Watercourse Convention may never enter into force and, if it does, the ambiguity in its language and the loopholes provided for some of its obligations will hamper its effectiveness. But, as with the Ramsar Convention, the process of producing and adopting the treaty may be beneficial its in own right, particularly in defining a set of internationally shared values such as equitable use and information sharing.

'The sponsors of the resolution containing the Convention declared that they were "convinced" that it "will contribute to the equitable and reasonable use of transboundary water resources and their ecosystems, as well as to their preservation, to the benefit of current and future generations," and that it "will contribute to enhancing cooperation and communication among riparian states of international watercourses."'[19]

'[T]he Convention will have value even if it does not enter into force because it was negotiated in a forum that permitted virtually any interested state to

participate…. It was adopted by a weighty majority of countries, with only three negative votes, indicating broad agreement in the international community on the general principles governing the non-navigation uses of international water courses.'[20]

NON-BINDING AGREEMENTS

The global community is increasingly investing in non-binding dialogues to produce recommendations addressing some of the world's most complex and divisive issues. There are two substantial advantages to this approach. First, the negotiation processes that produce non-binding agreements can be more inclusive than those that produce treaties. Interested individuals, NGOs, corporations and communities are often provided with the opportunity to participate, in addition to governments and international organizations. Second, the agreements that result from these negotiations may be more specific and less ambiguous than those applying to treaties.

The obvious disadvantage of non-binding agreements is that they are, well, non-binding. Neither governments nor any other entities are legally obligated to comply with the provisions established through the negotiations, and there are generally neither incentives nor sanctions created to elicit compliance. The following pages examine two very different processes, the World Commission on Dams and the World Water Vision, for indications of their effectiveness.

The World Commission on Dams

The process that culminated in the creation of the World Commission on Dams (WCD) began in 1994 when a coalition of 326 social movements and NGOs around the world endorsed a statement calling for a moratorium on World Bank funding of large dams. One of the conditions for lifting the proposed moratorium was that the World Bank would set up an independent and comprehensive review of Bank-funded, large dam projects to establish the actual costs, including the direct and indirect, economic, environmental and social costs and the actual realized benefits of the projects.[21] Six months later, the World Bank's Operations Evaluation Department (OED) announced that it was undertaking a review of World Bank-funded large dams in order to determine their development effectiveness and to answer the questions why dams cause so much concern and what the Bank should do about it.[22] The OED planned to execute a two-phase desk study, with phase one constituting a desk review of experiences with selected dams and phase two expanding the study to field evaluations.

The Bank completed the first phase in 1996, after reviewing 50 Bank-financed dams. The Bank concluded that resettlement was inadequate in half the dams funded, but that performance improved over time. The Bank rated environmental performance as 'mixed.' The Bank's study further noted that, while under prior social and environmental policies only 10 percent of the sample was unacceptable, had all projects been assessed under new policies, 26 percent would have been considered unacceptable and 48 percent would have been considered 'potentially acceptable.' The Bank's report concluded that, because the large majority of dams are yielding benefits that outweigh their costs, the World Bank should continue to fund large dams with heightened attention to environmental and social policies. The Bank considered the report a relatively minor, internal document unsuitable for public dissemination. The Bank's Board of Executive Directors agreed with the report's general conclusions, but urged the OED to ensure that the second phase reflected the views of civil society, including those of private investors and NGOs.

The International Rivers Network, an anti-dam, non-profit organization based in California, obtained a copy of the report and penned a stinging critique, which it circulated to its extensive network of NGOs around the world. Based on the IRN critique, 49 NGOs from 21 countries signed a letter to World Bank President James D. Wolfensohn demanding that the Bank reject the report's conclusions and that the review called for in 1994 be conducted by a commission of eminent people independent from the Bank. In March 1997, the First International Meeting of Peoples Affected by Large Dams, held in Curitiba, Brazil, also called for an independent review.[23]

Meanwhile, in 1994, the Bank had signed a partnership agreement with the IUCN[24] which had yet to be implemented. The Bank decided that the dams debate would be a suitable issue for the two organizations to take on together, and invited the IUCN to co-organize a workshop to discuss the findings of the report and the process and objectives for a more comprehensive second phase.

The two organizations convened the workshop at the IUCN's headquarters in Gland, Switzerland in April 1997. Thirty-nine participants attended, ranging from dam construction companies to anti-dam organizations. The workshop concluded that the second phase of the Bank's study must include all dams, not just those funded by the Bank, and agreed that the study must be conducted by an independent panel of eminent persons. Thus the Gland workshop launched the World Commission on Dams. The Commission's objectives were to review the development effectiveness of large dams and assess alternatives for water resources and energy development and to develop internationally acceptable criteria, guidelines and standards, where appropriate, for the planning, design, appraisal, construction, operation, monitoring and decommissioning of dams.[25]

Structure and Process

The World Commission on Dams had a simple structure. The Commission itself initially consisted of 13 members, including the Chair, Kader Asmal from South Africa's Ministry of Water Affairs and Forestry, and Achim Steiner, the Commission's Secretary-General.[26] The Commission was supported by a full-time secretariat stationed in Cape Town, South Africa, and also assembled a forum of stakeholders to provide continuing feedback on its work.

The Commission's work programme included four regional consultations, a series of detailed case studies on eight specific dam and river basin projects, two country studies,[27] and a series of 17 thematic reviews on topics ranging from social impacts to economic, financial and distributional analysis.

The regional consultations were structured to draw comment from people and organizations in South Asia, Latin America, Africa and the Middle East, and East and South-east Asia. A total of 1,400 people from 59 countries attended. In addition, the Commission organized 20 consultations at country and river basin level to discuss the case studies.

The Report

The final report issued by the Commission in November 2000 contained a broad review of the technical, financial and economic performance of large dams and concluded that a considerable number fell short of their physical and economic targets, but also that dams provide considerable services.[28] The report's evaluation of the environmental and social impacts of dams was more critical. The Commission concluded, for example, that the 'ecosystem impacts [of dams] are more negative than positive and they have led, in many cases, to irreversible loss of species and ecosystems.'[29] The Commission also found that 'the construction and operation of large dams has had serious and lasting effects on the lives, livelihoods and health of affected communities, and led to the loss of cultural resources and heritage.'[30]

Significantly, the Commission's report contained a chapter on alternatives to dams for achieving energy availability, food production and other objectives of water management. Passive and demand-side options, including energy conservation and non-structural floodplain management, were among the alternatives presented, as were water recycling and wind or solar energy.

The Commission's report went on to critique the conventional decision-making process that leads to dam construction. Their review found that, despite substantial procedural improvements since the 1990s, 'the influence of vested interests, legal and regulatory gaps, disincentives for compliance and lack of monitoring, participation and transparency amongst other things have combined to create significant barriers to reforms.' The Commission asserted that the world has a responsibility to increase efficiency, assess options more clearly, improve the lives of project-affected people, conduct more inclusive decision-making processes, resolve past inequities, monitor effects, and create recourse mechanisms in the dam construction, management and decommissioning process.[31]

The remainder of the report (chapters 7–9) contained specific recommendations for improving the dam construction, management and decommissioning process. The recommended basis for future decision making was 'rights and risks' assessment. The Commission indicated that recognition of rights and assessment of risk should be used to identify the interested and affected parties who have most at stake in decisions regarding large dams and who should, therefore, be encouraged to participate in the decision-making process. The report then laid out a series of strategic priorities for future decision making. These included, among others, comprehensive options assessments, sustaining rivers and livelihoods, and sharing rivers for peace, development and security. The report ended with a more detailed series of proposed criteria and guidelines designed to apply the strategic priorities.

Reaction and Follow-up

'The high stakes for diverse groups in the dams debate and the high expectations for the WCD report created a tense atmosphere for its launch and dissemination, and pressure for major industry and NGO players to respond. The tone of the initial responses ranged from glowing to scathing, with the majority being cautiously receptive. But one generalization is possible about the report's reception. Institutions and individuals around the world were reading it closely and felt compelled to respond publicly. In the words of one Forum member, "People are poring over it."'[32]

Perhaps predictably, extreme responses ranged from anti-dam groups who had hoped the Commission would condemn large dams wholesale to dam construction firms who felt that the report was responsible for triggering a call for a moratorium on dam construction by anti-development groups.[33] Responses from governments were varied. India, for example, opined that the report was a hypocritical attempt by industrialized countries to intervene in the sovereign affairs of developing countries. Nepal believed that an overhaul of its existing policies to incorporate the Commission's guidelines would be unworkable and would cause chaos and confusion. Other countries, including Norway, found the WCD guidelines to be consistent with their own existing policies to the extent that no change in domestic policy was necessary to comply with them. Many countries responded that the report and background documents provided good guidance and reference material, but made no commitment to implement the WCD's recommendations.[34]

On the other hand, in the two years that followed the Commission's report, many countries and organizations committed themselves to incorporating its recommendations into their policies. In South Africa, government and non-governmental organizations established a multi-stakeholder initiative to identify elements of the report that could be beneficially implemented or reinforced in various contexts, and to make recommendations on policy, regulation and legislation. Poland decided to use a multi-criteria assessment of options, based on the Commission's recommendations, to secure the safety of the Wloclawek dam on the Wisla (Vistula) River.

The African Development Bank planned to incorporate the Commission's criteria and guidelines during the development of the Bank's technical guidelines in support of its recently completed policy on Integrated Water Resources Management. The Asian Development Bank vowed to re-examine its own procedures, including environmental and social development policies, through a series of in-country workshops to determine the extent to which the Commission's recommendations may necessitate changes in their procedures. One construction firm, Skanska AB in Denmark, stated its intention to apply the Commission's guidelines to its hydropower projects.[35]

Continuing dialogue on the recommendations is the focus of a two-year project established by the United Nations Environment Programme.

The World Water Vision

In contrast to the relatively straightforward organization of the conventions discussed in the first section of the present chapter and that of the World Commission on Dams, the World Water Vision process is complex, obscure and convoluted.

Background

The story begins in 1996 with the self-genesis of two NGOs, the World Water Council and the Global Water Partnership. The former designated itself a global policy think tank on water issues.[36] The latter, a much more technical organization, claimed it was established to support countries in the sustainable management of their water resources.

The World Water Council undertook to organize international water fora every three years, and held its first World Water Forum in Marrakech in 1997. The aid donors, water companies and government agencies that dominated the forum charged the World Water Council with developing a global 'Vision for Water, Life and the Environment.' The Council responded by establishing a World Commission on Water for the Twenty-first Century to oversee the preparation of the Vision. Ismail Serageldin, a World Bank Vice-President, chaired the Commission. At the time, Serageldin was also the chair of the Global Water Partnership and the Consultative Group on International Agricultural Research (CGIAR). The Commission, in turn, set up a temporary 'Vision Unit' at the Paris headquarters of the United Nations Educational, Scientific, and Cultural Organization (UNESCO), and tasked it with organizing the vision process and drafting the vision document for presentation at the Second World Water Forum, scheduled for March 2000 in The Hague.

Structure and Process

In collaboration with the Commission, the Vision Unit designed and implemented a strategy for creating the vision – intended to be participatory, although its outcomes were largely predetermined by the Commission's leadership. The process began with an analysis of forces that would drive water management trends 25 years hence. These factors included energy, biotechnology, institutions and information. A panel of experts assessed each driving force. The panels on institutions and information objectively described their predictions for the structure and functions of institutions and information systems 25 years hence. The energy panel exhibited a strong preference for hydropower on the assumption that other renewable sources would not be economically feasible within a 25-year period and that, therefore, nuclear power and fossil fuels represented the only viable alternatives. Similarly, the Panel on Biotechnology advocated genetically engineered crops as a critical component of future water management strategies that would produce more 'crop per drop.'[37]

These analyses of driving forces fed into the generation of scenarios which, after several major revisions, framed the alternative futures for world water as (1) business as usual; (2) technology-driven; and (3) value-driven.[38] The scenarios, in turn, fed into regional and thematic consultations. The plan was for the thematic groups,[39] which initially comprised Water for Food, Water for People (concerning water supply and sanitation) and Water and Nature,[40] to complete their work first, so that this work could form the basis for regional consultations. However, largely because of the short timeframe involved and the staggering of income from various funding sources, the regional and thematic consultations took place roughly simultaneously. By the time the final vision document was due to enter the production process to meet the March 2000 deadline, the vision process had become a mass cacophony of conflicting positions.

Products

The Vision Unit produced several drafts of the vision document. The earlier drafts closely reflected the values of the World Water Council, advocating investments in biotechnology, increased allocation of water to irrigation, and privatization of water and water services. After butting heads with the environmental community and social justice movement, the final version of the vision document, subtitled 'Making Water Everybody's Business,' contained sympathetic references to these strategies, but avoided concrete recommendations directly advocating them. Instead, the vision recommended five key actions: (1) involve all stakeholders in integrated water management; (2) move towards full-cost pricing of all water services; (3) increase public funding for research and innovation in the public interest; (4) increase cooperation in international water basins; and (5) massively increase investments in water.[41]

In response to the relative lack of definitiveness in the Vision Unit's document, the Commission drafted its own report.[42] Unlike the Vision Unit's report, the Commission's report was very clear. It advocated actions under several categories. The first, policy recommendations, focused mostly on the need for full-cost pricing of water services. The second, institutions, pressed for a broader role for the private sector and a more limited role for government.

'Above all, they [governments] will be responsible for creating an enabling environment in which incentives for investors and for innovators are ensured and in which the interests of the public are secured.'[43]

The third category was research and data. Under this heading, the Commission suggested that 'a major increase in funding of national agricultural research systems and the International Agricultural Research Centers of the Consultative Group on International Agricultural Research [chaired, as we have seen, by Commission Chair Ismail Serageldin] would be a modest investment for the international donor community and would have enormous benefits to the world.'[44]

Under the fourth heading, investments, the Commission stated that

it is our judgement that with full-cost pricing no special incentives are needed for the private sector, with three (temporary) exceptions. There should be time-bound adjustments subsidies to facilitate the entry of private operations under conditions of very low tariffs, political risk guarantees (with private operators assuming the commercial risk) and bridging financing when local capital markets are unwilling to finance the long maturity instruments needed for this capital-intensive industry.

The Global Water Partnership produced its own document for the 2000 meeting in the Netherlands, titled 'Towards Water Security: A Framework for Action.' Interestingly, it contrasted the 'water movement' with the success of the environmental movement, implying that the two movements were in competition and that the environmental movement was antiquated and would be replaced by the water movement. For the most part, however, the Framework for Action was bland: it recommended the generation of 'water wisdom'; expanding and deepening dialogue among key stakeholders; strengthening the capacities of the organizations involved in water management; and ensuring adequate financial resources to pay for the many actions required.

The Second World Water Forum

As might have been expected, the Second World Water Forum became a bit of a circus, with NGOs staging high-profile and graphic protests, national governments advocating their own directions in regional presentations, and the host government providing mimes for entertainment purposes.[45]

'Private water companies used [the Hague] meeting as an opportunity to do business, turned the halls of the WWF [World Water Forum] into a frenzied flea market. Shoved into tiny exhibition booths, representatives of these companies screamed over one another to pitch their latest pipes, pumps, and water delivery schemes against backdrops of picture-postcard-quality shots of their most impressive projects. Deals were being cut on the floor, as water officials from developed and undeveloped countries prized instant discounts for construction and equipment from water sales reps who peddled nonstop. Business got brisker and brisker.'[46]

Two additional processes contributed in important ways to the outcome of the Second World Water Forum. First, there was an ad hoc meeting of NGOs, consisting primarily of environmental and labour groups, that strongly opposed the pro-corporate leanings of the Council, Commission, and Global Water Partnership. Second, and more important, was a conference of ministers held separately from, but parallel to, the World Water Forum.

The NGO community met in several sessions to develop a position on the documents and process of the World Commission on Water and the Global Water Partnership. They issued a final, biting document, signed by 60 organizations from all regions of the globe, on 21 March. Their statement combined a number of specific positions. It stated that universal human rights include a healthy environment and access to water and sanitation. It contended that food and water insecurity are intrinsically linked to the current, unfair global trade system embodied in World Trade Organization rules. It asserted a fundamental right to access to information. It called for debt cancellation in poor countries and demanded that water and sanitation services be under the control of local communities, and that the benefits stay within these communities. It avowed that the key to the sustainable provision of water for life is the maintenance and protection of ecosystems.[48]

'1. The NGO and Trade Union Major Groups, who have signed below do not accept:

The report of the World Water Commission

The Vision document produced by the World Water Council.

'We express serious concerns about the process and content to date of the Framework for Action. Although there are some positive action points and recommendations, such as community-based rights, the mechanisms for integrating them into an overall process are flawed. The process is dominated by technocratic and top-down thinking, resulting in documents which emphasize a corporate vision of privatization, large-scale investments and biotechnology as the key answers. The process gives insufficient emphasis and recognition of the rights of local people and communities and the need to manage water in ways that protect natural ecosystems, the source of all water....

'If the Global Water Partnership and the World Water Council are to continue, their work must be made accountable and transparent. Their governance must be *reconstituted* to be more transparent and legitimate. Their work must be regularly reviewed by the United Nations, through the Commission on Sustainable Development, and by the stakeholders themselves.'[47]

Riled by the NGO statement, the principals in the World Water Council and Global Water Partnership requested a meeting with the NGO Major Group caucus. With the Director of the World Water Vision Unit and several important leaders of the GWP in attendance, Ismail Serageldin himself addressed the group. Serageldin unapologetically offered the caucus the opportunity to join the Global Water Partnership. The NGOs rejected the suggestion that they join what is in their view an unrepresentative organization after the rules of the game had been set; instead they demanded a new process similar to the World Commission on Dams, where their voices would be heard. The forum ended in a stalemate, and the architects of the World Water Vision and Framework for Action established a new strategy of belittling the NGO statement, asserting that the NGO community was divided and that not all groups present at the Forum had signed the statement.

Meanwhile, the Netherlands as host country had organized a conference of ministers, a group with considerable clout whose decisions were sure to overshadow the recommendations of the World Water Council and Global Water Partnership. No fewer than 158 delegations participated, representing 130 countries and including 114 ministers, as well as heads of many international organizations. The document produced by this process, the Ministerial Declaration of the Hague: Water Security in the Twenty-first Century, drew from the documents prepared by the Commission, World Water Council, Global Water Partnership and NGO caucus, as well as from other sources and from the experiences of the delegates. It was decisively clearer and better balanced than the bulk of the documents that had been prepared in advance of, and for presentation at the World Water Forum.

'[T]ogether we have one common goal: to provide water security in the Twenty-first Century. This means ensuring that freshwater, coastal and related eco-systems are protected and improved; that sustainable development and political stability are promoted; that every person has access to enough safe water at an affordable cost to lead a healthy and productive life and that the vulnerable are protected from the risks of water-related hazards.'[49]

The ministers laid out what they considered to be the major challenges for a water-secure future:

- Meeting basic needs: to recognize that access to safe and sufficient water and sanitation are basic human needs and are essential to health and well-being, and to empower people, especially women, through a participatory process of water management.

- Securing the food supply: to enhance food security, particularly of the poor and vulnerable, through the more efficient mobilization and use, and the more equitable allocation of water for food production.

- Protecting ecosystems: to ensure the integrity of ecosystems through sustainable water resources management.

- Sharing water resources: to promote peaceful cooperation and develop synergies between different uses of water at all levels, whenever possible, within and, in the case of boundary and trans-boundary water resources, between states concerned, through sustainable river basin management or other appropriate approaches.

- Managing risks: to provide security from floods, droughts, pollution and other water-related hazards.

- Valuing water: to manage water in a way that reflects its economic, social, environmental and cultural values for all its uses, and to move towards pricing water services to reflect the cost of their provision. This approach should take account of the need for equity and the basic needs of the poor and the vulnerable.[50]

- Governing water wisely: to ensure good governance, so that public involvement and stakeholder interest are included in the management of water resources.

The declaration also contained commitments to more specific actions, such as establishing targets and strategies for addressing established threats, increasing the effectiveness of pollution control strategies, and adopting positions to enhance coherence in United Nations water-related activities. A few participants further backed up these commitments outside of the body of the declaration with very specific pledges. For example, Mali promised to meet 80 percent of its water needs by 2025. Malta stated that by 2005 it would treat all of its wastewater. The Netherlands pledged to double funding for water-related activities in developing countries over a four-year period. The United Kingdom vowed to double bilateral support for water and sanitation projects over a period of three years. Vietnam made a commitment to provide a domestic water supply to its entire population and irrigation water for 7 million hectares of cultivated land by 2025. Zambia promised to provide 75 percent coverage of water service in rural areas and 100 percent in urban areas by 2015.

Response and Follow-up

And what of the World Water Council? Apparently unperturbed by the lack of influence exerted by its documents and expensive vision process, it ambled merrily forward towards the Third World Water Forum, to be hosted by Japan in 2003. The Council disbanded the Vision Unit and replaced it with an Action Unit, to indicate that the process of resolving the world's water problems had shifted from conceptualization to implementation.

The Action Unit subsequently produced a document (*World Water Actions*) to convince 'the whole world community, especially the media and those who make decisions on policies and investments … that a world water movement is under way.'[51] In attempting to demonstrate the effectiveness of World Water Council activities in generating this movement, the report failed several tests of validity.

First, the report cited the effectiveness of the ministerial conference in inspiring a surge of activity designed to address the global water crisis, implying that the World Water Council was somehow responsible for the conference. In fact, the Netherlands organized the conference separately from the World Water Forum, and the documents prepared for the forum, including the Commission's report and the World Water Council's vision, were not even considered official input to the conference.

Second, the report lists, as evidence of the ministerial conference's influence, several actions taken by countries or international organizations, but does not provide evidence of a causal link between the conference and the subsequent actions. In many cases, the actions were ongoing before the conference, or were driven by factors other than the conference, such as the need to implement the European Union Framework Directive on Water.

Third, the report implied that the ministerial conference was responsible for increases in the adoption of expanded water assistance programmes by Germany, the Netherlands, Norway and the United Kingdom. All of these countries had active and growing international assistance programmes that included water portfolios prior to March 2000. The report failed to provide evidence that water programmes expanded significantly faster after than before the conference, which might at least have established a positive correlation between these two variables, if not exactly a causal link. Even in the cases of the Netherlands and the UK, both of which pledged to increase assistance during the ministerial conference (therefore establishing at least a correlation), it is unclear which variable was the causal force behind the other. For example, perhaps the countries were planning to expand their water-related aid programmes prior to the ministerial conference and participated in the conference because it provided them with a high-profile platform on which to announce their generous actions.

Fourth, the report implied that the activity by Japan in organizing the Third World Water Forum was the result of the Second World Water Forum and ministerial conference. Rather than resulting from these processes, however, the Japanese contributions were part of the process. This logical error is similar to concluding that life results from birth and death results from life, when, in fact, birth and death are merely components of the process of living. In fact, given that more Japanese corporations than sovereign countries are members of the World Water Council, the March 2000 events in the Hague might have been quite irrelevant to Japan's offer to host the Third World Water Forum.

Finally, the report mentioned that, in many cases, there is a vague similarity between the Ministerial Declaration and the water policies adopted by various countries. For example, the report said that 'Sweden acknowledged that the National Environmental Policy already covers the majority of fields covered by the Ministerial Declaration' and that the 'Sultanate of Oman has prepared a National Water Resources Master Plan that meets the requirements of the Hague Ministerial Declaration (2000).'[52] Such coincidences may have little or nothing to do with the conference or the declaration.

The World Water Vision process illustrates a key defect inherent in non-binding dialogues. This is that, without the official protocols required for the creation of treaties, coalitions of special interests have a free rein to organize processes and events to suit their purposes, even while masquerading as legitimate governmental or inter-governmental organizations.

'The title of the conference [the World Water Forum] sounded like an official United Nations meeting about conserving world water resources, but it wasn't. The World Water Forum was anything but. It was convened by big business lobby organizations like the Global Water Partnership, the World Bank, and the leading for-profit water corporations on the planet, and the discussions focused on how companies could benefit from selling water to markets around the world.'[53]

FREE TRADE AND MARKET FORCES

The international institutions with the most muscle by far concerning water management are the financial institutions set up by the United Nations Monetary and Financial Conference at Bretton Woods, New Hampshire, in 1944. These comprise the General Agreement on Tariffs and Trade (GATT), the International Bank for Reconstruction and Development (later renamed the World Bank), and the International Monetary Fund (IMF). The UN intended the conference to develop a platform for world peace based on an integrated and stable global economy and the availability of financial resources for post-war reconstruction. The institutions that emerged have grown in size and stature and are now the subject of much storm and stress for communities and NGOs that fear the repercussions of global domination by powerful corporations. The reasons for the unrest are presented below in the context of water management.

GATT, GATS and the WTO

'Environmental protection was not a major issue when the General Agreement on Tariffs and Trade was drawn up just after WWII.... Until recently, trade policy makers and environmental officials pursued their work on separate tracks, rarely perceiving their realms as interconnected. Today, environmental protection has become a central issue on the public agenda – trade and environmental policies regularly intersect and increasingly collide. This reflects the fact that the norms and institutions of international trade remain rooted in the pre-environmental era and there exists no international environmental regime to protect ecological values, to reconcile competing goals and priorities or to coordinate policies with institutions such as the GATT.'[54]

GATT was first signed in 1947, with the objective of providing an international forum that would encourage free trade between member states by regulating and reducing tariffs on traded goods and by providing a common mechanism for resolving trade disputes. GATT has since undergone eight revisions, called rounds. The first rounds dealt primarily with tariff reductions, while further rounds included areas such as anti-dumping provisions and non-tariff issues. The most recent revision – the Uruguay Round, launched in 1986 and concluded in 1994 – created the World Trade Organization (WTO) and the General Agreement on Tariffs and Services (GATS). Since 1995, GATT has become the WTO's umbrella agreement for trade in goods. It contains annexes addressing specific sectors, such as agriculture and textiles, and annexes dealing with specific issues such as state trading, product standards, subsidies and actions taken against dumping. GATS provides similar guidance for the services sector.

The World Trade Organization is the only global, international organization dealing with the rules of trade between countries. Currently, more than 130 countries, accounting for over 90 percent of world trade, are members.[55] The agreements that set the WTO's trade rules are negotiated and signed by the majority of the world's trading nations and ratified by their parliaments. The WTO's functions include administering trade agreements, serving as a forum for negotiations, settling trade disputes, and reviewing national trade policies. The WTO's top-level decision-making body is the Ministerial Conference, which meets at least once every two years. The next level is the General Council, comprising ambassadors and heads of delegations in Geneva, which meets several times a year at the WTO's Geneva headquarters. The General Council also meets as the Trade Policy Review Body and Dispute Settlement Body. The WTO is staffed by a 500-person secretariat headed by a director-general.

Enforcement Authority

Unlike the more typical treaties discussed above, the WTO and GATT have the ability to impose trade sanctions on countries that fail to comply with their rules. Countries may bring disputes to the WTO if they believe that their rights under the agreements are being infringed. Specially appointed, independent trade experts judge such cases based on interpretations of the agreements and of individual countries' commitments. The decisions of these panels are binding. If a panel finds that a member country's laws or regulations are protectionist and in violation of WTO rules, the WTO can require that country to reform its laws to comply with WTO standards. If the country fails to do so, the WTO can authorize the complainant nation to impose trade sanctions, which are generally prohibitions on imports from countries found to be violating WTO rules.

In the last decade the world's trading nations provided GATT with a muscular sanction authority, as well. During the Uruguay Round, GATT altered rules regarding the imposition of sanctions. Before this, any country involved in a GATT-related dispute had the power to veto the use of sanctions, including the country accused of violating the rules. The new rules stipulate that sanctions will go into effect automatically unless all GATT member nations, including the country that brought the initial complaint, agree to waive the sanctions.

Under GATS, companies are permitted to sue countries whose domestic policies prevent free-market entry.

Provisions Relating to Water

Under GATT, all potential commodities that may be subject to GATT agreements are defined and described in the Harmonized Tariff Schedule, which is used by all WTO members. Section 2201.90.0000 of the schedule defines freshwater (sea water is addressed in a different section) as '[o]ther waters, including natural or artificial mineral waters and aerated waters, not containing added sugar or other sweetening matter nor flavoured; ice and snow.' The existence of an entry for water in the schedule means that there is a mechanism under which shipments of fresh water can be processed by customs organizations of WTO member countries.

Once water is defined as a commodity subject to WTO rules, the GATT agreements kick in, potentially making the regulation of water exports and imports extremely difficult. For example, one of GATT's basic underlying principles is non-discrimination, which dictates that once a good has entered a country, it must be treated no differently from 'like' goods produced domestically.[56] The inability to discriminate on the basis of how a good is produced could prohibit governments from entering into certification programmes that would bestow an environmental label on water extracted in a sustainable, equitable and environmentally protective manner. It could also stop governments from prohibiting sales of water that had been unsustainably mined or excessively extracted, thus endangering ecosystems and human communities.

GATT Article 11 – 'General Elimination of Quantitative Restricts' – could be interpreted to prohibit import bans from any country whose private corporations choose to sell bulk water.[57] Section 1 of this article forbids restrictions other than duties, taxes or other charges by any contracting party on the importation of products from any other contracting party. This section also prohibits restrictions on the exportation of any product destined for the territory of any other contracting party by private companies. Therefore, if domestic industries initiate bulk water transfers, this article could constrain WTO member governments from establishing policies that would inhibit such transfers.[57]

Other provisions of GATT might be interpreted as limiting the applicability of Article 11 to water exports. Article 20 (b), for example, exempts national policies necessary to protect human, animal or plant life or health from Article 11. Article 20 (g) exempts national polices relating to the conservation of exhaustible natural resources if such measures are made effective in conjunction with restrictions on domestic production or consumption.[59] This clause could be interpreted as applying to non-renewable freshwater sources, such as fossil aquifers. GATT has conditioned Article 20, however, so that the article can only be applied in a non-discriminatory fashion and cannot be used as a disguised barrier to trade.[60] The application of this 'chapeau' to Article 20 could become extremely common because the WTO believes that there is no difference between the implications for competitiveness stemming from different environmental standards and the consequences for competitiveness of many other policy differences between member countries. According to the WTO, such policy differences in areas such as tax, immigration and education policies, for example, could allow each member country to impose special duties against whatever it objects to among the domestic policies of other contracting parties. Opponents of the WTO argue that countries often use violations of workers' rights and environmental standards to gain an economic advantage.

The World Bank and International Monetary Fund

Like the GATT, the World Bank and the IMF were products of the Bretton Woods conference. According to the conference, the chief purpose of the Bank was to 'guarantee loans made through the usual investment channels' and the Bank would make loans 'only when these could not be floated through the normal channels at reasonable rates.'[61] The conference established the IMF to facilitate international agreements on basic rules governing exchanges of national currencies and outlaw practices recognized as harmful to world prosperity.

The World Bank, headquartered in the capital of its largest donor, the United States, consists of two layers of governance. The Board of World Bank Governors includes one member from each member country. The second governing tier is made up of 25 executive directors, one from each of the most generous member countries – the US, Japan, Germany, France and Britain – and the others elected by the remaining 180 donors. The executive director appoints the Bank's president, typically for a five-year term.

The IMF, which has over 180 members, was created to maintain the stability of the world monetary system by buying and selling the currencies of member countries. When it was founded the IMF also served as a forum through which nations could notify each other of changes in domestic monetary policies liable to affect payments from one country to another. In modern times, the IMF is available to bail out countries that are facing difficulties in paying off their debts. Like the World Bank, the IMF is governed by a Board of Governors, which includes representatives from all member nations, and an Executive Board consisting of 24 directors either elected by the members or appointed by the five largest donors – the same five countries that dominate the World Bank.

Both the World Bank and the IMF have promoted a corporate role in water resources management. In 2002, the Bank reported that 'about 40 percent of current World Bank-funded urban water and sanitation projects involved some form of private sector participation.'[62] The reasons given by the Bank for supporting corporate involvement in water management focus on the poor quality of public services in a non-competitive, monopoly environment. The Bank believes, however, that in order to increase private participation in the water services sector, public subsidies are needed in the form of public–private partnerships. Some of the subsidies specifically promoted by the Bank are already part of normal operating procedure in most countries. These include subsidies for the up-front study of ecological, hydrological, social and economic conditions and options assessments, which the Bank argues are public responsibilities. What the Bank doesn't say is that the conduct of such assessments in most countries is already funded by the public sector but executed by the private sector, and is therefore already subsidized.

The Bank also promotes public payment for those portions of a project that provide public services, such as flood protection, while the private sector pays for the construction of infrastructure that will be privatized, such as the generation of hydroelectricity.[63] What the Bank doesn't say is that the public sector often needs the revenue from lucrative activities, such as hydropower generation, to pay for the loss-making activities of multi-purpose projects. In the western United States, for example, hydropower generation has long been considered the 'cash register' that allows the distribution of free or below-cost water to agriculture or flood protection to floodplain development – activities which already constitute subsidies to the private sector. Additional subsidies advocated by the Bank include assistance in managing foreign exchange risk and 'output-based aid,' in which subsidies are disbursed on the basis of actual service delivery by the private entity.[64]

'For all the billions of dollars that the [World Bank] has provided for water development projects – about 14 percent of the overall funding budget since its inception – most of the benefits have accrued to multinational construction companies and the largest local industries. Very little – well under 1 percent of the bank's spending – has been allocated for providing water to thirsty people.'[65]

The accumulation of loans from the World Bank and other multilateral development banks, along with poor rates of return on water resources and other projects funded by such loans, are partially responsible for driving cash-strapped countries to seek financial assistance from the IMF. In return, the IMF frequently requires recipient countries to undergo 'structural adjustment,' which often means the privatization of previously public services. A random review of IMF loan policies in 40 countries revealed that, during the year 2000, IMF loan agreements in 12 countries included conditions imposing water privatization or full cost recovery.[66] Examples include IMF-conditioned debt relief for Tanzania on the assignment of the assets of the country's water and sewage authority to private management companies. The IMF required Niger to privatize its four largest government enterprises, including water, as a condition for receiving debt relief. It obliged Rwanda to privatize its water and electricity company. Honduras was required to approve a 'framework law' for the privatization of water and sewage systems. The IMF demanded that Nicaragua increase its water and sewage tariffs by 1.5 percent a month on a continuous basis for the purpose of full cost recovery and required concessions for private management of water and sewage systems in four regions of the country.[67]

'If you take out a map of Africa and look on the left-hand side, just below where the continent bulges most, you will find a small country called Guinea-Bissau (population 1 million). There is little remarkable about the country – like many countries in Africa it is very poor – except its indebtedness. The value of the country's outstanding debt amounts to a horrendous 1,105 per cent of its exports (which are mostly cashew nuts). To service its debt Guinea Bissau would need to fork our more than two and a half times what it earns in exports.'[68]

'In the 1970s, Tanzania experienced a series of economic disasters: bad harvests and drought; a brief war with Uganda which cost over 250 million pounds; a fall in commodity prices and a rise in import prices.

'On top of all this, in 1977 the IMF advised Tanzania to cut its reserves of foreign currency to improve its chances of getting aid from donors. The money was used by some Tanzanians to buy non-essential goods. By the end of 1978 the country had only 10 days' worth of foreign currency reserves.

'The country was in economic crisis. In 1979, the IMF was called in to help Tanzania pay its debts. But of course this meant imposing a structural adjustment programme.

'Over the following years, the Tanzanian government has devalued the shilling – in 1986 it was devalued by 40 percent in one stroke. Overnight, people's money bought as little as half of what it had before. The government has exported more and imported less; pared down the civil service and privatized state owned companies; and spent less on health and education.

'In theory, hardships in the short term lead to benefits in the long term. But the economy has hardly benefited from the reforms because world prices for its products are so low. For example, in 1986 Tanzania had a good cotton harvest to export. But in July that year the world price of cotton halved, and Tanzania made no profit.

'The country is still struggling economically and cuts in health and education spending mean the poor have nothing to fall back on, and are worse off than ever.'[69]

Markets and Pricing

In an age of accumulating corporate clout, the debate continues to be waged regarding whether there is a positive or negative correlation between the welfare of human beings and their earthly environment and the power of the private sector. In contrast to the World Bank's view that public subsidies are necessary to lure the fantastically efficient private sector into the realm of water resources management, there is abundant evidence that the profits resulting from private investment provide plenty of incentives on their own. For example, the multinational water companies Vivendi and Suez Lyonnaise des Eaux were ranked at 91 and 118 respectively in the Global Fortune 500 in 2000. Between them, they own or have a controlling interest in water companies in over 130 countries on all five continents. Combined, these two corporations distribute water services to more than a hundred million people world-wide.[70] Between 1990 and 1997, there were nearly 100 cases of non-local, private companies taking over water supplies in developing nations. During the preceding six years, there had been only eight. Within the United States, the private water sector generates more than $80 billion each year in revenue, or four times the profit generated by Microsoft sales. According to the World Bank, global private water industry revenue was close to US$800 billion in 2000.[71]

Citizens around the world are expressing concern about the environmental and social consequences of water privatization in their writings[72] and in public protest. More serenely, meanwhile, the World Bank argues that 'once users have clear, transferable property rights, then they automatically consider whether they want to forego a particular use of water in exchange for compensation from another user who may place a higher value on the water.'[73] The Bank goes on to contend that reallocating water between willing buyers and willing sellers becomes a matter of voluntary and mutually beneficial agreements rather than a matter of confiscation.

In most of the world, however, water has been treated as a public good and the rights of individuals – let alone the rights of ecosystems – to water have not been established.[74] In most cases, therefore, the water belongs to the country or state through which it flows, in the absence of any international or interstate agreements stating otherwise. This situation puts the national or state government in the position of rights holder, potentially with communities and corporations bidding for the water. In such cases, it may not be a matter of which competing party values the water more, but which can pay the highest price for it. Corporations clearly have the power to outbid all but the wealthiest communities. Ecosystems, of course, have no legally defined rights to water, so the task for governments is even more complicated. In addition to calculating the quantities and timing of water needed to support ecosystems, a difficult and data-intensive task as described in Chapter 8, the government must estimate a bid on behalf of ecosystems based on some measure of that ecosystem's value. International agreements and laws can provide little succour to people and ecosystems at present, given that they are often weak and somewhat ineffective in comparison to the free trade rules establishing the rights of corporations.

In contrast, the powers behind global water corporations – such as the World Bank, the World Water Council and the Global Water Partnership – consider that water is a human need, rather than a human right. The difference, according to author Jeffrey Rothfelder, is that a 'right is an entitlement, it cannot be denied without sanction. A need, by contrast, is something that is necessary but by no means guaranteed.'[75]

Once corporations gain control of a water supply, the profit margin may replace public welfare as the primary objective for managing the resource. While there may be many different ways to organize the public–private sector relationships that arise from wholesale or partial water privatization, and no demand that domestic governments cede their regulatory authority over domestically produced goods, the desire to increase supply is likely to prevail over any tendency towards conservation.[76] In addition, as is reflected in the recent corporate scandals involving Enron, World Com and other major corporations, corporate executives are often less interested in the long-term sustainability of the business than they are in its short-term profitability. After all, they can always dump their stock if they expect the value of the company to decline, arranging lucrative severance and pension packages for themselves before the coffers, or the rivers, run dry.

CONCLUSION

The potential for a global water crisis is the result not of technological incapacity to sustain the global water cycle so much as of the weakness of political will to adopt sustainable technologies. The corporations that produce dams, irrigation equipment, sewage treatment systems, genetically altered crops, fertilizers, pesticides, barges and other water-related products are exerting a greater influence on governing bodies than are the human communities which suffer because their water sources are destroyed. The only way to avoid a global water crisis is for people to learn about sustainable alternatives to massive and ecologically destructive technologies, and to insist that their governments embrace these alternatives.

Notes

1 Ward, D.R., 2002. *Water Wars: Drought, Floods, Folly and the Politics of Thirst.* Riverhead Books, New York. p. 12.

2 Matthews, G.V.T., 1993. *The Ramsar Convention on Wetlands: Its History and Development.* Ramsar Convention Bureau, Gland, Switzerland. p. 89.

3 H.K. Jacobson & E. Brown Weiss, 2000. 'A Framework for Analysis.' Chapter 1 in E. Brown Weiss & H.K. Jacobson (eds.), *Engaging Countries: Strengthening Compliance with International Environmental Accords.* MIT Press, Cambridge, Massachusetts. p. 5.

4 'Soft' law comprises the resolutions, recommendations and guidelines adopted by the contracting parties to a convention which establish rules by which the parties consider themselves to be bound. In the case of the Ramsar Convention, soft law must be passed by the requisite majority of parties present and voting and are effective immediately. In contrast, 'hard' law refers to the content of the treaty itself, as amended, which legally binds the parties. To enter into force, amendments to the Ramsar Convention require both (1) passage by a majority of parties present and voting and (2) subsequent acceptance by two-thirds of all the parties.

5 Matthews, G.V.T., 1993. *The Ramsar Convention.* p. 4.

6 Bowman, M.J., 1995. 'The Ramsar Convention Comes of Age.' *Netherlands International Law Review*, 42: 1–52. Section 3.

7 Ibid.

8 Ibid.

9 Ramsar Resolution 7.18, Section 9.

10 Bowman, M.J., 1995. 'The Ramsar Convention.' Section 9.

11 Ibid.

12 Ibid.

13 The GEF, established in 1991, is the designated financial mechanism for international agreements on biodiversity, climate change and persistent organic pollutants. GEF also supports projects to combat desertification, protect international waters, and preserve the ozone layer. A joint project of the United Nations Development Programme, the United Nations Environment Programme, and the World Bank, GEF typically provides grants of millions to tens of millions to eligible projects.

14 The Standing Committee is a body consisting of representatives from the parties. The Regina Conference established the Standing Committee to oversee convention affairs and the activities of the Ramsar Bureau in the periods between party conferences. As originally established, the committee included nine members, seven from each region (Africa, Asia, eastern Europe, North America, Oceania, South America and western Europe), as well as the hosts of the previous and following conference of the parties. The San Jose Conference amended this composition to provide proportional representation of the regions (now defined as Africa, Asia, Neotropics, Europe, North America and Oceania) based on the number of contracting parties in each region.

15 Ramsar Bureau, 1998. 'Critical Evaluation of the Ramsar Small Grant Fund for Wetlands Conservation and Wise Use.' Gland, Switzerland. http://www.ramsar.org.

16 Ibid. It is important to note, however, that the value of contributions to the fund shrank considerably when the contributions were converted to Swiss francs.

17 Scheumann, W. & A. Klaphake, 2001. *The Convention on the Law of Non-navigational Uses of International Watercourses.* Deutsches Institut für Entwicklungspolitik, Bonn.

18 These include Turkey's South-eastern Anatolia irrigation project, which involves the construction of 22 dams, and China's plan to construct nine hydropower dams on the upper Mekong River.

19 McCaffrey, S.C. & M. Sinjela, 1998. 'The 1997 United Nations Convention on International Watercourses.' *American Journal of International Law*, 92 (1): 107.

20 Ibid. p. 106.

21 Dubash, N.K., M. Dupar, S. Kothari & Tundu Lissu, 2001. *A Watershed in Global Governance? An Independent Assessment of the World Commission on Dams.* World Resources Institute, Washington. p. 28.

22 Ibid., p. 29.

23 Ibid., p. 31.

24 IUCN is the World Conservation Union, formerly called the International Union for the

Conservation of Nature, an international organization whose membership includes both governmental and non-governmental organizations.

25 World Commission on Dams, 2000. *Dams and Development: A New Framework for Decision-Making*. Earthscan Publications Ltd., London and Sterling, Virginia. p. 28.

26 One commissioner, Shen Guoyi from China's Ministry of Water Resources, resigned while the WCD process was still under way.

27 Both India and China sponsored country studies as an alternative to permitting case studies of dams or river basins within their borders.

28 World Commission on Dams, 2000. *Dams and Development*. p. 68.

29 Ibid., p. 93.

30 Ibid., p. 129.

31 Ibid., p. 193.

32 Dubash, N.K., M. Dupar, S. Kothari & Tundu Lissu, 2001. *A Watershed in Global Governance?* p. 101.

33 http://www.unep_dams.org

34 Ibid.

35 Ibid.

36 While the World Water Council presents itself as a quasi-intergovernmental organization, it is actually dominated by corporations and coalitions of corporations. As of 20 September 2002, the council's website (http://www.worldwatercouncil.org) listed 44 countries and at least 112 corporations or corporate coalitions (for example, the European Desalinization Society) among its 300-plus membership. With at least 46 members represented, corporations and corporate organizations in Japan alone outnumber the countries that are members of the WWC.

37 Panel on Biotechnology of the World Commission on Water for the Twenty-first Century, 1999. *Biotechnology and Water Security in the Twenty-first Century*. Chennai, India.

38 Rijsberman, F. (ed.), 2000. *World Water Scenarios: Analyzing Global Water Resources and Use*. Earthscan, London.

39 The thematic groups proliferated substantially as the Vision process unfolded, and ultimately included numerous strands ranging from 'Water in Rivers,' which focused on instream uses such as hydropower, to themes based on gender and youth.

40 The water and nature subsector had been originally named 'water for nature.' The executing organization, IUCN, objected to the implication that nature was a competitor for, rather than the source of, water.

41 Cosgrove, W.J. & F.R. Rijsberman, 2000. *Vision Report: Making Water Everybody's Business*. Earthscan, London.

42 World Commission for Water in the Twenty-first Century, 2000. *A Water Secure World: Vision for Water, Life and the Environment*. By adopting the subtitle of the report that the World Water Council intended the Vision Unit to produce, the Commission's report relegated the Vision Unit's report to the back seat.

43 Ibid., p. 63.

44 Ibid., pp. 65–6.

45 While funding actors for entertainment, the Netherlands failed to pay for simultaneous translation of the sessions. As a result, the less wealthy representatives of communities and organizations from the developing world were quite limited in their ability to provide effective input.

46 Rothfelder, J., 2001. *Every Drop for Sale: Our Desperate Battle over Water in a World About to Run Out*. Penguin Putnam Inc., New York. p. 86.

47 Second World Water Forum NGO Major Group Statement to the Ministerial Conference, 21 March 2000, The Hague. (http://www.worldwaterforum.net/dossiers/docs/ngo_statement.pdf)

48 Ibid.

49 Ministerial Declaration of the Hague: Water Security in the Twenty-first Century.

50 Ibid.

51 World Water Council Action Unit, 2002. *World Water Actions*. Marseille, France. p. 6.

52 Ibid., p. 27.

53 Barlow, M. & T. Clarkem 2002. *Blue Gold: The Fight to Stop the Corporate Theft of the World's Water*. The New Press, New York, p. 79.

54 Esty, D.C. & C.F. Begsten, 1994. *Greening the GATT: Trade, Environment and the Future.* Institute for International Economics. Washington. p. 9.

55 http://www.wto.org

56 Barlow, M. & T. Clarkem 2002. *Blue Gold.* p. 166.

57 Gleick, P.H., G. Wolff, E.L. Chalicki and R. Reyes, 2002. *The New Economy of Water: The Risks and Benefits of Globalization and Privatization of Fresh Water.* The Pacific Institute for Studies in Development, Environment, and Security. Oakland, California. p. 16.

58 Ibid.

59 In an effort to protect the North American Great Lakes from GATT jurisdiction, the International Joint Commission of the United States and Canada issued a report that concluded that the Great Lakes were 'non-renewable.'

60 Barlow, M. & T. Clarke, 2002. *Blue Gold.* pp. 166–7.

61 Closing address of US Secretary of the Treasury, Henry Morgenthain, 22 July 1944.

62 World Bank, 2002. 'Water Resources Sector Strategy: Strategic Directions for World Bank Engagement.' Discussion Draft. Washington, DC.

63 Ibid., p. 38.

64 Ibid.

65 Rothfelder, J., 2001. *Every Drop for Sale.* p. 90.

66 Grusky, S., 2001. *IMF Forces Water Privatization on Poor Countries.* Globalization Challenge Initiative, Takoma Park, Maryland.

67 Barlow, M. & T. Clarke, 2002. *Blue Gold.* pp. 163–4.

68 Asian NGO Coalition, 1999. 'Jubilee 2000: For a Debt-free Start to the Next Millennium.' *Lok Niti*, September. p. 9.

69 Ibid., p. 10.

70 Barlow, M. & T. Clarke, 2002. *Blue Gold.* p. 85.

71 Rothfelder, J., 2001. *Every Drop for Sale.* p. 90.

72 See, for example, Barlow, M. & T. Clarke, 2002, *Blue Gold*; Rothfelder, J., 2002, *Every Drop for Sale*; and Shiva, V., 2002, *Water Wars: Privatization, Pollution, and Profit,* South End Press, Cambridge, Massachusetts.

73 World Bank, 2002. 'Water Resources Sector Strategy.' p. 26.

74 An exception to this rule includes much of the western United States, where the law of prior appropriation establishes essentially a first-come, first-served method for allocating quantified rights to water.

75 Rothfelder, J., 2001. *Every Drop for Sale.* p. 78. Other authors, such as the Pacific Institute's Peter Gleick, make the argument that water is indeed a human right. See, for example, Gleick, P., 1999. 'The Human Right to Water.' *Water Policy,* 1 (5): 487–503.

76 This is true as long as the marginal costs of producing and distributing an extra unit of water do not exceed the price that the market is willing to bear.

Index

Acadian people 146
Adriatic Sea 71-2
Afghanistan 121
Africa 44, 48, 83, 98, 102, 123, 162, 198,
203-4; East 18, 26-7, 192, 198, 273;
Great Lakes 201; North 98; Southern
43, 132, 144, 198; sub-Saharan 63;
West 170
African Development Bank 274
agriculture, agroecology 80-2;
agroforestry 84-5; ancient 38; and
carbon sequestration 210; declining
productivity of 63-4, 67; delta 26;
dryland 203; ecological pest management in 87-9; energy consumption in
81; on floodplains 133, 135, 234, 237;
genetically modified crops 64-5, 67,
275-6, 278, 288; global warming and
203-4; industrialization of 229; and
land degradation/exhaustion 63-4, 69;
mixed-crop 82-4; plant/animal 83-4;
pollution from 104-6, 108; proportional
water use 45-6, 63, 65-6, 75; rain-fed
32, 49, 79-80, 82, 100; and river-
training structures 173; and
sedimentation of rivers 174, 178, 184,
210; slash-and-burn 81, 240; soil and
water conservation in 85-6; sustainable
80-2; and waste disposal 121, 123,
125, 247; and waste water 125; and
watersheds 242-3, 247; *see also*
fertilizers, Green Revolution,
irrigation, pesticides
aid 275

Alaska 56
Albany 153
Alberta 168, 202
Alexander the Great 161
Alexandria 39
Algiers 98
Alice Springs 150
Allier River 248
alternative technologies 118-19
Amazon River/Basin 42, 240
American Rivers (conservation group) 247
Amman 266
Amu Darya River 50
Andean region 89, 120
Andhra Pradesh 144
Angola 120
Antarctic peninsula 195
Antofagasta region 120
Antwerp 163
Appalachicola River 177
Araguaia River 167
Aral Sea 50
Arctic Ocean/region 10, 23, 201-2
Argentina 164, 219
Arica 120
Arizona 101
Ascension Island 120
Asia 45, 66-7, 75, 79, 102, 105, 123, 134,
162, 195, 197, 202-3, 233; Central 27,
50, 144; East 194; South 57, 63, 204,
273; South-central 198; South-east 43,
57, 85, 146, 273
Asian Development Bank 274
Asmal, Kader 272

Assyria 39, 133, 161
Aswan dam 54, 101, 161, 229
Atchafalaya River 169
Athens 38
Atlantic Ocean, 10, 23, 55, 164
Australia 86, 101-2, 109, 150, 162, 197, 200, 211, 266
Austria 103
Azraq 266

Babbitt, Bruce 247-8
Babylon 38, 133, 161
Bagre dam 144
Bahamas 54
Baikal, Lake 26-7
Bainbridge 153
Balbina dam 205, 251
Balsas Basin 43
Baltic Sea 171
Bangkok 57, 195
Bangladesh 47, 70, 78, 88, 133, 138, 144, 146, 162, 197, 200
Baraboo River 247
Baro 170
Basel 141
Baton Rouge 162
Beijing 50, 107, 161, 219
Belgium 152, 162, 197
Benanga dam 144
Bengal, West 107, 142, 144
Benicasim 72
Beskidi Mountains 171
Bihar 107, 142
biodiversity 15-18, 27, 29, 31-2, 65, 78-9, 171, 175, 185, 200, 229-30, 232, 234-8, 240, 246, 253, 263-4
Black Sea 71-2, 168
Blackhoof River 184
Bombay 99
Bonn 141
Borden food company 125
Botswana 98
Bozek, Jacek 172
Brahmani Damodar Basin 43
Brahmaputra River 138, 146, 200
Brazil 119, 164, 167, 205-6, 214, 272
Brisbane 266
Bug River 171
Bulawayo 101
Burkina Faso 80, 103, 144

Burma *see* Myanmar
Bush, President George. W. 193
Butte Creek 247

Cajun people 146
Calcutta 47
California 57, 247, 272
Cameroon 237
Canada 18, 49-50, 86, 151, 168, 192, 195-6, 199, 202, 205, 207, 211, 219, 265-6
Canary Islands 120
Canete Valley 88
Cape Town 272
Cape Verde Islands 120
carbon sequestration 208-11
Careces 164
Caribbean region 98, 105, 118
Carlton County 184
Carthage 38
Caspian Sea 78
Cataract Canyon 239
Central America 119
Central Valley 247
Cernovca 251
Cerron Grande dam 54
Chandrabhaga watershed 100
channelization 141-2, 167-76, 182-5, 229, 245
Chao Phrya Basin 43
Chernobyl nuclear disaster 207
Chicago 222
Chico 247
Chile 120, 219
China 38, 43, 49-50, 52, 56, 64, 66-7, 79, 81, 85, 87, 107, 118, 139-40, 142, 154, 161, 163, 197, 212-13, 218-19, 269, 289n
Cologne 141
Colorado River 45, 66, 100, 200, 239, 254
Columbia 247
Columbia River 77
comets 8, 12, 43
Congo River 42
Consultative Group on International Agricultural Research (CGIAR) 275
Convention on Biological Diversity 264-5
Convention on International Trade in Endangered Species of Wild Fauna and Flora 265
Convention on the Law of the Non-

navigational Uses of International
Watercourses 261
Convention to Combat Desertification 265
coral reefs 29
Costa Rica 125, 220, 263
Crapper, Thomas 105
Curitiba 272
Cyprus 54, 242

Dakar 69
Damodar River 142
dams 3, 40, 52-5, 75-8, 91, 96, 100-1,
108, 111, 133, 142-5, 168, 170-1, 176-
8, 185-6, 229, 231, 233, 237, 242, 245-
9, 271-4, 288; World Commission on
Dams 53, 75, 271-4, 278, 289n
Danda watershed 100
Danube River 71, 104, 136, 168, 171, 251
Daschle, Thomas A. 177
deforestation 77, 101-2, 135-6, 174, 178,
193, 209, 229
Delta State 170
Denmark 208, 274
desalination 32, 48, 195
desertification 25, 63, 97, 101-3
dew harvesting 120
Dhaka 195
Diama dam 108
Dongting Lake 139
Dorback River 168
Douglas County 184
drought 58, 116, 194, 197-200, 202-4,
207, 246, 279
Dynamic River Management (DRM) 244

East Prairie River 168
ecosystems, and alternative technologies
118; channelization and 142, 168-74,
182-5, 229, 245; dams and 142, 171,
177-8, 185-6, 229, 245, 249; fertilizer
and 70-2; fisheries and 78-9; flood
damage to 142, 146-7; freshwater 23-
33; global warming and 193, 196, 199-
201, 222; and Green Revolution 67-79;
human domination of 133, 135, 156;
human waste in 97; industrial pollution
of 106; and inland waterways 160-88;
inshore 202; institutional protection of
258-88; irrigation and 68-70, 82, 200;
maintenance of 228-9; pesticides and

74-5; and pollution prevention 114-16;
rain-fed agriculture and 82; and recreation 47, 152, 185; reservoir operation
and 177-8, 185-6; resilience of 156,
185; restoration of 146, 153-4, 185,
233-55; sediment disposal and 175;
and sanitation 96, 123; valuation of
30-1; water conservation and 111-12;
and water rights 287-8; and
wastewater 125
Ecuador 27
Egypt 56, 101, 219, 229; ancient 38-9,
133, 161
El Salvador 54, 123
Elbe River 183
Emilia 72
energy 2-3, 47, 81, 179, 193-4, 204-22,
273, 275; energy efficiency 212-14;
fossil fuels 179, 193-4, 204-13, 215,
217, 219, 221-2, 275; geothermal
power 216, 220-1; hydrogen fuel cells
221-2; hydropower industry 3, 204-7,
222, 231, 237, 240, 245, 249, 274-5,
285, 289n; nuclear energy 204-5, 207-
8, 212, 217, 222, 275; renewable
energy 3, 213, 215-22, 273; solar
energy 3, 216-19, 273; wind energy 3,
207, 219-20, 273
Enron 288
Eritrea 120
erosion 3, 16-17, 27-8, 53, 65, 82, 85, 103,
116, 154, 166-8, 170-3, 178-9, 182-4,
210, 236, 238, 245
estuaries/deltas 21-3, 26, 29, 53-4, 71, 78,
105, 111, 117, 146, 164, 169-71, 175,
182, 228, 247, 251, 253, 269
Ethiopia 54, 80, 120
Euphrates River 45, 161, 269
Eurasia 10
Europe 27, 43, 45, 57, 63, 66, 75, 105,
123, 162, 171, 182, 195, 251; central
119, 121, 163, 213-14; eastern 86, 119,
121, 162-3, 213-14; northern 204;
southern 43, 204; south-eastern 102;
western 50
European Bank for Reconstruction and
Development 213; Energy Efficiency
Unit 213
European Union (EU) 210, 217, 219
eutrophication 16, 19-20, 70-2, 78, 199,

235, 252

evaporation 6, 8, 52-3, 68, 97, 100-1, 103, 196-8, 203

evapotranspiration 13-14, 66, 132, 192, 197-8, 200

Everglades National Park/region 117, 234

evolution 31, 238

fertilizers 70-2, 83, 88, 106, 121, 199, 235, 247, 288

fires 235-6

First International Meeting of Peoples Affected by Large Dams 272

fish 17, 19, 24, 26-8, 30, 50, 55, 67-8, 74-9, 84, 89-91, 123, 132, 147, 153, 168-9, 172, 174, 176-9, 185, 200-1, 203-4, 229-34, 237, 247-9, 252, 262, 264

Flint River 153

floodplains 12, 15-18, 24-6, 47, 53, 70, 100, 132-3, 135-6, 138-9, 141, 145-55, 167-8, 171-5, 178-9, 185, 200, 233, 236-7, 244-7, 285

floods 2, 12, 15-17, 24-7, 55, 69, 100, 102-3, 108, 116, 131-56, 167, 169, 175-6, 178, 182, 185, 197, 201-2, 204, 234-7, 250-1, 279, 285; damage reduction 2, 131-56

Florida 117, 202, 234

fog harvesting 119-20

Food and Agriculture Organization (FAO) 75, 89

food, declining productivity 63-4, 67; energy consumption in production of 81; and floods 133; global warming and 203; hunger 63, 133; imbalance of world production/consumption 66; meat preference in 66, 75; and the water cycle 62-91; water requirement 1, 65-6, 75, 111, 279; *see also* agriculture, fish, green revolution

fossil fuels *see* energy

Fouta Djallon 69

France 152, 162, 207, 248, 284

Friends of the Earth 266

Galapagos Islands 27

Ganges River 42, 47, 147, 200

Garwhal region 100

Gavins Point Dam 174

Gdansk 171

General Agreement on Tariffs and Services (GATS) 282

General Agreement on Tariffs and Trade (GATT) 282-3

genetic modification 64-5, 67, 275-6, 278, 288

Georgia State 153

Germany 118, 151, 162-3, 280, 284

Ghana 144

glaciers 12, 15, 18, 144, 195-6

Gland 272

Gleick, Peter 199

Glen Canyon dam 100, 239

Global Environment Facility 213, 220, 266, 289n

Global H_2O 56

Global Water Partnership 275, 277-8, 281, 288

global warming 23, 37, 53-4, 135, 155, 160, 179, 188, 192-222

globalization 39, 41, 47, 54, 179

Godavari Basin 43

Gordon River 248

Grand Canal 161

Grand Canyon 239

Grand Rapids dam 205

Grande de Santiago Basin 43

Greater Hermanus Water Conservation Programme 110-11

Greece 56; ancient 38

Green Revolution 44, 63-79

greenhouse effect *see* global warming

Groningen 266

groundwater 10-12, 14-15, 29, 56-7, 68, 97, 100, 102, 106-7, 111, 117-18, 125, 141, 154, 167-8, 176, 186, 195-6, 199, 207, 232, 241-2, 245, 251, 264, 269

Guateng Province 55, 98

Guinea-Bissau 286

Gujarat 80

Hai Ho Basin 43

Haiti 83, 99

Hangzhou 161

Hebei county 107

Hidalgo State 144

Himalaya Mountains 201

Honduras 80, 89, 119, 144, 286

Hong Basin 43

Hubei Province 139

Hunan Province 139
Hungary 107, 136, 269
Hurricane Mitch 144
hurricanes 132, 144
Hyderabad 144
Hydrovia Project 164, 167

Iceland 43, 220
Ilha do Bananal 167
Illinois 139, 177
Illinois River 179
India 43, 50, 52, 67, 80, 98, 100, 102, 107,
    118-19, 131, 133, 142-3, 147, 197,
    203, 214-15, 217, 219, 240, 274; north
    147; north-eastern 240
Indian Ocean 10
Indonesia 85, 144, 154, 163, 218, 220
Indus River 45, 133
industrialization 44-6, 104-6, 108, 194,
    229
Intergovernmental Panel on Climate
    Change 197, 209
International Council for Bird Preservation
    262
International Court of Justice 261
International Institute for Energy
    Conservation (IIEC) 213
International Monetary Fund (IMF) 282,
    284-7
International Rivers Network 272
International Union for the Conservation
    of Nature (IUCN) 230, 262, 272, 285-
    6n
International Water Management Institute
    50
International Waterfowl Research Bureau
    262
Iowa 174
Iran 261
Iraq 161
irrigation 1-2, 51, 63-4, 66, 68-70, 75, 79-
    80, 82, 106, 108, 125, 200, 203, 207,
    237, 240, 247, 276, 285, 288; micro-
    86-7
Israel 49-50, 56, 86, 118, 125, 269
Italy 57, 217, 220

Jakarta 195
Japan 52, 54, 63, 125, 207, 217, 220, 266,
    280-1, 284

Jebba 145
Jericho 38
Johannesburg 98
Jordan 98, 266, 269
Jordan River/Basin 269
Kaifeng 140
Kainji 145
Kalimantan State 144, 163
Kalsaka village 103
Kariba dam 144
Karlsruhe 141
Katsina State 145
Kazakhstan 203
Kebbi State 145
Keibul Lamjo National Park 240
Kenya 80, 89, 120, 123, 218, 220; western
    89
Kinneret, Lake 202
Koblenz 141
Kogi state 145
Korea 54, 207, 214
Kouris 242
Krishna Basin 43
Kuban-Kel Lake 144
Kugart River 144
Kushiro 266
Kuwait 32
Kwara State 145
Kyoto Protocol 210-11
Kyrgyzstan 144

La Esperanza dam 144
La Plata Basin 164
La Serena 120
lakes 12, 18-20, 26-7, 70, 103, 105, 116-
    17, 175, 193, 196, 199, 201-2, 228,
    231-2, 235, 238, 240, 252-3
Laos 43, 55, 83, 162
Latin America 86, 98-9, 105, 123, 164,
    194-5, 198, 273
Latvia 57
Lebanon 269
Lees Ferry 239
Lesotho 55, 98
Lesotho Highlands Water Project (LHWP)
    55
levees/polders/dikes 138-40, 167-8, 173,
    228, 233, 245-6, 251
Lewis and Clark Lake 177
Leyte-Luzon Geothermal 220

Libya 56
Limpopo Basin 43
Living Planet Index for 2002 230
Loire River/Valley 136, 248
Loktak Lake 240
Louisiana 47, 71, 146
Lovelock, James 5
Luzon State 144
Lyte-Cebu Geothermal 220

Machau II dam 143
Madagascar 120
Madi Basin 43
Madras 57
Mainz 141
Malawi, Lake 201
Malay Peninsula 85
Malaysia 146
Maldives 119
Mali 26, 108, 280
Malta 54, 98, 280
Malthus, Thomas 67
Manantali dam 108
Manavgat River 54
Manawatu River 142
Manila 57, 99, 144, 195
Manipur State 240
Manitoba 151
Mannheim-Ludwigshafen 141
market forces 3, 39, 58, 208, 287-8
Marrakech 275
Marshall Islands 119
Masions-Rouges dam 248
Mato Grosso state 164
Mauritania 108
McPherrin dam 247
Mediterranean region 102
Mediterranean Sea 57, 161, 229
Mekong River/Basin 42, 55, 83, 89, 269,
    289n
Memphis 38
MERCOSUR 164
Meuse River 152
Mexico 43, 65, 67, 81, 86, 107, 123, 214,
    218-20, 254; Gulf of 71
Mexico City 98, 110
Miami 57, 117
Michigan, Lake 230
Micronesia 119
Middle East 45, 48, 85, 98, 202, 273

Minnesota 138
Mississippi River/Basin 47, 68, 71, 137,
    139-40, 142, 146, 152, 162, 169, 179,
    181
Missouri 152, 177
Missouri River 142, 152, 173-4, 176-9,
    185
Mohenjo-Daro 133
Moldavia 57, 107
Mongolia 219
Montreux 262, 265-6
Morocco 120
Mozambique 237
multinational companies 56, 281, 287
Myanmar 162

Nabatean people 38
Nairobi 110
Nam Hinboun River 55
Namibia 55, 120
Nasser, Lake 54, 101
Ndumu game reserve 237
Negev desert 38
Nemadji River/Basin 184
Nepal 87, 197, 274
Netherlands 118, 140, 151-2, 162, 187,
    208, 220, 244, 266, 275, 277-8, 280-1
New Bussa 145
New Orleans 162
New South Wales 109
New Zealand 86, 142, 197, 202, 220
Newton 153
Nicaragua 89, 220, 286
Niger 162, 286
Niger River 26, 145, 162, 170, 200
Niger State (Nigeria) 145, 170
Nigeria 49, 99, 162, 170
Nile River 30, 45, 54, 66, 133, 161, 229
non-governmental organizations 260, 262,
    271-2, 274-5, 277-8
North America 10, 98, 105, 183, 195
North Dakota 177, 219
Northamptonshire 151
Norway 274, 280
nuclear power *see* energy
Nun (Babylonian god) 37

Odra River 171
Oman 120, 281
Onya 170

Orange River *see* Senqu River
Orinoco River 200
Ouse River 149
Oxfordshire 151

Pacific Ocean 10
Pacific region 134
Padma River 79
Pakistan 49, 67, 133
Palestine 51
Palmiter, George 239
Pampas 102
Pantanal 30
Papago people 38
Pará State 167
Paraguay 119, 164, 269
Paraguay River 164, 269
Parana River 164, 269
Paria River 239
Pearl River 79
Pedder, Lake 248-9
Pennine Mountains 149
Pepi I 161
Peru 43, 88-9, 120
pesticides 72-5, 83, 88-9, 103, 105-7, 201, 288
Philippines 67, 87, 99, 144, 195, 214, 220
Phongolo River 237
Pien Canal 161
Pine County 184
Po River 71
Poland 57, 171-2, 192, 274
pollution 2, 27, 29, 46-7, 65, 70, 77, 79, 97-9, 103-9, 112, 114-16, 141, 161, 165, 168, 172, 175-6, 193, 199, 201, 210, 212, 214-15, 229-30, 232, 241, 252, 269, 279
Pongolapoort 237
Ponnaujar Basin 43
population growth 1, 37-8, 40, 46, 48, 58, 62-7, 103, 109, 112, 116, 118, 133-4, 139, 156, 229
Portugal 125
Powell, Lake 239
Pretoria 98
privatization 109, 276-8, 285-8
Puerto Rico 54

Rabamarti Basin 43
rainfall, and agriculture 32, 49, 79-80, 82, 100; convective 132; in drylands 102-3; flood-causing 131-2, 141, 150, 153-4, 184; global statistics 9, 194-5; global warming and 194-5; harvesting systems for 118-21; Hindu god of 38; and inland waterways 176; land sponges capture 100; monsoon 42, 131-2, 197; pesticides 74; primal deluge 5; and river flow changes 198, 200; seasonality of 42, 200; source of 13; storms 116, 232; tropical 9
Ramsar Convention on Wetlands of International Importance 240, 260-8, 289n
Rasi Salai dam 67
recreation 2, 23, 26, 47-8, 152, 177, 185, 237
Red River Basin 151
Redefining Progress 230
Regina 263, 266, 289n
religion 34, 37-8
Renewable Energy and Energy Efficiency Fund 213
renewable energy *see* energy
Rhine River 48, 136, 138, 141, 146, 151-2, 163, 182, 229
River Basin Initiative on Integrating Biological Diversity, Wetland and River Basin Management 264
rivers 15-18, 25, 42-3, 52-4, 70-1, 77-9, 102-3, 105, 116-17, 131-2, 135-46, 149-9, 160-88, 200-1, 207, 228, 230-2, 236, 238-9, 245-7
Rogmagna 72
Romania 104, 107
Rome 98; ancient 38-9, 161
Rotterdam 163
Roxsagar dam 144
Russia 106, 211, 219
Rwanda 286

Saba, kingdom of 39
Sacramento Valley 247
Saint-Etienne-du-Vigan dam 248
Samabri 170
Samarinda 144
San Jose 263, 289n
sanitation 1, 46, 96-126, 204, 279-80, 285
Saudi Arabia 32
Scandinavia 43
Scotts Peak dam 248-9

sea level rise 29, 47
Seminole, Lake 177
Senegal 108
Senegal River 69
Senqu (Orange) River 55
Serageldin, Ismail 275-6, 278
sewage 47, 97, 100, 104-8, 112, 121, 123-
    6, 148, 172, 199, 235, 286, 288
Shandong county 107, 161
Sharpe, Lake 177
Shreve, Henry 169
Sichuan Province 154
Sierra Norte de Oaxaco Mountains 65
Signet shipping group 56
Singapore 99
Sioux City 174
Skanska AB 274
Slovakia 168
Small Grant Fund for Wetland
    Conservation and Wise Use 266-8
Snake River 77
snow 10, 120-1, 131, 141, 144, 149, 176,
    192, 195, 197
snow harvesting 120-1
Sokoto State 145
solar energy *see* energy
Somalia 120
South Africa 55, 86, 110-11, 120, 213,
    219, 237, 272, 274
South America 30, 43, 119, 164, 202
South Dakota 177, 219
Southern Conveyor Project (Cyprus) 242
Soviet Union, former 75, 78, 207, 268
Spain 43, 52, 57, 72
Spring Creek 184
Sri Lanka 84
St Charles County 152
St Louis 139, 142
Stakhiv, Eugene 199
Steiner, Achim 272
Stockholm Convention on Persistent
    Organic Pollutants 265
streams 12, 15-18, 25, 111, 132, 199, 231,
    245, 252
structural adjustment 286
Sudan 120
Suez Lyonnaise des Eaux 287
Sui dynasty 161
Superior, Lake 184
Surinam 43

sustainability 2-3, 12, 38, 80-2, 96, 103,
    105, 108-9, 116, 121, 125, 146, 153-4,
    234, 236, 241-2, 246, 255, 258, 263,
    268, 278-9, 284, 288
Suzah district (Kyrgyzstan) 144
Swaziland 237
Sweden 121, 123, 281
Switzerland 197, 262, 272
Sydney Water Corporation 109
Syria 269

Taita-Taveta 80
Taiwan 54
Taiz 98
Takhar Province 121
Tanganyika, Lake 201
Tanzania 120, 286
Tapti Basin 43
Tasmania 211, 248-9
tectonic plates 7-8, 23
Tegucigalpa 144
Tembe-Thonga people 237
Texas 138, 219
Thailand 68, 85, 89, 119, 214
Thames River 146
The Hague 1, 275, 277, 280-1
Theun River 55
Theun-Hinboun Hydropower Project 55
Three Mile Island nuclear disaster 207
Tianjin county 107
Tigris River 45, 133, 161, 269
Titcaca, Lake 202
transportation 22, 24, 26, 47, 136, 160-88,
    204
Tucuruidam 205
Tunis 125
Tunisia 125, 219
Turkey 54, 56-7, 269, 289n
Turkmenistan 50
typhoons 132

Uganda 80
United Kingdom (UK) 70, 136, 151, 219,
    280-1, 284; England 151, 195;
    Scotland 168; Wales 151
United Kingdom Environment Agency
    149
United Nations Educational, Scientific,
    and Cultural Organization (UNESCO)
    275

United Nations Environment Programme (UNEP) 201, 230, 274
United Nations Framework Convention on Climate Change 210, 265
United Nations Monetary and Financial Conference (Bretton Woods, 1944) 281-2, 284
United Nations Watercourse Convention 268-70
United States (US), 18, 20, 27, 40, 47, 49-50, 52, 56-7, 63, 66, 70-1, 75, 77, 81, 86, 106, 109, 115-18, 162, 173, 176, 183, 192, 194-5, 197, 207, 211, 217, 219-21, 234, 250, 260, 284-5; Army Corps of Engineers 169, 177; central 192; Department of Energy 217, 221; Environmental Protection Agency (US) 116; Fish and Wildlife Service 185-6; Great Lakes 18, 27, 115-16; Great Plains 102; midwestern 18, 20, 27, 115, 173, 177, 250; Pacific North-west 77; south-western 18; western 285
United States Agency for International Development 67
Ur 38
urbanization 46-7
Uruguay 164
Uzbekistan 50, 144

Vaal River 55
Vancouver 222
Varta River/Basin 171
Victoria, Lake 201
Vienna Convention for the Protection of the Ozone Layer 265
Vienne River 248
Vientiane 83
Vietnam 280
Vistula River see Wisla River
Vivendi 287
volcanoes 7-8, 18, 43

Waal River 244
Walter F. George reservoir 177
Warri 170
Warwickshire 151
waste, disposal 6, 47, 79, 97, 104-8, 114-15, 121-6, 187, 221, 229, 247, 280; see also sewage

water commodification 41, 54, 58, 276, 279, 287-8
water companies 275
water conservation 85-6, 109-14, 122-3, 239, 263-4
water crisis 2, 33, 37-59, 160, 179, 222
water cycle, and alternative technologies 118, 122, 125; channelization and 141-2, 167-74, 182-5, 229; dams/reservoirs and 142, 171, 177-8, 185-6, 229; defined 1; dynamics of 5-33, 197; and flood damage 135, 137, 141, 146; and food production 62-91; and freshwater ecosystems 23-33; global warming and 192-222; and Green Revolution 67-79; and inland waterways 160-88; institutional protection of 258-88; integrated approach to 146; irrigation and 68-9; living components of 13-23; mechanics of 5-23; non-living components of 6-13; nuclear power and 207; pesticides and 74; rain-fed agriculture and 82; restoration of 116-18, 153-4, 228-55; short-circuiting of 97; and waste disposal 122-3; and water conservation 111, 122-3
water origins 7-8
water quality 2, 19, 23, 27-8, 33, 44, 46, 48, 52-3, 56-7, 85, 99, 101, 103-4, 107, 116, 152-4, 161, 166, 178, 196, 201, 204, 229, 238, 245; drinking water 3, 25-6, 33, 39, 44, 48, 70, 96-104, 107-8, 118, 123, 130n, 168, 170, 204, 266
water treaties 259-71
water-related diseases 97, 104-8, 204
watersheds 3, 15-16, 28, 77, 100, 116, 131-2, 134-5, 144, 148, 150, 153-6, 161, 180, 183-4, 200, 239, 242-3, 245-7, 252
Waza-Logone project (Cameroon) 237
wells 38, 56-7, 118
West Bank 51
West Point Lake 177
West Prairie River 168
Wetland Conservation Fund see Small Grant Fund
wetlands 20-1, 27-8, 33, 105, 111, 117, 132, 135-6, 141, 154, 168-9, 171, 173, 179, 184, 199-200, 202, 228, 232-4, 237-8, 240, 242-3, 245-7, 250-2, 262-8

wildlife 26, 46, 55, 74, 117, 152-4, 168,
185, 232, 235, 237, 246-7
wind energy *see* energy
Wisconsin 184, 247
Wisla (Vistula) River 171, 274
Wloclawek 172, 274
Wolfensohn, James D. 272
World Bank 99, 143, 213, 271-2, 275,
282, 284-8
World Com 288
World Commission on Dams 53, 75, 271-
4, 278, 289n
World Commission on Water for the
Twenty-first Century 275
World Conservation Monitoring Centre
230
World Conservation Union *see*
International Union for the
Conservation of Nature (IUCN)
World Energy Council 208
World Health Organization 105, 123

World Trade Organization 278, 282-3
World Water Council 275-8, 280-1, 288,
290n
World Water Forum 275; Marrakech
(1997) 275; The Hague (2000) 1, 275,
277, 280-1; Japan (2003) 280-1
World Water Vision 271, 275-81
World Wide Fund for Nature 230

Yangtze River 50, 139, 146, 154, 161,
163
Yellow River 50, 140, 142, 161
Yemen 98
Yenisey River 106
Yorkshire 149
Yucatan 81, 107

Zambezi River 144
Zambia 280
Zamfara State 145
Zimbabwe 87, 101, 123, 218

Zed Books on Water Management

Dipak Gyawali
Water, Technology and Society:
Learning the Lessons of
River Management in Nepal
1 84277 276 7 Hb

Patrick McCully
Silenced Rivers: The Ecology
and Politics of Large Dams
(enlarged and updated edition)
1 85649 901 4 Hb
1 85649 902 2 Pb

Leif Ohlsson (ed.)
Hydropolitics: Conflicts over
Water as a Development
Constraint
1 85649 331 8 Hb
1 85649 332 6 Pb

Riccardo Petrella
The Water Manifesto: Arguments
for a World Water Contract
1 85649 905 7 Hb
1 85649 906 5 Pb